Industrialization and Urbanization

Industrialization and Urbanization

Studies in Interdisciplinary History

Edited by
Theodore K. Rabb and Robert I. Rotberg

Contributors
Thomas W. Africa
Jon Amsden
Stuart M. Blumin
Stephen Brier
Clyde Griffen
Michael R. Haines
Peter R. Knights
Virginia Yans-McLaughlin
Franklin F. Mendels
Daniel T. Rodgers
Gilbert Rozman
William H. Sewell, Jr.
Howard Spodek
Stephan Thernstrom
Paul Wheatley
Edward Anthony Wrigley

Princeton University Press
Princeton, New Jersey

Contents

INTRODUCTION

From its very first issue in 1970, the *Journal of Interdisciplinary History* has encouraged its readers radically to rethink the ways in which historians and social scientists have approached the development of cities— what happened in cities in the past, how cities operated, how cities influenced the lives of their inhabitants, and what contributions urbanization made to industrialization. The *Journal* has emphasized those focuses which were new and methodologically innovative and has also attempted to expand the usual horizon of urban studies to include cities outside the West.

This book is a collection of essays drawn from the first nine volumes of the *Journal*. Collectively and individually the essays exemplify the *Journal*'s approach and contribute directly to the long debates on the role of the city in the past and the origins of the industrial revolution.

Thomas Africa's article on violence in imperial Rome complements articles which appeared in the *Journal* (but are not reprinted here) on violence in France and violence in the United States. It uses the ancient sources imaginatively to survey four centuries of urban violence. In Rome there were bread riots foreshadowing the grain riots of medieval Egypt and modern France, but the angry tone of the Circus was more consciously political and controlled, than randomly obstreperous.[1] Africa's evidence serves to revise the received view of the Roman masses as lawless and fickle. The Roman mob, he concludes, often defended justice and legitimate government more effectively than the Senate, the soldiers, and the emperors.

England is the setting for E. A. Wrigley's painstaking attempt to unravel the true connections between industrialization and modernization, and between the rise of cities, the growth in literacy, new trends in fertility, and explanations for new trends in population growth. He shows how the development of the big cities of England affected the smaller cities and the countryside; how the changes in the markets of

---

[1] Daniel Calhoun, "Studying American Violence," *Journal of Interdisciplinary History*, I (1970), 163-185; Louise A. Tilly, "The Food Riot as a Form of Political Conflict in France," *ibid.*, II (1971), 23-57; Boaz Shoshan, "Grain Riots and the 'Moral Economy': Cairo, 1350-1517," *ibid.*, X (1979), 459-476. See also Pauline Maier, "Revolutionary Violence and the Relevance of History," *ibid.*, II (1971), 119-135; Jerome H. Skolnick, "Interpreting Violence," *ibid.*, III (1972), 177-185.

London, for example, had an impact on the agricultural practices of farmers in eighteenth-century Cambridgeshire; how sudden population growth in England had destabilizing effects in the wage sector; and how sources of energy, especially the shortage of wood, influenced the shape of England's modernization. Wrigley answers old questions in novel ways, asks new questions of the old material, and brings the technological insights of modern demography and economics to bear on a fundamental historical dilemma.

Two other essays in this volume, Franklin Mendels on "Social Mobility and the Phases of Industrialization" and William H. Sewell, Jr. on "Social Mobility in a Nineteenth-Century City," look at the Western European experience in detail. Mendels ranges over time and space to conclude that economic patterns did not determine patterns of social or worker mobility in Europe. Confusingly, social mobility in the past was a function of the stage of growth attained by a particular local, regional, or national economy. Mendels also suggests that industrialization was not a linear process—that a careful analysis of groups of artisanal industries necessarily must precede a thoroughgoing understanding of that lumpy, inconsistent, irregular, and diverting process which we today call the industrial revolution.

Sewell, for a later period, and especially for Marseille, finds low levels of upward mobility from the working class as a result of a voluntary refusal to compete for white-collar positions. Descendants of peasants had no such scruples and attained such levels more frequently than the sons of manual workers. Marseille, as Sewell points out, was very different from Boston. Yet he makes no facile connections between low social mobility and strong class consciousness (Marseille was and is a bastion of French socialism). Marseille was specifically not a place where the impossibility of individual betterment led workers to collective action (and socialism).

This volume also contains two articles on coal miners in Britain and the United States. Michael Haines demonstrates the persistence of fertility differences between miners in England and Wales and other socioeconomic and occupational groups. He shows how marriage patterns varied and how they explain fertility distinctions among mining populations in the nineteenth century. Jon Amsden and Stephen Brier look at American strikes, combining the approaches of social and economic history in a resolution of the problem of how and why trade unions took the form they did and emerged when they did in the coal mining sector. Their data suggest a consistent relationship between the growth of unionization and the peculiar pattern of coal strikes in the late nineteenth century. They see both as a part of the struggle for control between owners and employees.

There are five other articles on the urban experience in America. A classic, from our first number, is Stephan Thernstrom and Peter R. Knights, "Men in Motion," an assessment of and a method of resolving the problem of urban population mobility in the nineteenth-century city. Their method has since been widely used, adapted, and refined, not least by Thernstrom and other contributors both to the *Journal* and to this specific volume. Persistence, and how it can be measured, is at the heart of the article here reprinted. So are its seven conclusions, presented tentatively here but now central to the revisionist literature on American cities. The fifth, overturning the notion that there were closed ethnic or class ghettoes in the American cities, is further tested by Virginia Yans-McLaughlin's examination of the Italian experience in Buffalo. She supports the Thernstrom and Knights suggestion but focuses more directly on the impact of the city on the family. For Italians in Buffalo, she concludes, there was no radical disruption of family life. This was a revisionist notion when presented, but is now a widely accepted hypothesis being tested by a generation of new scholars. Daniel Rodgers' essay on the history of the American industrial worker is also a point of departure for new work. For him, working-class cultures were not made at a single time but refashioned, generation after generation, in the schools, in the homes, in play, and in the institutionalization and reinstitutionalization of values that is a characteristic of American life.

Gilbert Rozman is a sociologist. His view of Asian and European urban rise and decline is based on a synoptic examination of five functions of societal evolution: human resources (including demographic growth rates), patterns of settlement (including distinctly regular alterations in land use), organizational contexts (especially the transformation of family structure and the decline of kinship units), redistributive processes (marketing, mobility, migration, and taxation), and aspects of personal relationships (from the less to the more rational, universalistic, and functionally specific).

Howard Spodek's essay on post-colonial India demonstrates the relevance of Rozman's last paradigm. Even the modern Indian city underwent a formative stage when aggressive, bourgeois men wrested control from the landed princely classes. Their land use and patterns of family structure also altered, as Spodek's data and argument show.

Together these essays, and three review articles by Paul Wheatley,

Stuart Blumin, and Clyde Griffen, are suggestive (but not exhaustive) of the range of methodology and the kind of revisionist concern which has exemplified the study of the new urban history during the 1970s. Americanists have learned from those whose prime concern is Europe, Asia, or Africa, and those of the old hemisphere from innovative work in the new. The germ of that remarkable ferment is contained in the pages of this special reader in interdisciplinary history.

—R.I.R., T.K.R.

Industrialization and Urbanization

Thomas W. Africa

Urban Violence
in Imperial Rome
Bread, circuses, and an occasional riot—
such, we are told, were the main interests of the populace in Imperial
Rome: an indolent and debased people, glutted with free food and ad-
dicted to spectacles. Tacitus sneered at "the sordid plebs who hang about
the Circus and theaters,"[1] and Juvenal impaled them with an epigram:
"The people, who once bestowed republican offices, have now only
two interests, bread and games."[2] These charges have been echoed by
many modern authors, and even authorities of the stature of Rostovtzeff repeat them.[3]

Evidence for the history of the Roman commons is fragmentary,
but, even so, the record does not confirm the image of a spoiled, fickle,
and irresponsible people.[4] Since Roman history was written by men of
the senatorial class, or by those who had attached themselves to its interests, it is not surprising that Roman historians had little sympathy for
the lower classes. Tacitus employed an arsenal of invective against the
commons: *plebs sordida, vulgus imperitum, inops vulgus*[5]—they were a
vile, ignorant, wretched rabble. From his viewpoint, the Roman
masses were *canaille, Lumpen*, or, in Burke's words, "a swinish multitude."[6] Impudent and unruly, they seemed an amorphous mass,
potentially a mob. Yet even Tacitus made a subjective distinction
between the "respectable commons" who rejoiced at the fall of Nero
and the "riff-raff" who lamented the tyrant's passing.[7]

Thomas W. Africa is Professor of History at the State University of New York at
Binghamton. He is the author of *Phylarchus and the Spartan Revolution* (Berkeley, 1961),
Rome of the Caesars (New York, 1965), *Science and the State in Greece and Rome* (New York,
1968), and *The Ancient World* (Boston, 1969), and has published numerous articles in
learned journals.

1 Tacitus, *Historiae*, I, 4. Cf. *Dialogus*, 29.   2 Juvenal, X, 79–81.
3 Mikhail I. Rostovtzeff, *The Social and Economic History of the Roman Empire* (Oxford,
1957), I, 81–82. For a different view, see Thomas W. Africa, *Rome of the Caesars* (New
York, 1965), 14–17, and John P. V. D. Balsdon, *Life and Leisure in Ancient Rome* (New
York, 1969), 267–269.
4 Two recent studies which deal with the Imperial period are by Ramsay MacMullen,
Enemies of the Roman Order (Cambridge, Mass., 1966), 163–191, and Zwy Yavetz, *Plebs
and Princeps* (Oxford, 1969). Though both are valuable, the former is concerned with the
empire more than with the city of Rome, and the latter is limited to the period ending in
A.D. 68.
5 Tacitus, *Historiae*, I, 4; III, 31; *Annales*, II, 77. See the excellent discussion of the sub-
jectivity of Tacitus' terms by Yavetz, *Plebs and Princeps*, 141–155.
6 Edmund Burke, *Reflections on the Revolution in France* (Chicago, 1955), 115.
7 Tacitus, *Historiae*, I, 4.

Rhetoric should not be confused with historical evidence, and a crowd is not a mob merely because historians label it so when they disapprove of the masses' actions. While Imperial Rome had its share of social scum and criminals, the people who demonstrated in the Circus, and who sometimes took to the streets in riots, were not the dregs of society. The Roman "mob" was generally composed of shopkeepers, craftsmen, and workers (particularly in transportation and the building trades)[8] who had grievances to air. The Principate had wiped out all but the formalities of republican government. No longer able to effect decisions through republican channels, the Roman commons could only petition the emperor through mass demonstrations, and, if he failed to heed their demands, they sometimes resorted to violence.

In assessing urban violence in Imperial Rome, one must not lose sight of its causes, nor of the grievances and loyalties that prompted humble men to challenge tyrants, and civilians to battle professional soldiers. The environment and values of the Roman masses must be considered, as well as their composition and actions. Clichés about "bread and circuses" throw little light on the lives or aspirations of the urban masses.

Imperial Rome was a city of about one million inhabitants.[9] Filled with palaces, monuments, and slums, it was a city of contrasts where splendor and squalor existed side by side. Short of space, Rome had expanded vertically as well as horizontally, and much of the population lived in multistoried tenements. Most housing was poorly built, and the collapse of apartment houses was not uncommon. Yet, since living space was at a premium, rents were high. Fires were frequent and destructive. Although the city contained many large public baths, sanitation was poor. Congested and noisy, Rome had grown without

8 Peter A. Brunt, "The Roman Mob," *Past and Present*, XXXV (1966), 3–27, esp. 24. Cf. George Rudé, *The Crowd in History* (New York, 1964), 204–205. For the purposes of the present paper, a crowd becomes a mob when it turns to violence. Its social composition is irrelevant, for the mob that lynched Tiberius Gracchus included the Pontifex Maximus and many nobles and equites.

9 Karl J. Beloch, *Die Bevölkerung der griechisch-römischen Welt* (Leipzig, 1886), 392–412, estimated the population of Augustan Rome as about 800,000; in "Die Bevölkerung Italiens im Altertum," *Klio*, III (1903), 489–490, he raised it to about 1,000,000. Whitney J. Oates, "The Population of Rome," *Classical Philology*, XXIX (1934), 101–116, argues for 1,250,000, but see now James E. Packer, "Housing and Population in Imperial Ostia and Rome," *Journal of Roman Studies*, LVII (1967), 80–95, who favors under a million. Tenney Frank, *An Economic Survey of Ancient Rome* (Baltimore, 1940), V, 218, and Jerome Carcopino, *Daily Life in Ancient Rome* (New Haven, 1940), 16–20, agree on about 1,000,000. Henry T. Rowell, *Rome in the Augustan Age* (Norman, Okla., 1962), 102–106, is rightly cautious of ancient statistics and modern calculations.

planning, and its streets were narrow and winding—a factor that aided
rioters. Like modern capitals, Rome depended on imported food, and
a delay in the arrival of the grain fleet could reduce the city to famine
and bread riots.

As the cosmopolitan center of a world state, the population of
Rome was mixed, for freedmen of varied ethnic backgrounds were absorbed into the body politic as citizens.[10] The city also included a large
number of non-citizens and probably 100,000 slaves. Though upper
class Italians were contemptuous of provincials in general, and Eastern
peoples in particular, Roman society was not marred by overt racial or
ethnic discrimination. Organized in guilds, craftsmen and tradesmen
often lived together on the same streets, thus affording them a sense of
sodality.

In Imperial Rome, crime was commonplace, and some of it was
organized. Domitian broke up a ring of professional murderers who
killed their victims with poisoned needles, and who operated both in the
city and throughout the empire. Under Commodus, there was a revival
of the same gang, but it was soon suppressed.[11] Most criminals at Rome
followed more traditional pursuits, and the city was plagued with
housebreakers, pickpockets, petty thieves, and muggers. Juvenal gives a
vivid description of the many dangers of Rome at night.[12] Yet, despite
the inconveniences of life in the great city, Juvenal and a million others
found Rome too exciting to leave.

The attractions of Rome included bread for some and circuses for all.
Occasionally, the emperors would distribute gifts of cash or grain to the
citizenry. In 5 B.C., for example, 320,000 citizens of Rome received a
cash gift from Augustus.[13] More important was the monthly dole
which the state furnished to a fixed number of citizens, who were
issued a square wooden chit redeemable for five *modii* (about $1\frac{1}{4}$ bushels) of
grain.[14] A holdover from the Republic, the grain dole was not welfare,

10 Sepulchral evidence would suggest that freedmen outnumbered freeborn men by
three to one, but these statistics ignore the fact that the freeborn poor could not afford
epitaphs, and that wealthy freedmen were anxious to boast of their acquired citizen
status. See Lily R. Taylor, "Freedmen and Freeborn in the Epitaphs of Imperial Rome,"
American Journal of Philology, LXXXII (1961), 113–132. Susan Treggiari, *Roman Freedmen
in the Late Republic* (Oxford, 1969), has an excellent discussion of the ethnic composition
(5–11) and numbers of freedmen in Rome (31–36).
11 Cassius Dio, LXVII, 11.6; LXXIII, 14.4.
12 Juvenal, III, 268–308.
13 Augustus, *Res Gestae Divi Augusti*, 15.
14 Suetonius, *Augustus*, 40. Frank, *Economic Survey* (Paterson, N.J., 1959) I, 328–330,
assembles the evidence for the dole under the Republic.

or even philanthropy, but was viewed as the hereditary privilege of the descendants of the Romans who had conquered the world and were entitled to its tribute. The privilege was confined to citizens who resided in the city, and only the poor relied on the dole.[15] No man could live on the dole alone, however, much less depend upon it to feed his family, and rent and clothing required money. The Roman masses worked hard for a living, and at the most the dole only supplemented their meager incomes. In all periods, the dole and its recipients have been criticized by well-fed moralists, but the Roman commons were not lazy parasites feeding at the public trough—they were working men who received a food supplement and little else from their imperial masters.

Like all peoples, the Romans enjoyed shows and games, and the more spectacular they were, the better. Much, though not all, of the public entertainment at Rome was free, and holidays were frequent, for the ancients did not subscribe to the Puritan ethic. Under Claudius, ninety-three days per year were devoted to spectacles at government expense; in the third century A.D., the figure almost doubled.[16] How much time a working man could afford to waste on amusement is open to speculation, though common sense suggests some obvious limitations. The city boasted many large theaters which offered pantomimes, ballets, and operas of sorts. However, the main centers of public entertainment were the Circus Maximus and (after Vespasian) the Colosseum. Many Romans were passionately devoted to the races in the Circus, and rivalries were strong between the fans of famous teams of charioteers. Best known are the partisans of the Blues and the Greens, who were also active in Antioch and other cities, especially later at Constantinople. (A comparable phenomenon is the rabid devotion to soccer

15 Though not originally intended as economic aid, the dole made life in a preindustrial city of the size of Rome tenable for the poor. In 2 B.C. a little over 200,000 men were on the dole registers (Augustus, *Res Gestae*, 15). By A.D. 202 the number seems to have dropped by a few thousand (Cassius Dio, LXXVI, 1.1.; cf. *Scriptores Historiae Augustae*, "Septimius Severus," 23.2). In the troubled third century, Aurelian substituted baked bread and added a ration of pork and oil (*Scriptores Historiae Augustae*, "Aurelian," 35.1, 48.1–4. See also Rostovtzeff, *Social and Economic History* [Oxford, 1963] II, 735, n. 39). Though the additional items may have been relief measures for refugees, they soon became fixtures in the dole. In A.D. 369 Valentinian substituted six loaves of high quality bread for twenty coarse loaves (*Codex Theodosianus*, XIV, 17.5). In A.D. 419 the pork ration was five pounds per month for five months out of a year (*Codex Theodosianus*, XIV, 4.10,3). At this time, about 120,000 men were on the dole at Rome, a figure which may reflect a general drop in the city's population (Arnold H. M. Jones, *The Later Roman Empire* [Norman, Okla., 1964], I, 696; II, 1289, n. 35).

16 Carcopino, *Daily Life*, 205–206. See also Balsdon, *Life and Leisure*, 245–248.

teams in Latin American countries today.) While not edifying, the
races were hardly demoralizing, and even Fronto admits that all classes
were fond of them.[17] Originally, the Circus seated 150,000 spectators;
later, it accommodated 250,000.[18] When a crowd of this size chanted a
grievance to the imperial box, the emperor did well to pay attention.
The Colosseum held about 50,000 spectators[19] and featured games with
rare beasts from foreign lands. It also provided grislier fare with gladiatorial combats and the staged executions of criminals. Though always
bloody, not all gladiatorial fights were to the death, for many gladiators
were popular with the crowds, and no impresario would allow the
slaughter of a champion who had many fans. Nevertheless, death was
part of the scene in the arena. While such sports degraded men, it was
an age not squeamish to pain and hand-to-hand combat.[20] In any case,
the aristocracy flocked to the arena as eagerly as did the masses, and the
Romans have not been the only people in history to enjoy violent
sports.

In Roman society, violence was endemic and had been accentuated
by the political chaos of the Late Republic.[21] Like other Italians, the
Romans were emotional and volatile. Though the state could usually
cope with major disorders,[22] personal violence plagued the city. Under
the Republic, the police powers of the state had been rudimentary, with
a few officials and their limited staffs trying to maintain a semblance of
order.[23] Without a police force, Romans traditionally had to rely on
relatives and friends when violence entered their lives. While a commoner would call upon his friends and neighbors to assist him, a noble
could also summon a throng of clients to do battle for him.[24] In rural

17 Fronto, *Principia Historiae*, 17.
18 Dionysius, *Antiquitates Romanae*, III, 68. Pliny the Elder, *Historia Naturalis*, XXXVI, 102.
19 Carcopino, *Daily Life*, 235.
20 Though Seneca, *Epistulae ad Lucilium*, VII, 3–5, considered the gladiatorial games re-
volting and sadistic, Pliny the Younger, *Panegyricus*, 33, excused them on the grounds
that such spectacles conditioned the audience to scorn wounds and death.
21 Andrew W. Lintott's *Violence in Republican Rome* (Oxford, 1968) has been reviewed
severely by G. V. Sumner, *Phoenix*, XXIV (1970), 88–92, but enthusiastically by Adrian
N. Sherwin-White, *Journal of Roman Studies*, LIX (1969), 286–287.
22 See Tacitus, *Annales*, I, 77, for the government's reaction to the theater riots in
A.D. 15.
23 Lintott, *Violence in Republican Rome*, 89–106. Edward C. Echols, "The Roman City
Police: Origin and Development," *Classical Journal*, LIII (1958), 377–384, is more san-
guine and argues that the Republic had a police force of *custodes urbis*.
24 Lintott, *Violence in Republican Rome*, 6–16, 66. See now his "The Tradition of
Violence in the Annals of the Early Roman Republic," *Historia*, XIX (1970), 12–29.

areas, the situation was worse, and landowners hired armed bands to protect them and intimidate their foes. In the 50s B.C., Clodius and Milo had headed private armies of thugs at Rome, but such gangs were banned by the Principate. Even when public violence was at a low ebb, the average Roman felt it quite natural to call upon his friends to help him resist an assault—or to commit one.

One of the major achievements of Augustus was the establishment of effective military and paramilitary forces to police Rome. Within or near the city were stationed about 12,000 professional soldiers. Nine cohorts of Praetorian Guards served as the household troops of the emperor, while three urban cohorts policed the city, although they functioned mainly as riot troops.[25] The 3,000 troopers of the urban cohorts were under the command of the urban prefect, who was responsible for public order in the city. A fourth urban cohort was added, probably by Caligula,[26] and a total of seven was reached under Claudius.[27] During the civil wars of A.D. 69 the Praetorians and the urban cohorts gambled in politics, and both units backed Otho against Vitellius. After defeating Otho, Vitellius reduced the urban cohorts to four but increased the Praetorian cohorts to sixteen by adding his own troops. When Vespasian's brother, the urban prefect Sabinus, rose against Vitellius, the urban cohorts supported the prefect, and most died in his abortive attempt to hold the Capitol.[28] In A.D. 70 the victorious Vespasian restored the number of cohorts to four urban and nine Praetorian.[29] His son Domitian added a tenth Praetorian cohort,[30] and the number ap-

25 Tacitus, *Annales*, IV, 5. Cassius Dio, LIII, 24.6, assigns 10,000 soldiers to guard the emperor and probably includes a corps of personal bodyguards; he also lists four urban cohorts with a strength of 6,000. Echols, "The Roman City Police," 381, would include 3,000 *custodes urbis* in this figure. Dio's statistics may reflect the Severan era. The actual strength of a cohort is controversial. Marcel Durry, "Praetoriae Cohortes," *Realenzyklopädie der klassischen Altertumswissenschaft*, XXII, col. 1613–1614, argues that the figure was 500 before Septimius Severus doubled it. (Thus, Tacitus, *Historiae*, II, 93, deals with an exception.) However, Alfredo Passerini, *Le coorti pretorie* (Roma, 1939), favors a strength of 1,000 from the beginning of the Principate. The latter figure seems more realistic, for it would insure the Princeps the equivalent of two legions at his disposal.
26 Josephus, *Antiquitates Judaicae*, XIX, 188, but he mentions three urban cohorts in *Bellum Judaicum*, II, 205.
27 Echols, "The Roman City Police," 382. Apparently, Claudius also increased the number of Praetorian cohorts to twelve—*Cambridge Ancient History*, X, 232, n.3.
28 Tacitus, *Historiae*, II, 93; III, 57, 69, 73. One cohort deserted to Vespasian; three died with Sabinus. In A.D. 41 the urban cohorts had briefly backed the short-lived "restoration" of the Republic—Josephus, *Antiquitates Judaicae*, XIX, 188.
29 Echols, "The Roman City Police," 383.
30 *Cambridge Ancient History*, XI, 135, n.2.

parently remained fixed.[31] While available in an emergency, the Praetorian Guards were an elite corps, and the actual policing of the city fell on the urban cohorts.

The "police force" of Rome was augmented by a quasi-military fire brigade, the *vigiles*, who served as both firemen and nightwatch-men and often in a police capacity as well. In A.D. 6 Augustus established seven cohorts of freedmen[32] as *vigiles*, with a strength of about 7,000.[33] In the second century, however, the *vigiles* were largely recruited from freeborn citizens.[34] (Frequently, the office of prefect of the *vigiles* was a stepping-stone to the choice Praetorian prefecture.[35]) When Tiberius engineered the overthrow of the powerful Praetorian prefect Sejanus in A.D. 31, neither the Praetorians nor the urban cohorts could be trusted, so *vigiles* guarded the crucial meeting of the Senate where Sejanus was deposed.[36] Yet, during the great fire of A.D. 64, some *vigiles* behaved un-professionally, looting and spreading fires themselves.[37] Discounting the Praetorians, the "police force" of Rome, including *vigiles*, num-bered about 10,000 in the Augustan age, and later about 11,000.[38] With a third of the population of Chicago, Imperial Rome had a police force of about the same size as that of the modern city. By present standards, Rome was heavily policed in terms of numbers, but much of that force was occupied with fire fighting, and the core of the police were riot troops, not patrolmen. When the average resident of Rome was in difficulty, he stood little chance of aid from a policeman and called upon his neighbors for help. When he had a grievance against the state, he was likely to do the same.

Under an authoritarian regime, it is not easy for a citizen or even a group of citizens to communicate with the head of state. Absorbed in the awesome task of running the empire, the emperor at Rome was gener-ally inaccessible to his subjects. It was equally difficult for him to learn of their needs and wishes, for the ruler was surrounded by secretaries

31 Herodian, III, 13.4, says that Septimius Severus quadrupled the forces at Rome, but this is an unlikely figure even including the legion at Albano and assuming that Severus doubled the numbers in the Praetorian and urban cohorts.
32 Cassius Dio, LV, 26.4–5. Suetonius, *Augustus*, 30. Strabo, V, 3.7.
33 Cassius Dio, LV, 24.6, says 6,000.
34 P. K. Baillie Reynolds, *The Vigiles of Imperial Rome* (London, 1926), 67–68.
35 Note the career of Ofonius Tigellinus—Tacitus, *Historiae*, I, 72.
36 Cassius Dio, LVIII, 9.3–5.
37 Cassius Dio, LXII, 17.1.
38 Mason Hammond, *The Antonine Monarchy* (Roma, 1959), favors a strength of 500 for an urban cohort or one of the *vigiles*. This figure results in a police force of 5,500, equivalent to that of Los Angeles.

and courtiers. The great exception to the isolation of the emperor was his appearance at the Circus or the theaters. To display their affinity with the people, even rulers who were bored by shows and games made token appearances, although Marcus Aurelius, like Caesar, annoyed the audience by reading and dictating letters.[39] Augustus, on the other hand, frankly enjoyed the shows,[40] and so did most of his successors. When the emperor was present, the crowd took full advantage of the opportunity to attract his attention. In the anonymity of a mass audience, it was safe to be impudent and call out witticisms that bordered on sedition. In the sheer numbers which filled the Circus, there was great power, both in the psychological force of noise itself and in the latent possibility of a riot. Claques organized rhythmic chants and clapping in unison and were often joined by other spectators, who were caught up in the compulsive excitement of a crowd atmosphere. Sometimes the cries and requests were flippant, but often matters of import were brought to the ear of the ruler. Though freedom had long since vanished from Rome, the emperors could not afford to disregard public opinion when it was howled by an immense throng. Even the dour Tiberius, who loathed the games and the crowds, was forced by their cries to grant freedom to a slave comedian and to restore a statue which had been taken from a public building.[41] When the crowds blamed him for high grain prices, however, the emperor ordered the Senate to issue an official censure of the populace for their impudence.[42]

Toward the Circus crowds, the tyrannical Caligula was less forbearing than Tiberius. From a good Roman source (possibly Cluvius Rufus), Josephus preserves an account of a clash between Caligula and the masses in the Circus:

There, the assembled throngs make requests of the emperors according to their own pleasure. Emperors who rule that there can be no question about granting such petitions are by no means unpopular. So in this case, they desperately entreated Gaius to cut down imposts and grant some relief from the burden of taxes. But he had no patience with them, and when they shouted louder and louder, he dispatched agents among them in all directions with orders to arrest any who shouted, to bring them forward at once, and to put them to death. The order was given and . . .

39 *Scriptores Historiae Augustae*, "Marcus Aurelius," 15.1.
40 Suetonius, *Augustus*, 45.
41 Suetonius, *Tiberius*, 47. Pliny the Elder, *Historiae Naturalis*, XXXIV, 62.
42 Tacitus, *Annales*, VI, 13.

carried out. The number of those executed in such summary fashion was very large. The people, when they saw what happened, stopped their shouting.[43]

When faced with a resolute tyrant, Cassius Dio remarks of this episode, the people can only be sullen and mutter.[44] Yet most emperors were receptive to public opinion as represented by the multitude in the Circus. When the masses in the Circus and theaters cried for the death of Nero's hated henchman, Tigellinus, Galba quieted them by announcing that their foe was dying of disease.[45] Later, the crowds in the Circus and theaters—where, Tacitus adds, "they have less restraint"—compelled Otho to order Tigellinus' death.[46] Only foolhardy tyrants like Caligula totally disregarded the voice of the people in the Circus.

When civil war broke out between Septimius Severus and Clodius Albinus in A.D. 196, Dio witnessed an extraordinary display of crowd discipline during a demonstration for peace that took place at the Circus:

> While the entire world was disturbed by this situation, we senators remained quiet, at least as many of us as did not, by openly inclining to the one or the other, share their dangers and their hopes. The populace, however, could not restrain itself but indulged in the most open lamentations. It was at the last horse race before the Saturnalia, and a countless throng of people flocked to it. I, too, was present . . . and I heard distinctly everything that was said. . . . They had watched the chariots racing . . . without applauding, as was their custom, any of the contestants at all. But when these races were over and the charioteers were about to begin another event, they first enjoined silence upon one another and then suddenly all clapped their hands at the same moment and also joined in a shout, praying for good fortune for the public welfare. . . . Then, applying the terms "Queen" and "Immortal" to Rome, they shouted: "How long are we to suffer such things?" and "How long are we to be waging war?" And after making some other remarks of this kind, they finally shouted, "So much for that," and turned their attention to the horse race.[47]

Dio adds that divine inspiration must have prompted the demonstration, for how else could so many men have cooperated?[48] It may well

43 Josephus, *Antiquitates Judaicae*, XIX, 24–26, in (trans. Louis H. Feldman) *The Works of Josephus* (Cambridge, Mass., 1965), IX, 227–229.
44 Cassius Dio, LIX, 13.4.
45 Plutarch, *Galba*, 17.4.
46 Tacitus, *Historiae*, I, 72; Plutarch, *Otho*, 2.2.
47 Cassius Dio, LXXV, 4.2–5, in (trans. Earnest Cary) *Dio's Roman History* (Cambridge, Mass., 1927), IX, 203–205.
48 Cassius Dio, LXXV, 4.5–6. In other cities, the Circus was also the scene of dis-

be that *vox populi* is *vox dei*, but the senator was not privy to the organizations among the masses that could produce such a disciplined display of peace sentiment from perhaps 250,000 people. Critics of the commons can note with satisfaction that the masses soon turned their attention to the races, but the Roman people had made known their desire for peace in a most impressive manner. Unfortunately, Severus was not swayed by the people's weariness with war, for his throne was at stake.

In Imperial Rome, safety to shout en masse was not an idle thing, for the individual was helpless when confronted with the massive power of the state and its ubiquitous secret police. Originally, the secret police were soldiers in civilian clothes, but they soon became a separate adjunct of the Principate, working closely with the urban cohorts.[49] "Their titles, like those of their twentieth-century equivalents, are the more terrifying for their blandness: *curiosi, frumentarii, agentes in rebus*."[50] The secret police not only ferreted out subversive courtiers,[51] but also lured common people into making disloyal remarks. Epictetus warns his fellow Romans to beware of strangers who strike up a conversation and begin to criticize the emperor, for they are surely secret agents and, if the unwary victim joins in berating the ruler, he will be arrested for sedition.[52] Historians have preserved accounts of prominent figures who were denounced by informers, but how many more commoners were trapped by the secret police and perished for their indiscretion?

A frequent cause of popular discontent at Rome was food shortages. At best, prices rose, and, at worst, the city was brought to the brink of famine. When the situation became critical, a bread riot could break out. In 41 B.C. the fleets of Sextus Pompeius cut off the food supply for Rome, and the hungry citizenry staged a massive strike, closing all shops and protesting loudly to the government to provide food.[53] Two years later, when the city again faced famine, the entire populace rose to complain of hunger and high taxes. Angry mobs

---

ciplined demonstrations and occasional riots. See, for example, John B. Bury, *History of the Later Roman Empire* (New York, 1953), II, 39–48, 71–74, and Robert Browning, "The Riot of A.D. 387 in Antioch," *Journal of Roman Studies*, XLII (1952), 13–20.

49 William Sinnigen, "The Roman Secret Service," *Classical Journal*, LVII (1961), 65–72, esp. 68.

50 MacMullen, *Enemies of the Roman Order*, 336, n.2.

51 *Scriptores Historiae Augustae*, "Hadrian," 11.4–6.

52 Epictetus, *Dissertationes*, IV, 13.5, specifies that the *agent provocateur* is a soldier in mufti.

53 Appian, *Bella Civilia*, V, 18.

threatened to stone those who did not join them and to burn the houses of those who held aloof. When he tried to calm them in the Forum, Octavian was stoned and wounded by the rioters, who also hurled rocks at Antony when he tried to intercede. Seeing that the mob could not be restrained, Antony summoned a detachment of troops and charged into the crowd to rescue the bloodstained Octavian. The soldiers then began to massacre the civilians and soon cleared the streets. Appian notes that the rioters had included "men of the better class."[54] Though the people of Rome paid a high price in casualties, the riot forced Antony and Octavian to come to terms with Sextus Pompeius in order to relieve the situation that had caused the disorders.[55]

So crucial was the problem of food for the capital that the Principate took great care to ensure prompt and sufficient deliveries of grain for the city.[56] In A.D. 51 a delay in the arrival of the grain fleet caused a serious food shortage, for only a fifteen-day supply was left in Rome. An angry crowd surrounded Claudius in the Forum and pelted him with stale crusts of bread until soldiers rescued the emperor and hurried him away to the palace.[57] Yet Claudius was most conscientious with projects to provide adequate supplies for the city.[58] In A.D. 68 food shortages at Rome helped to topple Nero from his throne.[59] In A.D. 189 the Praetorian prefect Cleander was hoarding grain to raise the price, and his political enemies cut the city's supply even more to bring on famine and riots which could unseat the unpopular prefect. Exasperated by hunger, the masses rose and demanded that Commodus execute Cleander. When the emperor sent out the cavalry to disperse the crowds, heavy street fighting ensued. The Praetorian Guards, however, backed the rioters, and the combined force of infuriated citizens and professional soldiery compelled Commodus to accede to the demands and behead the hated Cleander.[60] In the bread riots, the violence of the mob resulted from impatience with a government that had failed to fulfill one of its major responsibilities.

It is often said that the masses are incapable of acting on behalf of abstract principles, for common men are stupid and crowds are

54 Appian, Bella Civilia, V, 67–68.
55 Cassius Dio, XLVIII, 31.5–6.
56 Guy E. Chilver, "Princeps and Frumentationes," American Journal of Philology, LXX (1949), 7–21.
57 Tacitus, Annales, XII, 43; Suetonius, Claudius, 18.
58 Frank, Economic Survey, V, 41, 268–269.
59 Suetonius, Nero, 45.
60 Cassius Dio, LXXII, 13.1–6; Herodian, I, 12–13.

aggregates of the irrational. In his classic study, *The Crowd*, Le Bon pontificates: "The powerlessness of crowds to reason aright prevents them from displaying any trace of the critical spirit, prevents them, that is, from being capable of discerning truth from error, or of forming a precise judgment on any matter."[61] Such a generality is as worthless as the snobbish quips of ancient writers on the fickleness and irrationality of the masses.[62] Even Tacitus, who was no friend to the commons, reports a striking example of the masses challenging the state on behalf of a very abstract principle—justice for slaves. In A.D. 61 an unsavory official was murdered by one of his slaves, which by law required the arbitrary execution of all slaves in the household, innocent and guilty alike. When it was learned that the full measure of the law was to be employed, a large crowd gathered to protest and demand that the innocent slaves be spared. While the matter was being debated in the Senate, the crowds besieged the building and encouraged those senators who spoke in favor of moderation and justice. The majority of the Senate voted to carry out the letter of the law, however, whereupon the crowd armed itself with stones and torches and tried to prevent the executions. To uphold the authority of the state, Nero dispatched troops and lined with soldiers the route where the luckless slaves were led to death.[63] The riot had not been a protest against slavery but against a glaring injustice. Apparently, the Roman masses cherished the principle of justice more dearly than did most of the haughty senators. When evaluating clichés about the "debased" Roman commons, this episode should not be forgotten.

How many comparable episodes went unrecorded or, if recorded, have been lost, can only be conjectured. A year later, the masses loudly protested Nero's divorce and degradation of Octavia, and rioters overthrew statues of her successor, Poppaea.[64] How much of their devotion was inspired by loyalty to the family of Claudius and how much was due to sympathy for a wronged and virtuous wife is open to argument, but the masses had already displayed a fine sense of justice in the affair of the slaves. After the great fire of A.D. 64 Nero blamed the disaster on Christians and executed a number of them as enemies of society. The

---

61 Gustave Le Bon, *The Crowd* (London, 1947), 66–67.
62 See, for example, Polybius, VI, 56.11, and the note by Frank W. Walbank, *A Historical Commentary on Polybius* (Oxford, 1957), I, 742.
63 Tacitus, *Annales*, XIV, 42–45.
64 Tacitus, *Annales*, XIV, 59–61. See also the contemporary play, *Octavia*, which is usually included in editions of Seneca's tragedies, though Seneca himself appears as a character in the drama.

emperor invited the public to view the torments which he inflicted on the unpopular sectarians, but the masses were not amused: "Compassion arose because they were being sacrificed to the fury of one man and not for the public good."[65] Admittedly, such examples are rare, but not because the masses were insensible to the principle of justice. Rather, the sources for ancient history (especially for social history) are fragmentary at best, and the historians of antiquity, preoccupied with rulers and the upper classes, disdained the attitudes of the faceless "mob."

In the early Principate, there was still a residue of republican sentiment among the common people. In A.D. 19, when news of the death of Tiberius' heir Germanicus reached the capital, the entire populace closed their shops and went into mourning before the Senate had time to proclaim a public display of grief. Part of Germanicus' popularity was based on a belief that he had intended to "restore the liberties of the Roman people with equal rights for all."[66] Such egalitarian views were not shared by the conservative "senatorial opposition," who yearned for the oligarchic realities of the Republic, but among all classes the image of the Republic was still popular. Augustus had been in his grave for only five years, and the assemblies still functioned at least as formalities.[67] At any rate, Germanicus had seemed a symbol of egalitarian republicanism to the masses. No doubt, these hopes were ill placed, for Germanicus was a shallow mediocrity and surely no democrat, but nonetheless he represented to many Romans the possibility of a republican restoration.

With the passage of time, the aura of the Republic faded, and the masses became attached to the concept of legitimate emperors and dynastic loyalty. In theory, the emperor was still a republican magistrate, but to the people he was a "just king" who embodied the general will. Dynastic sentiment increased devotion to the ruler. When Caligula was assassinated in A.D. 41, the Senate wished to seize power by "restoring the Republic," and the "restoration" received some support from the urban cohorts, but the masses rallied in support of Caligula's uncle,

65 Tacitus, *Annales*, XV, 44.
66 Tacitus, *Annales*, II, 82; Suetonius, *Caligula*, 5–6. Supposedly, he derived these sentiments from his father, Drusus—Tacitus, *Annales*, I, 33. Suetonius, *Claudius*, 1. See Sir Ronald Syme, *Tacitus* (Oxford, 1958), I, 418, on the pro-Germanicus tradition.
67 Arnold H. M. Jones, "The Elections under Augustus," *Journal of Roman Studies*, XLV (1955), 9–21, believes that Augustus allowed considerable freedom to the assemblies; but Peter A. Brunt, "The Lex Valeria Cornelia," *Journal of Roman Studies*, LI (1961), 71–83, is more cautious and rightly so. At any rate, the forms of the Republic were in evidence. For a lively meeting of the *comitia tributa* as late as A.D. 41, see Josephus, *Antiquitates Judaicae*, XIX, 158–159.

Claudius, as emperor.[68] Once the commons had accepted the principle of dynastic legitimacy, even a despot could be viewed as a "just king" if he was legitimate and had not offended the masses. Thus Nero, though hated by the aristocracy, was popular with the commons, and many people regretted the overthrow of the last of the Julio-Claudian house. For years his grave was strewn with flowers.[69] In the fierce power struggles of A.D. 69, the masses generally held aloof, for the armies decided who would occupy the throne. Yet Otho took great pains to exploit legitimist sentiment by identifying himself with Nero.[70] After Otho's suicide, Vitellius was viewed as a legitimate emperor, and the masses demanded arms to defend him when the Flavian armies were approaching Rome. Tacitus expresses some surprise at the episode and notes with satisfaction that the support of the people soon melted away.[71] Understandably, the civilian militia hesitated to stand up to legionary veterans in a pitched battle.

At times popular indignation erupted into open violence, and the people of Rome rose against tyrants and usurpers. Ideologically, the masses rallied in the name of a "just king," and the disorders at Rome resemble what Hobsbawm calls "Church and King" riots.[72] According to Rudé, "the target of 'Church and King' is nearly always 'the rich' or the wealthy middle class, and the ideas and institutions that they espouse."[73] Usually, the element of social protest was lacking in the Roman riots, or at least our scanty accounts make little mention of it. In A.D. 193, following the assassination of Commodus, the Senate elected the able and popular Pertinax as emperor, but, after only eighty-seven days, the mutinous Praetorians murdered him and auctioned the throne to a wealthy senator, Didius Julianus. Though the supine Senate

---

68 Josephus, *Antiquitates Judaicae*, XIX, 166–189, 227–228. Suetonius, *Caligula*, 60; *Claudius*, 10. Josephus mentions that the commons feared a revival of the civil wars. With or without their support, Claudius' success was guaranteed by the swords of the Praetorians and the diplomacy of Herod Agrippa.

69 Suetonius, *Nero*, 57. Cf. Tacitus, *Historiae*, I, 4. The false Neros who soon appeared in the East confirm the popularity of the fallen emperor in the provinces. See Tacitus, *Historiae*, I, 2; II, 8; Cassius Dio, LXIV, 9.3; LXVI, 19.3; Suetonius, *Nero*, 57. Despite the "bad press" that he received from senatorial historians and Christian propagandists, Nero became "the once and future king" in the popular mind.

70 Suetonius, *Otho*, 7; Plutarch, *Otho*, 3.1–2. The ambitious Praetorian prefect, Nymphidius Sabinus, had tried to create a claim on the throne by posing as Caligula's bastard—Plutarch, *Galba*, 9.1.

71 Tacitus, *Historiae*, III, 58. See Zwy Yavetz, "Vitellius and the 'Fickleness of the Mob,'" *Historia*, XVIII (1969), 557–569.

72 Eric J. Hobsbawm, *Primitive Rebels* (New York, 1959), 108–125.

73 Rudé, *The Crowd in History*, 138.

accepted the coup, the masses were furious over the murder of Pertinax and the degradation of the imperial office. Denouncing Julianus, the common people spurned his offers of cash gifts and threw stones at him until the soldiers came to his rescue. After some street fighting, the mob seized the Circus Maximus and held it for a night and a day without food or water, calling upon the frontier generals to overthrow Julianus. Since they had no provisions, the crowds then dispersed.[74] The opportunistic generals pretended to heed the voice of the people, though regardless of the disorders at Rome the legionary commanders would not have allowed the Praetorians to impose Julianus on them. However, the popular rising in the capital had added a tone of legitimacy to a new crop of usurpers. Septimius Severus won the scramble for the throne by marching rapidly to Rome, where Julianus was immediately deposed. An astute politician, Severus posed as the avenger of Pertinax and disbanded the guilty Praetorians, replacing them with his own troops.[75] Later, to legitimize his regime, Severus deified the late Commodus and attached himself and his sons to the Antonine family.[76] Whatever his faults, Commodus had been the son of the beloved Marcus Aurelius. By claiming to represent the Antonine dynasty, Severus assumed the aura of the "just king," dear to the hearts of the Roman people. Even without the riot at Rome, the generals would surely have toppled the puppet Julianus, but nevertheless the Roman "mob" had defended the cause of justice and honor while the Senate was groveling before a usurper.

In the third century A.D. there were more incidents of urban violence, though the sources for this period are especially poor. For some obscure reason, the people battled the Praetorians for three days during the reign of Severus Alexander, and the riots ended only when the soldiers threatened to set fire to the city.[77] In A.D. 238 disorders broke out which were true "Church and King" riots with an undertone of attacks on the rich. Rome was languishing under the despotism of Maximinus Thrax, who had overthrown the last of the Severan house. At a false rumor that the tyrant was dead, the Senate elected Gordian as emperor, and mobs swept through Rome overturning statues of

74 Cassius Dio, LXXIV, 13.3–5. Cf. Herodian, II, 7.2–3, and *Scriptores Historiae Augustae*, "Didius Julianus," 4.2–5.
75 Cassius Dio, LXXV, 1.1, 4.1. Herodian, II, 10.1. Cassius Dio, LXXV, 1.4–5, witnessed the enthusiasm of the crowds for Severus when he entered the city.
76 Cassius Dio, LXXV, 7.4; LXXVI, 9.4. *Scriptores Historiae Augustae*, "Septimius Severus," 10.3–6. Herodian, III, 10.5.
77 Cassius Dio, LXXX, 2.3.

Maximinus and lynching his henchmen. Herodian notes that "without warning, men broke into the houses of their creditors and their opponents in lawsuits, indeed into the house of anyone they hated for some trivial reason; after threatening and abusing them as informers, their attackers robbed and killed them."[78] When Gordian was defeated by Maximinus' supporters in Africa, the Senate elected Balbinus and Pupienus as emperors. The latter, however, was unpopular with the Roman masses, who rioted until the two emperors proclaimed Gordian's grandson, Gordian III, as their heir.[79] While Balbinus and Pupienus marched against Maximinus, the Praetorians at Rome were still loyal to him, but the masses were fiercely opposed to Maximinus. After attacking the soldiers with stones in the streets, a large mob seized arms and laid siege to the Praetorian camp.[80] When the rioters cut off the water supply to the barracks, the soldiers made a sally from the camp. Herodian vividly describes the street fighting:

> A sharp skirmish resulted and, when the mob fled, the guards pursued and drove them into all parts of the city. Bested in the hand-to-hand fighting, the people climbed to the housetops and rained down upon the Praetorians tiles, stones, and clay pots. In this way, they inflicted severe injuries upon the soldiers, who, being unfamiliar with the houses, did not dare to climb after them, and, of course, the doors of the shops and houses were barred. The soldiers did, however, set fire to houses that had wooden balconies, and there were many of this type in the city. Because a great number of houses were made chiefly of wood, the fire spread very rapidly and without a break throughout most of the city. . . . A great many people died in the fire, unable to escape because the exits had been blocked by the flames. All the property of the wealthy was looted when the criminal and worthless elements in the city joined with the soldiers in plundering. And the part of Rome destroyed by fire was greater in extent than the largest intact city in the empire.[81]

In the conflagration, the riot ended and looters replaced the crowds who

---

78 Herodian, VII, 7.3, in (trans. Edward C. Echols) *Herodian of Antioch's History of the Roman Empire* (Berkeley, 1961), 185. Herodian, VII, 3.5, attributes the resentment of the masses to Maximinus' expropriation of public funds earmarked for games and entertainment. Relying on Herodian, VII, 3.1–6, Rostovtzeff, *Social and Economic History*, I, 452–453, views Maximinus as primarily a relentless foe of the *bourgeoisie*. Apparently, the pro-Gordian riot got out of hand when the poor began to attack the homes of the rich.
79 Herodian, VII, 10.5–9.
80 Herodian, VII, 11.6–12.4. Cf. *Scriptores Historiae Augustae*, "Maximini Duo," 22.6; "Gordiani Tres," 22.7–23.1; "Maximus et Balbinus," 9.1–10.8.
81 Herodian, VII, 12.4–7, in (trans. Edward C. Echols) *Herodian*, 196.

had fought against the troops of the "unjust king." However, the masses had once again defended the cause of legitimate government.

Another clash between civilians and Praetorians took place in A.D. 311. While fire swept the Temple of Fortuna, a soldier, possibly a Christian, blasphemed and was promptly lynched by a mob. The Praetorians then attacked the crowd and slew many until they were restrained by the "emperor" Maxentius.[82] In this episode, the masses were not defending a "just king," but the "true gods."

In the fourth century the city of Rome was demilitarized and outbreaks of urban violence increased. Because the troops in the capital had backed his rival, Maxentius, the victorious Constantine disbanded both the Praetorians and the urban cohorts and did not replace them with a military force.[83] The date is uncertain, but it occurred perhaps by A.D. 318 and surely by A.D. 331.[84] "A similar fate must have befallen the *vigiles*,"[85] for they too vanished from the scene, and artisan clubs assumed the duties of fire fighting.[86] Deprived of both professional troops and a police force, the urban prefects had to maintain order with only the aid of their limited staffs. Imperial Rome reverted to the hectic insecurity which had characterized the city under the Late Republic.

The extant books of Ammianus Marcellinus cover only the years 353–378, but they record a number of outbreaks of urban violence. Throughout the century, there were obviously many more riots, for in A.D. 388, Ambrose dryly remarked: "Do you remember, O Emperor, how many homes of prefects at Rome have been burned, and no one exacted punishment?"[87] Some prefects had managed to assert authority by displays of bravado. In A.D. 356, a riot broke out over the arrest of a popular charioteer, and the prefect's aides seized a few of the rioters. A few days later, a major disorder erupted over a wine shortage, but the prefect Leontius drove into the crowd, personally arrested the ringleader, and had him flogged on the spot, whereupon the mob melted away.[88] In A.D. 358 there were more disturbances, but Ammianus

82 Zosimus, II, 13. Naturally, Eusebius, *Historia Ecclesiastica*, VIII, 14.3, considers Maxentius responsible for the massacre. Cf. Aurelius Victor, *de Caesaribus*, 40.
83 Aurelius Victor, *de Caesaribus*, 40. Zosimus, II, 17.
84 William Sinnigen, *The Officium of the Urban Prefecture during the Later Roman Empire* (Roma, 1957), 35, n.11; 91, 92, n.21.
85 *Ibid.*, 92–93.
86 Jones, *The Later Roman Empire*, I, 695.
87 Ambrose, *Epistulae*, 40.13, in (trans. Sister Mary Beyenka) *Letters* (Washington D.C., 1954), 11.
88 Ammianus Marcellinus, XV, 7.2–4.

provides no details.[89] During a bread riot in the following year, the prefect Tertullus could only calm the mob by offering his own children as hostages. Shamed by the gesture, the crowd dispersed.[90] In A.D. 364 a mob burned down the house of the prefect Symmachus, who had threatened to destroy his stock of wine rather than sell it at reduced prices.[91] A year later, a mob fired the house of the prefect Lampadius, who was vain, high-handed, and hated by the poor. Since there were no police, neighbors drove off the rioters, but the prefect still thought it prudent to flee from the city.[92] During the disputed papal election of A.D. 366, fierce fighting broke out between the followers of Damasus and those of his rival for the bishopric. In one engagement alone, 137 fatalities occurred. Despairing of the strife, the prefect Viventius withdrew to the suburbs, and order was only slowly restored to Rome.[93] While such outbreaks were detrimental to public order, the contested episcopal elections at Rome and in other cities were rowdy exercises in democracy, one of the few opportunities for the people to make their own decisions under the stifling despotism of the Late Empire.[94] In the absence of police and troops, demonstrations easily degenerated into riots.

Surveying four centuries of urban violence in Imperial Rome, it is obvious that "bread and circuses" played a major role, but not as corruptive factors as the moralists would have it. Since the city depended upon imported food, hungry crowds sometimes engaged in bread riots. While the Circus and theaters may have tempted some Romans to idle amusements, the poor could not afford much absence from work. Though partisanship between the Blues and Greens often grew overheated, the Circus was more important as the principal means for the masses to communicate with the emperor. Often the roar of the crowd was political in tone, protesting high prices and unfair taxes, appealing for justice, and even demonstrating for peace. When the Circus crowds complained about discrimination between social classes in matters of punishment, Diocletian growled to his councillors: "The empty voices of the people are not to be heeded."[95] Less despotic rulers did heed the

89 Ammianus Marcellinus, XVII, 11.5.
90 Ammianus Marcellinus, XIX, 10.1–4.
91 Ammianus Marcellinus, XXVII, 3.4.
92 Ammianus Marcellinus, XXVII, 3.8–9.
93 Ammianus Marcellinus, XXVII,3.11–13.
94 At Milan in A.D. 373, the governor, Ambrose, tried to quiet the rowdy electorate and wound up being elected bishop. Paulinus, *vita Ambrosii*, 6–7.
95 *Codex Justinianus*, IX, 47.12.

voices of the people, who, if too long ignored, might resort to violence. When the masses took to the streets, the mobs were largely made up of ordinary citizens, "little people" driven to desperate action, though obviously criminals and social scum readily joined in the violence in hopes of looting. It is too often overlooked that the majority of episodes of urban violence at Rome were either provoked by food shortages or prompted by ideological attachments to abstract justice or the cause of a "just king." Were the sources more complete and less warped by class bias, even more episodes might come to light. Though most ancient (and some modern) writers dismiss the masses as lawless and fickle, the records of even unsympathetic historians tell a different story. To a large extent the history of the Roman Empire is a grim chronicle of military despotism in the name of law and order, cringing servility on the part of the Senate, and irresponsible opportunism by the armies. In defense of justice and legitimate government, the Roman "mob" often acquitted itself better than its social superiors.

E. A. Wrigley

The Process of Modernization and the
Industrial Revolution in England   Modernization and
industrialization are terms widely used in descriptions of the changes
which have occurred in Western societies over the last two or three
centuries. Whether they represent concepts able to sustain adequately
the explanatory and descriptive loads borne by them is disputable. Yet
they enjoy very wide currency and form the most convenient point of
departure for a general discussion of the Industrial Revolution in
England.

In this essay I shall describe a view of the relationship between
modernization and industrialization which seems to me to be both
widespread and unfortunate when applied to the Industrial Revolution
in England. In particular, I shall argue that the connection between the
two is contingent rather than necessary. I shall begin by offering brief
definitions of modernization and industrialization as a preliminary to a
discussion of the way in which the assumptions which underlie the use
of the terms have clouded our appreciation of the Industrial Revolution. The definitions will serve to introduce both a discussion of the
views of percipient contemporaries, especially Adam Smith and Karl
Marx, and an examination of some features of the Industrial Revolution itself. I have tried to present the definitions in the form in which
they are most widely held—what might be called highest common factor definitions. This means a loss of rigor, but it conforms to the requirements of the essay. At times, it will be evident that the definitions of
modernization and industrialization offered are used as stalking horses
as much as chargers, underlining the point that they are at once convenient and yet inadequate.

E. A. Wrigley is a Fellow of Peterhouse, Cambridge, England, and a Member of the
Cambridge Group for the History of Population and Social Structure. He is the author of
Industrial Growth and Population Change (Cambridge, 1961), and *Population and History*
(London, 1969), and editor of *An Introduction to English Historical Demography* (London,
1966) and *Nineteenth Century Society* (Cambridge, 1972).

This essay was written during a year spent at the Institute for Advanced Study in
Princeton. The author's work for that period was supported by a grant from the Carnegie
Corporation and the Russell Sage Foundation. He wishes to make grateful acknowledg-
ment of their generosity. The author also benefited greatly from the discussion of an early
draft of this essay at an Institute seminar. He is especially grateful to Carl Kaysen, Theodore Rabb, and Fred Weinstein for their helpful comments on that draft, and to Michael
Anderson, Bob Coats, Geoffrey Hawthorne, Alan Macfarlane, and Quentin Skinner for
their excellent advice on a later draft.

The views of contemporaries are of great value in this regard. Smith and Marx stood closer to the Industrial Revolution than we do today. I shall argue that they identified the salient characteristics of their times in a manner from which we can still learn much—that we have been partially blinded by our knowledge of subsequent events, and so see some things less clearly than they. Finally, I shall point to some parallels and differences between English history and that of her neighbors, France and Holland, in order to throw into relief those features of English experience which set it apart from the continent and have a peculiar relevance to the question of the relationship between modernization and industrialization.

Economists and sociologists have perhaps had the most to do with attempts to define the concepts connoted by the words modernization and industrialization, but the terms are also much used by historians, political scientists, social anthropologists, geographers, and others. It is not surprising, therefore, that the two words have been put to so many different uses. Often they are simply convenient umbrellas to shelter a miscellany of less ambitious ideas.

Of the two terms, industrialization is the narrower in scope and presents fewer difficulties of definition. This is because industrialization has come to be used as a synonym for sustained economic growth. It is said to occur in a given country when real incomes per head begin to rise steadily and without apparent limit, and is always associated with major and continuing changes in material technology, including the tapping of new sources of energy. The prospect of rising real incomes per head has caused industrialization to be widely and ardently pursued. To free men from the dread of periodic cold, privation, famine, and disease, and from the hardship of long bouts of heavy labor in the fields or at the loom by creating the means to meet men's main wants and many of their fancies implies a vast change from the preindustrial past. It has placed the golden age in the future and the lure has proved universal and irresistible.

Expansion of total output alone is not a sufficient criterion of industrialization since, if population is rising more rapidly than output, it is compatible with declining real incomes per head. Nor can mere abundance of capital and land (which might give rise for a time to growing real incomes per head) produce a growth in the economy which can be described as industrialization if material technology remains unchanged. A country which retains a large, even a predominant, agricultural sector may be described as industrialized if real incomes rise and technology changes. New Zealand is an example of this possibility, although the proportion of the labor force engaged in agriculture has now fallen to a modest level. The popularity of Rostow's analogy between the behavior of an economy during industrialization and the takeoff of an airplane speaks to the same point. The crucial change is identified as a rise in the proportion of net national product invested (say from 5 to 10 per cent), but it is implicit in the selection of this criterion that population growth rates and capital-output ratios shall be such that real incomes rise, and rapid technological change is also assumed to take place.[1]

Associated with industrialization are a number of economic and social changes which follow directly from its defining characteristics. For example, as real incomes rise, the structure of aggregate demand will change, since the income elasticities of demand for the various goods available differ considerably. Again, and partly for the same reason there will be a major, sustained shift of population from the countryside into the city. These, and many other related changes, are generally understood to accompany industrialization, but whereas there is room for argument about the length and makeup of any list of the concomitants of industrialization, there is near unanimity upon the central identifying characteristic: the rise in real income per head.[2]

There is also general agreement that industrialization is possible only as part of a wider set of changes in a society which have come to be

1 "The process of take-off may be defined as an increase in the volume and productivity of investment in a society, such that a sustained increase in *per capita* real income results." Walt W. Rostow, *The Process of Economic Growth* (Oxford, 1953), 103–104.

2 For example, Kindleberger's discussion of what he calls economic development, in which he is at pains to be authoritative without provoking controversy, runs along these lines. "Economic growth is generally thought of as unidimensional and is measured by increases in income. Economic development involves as well structural and functional changes. In the absence of effective measures of the latter, however, states of development are estimated by levels of income, and rates of development by the growth of income." Charles P. Kindleberger, *Economic Development* (New York, 1965; 2nd ed.), 15. As Bruton remarks, "Per capita income is chosen as the main measure of growth for two simple reasons: One, almost all writers direct attention to this variable; two, despite some obvious weaknesses in its use there does not seem to be a practical alternative." Henry J. Bruton, "Contemporary Theorizing on Economic Growth," in Bert F. Hoselitz, et al., *Theories of Economic Growth* (Glencoe, 1960), 241. See also W. Arthur Lewis, *The Theory of Economic Growth* (London, 1955), 201–303.

known collectively as modernization. Indeed, in discussions of the developing world today, industrialization and modernization are often used interchangeably,[3] or the former is treated as one aspect of the latter. Much the same point can be made in a different way by noting that almost everyone regards modernization as a necessary condition of industrialization, and that many writers implicitly treat it as also a sufficient condition.

If these assumptions cause difficulty in the study of the Industrial Revolution in England, it is not because historians have been unwary enough to transfer to past time ideas developed by economists and sociologists with only the present in mind. Adam Smith, Marx, and Max Weber, prominent among the host of those who have helped to fashion the concepts now known as industrialization and modernization, had the history of Western Europe chiefly in mind when they wrote. The discussion of change in Asia and Africa today is more often conducted in categories devised for the European past than *vice versa*. Yet, ironically, it may be that the understanding of European history has suffered the more.

It is less easy to define modernization in a way that is likely to command a wide acceptance than is the case with industrialization. There is no equivalent to the measurement of real income per head that can serve as a touchstone for the extent and rate of advance of modernization. It is usually regarded as a congeries of changes which are found together and are related to each other, but the length, composition, and ranking of the list of associated changes vary. The nature of the relationship between the changes is also much disputed. A cynic might say that modernization has come to be a term of convenience used by those who are aware of the profound difference between traditional and modern society, and need a word which can convey their appreciation of its importance, but which does not commit them to any one interpretation of the causes or the course of change.

3　The two terms are often used almost as synonyms. Hoselitz, for example, in his "Main Concepts in the Analysis of the Social Implications of Technical Change" (11–31), writes: "The use of pattern variables has had the advantage of putting some of the strategic mechanisms of social change associated with industrialization and technical progress into sharper focus. Universalistic norms need not generally replace particularistic ones. However, the transitions from allocating economic roles according to a system of ascription to assigning them on a basis of achievement, and the replacement of functionally diffuse by functionally specific norms for the definition of economic tasks, appear to have occurred in all cases of successful modernization." Bert F. Hoselitz and Wilbert E. Moore (eds.), *Industrialization and Society* (Paris, 1963), 18–19.

In what follows, I shall do little to allay the suspicions of such a cynic. My description of modernization contains no new features. It is eclectic and is intended simply to summarize views that have often been expressed about the changes underlying the transformation of Western European society between the sixteenth and nineteenth centuries. To proceed in this way cloaks issues of the greatest importance since it tends to imply that all concepts of modernization are equivalent, that the apparent differences between Adam Smith, Marx, Ferdinand Tönnies, Weber, Sigmund Freud, Talcott Parsons, and others are more terminological than substantial. In a different context, this would be tendentious if not absurd. In this essay, however, my purpose is simply to provide a backcloth for a discussion of the relationship between modernization and the Industrial Revolution in England, and this must be my excuse for glossing over matters which would otherwise require fuller treatment.

That modernization and greater economic efficiency are closely linked is universally accepted, and the connection is usually made explicit. For this reason, the concept of rationality which underpins much of the discussion of the modernization of Western European society has acquired a limited, almost technical, meaning. Given the values which obtain in a traditional society, for example, it may be perfectly "rational" to retain in a family group, living on a small peasant holding, adult male kin who produce less than they consume. To expel them would do violence to the social system, and cause damage not offset in the eyes of members of the family by any gain in income per head for those who remained on the holding.[4] Such behavior, however, would be counted irrational in the context of modernization because marginal labor productivity in agriculture is held down as long as attitudes like this persist. Rational behavior has come to be defined as that which maximizes economic returns either to the individual, to the nuclear family, or to the state (the interests of the three do not, of course, necessarily coincide, and this has been and still is a source of difficulty with the concept). In comparison with traditional societies, the utilities to be maximized are concentrated in a narrower band and are pursued with a new urgency.[5]

4 It is sometimes argued, following Ferdinand Tönnies, that the essential difference between modern and traditional attitudes lies less in the degree of rationality involved in decisions of this type than in the degree of consciousness on the part of the individual of the moral bases of his actions. Perhaps we overstate the uniformity of traditional societies in this respect. See the brief description of Tiwi life (below) in this connection.
5 This changing emphasis is well illustrated in the chapter by Joseph J. Spengler, "Mercantilist and Physiocratic Growth Theory," in Hoselitz, *Theories of Economic Growth*,

In order to achieve this end, there must be a common measure of value, a means by which all goods and services can be related to a common yardstick, and a calculus by which alternative courses of economic action can be compared. Money provides a common measure of value and will solve the first problem if most goods and services are bought for money rather than bartered. The operation of the market in such an economy will enable goods and services to be valued on an interval scale, and so solve the second problem. And monetary accounting, if sufficiently developed, makes it feasible to estimate the costs and returns of every possible course of economic action; to balance a given present utility against some greater future utility; and to compare the potential returns from a capital sum which may be invested in several different ways, thus meeting the third requirement.

Arbitrary action and any circumstance which makes prediction difficult are held to be antipathetic to rational behavior. The greater the accuracy with which the outcome of alternative courses of action can be foreseen, the greater the scope for rational choice and the incentive to employ rational accounting. Hence the stress first upon the importance of replacing customary arrangements by legally enforceable and specific contractual obligations, and second, upon the attractiveness of a sophisticated governmental bureaucracy to nascent capitalism striving to reduce the range of the incalculable. A government which is unable or unwilling to enforce the law and maintain public order, or which levies large exactions arbitrarily and without due notice, will inhibit rational calculation and is incompatible with modernization.

If rationality is defined along these lines and is regarded as central to the modernization process, it is possible to examine each aspect of social structure and function and, in many cases, define pairs of polar opposites, one of which is regarded as congruent with modernization and likely to further it, while the other is inimical to it and apt to prevent its development. Mention of three such pairs will suggest what is at issue. They are widely held both to be particularly important and also to be closely interlocked. Needless to say, no society has ever been either perfectly "rational" or "irrational" in regard to them. They represent

---

3–64, esp. in the appendix to the main chapter. It is, of course, the total social context which determines what is "rational" in each society. There are no absolute touchstones: Hence such charming ironies as the effect of a rise in the price of beaver fur upon the supply of pelts in French Canada. Since the Indians who caught the beaver wanted little from the French—a gun, a blanket, or a knife—they were able to satisfy their wants by trapping fewer animals when prices were high, a rational if inconvenient response.

limiting possibilities and each pair defines a spectrum on which, in principle, each society may be placed.

The first pair concerns the way in which men are recruited to discharge roles within a society. The rational method of selection is to consider only the fitness of the candidate to carry out the tasks associated with the role regardless of his parentage, kin, status, age, nationality, religion, race, or sex. At the other extreme, recruitment to a particular role is confined to a restricted group within the whole population, which in the limiting case might contain only one member. The group may be defined by kinship, status, race, or in any other way which has gained the sanction of social consent. Open, competitive examination for a governmental administrative post is an example of the first type of recruitment, while entry into a craft with preference given to sons of present members is an instance of the second. The opposite ends of the spectrum are sometimes termed achievement and ascription. The former both favors modernization and helps to define it, while the latter is the dominant form of recruitment in traditional societies.

Rationality bears not only on methods of recruitment to social and economic roles, but also on the definition of the roles themselves. The criteria for recruitment can be more exactly specified, and, at the same time, greater economic efficiency achieved if roles are strongly differentiated. A jack-of-all-trades is master of none. Division of labor tends both to increase productivity and to help ensure that the men appointed to each job are well qualified to discharge it efficiently. This is one aspect of the second spectrum, that which runs between functional specificity and functional diffuseness. In traditional societies, a man may be called upon to perform a number of different roles because of his position in society. Actions and attitudes toward him will be conditioned by the consciousness of this fact. If he is a merchant, for example, men's behavior toward him may be affected not simply by the type and price of the wares he has to offer, but by the status of merchants in the society generally, by his kinship ties, by his religion, and so on. Similarly, his attitude to his customers may be influenced by considerations other than their financial means. And what is true of merchants, is true a fortiori of peasants or craftsmen. In economic relations, these influences are compounded by the fact that in traditional societies, the play of the market is limited and transport costs are high. Specialization of economic function cannot, therefore, be carried very far either on the peasant holding, where a substantial measure of self-sufficiency in food and simple consumer goods may be necessary, or in the craft workshop, where the size of the market and the personal predilections of customers prevent long production runs of standard products, and hence division of labor.

It is a short step from these first two polar pairs to the third, which deals with the criteria for membership of a group. At one extreme, this may be particularistic; at the other, universalistic. The latter is typified by the view that all men should be equal before the law and that the law should be the same for all men. It is at odds with this universalistic principle, for example, that a priest in holy orders should be able *qua* priest to invoke immunity from the civil courts, or that because a man is born a serf he should suffer disabilities before the law. Again, the long struggle by local communities in France to retain control of the grain supply within their areas, setting its price and limiting its export as seemed best in their interest, was particularistic in spirit. The central government moved toward the view that trade in grain should be free, with the market being the sole arbiter of price and the movement of grain no longer inhibited by local regulation.[6] In this it was exemplifying the universalistic principle that all franchises, liberties, and privileges which distinguished particular groups, areas, or communities were to be deplored. Formal equality is mandatory.

Consideration of the several linked aspects of social and economic behavior which change during modernization has, in turn, produced paired terms intended to connote the changes as a whole: feudal-capitalist, traditional-modern, and *Gemeinschaft-Gesellschaft*. When the elements of change are analyzed, and especially when their causes are discussed, major differences of interpretation appear, but the definition of modernization may be extended a little by referring to some further points which are common ground to most views of modernization.

Self-interest is the twin pillar to rationality in supporting the concept of modernization. Self-interest is held to be the guiding principle of action in a modernized society to a degree which would appear both aberrant and abhorrent in traditional communities. Like the idea of rationality, self-interest has acquired a special meaning in these discussions. It is perfectly possible to argue that a man in a traditional community who acknowledges a very wide range of kinship obligations and devotes much of his time and energy to promoting the well-being, security, and status of his relatives, his dependents, or his lord, is just as much actuated by self-interest as any Scrooge. The difference lies

6 See Louise A. Tilly, "The Food Riot as a Form of Political Conflict in France," *Journal of Interdisciplinary History*, II (1971), 23–57.

in the nature of the rewards that are sought, not in the degree of self-interest involved. It may also be argued that some traditional societies were so constituted as to put a high premium not only upon the pursuit of self-interest, but also upon a long-term calculation of advantage which in a different context might have gained the approval of Samuel Smiles. Among the Tiwi in northern Australia, for example, a man's status depended above all upon the number of his wives. No man could achieve high status in this way before his late forties, but he had to lay the foundation of his later success two decades earlier by forming links with powerful men who were willing to promise him female children born or as yet unborn as his future wives in return for present services. Twenty years is a long time to wait for an investment to mature, especially where there is a high risk that the premature death of infants, or an unfortunate run of male offspring, will make it impossible for the older man to fulfil his obligations.[7]

Whatever the justice of the prevailing stereotype of traditional societies, in the context of modernization, self-interest has come to mean the adoption of a calculus of advantage. In the calculus, the unit is the individual, or, at the widest, the nuclear family, and the accounting scale is pecuniary gain.

Tönnies, an early and extreme protagonist of the view that modern and traditional societies differ profoundly, wrote in Gemeinschaft und Gesellschaft: "The will to enrich himself makes the merchant unscrupulous and the type of egotistic, self-willed individual to whom all human beings except his nearest friends are only means and tools to his ends or purposes; he is the embodiment of Gesellschaft."[8] He thought the pressure toward atomistic individualism to be so acute that he added: "The family becomes an accidental form for the satisfaction of natural needs, neighbourhood and friendship are supplanted by special interest groups and conventional society life."[9] These attitudes eat like acid into the fabric of traditional society, destroying solidary groups. When this

7 "To become a really big man or even a minor figure among the elders, a Tiwi had to devote all his adult life to that goal. Careers were built up and influential positions gained not by executing spectacular coups at any one time, but by slow, devious maneuvering and dealing in influence throughout adulthood. Men in their early thirties invested their very small assets in the hope of large returns twenty years later." Wives, mothers, sisters, and daughters were all "investment funds in [a] career of influence seeking." C. W. M. Hart and Arnold R. Pilling, The Tiwi of North Australia (New York, 1960), 51, 52.
8 Ferdinand Tönnies (trans. and ed. Charles P. Loomis), Community and Society [Gemeinschaft und Gesellschaft] (East Lansing, 1957), 165.
9 Ibid., 168.

happens, old values and attitudes are no longer internalized by the young, and the web of rights and obligations which binds together small traditional communities weakens and, in time, dissolves.

Other attributes of modernization may be inferred from its major characteristics. Social, occupational, and geographical mobility will tend to increase with the decline of ascriptive recruitment. Rights and obligations linked to kinship become less extensive and less easily enforceable, except perhaps within the nuclear family.[10] Structural differentiation at the institutional level parallels the specialization of individual roles. Again, modernization promotes the growth of towns, and in towns its attributes are more widespread, prominent, and pervasive than in the countryside. Its development fosters the spread of literacy and numeracy through a population.

There remain two aspects of modernization which are widely held to be important when assessing its relationship to industrialization in Western Europe. Both have received increased attention in recent years.

The first concerns the actions of the nation state. The close connection between rationality and bureaucratic method, which Weber frequently stressed, has already been remarked.[11] It is only one facet of the stimulus afforded by the state to modernizing tendencies. The state provides the sanction for the enforcement of contractual obligation. and the maintenance of order. Since it encourages the growth of a bureaucracy recruited by achievement rather than by ascription, it is apt to oppose particularistic interests, and to provide an administrative framework within which rational action can flourish. The bourgeois and the nation state are congenial to each other. Impediments to commerce, to the free movement of capital, to unrestricted discretion in the use of private property, and to the treatment of labor simply as a production factor, impediments which inhibit the growth of capitalism and which display a notable persistence in the face of change, can all be reduced to the vanishing point by a vigorous state acting in the bourgeois interest, which is also its own.[12]

Other forms of state action may also increase the momentum of

10 It may be as well to note that the prevalence of the extended family is one of several assumptions about the universal characteristics of traditional society which are disputable in the case of Western Europe.

11 See, e.g., Max Weber (trans. A. M. Handerson and Talcott Parsons; ed. Talcott Parsons), *The Theory of Social and Economic Organization* (New York, 1964), 329–341.

12 Such at least is the "pure type" of action by the state. It is, of course, unlikely to be paralleled exactly in any particular case.

modernization, which is further speeded as groups whose interests lie in accelerating change force an entry into the polity.[13] Taxation, for example, unless payment in kind or labor is accepted, forces the peasant into the market to raise cash. The maintenance of standing armies, like the growth of cities, enlarges the market for foodstuffs and textiles, and encourages specialization of economic function. Or, again, the actions of the state may undermine alternative and older institutional frameworks. The English Poor Law, for example, enshrined the view that if a man or a family fell upon evil times, responsibility for their support ultimately devolved upon the parish. It is evidence of the state's desire that all men who could work should do so, but it is also an acknowledgement of the responsibility of the state toward individuals in distress. Kinship ties and local custom were no longer the sole basis of all help and support in bad fortune. Nor was the lord of the manor expected to provide for his own in return for the services owed him by his men. Instead, the state created a statutory framework within which local communities were to make provision for the sick and needy.

Second, economic and social change produces tension not only between individuals, but also within them. For individuals to act rationally (always in the restricted sense described above), they must achieve rational control of affect and much greater autonomy than is needed or would be acceptable in a traditional society. In traditional society, authority is perceived as protective and nurturant. Hierarchical authority structures are acceptable as long as this holds true, and the values internalized by individuals legitimate the system. Affectual ties are strong and personal, and personal dependency does not involve severe conscious stresses in relation to authority figures. When, however, authority appears to be failing to fulfill its side of the bargain upon which a hierarchical structure of authority rests, hostility toward it, which was once successfully repressed, may surface. A competing set of values appropriate to individual autonomy may be internalized by a part of the population, and conflict between the old and new values will occur.[14] Institutional (social and economic) and internal (psychic)

13 It is sometimes argued that just as formal equality before the law is mandatory, so formal equality in political participation is ultimately inevitable, or at least that competing political groups should stand toward the polity much as competing firms do to the market. There is perhaps something of this in Burke's teaching about political party. The old parallel between party in the state and schism in the church was no longer acceptable.
14 On this aspect of modernization, see, e.g., Everett E. Hagen, *On the Theory of Social Change: How Economic Growth Begins* (Homewood, Ill., 1964); Fred Weinstein and Gerald M. Platt, *The Wish to be Free: Society, Psyche, and Value Change* (Berkeley, 1969).

changes both occur during modernization. If they get out of step with each other, tension and violence are likely to increase.[15]

Once any considerable number of men have ceased to internalize the values upon which traditional society rests, their behavior is certain to impede the smooth functioning of traditional authority and to call its legitimacy and its ability to protect and nurture further in question. Hence the belief that changes in the value systems of small groups of men, such as the early Calvinists, may have an importance in producing massive changes at a later date which might appear at first sight to be quite out of proportion to their number or political power. There is, of course, no reason why the later changes should necessarily follow the same pattern, for greater autonomy and control of affect may be achieved by internalizing value systems other than ascetic Protestantism. But the first successfully established alternative to the traditional ethic, if such it was, holds a special interest.

Not all analyses of modernization contain all of the elements described above. In part, this is an accident of chronology. Marx's analysis, for example, obviously could not be cast in a form which took account of the insights of Freud. Hence, psychic structural changes inevitably figure less prominently than those in social and economic structure. In part, it is a matter of terminology rather than substance. Unquestionably differences remain despite these two considerations, but there is at least tolerable unanimity that the several changes were closely interlocked and that they tended to reinforce each other. Latterly it has also been common to assume that an adequate understanding of modernization in Western Europe would entail *ipso facto* an understanding of the occurrence of the Industrial Revolution in England and its counterpart a little later on the continent.

In this view, the Industrial Revolution is a dramatic culmination to a long-gathering process of change, rather as the cylinder may be charged with a head of steam quite quickly but only if the water has long been heating. Geertz puts the matter succinctly. "In one sense, of course," he writes, "increasing per capita income *is* economic growth, not a mere index of it; but in another, it is clear that such increases are but one highly visible resultant of a complex process. . . . Though it may be true that, as an economic process, development is a dramatic,

---

15 On this argument, the attempt to impose new institutional forms by *force majeure* from the center not only offends local interests at the conscious level, but also stirs up large anxieties which are the harder for the individual to quell precisely because they are imperfectly accessible to him at the conscious level.

revolutionary change, as a broadly social process it fairly clearly is not. What looks like a quantum jump from a specifically economic point of view is, from a generally social one, merely the final expression in economic terms of a process which has been building up gradually over an extended period of time."[16]

This view is certainly plausible. The very concept of rationality as it has come to be used in the discussion of modernization is intimately related to the promotion of economic efficiency. All modernizing countries have enjoyed economic growth. The early stages of modernization produce, in Rostow's terminology, those changing propensities necessary for takeoff, after which takeoff itself occurs. Exponential economic growth gets under way. Real incomes rise. Material technology advances. Cities swell in size and population. Literacy becomes universal. As living standards rise, the death rate falls, presaging in its turn the control of fertility. Societies come to resemble more and more the late-twentieth century world.

It is my thesis in this essay that it is unwise to view the connection between the Industrial Revolution in England and the changes known as modernization in this manner. I shall argue that, although modernization may be a necessary condition for industrial revolution, it is not a sufficient condition; or, to put the same point in a different way, it is reasonable to argue that a society might become modernized without also becoming industrialized. I shall review in some detail what two major contemporary writers, Smith and Marx, had to say on this subject. It is convenient to do so because their account of the changes going on about them is a valuable corrective to some elements of the conventional wisdom about modernization and industrialization today. It is also a good base from which to explore further the evidence on which the competing explanations rest.

The *Wealth of Nations* might be described as the bible of modernizing man. Rationality and self-interest are made the guiding principles of action. No one has written more trenchantly and persuasively in their favor than Smith. He caught to perfection the capitalist ethic, as well as analyzing the advantages of a capitalist system in producing wealth:

16 Clifford Geertz, *Peddlers and Princes: Social Change and Economic Modernization in Two Indonesian Towns* (Chicago, 1968), 2.

... man has almost constant occasion for the help of his brethren, and it is vain for him to expect it from their benevolence only. He will be more likely to prevail if he can interest their self-love in his favour, and show them that it is for their own advantage to do for him what he requires of them. ... It is not from the benevolence of the butcher, the brewer, or the baker that we expect our dinner, but from their regard to their own interest. We address ourselves, not to their humanity but to their self-love, and never talk of our own necessities but of their advantages. Nobody but a beggar chooses to depend chiefly upon the benevolence of his fellow-citizens.[17]

Smith used a less technical and more telling prose than those who write of modernization today, but there is little in recent discussions of the topic which does not find a parallel in the *Wealth of Nations*.

Many later descriptions of the advantages of functional specificity in economic affairs and of the gains which flow from the division of labor refer to Smith's pinmakers. He was also insistent upon the importance of removing particularistic restrictions in the interest of higher overall efficiency. He advocated the abolition of the apprenticeship system. He opposed all regulations in restraint of trade, and legal incorporations. "The pretence that corporations are necessary for the better government of the trade is without any foundation. The real and effective discipline which is exercised over a workman is not that of his corporation but that of his customers."[18] He favored free trade in foodstuffs, including corn. The settlement laws were castigated: "There is scarce a poor man in England of forty years of age, I will venture to say, who has not in some part of his life felt himself most cruelly oppressed by this ill-contrived law of settlements."[19]

Adam Smith urged the fundamental importance of formal equality with great vigor. In a passage dealing with colonial trade, he finds its prosperity to be due above all to "that equal and impartial administration of justice which renders the rights of the meanest British subject respectable to the greatest, and which, by securing to every man the fruits of his own industry, gives the greatest and most effectual encouragement to every sort of industry";[20] a splendid text.

The *Wealth of Nations* also makes vividly clear the close connection

17 Adam Smith, "An Inquiry into the Nature and Causes of the Wealth of Nations," in *Great Books of the Western World* (Chicago, 1952), 7.
18 *Ibid.*, 56.
19 *Ibid.*, 61.
20 *Ibid.*, 264.

which Smith saw between modernization and firm, ubiquitous, reliable government. "Thirdly, and lastly," he remarks in a chapter entitled "How the Commerce of the Towns Contributed to the Improvement of the Country," "commerce and manufactures gradually introduced order and good government, and with them the liberty and security of individuals, among the inhabitants of the country, who had before lived almost in a continual state of war with their neighbours and of servile dependency upon their superiors. This, though it has been the least observed, is by far the most important of all their effects."[21] This chapter is one of the most interesting in the whole work, containing an account of the relationship between feudal law and medieval property and manners; a vignette of the redoubtable Cameron of Lochiel who in the mid-eighteenth century still exercised "the highest criminal jurisdiction" over his people "with great equity, though without any of the formalities of justice";[22] and an analysis of the way in which surplus income is disposed of in a country lacking commerce and manufactures —echoed more than a century later in Weber's discussion of the disposal of surpluses where "an expansion and refinement of everyday wants has not taken place."[23] There is even a passage in which Smith's diatribes upon the iniquities of the wealthy and powerful have a Marxian sting. Both believed that their follies and greed must bring about a revolution, though they had very different revolutions in mind.

> A revolution of the greatest importance to the public happiness was in this manner brought about by two different orders of people who had not the least intention to serve the public. To gratify the most childish vanity was the sole motive of the great proprietors. The merchants and artificers, much less ridiculous, acted merely from a view to their own interest, and in pursuit of their own pedlar principle of turning a penny wherever a penny was to be got. Neither of them had either knowledge or foresight of that great revolution which the folly of the one, and the industry of the other, was gradually bringing about.[24]

The proprietors and merchants were not alone in their ignorance of an impending revolution, for Smith himself was unaware of the immense changes already in train when the *Wealth of Nations* was written. Indeed, the implication of the arguments he used would rule

21 *Ibid.*, 175–176.
22 *Ibid.*, 177.
23 Weber, *Social and Economic Organization*, 189.
24 Smith, *Wealth of Nations*, 179.

out the possibility of rapid and sustained economic growth. The great revolution of which he wrote was an economic revolution, and was brought about by the group of changes now called modernization, but it was not an *industrial revolution* as that term has come to be used. If one were to characterize the difference between the two revolutions in a single phrase, one might say that whereas a defining characteristic of an industrial revolution is exponential economic growth, the expected outcome of modernization in Smith's view was asymptotic growth.

He believed that economic growth had been continuous during much of the same period as that in which the chief features of modern England took shape. "Since the time of Henry VIII the wealth and revenue of the country have been continually increasing, and, in the course of their progress, their pace seems rather to have been gradually accelerated, than retarded. They seem not only to have been going on, but to have been going on faster and faster. The wages of labor have been continually increasing during the same period, and in the greater part of the different branches of trade and manufactures the profits of stock have been diminishing." [25] This is a more optimistic picture of English economic history than would be thought orthodox today, but it did not lead Smith to an equally optimistic assessment of the future.

His doubts sprang in part from his analysis of the limitations upon the profitable employment of capital, and in part from his views on population trends. Like many of his contemporaries, he read, in recent Dutch experience, lessons about the future of other countries. Holland he held to be a richer country than England and one in which wage rates were higher, but the rate of interest lower than in any other country. "The government there borrows at two per cent, and private people of good credit at three." [26] Comparable rates in England were three and four per cent; in France higher still. Relative abundance of capital seeking profitable employment kept interest rates very low in Holland (and explained the large Dutch holdings in English and French funds); its relative scarcity meant much higher rates in Scotland and France. In general, he observed that high wages accompanied low interest rates, as in Holland, and *vice versa* as in France. Exceptionally, in colonies of recent settlement, both might be high together, although this happy state could not last long. But both might also be low, and Smith envisaged this as the most likely state toward which an economy might move. "In a country which had acquired that full complement of riches

25 *Ibid.*, 38.
26 *Ibid.*

which the nature of its soil and climate, and its situation with respect to other countries, allow it to acquire; which could, therefore, advance no further, and which was not going backwards, both the wages of labor and the profits of stock would probably be very low."[27]

The profits of stock would be low in this limiting case because investment opportunities had been exhausted. Wages would also tend to low because, as Smith put it in a passage which foreshadowed in part the views of Malthus: "Every species of animals naturally multiplies in proportion to the means of their subsistence."[28] A country might be wealthy but no longer growing in wealth. "If in such a country the wages of labour had ever been more than sufficient to maintain the labourer, and to enable him to bring up a family, the competition of the labourers and the interest of the masters would soon reduce them to this lowest rate which is consistent with common humanity."[29] Labor does best during the middle stages of modernization in Smith's analysis, because for a time capital finds the opportunity for fair profit while simultaneously labor may be relatively scarce.

> It is in the progressive state, while the society is advancing to the further acquisition, rather than when it has acquired its full complement of riches, that the condition of the labouring poor, of the great body of the people, seems to be the happiest and most comfortable. It is hard in the stationary, and miserable in the declining state. The progressive state is in reality the cheerful and hearty state to all the different orders of the society. The stationary is dull; the declining, melancholy.[30]

As modernization grew more complete, the prospects for both capital and labor would dim. The most favorable outcome that could be readily envisaged was one in which the material necessities of laboring men were set by social convention at a level well above that of bare subsistence. The least favorable might be very bleak. Both were equally consonant with what is now called modernization. Both David Ricardo, a generation later, and Marx after a further half-century, shared Smith's doubts about the prospect for the real wages of working men. The wages fund doctrine leaves little room for hope on this score. Yet, by definition, if real wages fail to rise, and a fortiori if they fall, industrialization is not taking place. A secular rise in real income per head is more a utopian ideal than an object for practical endeavor if economies

27 Ibid., 40.
28 Ibid., 34.
29 Ibid., 30.
30 Ibid., 34.

develop during modernization in the way Smith adumbrated—and his views on the matter were echoed by most of his successors until late in the following century. Marx, for instance was firm in his retention of Ricardo's argument on this point. "The value of labour-power is determined by the value of the necessaries of life habitually required by the average labourer. The quantity of these necessaries is known at any given epoch of a given society, and can therefore be treated as a constant magnitude."[31]

The course of events for many decades after the publication of the *Wealth of Nations* contained little to shake the convictions of those who doubted that the lot of working men could be greatly ameliorated. It is ironic, in view of the doctrine which links industrialization to rising real income per head, that there is clearer evidence for rising real wages in England in the first half of the eighteenth century and the second half of the nineteenth than for the intervening period during which the Industrial Revolution is usually supposed to have occurred. To save the phenomena, if rising real incomes are to be a defining characteristic of industrialization, their appearance must be conceded to be a heavily lagged effect.

It is clear enough why it was that Smith was mistaken in ruling out any hope of industrialization (in the sense the term is used in this essay). He failed to foresee the phenomenal productive powers which the new forms of fixed investment made possible. It was inventions like the steam engine, the coke-fired blast furnace, and the railway which proved him wrong in time, rather than some flaw in his logic or failure to perceive the nature of the modernization process, unless indeed this last is taken to imply the sort of technological advance which actually took place.

By Marx's time, the productive power of the new machines was already a dominant feature of the economic scene. This obliged him to treat the future prospects of man very differently from Smith, quite apart from any differences which might have sprung from their different attitudes to the modernization process in general. Factory industry appeared to Marx to be creating both greater misery and greater scope for future improvement than was conceivable without it. "Fanatically bent on making value expand itself, he [the capitalist] ruthlessly forces the human race to produce for production's sake; he thus forces the

31 Karl Marx (trans. from 3rd German ed. by Samuel Moore and Edward Aveling; ed. Friedrich Engels; rev. according to 4th German ed. by E. Untermann), *Capital: A Critical Analysis of Capitalist Production* (New York, 1906), 568.

development of the productive powers of society, and creates those material conditions, which alone can form the real basis of a higher form of society, a society in which the full and free development of every individual forms the ruling principle." [32] Meanwhile, productive potential was being perverted because of the way wealth was being dissipated: "the extraordinary productiveness of modern industry. . . allows of the unproductive employment of a larger and larger part of the working class, and the consequent reproduction, on a constantly extending scale, of the ancient domestic slaves under the name of a servant class, including men-servants, women-servants, lackeys, etc." [33]

Marx wrote *Capital* at a time when real wages were at the start of a period of steady and substantial growth. Had he written, say, twenty years later, he might have been tempted to apply to the later nineteenth century an observation he made about the fifteenth and early eighteenth centuries: "under special stimulus to enrichment, such as the opening of new markets, or of new spheres for the outlay of capital in consequence of newly developed social wants, etc., the scale of accumulation may be suddenly extended—[and]—the demand for labourers may exceed the supply, and, therefore, wages may rise." [34] Later in the chapter in which this passage occurs, however, Marx gives reasons for supposing that such a situation must prove temporary because of the basic defects of the capitalist system. [35]

In fact, real wages have risen steadily in the century since the publication of *Capital*, with only intermittent checks, and the assumption that this may be expected to continue, is deeply rooted in popular attitudes and in academic analysis (the prevailing definition of industrialization reflects this assumption). Over the same period during which real wages have been rising, mortality rates in urban areas, a measure which Marx sometimes used as a proxy for misery and degradation, have turned strongly downward; there has been a shift in the structure of aggregate demand which has combined with social preferences to reduce the numbers in domestic service drastically; the era of high mass consumption has dawned; "mixed" economies have become common. [36]

32 *Ibid.*, 649.
33 *Ibid.*, 487.
34 *Ibid.*, 672.
35 *Ibid.*, 680.
36 The possibilities latent in the last of these developments is suggested by Marx himself, although it was still too early for him to assess its longer term significance. In discussing the effects of the Factory Acts of 1850 and 1853, he wrote: "Their wonderful development [that of the industries affected by the Acts] from 1853 to 1860, hand-in-

Marx had the advantage over Smith in being able to observe very clearly that production *could* grow exponentially rather than tending to level off to some asymptote reached when the modernization process had exhausted the openings for profitable investment. He saw, in the tension between exponential growth in productive capacity and the asymptotic tendency of real wages among the vast majority of mankind, the certainty of violent, revolutionary change. Today, as far distant in time from *Capital* as *Capital* was from the *Wealth of Nations*, we can see that the secular trend of real wages is no more bound to be asymptotic than that of total production, but that, on the contrary, the two (when growth in total production is measured *per caput*) have marched closely together across the graphs of the last century.

With the benefit of hindsight, it may be said, the linkage between modernization and full-blown industrialization is evident, however it may have seemed to Smith at the onset of the Industrial Revolution or to Marx part-way through it. But hindsight is not always clear, and its benefit is sometimes questionable. In a rather trivial sense, since modernization was taking place in England from the sixteenth century onwards (Smith, Marx, Weber, and many lesser men are in substantial agreement here although their descriptive vocabularies differ), and was followed by the Industrial Revolution, it may be true that Smith's analysis was mistaken. But this is to say only that what happened, happened. We know that modernization *may* be followed by industrialization, but not that it *must*, or even that such a sequence of events is likely.[37]

Marx's account of the transition from handicraft industry to large-scale power-driven factory industry is interesting in this connection, since in his view the crucial change came before the use of inanimate sources of power on a large scale. He distinguished between tools and machines, the one characteristic of manufacture (handicraft industry), the other of modern industry. "The machine proper. . . is a mechanism that, after being set in motion, performs with its tools the same operations that were formerly done by the workman with similar tools.

---

hand with the physical and moral regeneration of the factory workers, struck the most purblind." Marx, *Capital*, 323–324.

37 The concatenation of changes which comprise the Industrial Revolution are a good example of what Hayek had in mind in writing: "Many of the greatest things man has achieved are not the result of consciously directed thought, and still less the product of a deliberately co-ordinated effort of many individuals, but of a process in which the individual plays a part which he can never fully understand," Friedrich August von Hayek, *The Counter-Revolution of Science: Studies on the Abuse of Reason* (New York, 1964), 84. The act of comprehension is almost as taxing as that of creation.

Whether the motive power is derived from man, or from some other machine, makes no difference in this respect. From the moment that the tool proper is taken from man, and fitted into a mechanism, a machine takes the place of a mere implement. The difference strikes one at once, even in those cases where man himself continues to be the prime mover." [38] Again, "The machine, which is the starting point of the industrial revolution, supersedes the workman, who handles a single tool, by a mechanism operating with a number of tools, and set in motion by a single motive power, whatever the form of that power may be." [39] The distinction between animate and inanimate sources of power Marx held to be unimportant. "The steam engine itself, such as it was at its invention, during the manufacturing period at the close of the seventeenth century, and such as it continued to be down to 1780, did not give rise to any industrial revolution. It was, on the contrary, the invention of machines that made a revolution in the form of steam-engines necessary." [40]

In a sense, the essence of the modernization/industrialization question lies in this last sentence. As rationality spreads and markets broaden, productivity in many branches of industry will increase by the division of labor and the adoption of machinery. If the "right" invention inevitably appears to match every opportunity as it emerges, the smallest gains will tend to be cumulative. Marx's view of the introduction of the steam engine by factory industry is reminiscent of Voltaire's aphorism about God—if He had not existed, He would have had to be invented. Rostow takes a similar line.[41] Smith vividly described how this process might become institutionalized. Having noted how many machines had been designed by workers to save themselves labor, he continues: "Many improvements have been made by the ingenuity of the makers of machines, when to make them became the business of a peculiar trade; and some by that of those who are called philosophers or men of speculation, whose trade it is not to do anything, but to observe everything; and who, upon that account, are often capable of combining together the powers of the most distant and dissimilar objects." [42]

38 Marx, *Capital*, 408.
39 *Ibid.*, 410.
40 *Ibid.*, 409–410.
41 "The appropriate general proposition concerning the composition of innovations seems to be that necessity is the mother of invention." Rostow, *Economic Growth*, 83.
42 Smith, *Wealth of Nations*, 5.

If, however, technological advance were a more wayward and circumstantial matter, and there were no automatic response to opportunity, it is incautious to assume that the issue can be passed over so lightly. It is interesting that Rostow takes exception to Schumpeter's discussion of innovation, quoting a passage which bears repeating:

> It might be thought that innovation can never be anything else but an effort to cope with a given economic situation. In a sense this is true. For a given innovation to become possible, there must always be some "objective needs" to be satisfied and some "objective conditions"; but they rarely, if ever, uniquely determine what kind of innovation will satisfy them, and as a rule they can be satisfied in many different ways. Most important of all, they may remain unsatisfied for an indefinite time, which shows that they are not in themselves sufficient to produce an innovation.[43]

Ironically, the same passage in *Capital*, from which Marx's observations about tools, machinery, and the steam engine were drawn, contains an aside which might suggest a very different conclusion from that which Marx drew. He refers to the drainage of the Haarlemmermeer by steam pump in 1836–37, noting that the machinery used the same principle as an ordinary pump and differed only in that it was driven by "cyclopean steam-engines."[44] In a footnote he describes the earlier history of drainage in Holland.

> It was partly the want of streams with a good fall on them, and partly their battle with a superabundance of water in other respects which compelled the Dutch to resort to wind as a motive power. The windmill itself they got from Germany, where its invention was the origin of a pretty squabble between the nobles, priests, and the emperor, as to which of those three the wind "belonged." The air makes bondage, was the cry in Germany, at the same time that the wind was making Holland free. What it reduced to bondage in this case, was not the Dutchman, but the land for Dutchmen.[45]

The perennial drainage problem which has plagued Dutch history is technically similar to the problem of evacuating water from coal mines, for which the Newcomen engine was developed in England. In both

43 Joseph A. Schumpeter, *Business Cycles: A Theoretical, Historical, and Statistical Analysis of the Capitalist Process* (New York, 1939), I, 85n.
44 Marx, *Capital*, 409.
45 *Ibid.*, 409n.

cases, a basic factor of production was in danger of destruction (or at least of becoming inaccessible) unless huge volumes of water could be pumped away. That the steam engine represents a better solution than the windmill to the drainage problem in Holland is clear from the eagerness with which it was adopted at the Haarlemmermeer and elsewhere, but that it would have been developed independently in Holland is highly doubtful, even though more was at stake for Holland than for England, and Holland was perhaps a more fully modernized country than England in the early eighteenth century.

If it is true that certain important technological innovations first introduced in the eighteenth century, such as the steam engine and the coke-fed blast furnace, were the product of special, local circumstances;[46] and if it is also true that without them, productivity, handicapped by a lack of power and precision in the available machinery, could have risen only moderately, then the connection between modernization and industrialization appears much more a matter of happy coincidence than of ineluctable necessity. It is not what was common to all modernizing countries, but what was peculiar to England which then appears important. And what is explained is not simply why the Industrial Revolution occurred in England earlier than elsewhere, but why it occurred at all.

The two conditions which must be satisfied if this conclusion is to follow are plausible but not conclusively demonstrable. It is likely on general grounds that a very large part of the total gain in productivity during the Industrial Revolution sprang from technological advances.[47] It is also reasonable to suppose that the relative scarcities of important raw materials in England, combined with local factor endowment, served both to produce an unusual range of problems at an early stage in industrial expansion and also to permit solutions whose long-term implications were not apparent at their first adoption. I have discussed these circumstances and their outcome elsewhere,[48] and wish in this

46 See E. A. Wrigley, "The Supply of Raw Materials in the Industrial Revolution," *Economic History Review*, XV (1962), 1–16.
47 For the class of reasons discussed, for example, by Robert M. Solow, "Technical Change and the Aggregate Production Function," *Review of Economics and Statistics*, XXXIX (1957), 312–320.
48 See n. 46, above.

essay to concentrate mainly on giving a context to the English experience by commenting on events elsewhere in Western Europe. However,
it may be useful to refer briefly to those peculiarities of English economic life which had a bearing on the development of the steam engine
and a new technology of iron production.

Shortage of wood made England increasingly dependent on coal
for domestic and industrial fuel from the late sixteenth century, and,
until well into the nineteenth century, English coal production dwarfed
that of continental Europe. The coal industry's growth involved severe
difficulties from the start, connected above all with mine drainage as the
pits went deeper. Immense pains were taken to overcome them. Three-
fourths of all patents issued between 1561 and 1668 are said to have been
related to the coal industry's problems in some degree, and one-seventh
was taken up with drainage. The engines of Savery and Newcomen
were late entrants into the competition to find an answer to this problem. By the early eighteenth century, Newcomen engines had been
developed to the point where they were reliable and necessary adjuncts
to coal production, at once essential to its continued expansion and
unusable without a local supply of coal. James Watt's refinement of the
new machine made it the means of revolutionizing transport and transforming production in industry after industry as the nineteenth century
drew on.[49]

The fuel problem also loomed large in iron production. In the first
three-quarters of the eighteenth century, iron production made little
progress in England due to a lack of charcoal or an acceptable substitute.
In France at the same time, iron production, using traditional methods,
expanded more rapidly and eventually surpassed English levels substantially. It was clear to many men that coal or coke might provide a
good solution to the problem of finding a charcoal substitute, but it
proved very hard to produce iron of acceptable quality in this way
because of the difficulty of keeping the chemical impurities in the iron
sufficiently low. Once the trick was learned, however, old limitations

49 On the question of patents, see Stephen F. Mason, *A History of the Sciences: Main
Currents of Scientific Thought* (London, 1953), 217. Levasseur made an interesting calculation to drive home the significance of the steam engine in extending man's productive
powers. He noted that, on the assumption that the amount of work done by one steam
horse-power was equal to that of twenty-one men, France had at its disposal just over
one million slaves of a new mechanical kind in 1840. By the middle 1880s, the figure had
risen to 98 million, or two and one-half slaves for every inhabitant of France. Emile
Levasseur, *La population française: Histoire de la population avant 1789 et démographie de la
France comparée à celle des autres nations au XIXè siècle* (Paris, 1892), III, 74.

upon the scale of iron production disappeared. Mineral sources of heat and power, unlike the vegetable and animal alternatives which they supplanted, could be tapped in larger and larger quantities without driving up the marginal costs of production. Industry at long last escaped from the limitations under which it had labored as long as it was dependent upon the productivity of the land. Inanimate sources of heat and power offered great advantages over animate sources for this reason.

The steam engine and the coke-fired blast furnace were the result of a long defensive struggle against intractable production difficulties. They did not occur when production was rising unusually fast. In the second case, production was barely holding its own when the crucial innovations were made. This makes a contrast with the course of change in the cotton industry, where the burst of innovations occurred at a time of rising production and bright prospects. The water frame and spinning jenny came into use in the 1770s (the patents were dated 1769 and 1770) at a time when cotton production was already growing fast. Retained imports of raw cotton had doubled in the previous quarter century.[50] They were the result of a clear opportunity to expand rather than the wish to avoid contraction, and they presaged a period of much more hectic growth. The cotton industry during this period progressed in a manner which conforms well to Smith's view of "the progressive state." Considerable growth is clearly possible in this state and is linked to modernization, but for an industrial revolution to occur, there must be a switch to a new energy source.

The power requirements of the new textile machines were so modest that the steam engine was no more than a useful alternative to a waterfall for many years. The overshot wheel provided all the power that was needed to drive them. But there came a time when greater power was needed and unused waterfalls with a sufficient head were few and remote. Even in the textile industry, and still more in industrial production at large, it is reasonable to assume that the factory would not have become the predominant unit of production without the new technology of coal, steam, and iron. The unexampled and continuous growth in production per head which fascinated Marx's generation was based upon it.[51]

---

50 Phyllis Deane and W. A. Cole, *British Economic Growth, 1688–1959: Trends and Structure* (Cambridge, 1962), 51.

51 Jevons published a work which reflects this interest and the new attitude to the creation of wealth very well at almost exactly the same time as *Capital*. W. Stanley

If it were always a case of "Cometh the hour, cometh the engine," it would matter little how the new technology first came into being, since the need for a cheap, reliable source of energy to magnify the productive power of the new machines would have ensured its development. If, on the contrary, technological advance in a prescientific age is far from automatic, whatever the "objective" possibilities of the time—if Schumpeter's view is more just than Rostow's—if the development of power sources for textile machinery might have stopped short with water power as Dutch drainage did with the windmill, then the particular course of events in England will repay close attention. So, too, will the circumstances of other European countries at the same time, for they suggest other possibilities within the general framework of modernization.

Smith wrote not only of the relative abundance which was attainable in the progressive state, but also of stationary and declining states in which the lot of men was far less enviable. And it appears from the context of his remarks that he thought that a country could be modernized and yet find itself in one of the two latter states as easily as in the progressive. Europe in the eighteenth century affords examples of all three and also of more mixed conditions. Comparison with continental Europe offers some indirect warrant for thinking that England was fortunate to have remained in a progressive state.

Smith appears to have believed that Holland was in what he called a stationary state, having moved close to the asymptote which represented the full extent of growth possible in the circumstances of the day. The principal evidence for this was the prevailing rate at which money could be borrowed on good credit, and he found it necessary to remark that there was no good reason to suppose that business in Holland had actually declined, fearing that his readers would draw this inference.[52] In his view, Holland was the country with the highest real income per head of any in Europe, but was, for that reason, the more likely to be at or close to the limit of growth, rather than being poised for a continuing surge of expansion. That Holland had reached a high degree of rationality in economic affairs seems indisputable. Nor was this just an urban phenomenon, leaving the countryside largely untouched. A very telling example of the suffusion of the countryside by advanced forms of

---

Jevons, *The Coal Question: An Inquiry Concerning the Progress of the Nation, and the Probable Exhaustion of our Coal-Mines* (London, 1865).
52 Smith, *Wealth of Nations*, 38.

economic organization is to be found in Roessingh's recent analysis of a set of tax records relating to the Veluwe in 1749.[53]

The Veluwe lies in central Holland south of the Zuider Zee. It had never attained the degree of commercial or industrial development found in the west of Holland, and particularly in the province of Holland itself. It was an agricultural area with no large town, whose soils were at best of moderate quality. Yet Roessingh's study shows that even small settlements from 400 inhabitants upward almost invariably had a village shop (at a time when shops were still rare in England in places of similar size), a tailor, a shoemaker, and very often a weaver and baker, as well. All were frequently found in much smaller villages, too, and the hierarchical pattern of service function by settlement size was very well ordered. This was an economy in which division of labor had been pushed very far; in which money and the market entered into the lives even of small men to a degree which supported shops in small villages and caused wives to cease baking at home. The villages of the Veluwe were far removed from the type of communities which Tönnies had in mind in describing the nature of *Gemeinschaft*, even though theirs was largely an agricultural economy in a strictly rural setting. The Veluwe was part of an economy which had been modernized but not industrialized. Such an economy does not necessarily mean steadily rising real incomes, nor does it imply a move towards industrialization. When rationality prevails and men's actions are informed by self-interest, there must be gains in efficiency, but there is no certain and permanent rise in living standards for the bulk of the population.

At much the same time that the Veluwe census was taken, in another part of the Low Countries—in Belgian Flanders—the local economy was about to enter into what Smith might have called a declining state, as the work of Deprez and Mendels has shown.[54] They describe the instability of an economy, already substantially modernized, which becomes heavily dependent upon cottage industry to supplement income from agriculture. What begins as a useful addition to farming income comes to be, for many men, their prime or sole means of support. Population growth accelerates when checks upon early marriage

53 H. K. Roessingh, "Village and Hamlet in a Sandy Region of the Netherlands in the Middle of the Eighteenth Century," *Acta Historiae Neerlandica*, IV (1970), 105-129.
54 P. Deprez (trans. Margaret Hilton), "The Demographic Development of Flanders in the Eighteenth Century," in D. V. Glass and D. E. C. Eversley (eds.), *Population in History: Essays in Historical Demography* (Chicago, 1965), 608-630. Mendels' work is summarized briefly in Franklin F. Mendels, "Industrialization and Population Pressure in Eighteenth Century Flanders," *Journal of Economic History*, XXXI (1971), 269-271.

and high fertility, which are more powerful in a landholding community, lose their force. With the labor force growing more rapidly than opportunities for profitable employment, real incomes fall and the bitterly impoverished population is pushed down toward the lowest levels of subsistence. The lives of most men in the Vieuxbourg area, where conditions were especially bad, were indeed "melancholy," to use Smith's adjective for the declining state, by the end of the eighteenth century. In the Twente region of the province of Overijssel in east Holland, the declining, or at best stationary, state supervened about 1750. As in Flanders, the local linen industry proved unable to expand its markets as quickly as was needed to keep pace with the growth of the rural industrial population.[55] The economic history of early modern Europe contains many examples of areas at various stages along the road to modernization where change was accompanied by falling real incomes per head.[56] Eighteenth-century Holland represents as a whole a relatively happy outcome to this challenge in that real wages were maintained at a fairly high level.[57] Rationality in economic life neither led to a takeoff, nor plunged the population into misery.

Smith would not have been surprised at events in Flanders and elsewhere. Like Malthus and many later writers, including Marx, he saw dangers to living standards in rapid population growth and was inclined to regard population growth as dependent upon economic conditions. If the opportunities for employment grew, the labor supply could be relied upon to increase commensurately and was only too likely to increase more than commensurately. Marx expressed a view about what determines wage levels which is, in substance, the same as that of Smith or Malthus, although he had a special reason for taking a somber view of their secular trend. On the former point he wrote. "The value of labour-power is determined, as in the case of every other commodity, by the labour-time necessary for the production, and

55 B. H. Slicher van Bath, *Een samenleving onder spanning; geschiedenis van het platteland in Overijssel* (Assen, 1957). His conclusions are summarized in J. A. Faber, et al., "Population Changes and Economic Developments in the Netherlands: A Historical Survey," *Afdeling Agrarische Geschiedenis Bijdragen* (Wageningen, 1965), XII, 47–113, esp. 72–89.
56 Braun's study of an upland Swiss area is an example of the type of change which can easily produce this result. Rudolf Braun, *Industrialisierung und Volksleben: die Veränderung der Lebensformen in einem ländlichen Industriegebiet vor 1800* (Zurich, 1960).
57 It also illustrates a point which can hardly be made too strongly—that economic fortunes were at least as much a matter of region as of country in early modern Europe. They remained so during the early stages of the Industrial Revolution. I have traced one example of this in E. A. Wrigley, *Industrial Growth and Population Change* (Cambridge, 1961).

consequently also the reproduction, of this special article. . . . Given the individual, the production of labour-power consists in his reproduction of himself or his maintenance. . . . in other words, the value of labour-power is the value of the means of subsistence necessary for the maintenance of the labourer."[58] Convention may, however, play a part in determining the subsistence level.

> His natural wants, such as food, clothing, fuel, and housing, vary according to the climatic and other physical conditions of his country. On the other hand, the number and extent of his so-called necessary wants, as also the modes of satisfying them, are themselves the product of historical development, and depend therefore to a great extent on the degree of civilisation of a country, more particularly on the conditions under which, and consequently on the habits and degree of comfort in which, the class of free labourers has been formed. In contradistinction therefore to the case of other commodities, there enters into the determination of the value of labour-power a historical and moral element. Nevertheless, in a given country, at a given period, the average quantity of the means of subsistence necessary for the labourer is practically known.[59]

This was very much Smith's view, too. He felt the disquiet to which Malthus was later to give fuller expression, although his doubts were tempered by his appreciation of the complexity of the process of growth, which gave some ground for optimism. Nevertheless, if population is sensitive to economic stimuli and grows readily when conditions improve (for example, because young people marry when wheat is cheap), and if the rate at which population can grow exceeds the rate at which the economy can expand, then there is little hope of increasing subsistence wages set at some conventional standard, and a pressing fear that a volatile population growth may cause the conventional standard to be eroded. There was no warrant in past experience for expecting an economy to grow steadily at, say, 3 per cent per annum, a rate which would ensure that production grew more rapidly than population, and so enable real incomes to rise in spite of growing numbers.

By Marx's day, it had become clear that a rapid and sustained growth in industrial production was possible, but in his analysis, labor, by one of the crucial paradoxes of the capitalist mode of production, is

58 Marx, *Capital*, 189–190.
59 *Ibid.*, 190.

actually worse off as a result, both in income and in the general nature and conditions of work. His analysis depends upon his insistence that each historic mode of production has its own special population laws.[60] In a capitalist society, the industrial reserve army grows. Its relative size determines wage levels, and "The fact that the means of production, and the productiveness of labour, increase more rapidly than the productive population, expresses itself, therefore, capitalistically in the inverse form that the labouring population always increases more rapidly than the conditions under which capital can employ this increase for its own self-expansion."[61]

Given that over-rapid population growth may be a cause of economic distress (as it seems to have been in England in the late sixteenth and early seventeenth century), it is of interest that England in the second half of the eighteenth century was perhaps in greater danger than France or Holland, the two other countries in which modernization had progressed furthest.[62] The threat to wages posed by population growth had been increasing in most of Europe in the later eighteenth century. Ireland had embarked on a period of her history which brings to mind the process which Geertz calls agricultural involution, which "resembles nothing else so much as treading water. Higher-level densities are offset by greater labour inputs into the same productive system, but output per head (or per mouth) remains more or less constant."[63] The pool grows larger, but the numbers treading water in it increase at least as quickly.[64] Many other countries, especially in eastern and southern Europe, where population growth rates were often high, would eventually have met a fate like that which devastated Ireland, but for the safety valves afforded by industrialization in Western Europe and the possibility of emigrating to countries of European settlement outside Europe. But in France, there were signs that rationality was beginning to affect reproductive behavior.

60 Ibid., 692–693.
61 Ibid., 708.
62 In Holland, population increased hardly at all in the eighteenth century. In 1700, the total lay between 1.85 and 1.95 million; in 1795, 2.08 million (Faber, Afdeling, XII, 110). In France, the growth was faster but much less fast than that in England. The French population rose from 19.3 to 26.3 million between 1700 and 1789 (Marcel R. Reinhard, et al., Histoire générale de la population mondiale [Paris, 1968; 3rd ed.], 252, 683). The population of England and Wales grew from c. 5.5 to 9.2 million between 1700 and 1800.
63 Clifford Geertz, Agricultural Involution: The Process of Ecological Change in Indonesia (Berkeley, 1963), 78.
64 Ibid., 95.

Perhaps it is symbolically appropriate that the first group which is known to have adopted effective and conscious family limitation as part of their habit of life should have been the bourgeoisie of Geneva, the city of Calvin. This pattern of behavior was firmly established by the end of the seventeenth century.[65] A century later it was growing common throughout much of France. Characteristically, it seems to have begun in small towns before the surrounding countryside was affected, but very early in the nineteenth century there were several large areas in which family limitation was widespread among peasant populations.[66] In consequence, French population growth was much more modest in the nineteenth century than that of any other major European state. By the end of the century, this had become a matter for the keenest regret among many French writers, an attitude still evident in the work of recent French scholars.[67] If the Industrial Revolution had not occurred, however, France might have been the envy of Europe. French population trends were much safer than English in the economic world which Smith depicted. The principles of rationality and self-interest which inform the entire range of changes during modernization point to fertility control within marriage as surely as to the division of labor or to the principle of universalistic criteria for group membership.

The process of modernization may also have affected fertility levels in other countries earlier than in England.[68] It may prove to be the case

65   Louis Henry, *Anciennes familles genevoises: étude démographique, XVIe–XXe siècle* (Paris, 1956), 77–78, 94–110, 127–142.
66   There is an excellent brief review of early modern French demographic history in Pierre Goubert, "Historical Demography and the Reinterpretation of Early Modern French History: A Research Review," *Journal of Interdisciplinary History*, I (1970), 37–48. Antoinette Chamoux and Cécile Dauphin, "La contraception avant la Révolution française. L'exemple de Châtillon-sur-Seine," *Annales, E.S.C.*, XXIV (1969), 662–684. Etienne van de Walle of the Office of Population Research, Princeton University, tells me that the large-scale study of nineteenth-century fertility in progress in that Office shows that by about 1830, when marital fertility was already low in parts of the south-west and Normandy, there was in those areas a very marked association between low marital fertility and early marriage—a very "rational" pattern of behavior in the sense that ability to limit family size within marriage removes what would otherwise be a telling "rational" argument against early marriage. There is some discussion of this point for a later period in his article, "Marriage and Marital Fertility," *Daedalus*, XCVII (1968), 486–501.
67   See, for example, Alfred Sauvy, *General Theory of Population* (London, 1969), 272–282.
68   I have found some evidence of family limitation in Colyton, Devon, in the second half of the seventeenth century, but it is not yet possible to say how widespread this was. And all trace of it had disappeared in Colyton by the middle decades of the eighteenth century. See E. A. Wrigley, "Family Limitation in Pre-Industrial England," *Economic History Review*, XIX (1966), 82–109.

that in parts of Holland there was restriction of family size at an early date. Van der Woude's tabulations for certain settlements in the province of Holland show that household size was unusually small in the late seventeenth and eighteenth centuries, and the number of children per family somewhat lower than in England.[69] This was an area deeply involved in commerce, with a high proportion of the population literate, perhaps the most thoroughly modernized part of that country which contemporaries regarded as the furthest advanced in modernization. Dutch church registers do not easily lend themselves to family reconstitution so that clear-cut confirmation of low marital fertility is hard to obtain, but it is at least possible that here, as in Geneva, rationality produced a lowering of fertility in marriage among some elements in the population. There is also evidence that a substantial proportion of men and women never married. Postponement or avoidance of marriage is an equally effective "rational" strategy (although it may also occur for other reasons). Early in the nineteenth century, a tendency toward modern patterns of marital fertility appeared among the native-born in New England.[70] It was well established half a century before the same pattern appeared in England.

Population growth in England accelerated sharply in the mid-eighteenth century and remained at a high level until late in the nineteenth, at or a little over 1 per cent per annum. If incomes were not eventually to suffer as a result, production had to increase at least as fast as the population. To Smith, the chance of tripling the national product in a century (roughly the scale of increase needed merely to offset population growth) would have seemed slight; and time for a solution was short when growth was so rapid. Over-rapid population growth brings great dangers to a modernizing society, although in an industrializing society, population growth may even confer benefits. It was England's good fortune that the Industrial Revolution rescued her from

69 A. M. van der Woude, "De omvang en samenstelling van de huishouding in Nederland in het verleden," *Afdeling Agrarische Geschiedenis* (1970), XV, 202–241.

70 See, e.g., Peter R. Uhlenberg, "A Study of Cohort Life Cycles: Cohorts of Native Born Massachusetts Women, 1830–1920," *Population Studies*, XXIII (1969), 407–420, esp. Tables 1 and 2. Evidence of family limitation among small groups within the settled American population may be found in Robert V. Wells, "Family Size and Fertility Control in Eighteenth Century America: A Study of Quaker Families," *Population Studies*, XXV (1971), 73–82. There is inconclusive but suggestive evidence that marital fertility fell at the end of the eighteenth century among high-status Dutch settlers in the Hudson valley in Alice P. Kenney, "Patricians and Plebians in Colonial Albany," *Halve Maen: Quarterly Magazine of the Dutch Colonial Period in America*, XLV (1970–71), 1: 7–8, 14; 2: 9–11, 13; 3: 9–11; 4: 13–14; XLVI (1971), 1: 13–15.

what must otherwise have been a period of great stress due to the pace of population increase.

Smith regarded investment in land as the surest way of increasing national wealth. "The capital employed in agriculture, therefore, not only puts into motion a greater quantity of productive labour than any equal capital employed in manufactures, but in proportion, too, to the quantity of productive labour which it employs, it adds a much greater value to the annual produce of the land and labour of the country, to the real wealth and revenue of its inhabitants. Of all the ways in which a capital can be employed, it is by far the most advantageous to society."[71] The extent of the growth in industrial production was, in his view, geared to agricultural expansion. But land was in virtually fixed supply and the increases in production attainable from land in farms were limited and usually secured only over a long period. Therefore growth in general must be limited, or, in the terminology I have used in this essay, asymptotic. Modern industry based on the steam engine, a new iron technology, and the organization of production in factories, came just in time to save the day. Whether the further development of the sources of increased productivity familiar to Smith could have achieved the same success is highly doubtful. The Industrial Revolution represented a break in the working out of modernizing tendencies in Europe, a break which ultimately generalized and extended the scope of modernization while at the same time modifying it, but which was initially ill-matched with it.

Capital is, in a sense, a commentary on the severity of the tensions which were produced by the uneasy marriage of industrialization and modernization, a marriage in which the former proved to be the salvation of the latter in England by giving it a vastly larger economic base and freeing it from restrictions which had earlier seemed inescapable. But the price was high. Marx made an attempt to categorize the lessons to be learned from the turmoil of the first half of the nineteenth century in England, and to glean from this experience an insight into the future. His message was clear. The marriage was intolerable and must be dissolved if the benefits made possible by industrialization (but denied to the masses by the capitalist system set in a bourgeois state) were ever to be distributed equitably. The marriage proved more durable than Marx expected, and it became the object of widespread emulation. As time passed, the characters of the two partners merged into each other,

71 Smith, *Wealth of Nations,* 157.

and the early difficulties faded from memory. What had seemed inconceivable to Smith and intolerable to Marx developed into an acceptable commonplace. National product could rise without apparent limit, and was so divided as to assure most men of rising real incomes.

Some of the differences between the gradual development of modernization and the novel changes produced by the Industrial Revolution are epitomized in the contrast between old and new urban growth in England. London grew steadily throughout the period of modernization in England from the sixteenth century onwards. By the end of the eighteenth, it was already a big city with a population close to one million. London's development was relatively smooth and continuous. The city grew no faster in the nineteenth than in the seventeenth century. Already in 1700 very complex arrangements were needed to sustain it, and the London market helped to cause notable changes in areas at some distance from London—in the agriculture of Fen-edge villages in Cambridgeshire, for example, or in those Leicestershire villages which became the home of the framework knitting industry. The growth of London was made possible by the economic and social changes of modernization, which were in turn fostered by it.[72] Defoe's London at the beginning of the eighteenth century, like Dicken's London in the mid-nineteenth, might be termed modernized, but not industrialized (there was, of course, a very large employment in industry, but the production units were usually tiny, often the home itself). Literacy was higher than elsewhere in England,[73] and the economic and social functioning of the city conformed well to what would be expected from a checklist of modernization—the chief concomitants of rationality and self-interest were eminently visible, while some of the most perturbing results of sheer size became less serious toward the end of the eighteenth century. Mortality rates, for example, had fallen considerably from the peak reached in the early decades of the century.

In contrast to the pattern of city growth in London, the large urban sprawls which unrolled across the industrial north and midlands from the end of the eighteenth century might almost be described as industrial but not modern. In these areas, levels of literacy were often very low, as poor as in the most backward rural areas of the country, and

---

72   See E. A. Wrigley, "A Simple Model of London's Importance in Changing English Society and Economy," *Past and Present*, XXXVII (1967), 44–70.

73   This is evident from the materials assembled by R. S. Schofield at the Cambridge Group for the History of Population and Social Structure. Schofield hopes to publish the results of his analysis of this material shortly.

mortality rates frequently very high. Even the free play of the market and the universal use of money as a means of exchange were threatened by the spread of truck systems of payment and the tying of employees to the company shop. Consumption standards were low and of limited scope. Tight-knit industrial and mining villages were almost solely of one class and there were few visible "betters" whose patterns of consumption could be aped. Rationality and self-interest had small room to flourish among men and women in the areas of working-class housing which grew up in knots round the factory or the pithead. This was a far cry from the capitalism of myriad small producers and consumers. It is not purely fanciful to see in communities of this type as many of the features which are held to go with *Gemeinschaft* as with *Gesellschaft*.[74] Industrialization brought with it major regressive features judged by the measuring rods of modernization.

In time this could be seen as a case of *reculer pour mieux sauter*, but it is hardly surprising that it was seldom seen in this way at the time. In hindsight, the magnitude of contemporary hazards and uncertainties tends to be lost to view. All one-piece theories of modernization/ industrialization, such as the analogy with the takeoff of an airplane, bear too heavily the marks of *ex post facto* summary to do justice to the Industrial Revolution. There is much to be learned from both Smith and Marx about the surprising and uncertain course taken by events. The fact that neither was right in the long run is not a good reason for ignoring their arguments. It is quite possible for a man to have, say, a one-in-fifty chance of hitting the jackpot and yet still win it. The relationship between modernization and industrialization cannot be reduced to simple odds, of course. Perhaps the analogy is misleading, but it will have served a useful purpose if it underlines the absence of any inevitability about the transition from a modernized but preindustrial economy to the postindustrial world.

74 Much of this has remained and is reflected in descriptions of the life of the industrial working classes in the recent past. See, for example, Richard Hoggart, *The Uses of Literacy: Aspects of Working-Class Life, With Special Reference to Publications and Entertainments* (London, 1967).

Franklin F. Mendels

Social Mobility and
Phases of Industrialization

The study of historical patterns of social mobility inevitably leads to questions about its determinants and to the search for correlations between mobility and industrialization. This paper is not based on any new empirical research on social mobility. Neither can it pretend to be based on an exhaustive reading of the extant literature. Rather, it focuses on the process of industrialization to provide some thoughts on social mobility during the passage of Western societies from the pre-industrial to the industrial age. Included here in social mobility are occupational, status and geographical, and inter- as well as intra-generational mobility. The discussion covers any of these three facets of social mobility when appropriate. A last caveat: this paper includes a typology of industrialization which is not fully and rigorously developed. Rather, the typology is used loosely with the sole purpose of emphasizing certain differences between phases or types of industrialization which are relevant to the study and understanding of social mobility in its various aspects.

The concept of industrialization usually refers to a dichotomy between traditional and modern society and to a more or less drawn-out transition from the former to the latter. For the purpose of analyzing the interactions between industrial change and mobility, it is useful first to recall how social mobility operates in pre-industrial societies. Second, it seems essential to take a close look at the process of industrialization itself and distinguish in it several phases (or types). Finally, it would be one-sided and

Franklin F. Mendels is Associate Professor of History at the University of Maryland Baltimore County.

This is a revised version of a paper I was asked to prepare for presentation at the Mathematical Social Science Board Conference on International Comparisons of Social Mobility in Past Societies, 1972. I have benefited from the comments and suggestions of Rondo Cameron, Paul Hohenberg, Hartmut Kaelble, Hans Medick, Iris Mendels, and Jürgen Schlumbohm. The ideas expressed in the first part of the article are a by-product of long discussions with Lutz K. Berkner about our joint work on "fertility and family law in Western Europe." Work for this paper has been supported by U.S.P.H.S. Grant HD 5586 and a grant under the Ford and Rockefeller Foundations Program in Support of Social Science and Legal Research on Population Policy. Of course, I alone am responsible for the opinions expressed here.

perhaps misleading to consider industrialization and economic development only as exogenous causal factors with respect to social mobility. Industrial development in Western countries was itself shaped in many ways by the stratification within respective countries, by the system of values of their various strata, and by the possibilities for the movement of individuals and groups— movement from employment in low-efficiency, low-earnings, or low-status occupations to employment in occupations with higher efficiency, earnings, or status; or movement from undifferentiated, unspecialized work to the kind of tasks needed in the factory system. Not all societies were endowed with the social and political structure which made such movements possible. To some extent, this structure adapted itself to economic forces and opportunities, but national or regional traditions, or the forces of vested interests, were sometimes persistent enough to slow down or postpone structural adaptation to a rapidly changing environment.

If in the study of social mobility we started from the work of Kuznets and others, we would define the epoch of modern economic growth (or modern industrialization) as one characterized by a "sustained increase in income per capita . . . most often accompanied by an increase in population . . . and by sweeping structural changes. The latter included a reallocation of resources toward non-agricultural activities (industry and services), a massive urbanization of the population, and changes in the relative economic position of groups defined by employment status, attachment to various industries, and level of per capita income."[1] At its own level of abstraction, this is an excellent definition. It means that a functional prerequisite of modern economic growth is a mobility which permits an initially rural, peasant agricultural society to transform itself over time into one where most people live in cities and work in industry and services.

Unfortunately, to look at change in this manner does not help uncover underlying mechanisms with any precision. A given rate of *net* occupational mobility between two dates may conceal much larger and more complex gross flows in and out of occupations. Similarly, the rural-urban transition of the early phases of industrialization resulted from much larger migration flows than would

---

[1] Simon Kuznets, *Modern Economic Growth* (New Haven, 1966), 1. The complete definition given by Kuznets is not relevant here.

appear from merely looking at the changing share of the population that was urbanized. As Wrigley has shown, the growth of London from 7 to 11 percent of the English population between 1650 and 1750 implies that the survivors of at least 17 percent of all the births taking place in the country eventually moved to London. If one could take account of the large movement of return migration, this figure would be even higher. Why such large gross flows were necessary to generate much smaller net changes is explained by the negative natural increase of cities, itself the result of the high urban mortality which prevailed in all European towns until the development of modern hygiene. For instance, the age of continuous growth by natural increase did not begin in Nottingham until 1740.[2] Similarly, the observed decline of the agricultural and the rise of the industrial labor force cannot be attributed to mobility alone on *a priori* grounds. It could have taken place without mobility by the simple effect of differential replacement rates between agriculturalists and industrial workers. As for the rise of services, that could have taken place through the succession by the numerous sons and daughters of the service workers of each generation. This is not what happened. The growing number of vacancies in industry, in the white collar positions, in public and private bureaucracies, and in the professions, was taken up to a large extent by the offspring of other occupational and status groups.[3]

Recent and current historical studies of social mobility during industrialization try to ascertain, by following the mobility pat-

[2] Otis D. Duncan, "Methodological Issues in the Analysis of Social Mobility," in Neil J. Smelser and Seymour M. Lipset (eds.), *Social Structure and Mobility in Economic Development* (Chicago, 1966), 51. E. A. Wrigley, "A Simple Model of London's Importance in Changing English Society and Economy, 1650–1750," *Past &Present*, 37 (1967), 44–70. Wrigley's partly theoretical computations are confirmed by the experience of the town of Cardington, 45 miles from London. R. S. Schofield, "Age-Specific Mobility in an Eighteenth-Century Rural English Parish," *Annales de Démographie Historique, 1970* (Paris, 1971), 271. Jonathan D. Chambers, "Population Change in a Provincial Town. Nottingham 1700–1800," in David V. Glass and David E. C. Eversley (eds.), *Population in History* (Chicago, 1965), 334–353; Adna Ferrin Weber, *The Growth of Cities in the Nineteenth Century* (New York, 1899), 230ff; Louis Chevalier, *La formation de la population parisienne au XIXe siècle* (Paris, 1950), 48.

[3] A mathematical treatment can be found in Judah Matras, "Differential Fertility, Intergenerational Occupational Mobility, and Change in the Occupational Distribution: Some Elementary Interrelationships," *Population Studies*, XV (1961), 187–197. See also Nathan Keyfitz, "Individual Mobility in a Stationary Population," *Population Studies*, XXVII (1973), 335–352.

terns of well-defined groups during well-defined periods, precisely the manner by which the new vacancies were being filled.[4]
Since they carefully measure the regional and temporal variations
in the rates and ranges of various types of mobility, the vision of
industrialization which is exemplified by the definition quoted
above is not congruent with the level of analysis needed in the new
studies of mobility. I will propose here a taxonomy of industrialization and suggest for each phase (or type) actual or plausible
relationships between selected aspects of social mobility and certain economic forces.

In order to enhance one's understanding of the effect of industrialization on social mobility, consider how, by contrast, social
mobility operated in a pre-industrial society. One's grasp of the
mechanisms at work will be tighter if one imagines an ideal-type
"medieval" society predominantly made up of a homogeneous
peasantry. There are some craftsmen, churchmen, soldiers, and
men of government, but their small numbers are fixed by guild restrictions or other statutory norms.[5] This mythical society is
peaceful and placid, so that great redistributions of land or status
which result from plunder, murder, war, epidemics, famine,
riots, or mass migration do not occur. The land available for agriculture is abundant but entirely settled and used, and is transmitted hereditarily, for there is no land market, or leasing of land by
one peasant to another. It appears that in this mythical medieval
society status and occupational and geographical mobility work
hand in hand with the inheritance system, the population's net rate
of reproduction, and its family structure. One can illustrate this
from the demographic pattern. Assume that families have many
children surviving to adulthood—as determined by some combination of fertility and mortality—but only one heir to the father's

4 Stephan Thernstrom, *Poverty and Progress* (Cambridge, Mass., 1964); the essays in
Stephan Thernstrom and Richard Sennett (eds.), *Nineteenth-Century Cities* (New Haven,
1969); Michel Papy, "Professions et mobilité à Oloron sous la Monarchie Censitaire d'après
les listes de recrutement militaire," *Revue d'histoire économique et sociale,* XLIX (1971), 225–
264; P. E. Razzell, "Statistics and English Historical Sociology," in R. M. Hartwell (ed.),
The Industrial Revolution (Oxford, 1970), 101–120. The common methodology is described
in Thernstrom, "Reflections on the New Urban History," in Felix Gilbert and Stephen R.
Graubard (eds.), *Historical Studies Today* (New York, 1972), 320–336.
5 See Lutz K. Berkner and Franklin F. Mendels, "Inheritance Systems, Family Structure,
and Demographic Patterns in Western Europe (1700–1900)," in Charles Tilly and E. A.
Wrigley (eds.), *Historical Studies of Fertility* (forthcoming).

farm, occupation, and status: then all the children but one, the heir, will experience mobility.

Figure 1 shows all the possibilities for non-heirs in a modern setting where non-agricultural employment is not rigidly constrained. Thus, in thirteenth-century Weston (Lincolnshire) where land partibility was limited, out of sixty-eight sons, nine entered the church and twenty-six (38 percent) emigrated from the village. In the neighboring village of Moulton, where partibility prevailed, the percentage of departures was only 23 percent. But was not mortality so high in a medieval village that replacement rates rarely surpassed 1.0? Data for 1270 show that the average Weston family produced 1.86 live adult sons and Moulton families produced 2.5. English replacement rates did fall below 1.0 in the period 1348–1450, but that was an exceptional time of plague and suffering.[6] Postan has explicitly made the link between replacement rates and mobility through opportunity for young men to find land. "When men were so plentiful, and land so scarce, the normal advancement of men by succession was denied to many—perhaps most—of the young people."[7]

Suppose, on the one hand, that extended families are the norm, while replacement rates are high. The non-heirs stay on the farm with the inferior status of celibate helper, except for those who move out, marry an heir, or obtain an occupation in a craft, in the church, or in the army. If, on the other hand, nuclear families are the norm, then the heir hires servants and workers instead of his unmarried kin to help on the farm. These servants and workers are themselves non-heirs from other peasant lineages. The loss of status that non-heirs suffer in comparison with their own father's is probably more serious if they have to hire themselves out as servants and laborers than if they stay celibate on the ancestral farm as in the case of the extended family. Moreover, geographical mobility is higher since there is a crossing of village limits to find positions. One can see that in this type of society the predominant status mobility flow for the largest section of the

6 H. E. Hallam, "Some Thirteenth-Century Censuses," *Economic History Review*, X (1958), 340–361. Sylvia Thrupp, "The Problem of Replacement Rates in Late Medieval English Population," *ibid.*, XVIII (1965), 101–119. T. H. Hollingsworth, *Historical Demography* (Ithaca, 1969), 378–379.
7 M. M. Postan, *The Cambridge Economic History of Europe*, (Cambridge, 1966, 2d ed.), I, 564.

Fig. 1 Career Paths for Farmers' Children

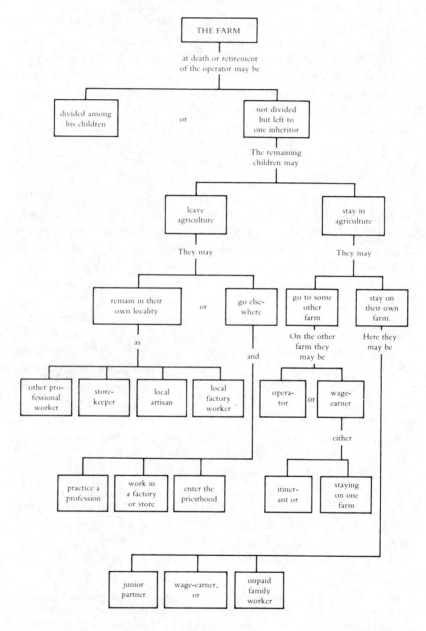

SOURCE: Nathan Keyfitz, "Population Problems," in Marcel Rioux and Yves Martin (eds.), *French-Canadian Society* (Toronto, 1964), I, 225; reprinted by permission of McClelland and Stewart, Ltd., Toronto, and the Carleton Library Board.

population, the peasantry, is downward. Chances of status improvement exist for the peasantry but are confined to the replenishment of the ranks of the church and army and to marriage with an heir. The higher the net reproduction rate, the stronger the downward flow.

If partible inheritance prevails, however, all the male offspring split the land at each generation. Male geographical mobility is constrained.[8] All of the sons stay in the village and acquire the father's occupation and status of a German *Bauer*, a Flemish *landsman*, an English yeoman, or a French *laboureur*. The prevailing norm of family organization determines whether farms are actually split or not by the division of property. Partible inheritance does not result in splitting of farms in the (relatively rare) case where all the heirs stay together as joint households. Fragmentation takes place if families are nuclear. A downward trend of status mobility is experienced to the extent that nuclear families are formed in the context of a high net rate of reproduction, since farms eventually become very small. However, if all lineages reproduce themselves at the same rate, the contraction of holding size depresses the income of all the peasants proportionately, without affecting their relative position.

In order to accommodate a rapidly growing population, the society may split into a class of heirs and one of non-heirs, thereby

---

8 In reality, the range of variation in inheritance systems is much broader than the opposition presented here between strict partibility and strict impartibility. Moreover, some additional possibilities are neglected, for instance the variation of retirement customs. In some cases the father handed over the land to his heir at the time of the latter's marriage in exchange for a written promise of support. In others, inheritance only occurred after the father's death. See Berkner, "The Stem Family and the Developmental Cycle of the Peasant Household: An Eighteenth-Century Austrian Example," *American Historical Review*, LXXVII (1972), 398–418. In some places, it was the custom to send the children off as servants of other households, perhaps temporarily. This fact introduces another dimension to the relationships between family structure and mobility. See Schofield, "Age-Specific Mobility," 261–271; Peter Laslett, *The World we have lost* (London, 1965), 14ff; Peter Laslett and John Harrison, "Clayworth and Cogenhoe," *Historical Essays 1600–1750, presented to David Ogg* (London, 1964), 170. For extensive discussions of inheritance systems in relation to family structure or demographic patterns, see, among others, Berkner and Mendels, "Inheritance Systems"; G. C. Homans, *English Villagers in the Thirteenth Century* (Cambridge, Mass., 1942), 109–222; Rosamond Jane Faith, "Peasant Families and Inheritance Customs in Medieval England," *Agricultural History Review*, XIV (1966), 77–95; Philip J. Greven, Jr., *Four Generations: Population, Land, and Family in Colonial Andover, Massachusetts* (Ithaca, 1970); H. J. Habakkuk, "Family Structure and Economic Change in Nineteenth-Century Europe," *Journal of Economic History*, XV (1955), 1–12.

generating a distinct social stratification. Or it may preserve a fairly homogeneous peasant class at the cost of depressing the incomes of all. As Smith observed, "How property is divided among heirs is always one of the determinants of class structure, powerful in proportion as other ways to wealth are closed. When completely closed, what a man inherits must fix his class position permanently and perhaps even that of his descendants through several generations. This situation was approximated in most parts of rural Japan in the seventeenth century."[9]

The pace at which class structure shapes itself depends on demographic determinants. The reasoning presented here assumes that the latter are given from the start, as well as the inheritance practices and family structure, an assumption only used for expository purposes. One must realize that these three data in fact interact. We simply do not know that any one set of them is more stable or at least more "given," thus more determining, than the others.[10]

The model which has been developed here is overly simple and its assumptions constraining. However, it is useful in the sense that relaxing its underlying premises is somewhat analogous to reading descriptions of social and economic changes that historians give of European countries emerging from the Dark Ages. New land is cleared in Europe or conquered overseas. Agricultural technology permits a better utilization of the existing land. Industrial occupations as well as positions in the tertiary sector of the economy are opened up. Cities grow, commodity markets expand, and a market in land is established. For instance, next to Weston and Moulton in Lincolnshire, the village of Spalding had deviated considerably from the ideal type as early as the thirteenth century. Out of 180 freemen, 25 percent bore the names of trades or professions. Most of the land was fragmented into tiny holdings and 20 percent of the 426 tenants lived on bought land. Many people settled in cottages along the river banks or the market place, and it appears that "commercial and industrial factors were

9   Thomas C. Smith, *Agrarian Origins of Modern Japan* (Stanford, Cal., 1959), 37.
10   The choice of an exogenous and determining variable is somewhat arbitrary but often seems related to one's relative ignorance. The more superficial one's understanding of a variable is, the more likely one is to treat it as given and determining.

more important in deciding the social structure of Spalding than inheritance customs."[11]

These changes have one effect in common, namely, to disengage occupational, status, and geographical mobility processes from the mechanism by which land is obtained, improved, increased, and passed along to the next generation. Indeed, it is very hard to find in a country such as France a small area in which the importance of inheritance rules is not mitigated, in early modern times, by the existence of leaseholds, by a land market, by nearby rural industries, let alone by the presence of a growing town. Even apparently isolated Pyrenean valleys, such as the valleys of the Ariège near Foix, the Bigorre, or the Valley of Aure, with their abundant sources of water power, provided a fertile ground for iron and textile industries.[12] This is not to say that the family-inheritance-population links cease to operate; only that they operate in a much larger network of interacting forces and therefore lose most of their determining power. It would therefore be an enormous task to construct a single model of mobility for an industrializing society. Presented instead are some thoughts on how the processes of mobility were linked with economic change according to the phase or type of industrialization in which an economy was engaged.

Well before the Industrial Revolution, various regions of Europe experienced an unprecedented growth in manufacturing. This type of "industrialization," however, was still remote from what is usually meant by the term. In particular, it was not carried out in factories and with machines coordinated to one source of power. There was nothing that prefigured the assembly line, yet it was not merely a growth of handicrafts for local markets. This causes some semantic ambiguity and has led me to define a phase of "proto-industrialization."[13] A number of features characterizes this phase and separates it from other subsequent phases of indus-

11 Hallam, "Some Thirteenth-Century Censuses," 348. Paul R. Hyams, "The Origins of a Peasant Land Market in England," *Economic History Review*, XXIII (1970), 18–31.
12 In eighteenth-century Flanders, inheritance law was far less important to explain what happened than market forces: Mendels, "Agriculture and Peasant Industry in Eighteenth-Century Flanders," in William N. Parker and E. L. Jones (eds.), *European Peasants and Their Markets* (Princeton, 1975), 179–204. Michel Chevalier, *La vie humaine dans les Pyrénées ariégoises*, (Paris, 1956).
13 Mendels, "Proto-industrialization: The First Phase of the Process of Industrialization," *Journal of Economic History*, XXXII (1972), 241–261.

trialization. On the one hand, the industrial role of cities was confined to a rather small share of manufacturing employment. One could thus say that there was industrialization without cognate urbanization. On the other hand, it was in the cities that the final stages of various production processes were carried out, e.g., those which were most intensive in the use of highly skilled craftsmen commanding high wages. The cities also gathered the men of enterprise who "put out" the work to be done by the peasants of the outlying districts or by urban craftsmen, or who purchased the finished goods sold by independent self-employed peasants at the weekly market and organized their sale to other regions or countries. Towns traded in agricultural goods and accommodated the *rentiers,* the professional men, and the men of government. And of course all these functions created employment opportunities for domestic servants and shopkeepers.

The growth of cities and the opportunities thus created for upward social mobility within them, as well as for movement into the city from the surrounding countryside, were small during this phase in comparison with what was to come later. But, as we have seen, the fact that growth was sluggish did not preclude a sizeable fraction of the surrounding rural population from moving to the city anyway. Undoubtedly, many of these migrants were pushed out rather than pulled in; they simply joined the ranks of the vagrants and beggars and came to the cities because the charitable institutions and asylums were there. But, as capital requirements in both trade and industry were very small, and as the level of skills required for success in business and industrial ventures did not go far beyond literacy, both capital and skills could be acquired in a few years. Therefore, artisans with some spirit of enterprise could become merchant-manufacturers more easily than in the early seventeenth, and certainly more easily than in the late nineteenth century.[14]

If we now look at the situation in the countryside during this period, what is characteristic of the regions which are launched on the path of proto-industrialization is the domination of strong forces favoring downward social mobility. The introduction of new opportunities for land-saving occupations in the village considerably modified the mechanisms through which wealth and

14 See Dorothy Marshall, "La structure sociale de l'Angleterre du dix-huitième siècle," in Roland Mousnier (ed.), *Problèmes de stratification sociale* (Paris, 1968), 101–116.

status were passed on from one generation to the next. A cottage industry made it possible for families to survive in the countryside on very small holdings of land, since the produce of that land could be supplemented by another source of sustenance. This might have led to improved standards of living. But some demographic studies show that areas which turned to cottage industry tended to attract immigration, had earlier and more marriages, and had higher fertility than other rural areas. And there are many regions of Europe where an impressive growth of this type of manufacturing was accompanied by equally impressive poverty. This seems to have been the case among the peasants in the interior of Brittany, in Bas-Maine, the Beauvaisis, the interior of Flanders, Limburg, Overijssel, Ulster, and many other regions. In these European societies, where status was closely associated with ownership or control over landed property, if, from generation to generation, an increasing percentage of families did not have enough land to support themselves—although often too much to be called landless—downward status mobility would result. Furthermore, this loss of land was compounded in some areas by the loss of control over the tools of their industry by peasants who previously had owned them. This was another step downward on a path which ultimately led to a total dependence on wages and the labor market.[15]

Another process led in the same direction. Agricultural progress in regions of commercial farming was as characteristic of the phase of proto-industrialization as was the growth of cottage industry in areas of subsistence farming. The form of agricultural progress in this phase had certain effects on social mobility. The consolidation of plots and the appropriation of common lands resulted in pushing many of those who were already at the lower rungs further down to the ranks of landless wage earners. This did not necessarily mean a loss of income or employment. On the contrary, since the process of "enclosures" was accompanied, in-

15 Mendels. "Proto-industrialization," 249–253; G. E. Mingay, *Enclosure and the Small Farmer in the Age of the Industrial Revolution* (London, 1968), Karlheinz Blaschke, "Soziale Gliederung und Entwicklung der sächsischen Landbevolkerung im 16. bis 18. Jahrhundert," *Zeitschrift für Agrargeschichte und Agrarsoziologie,* IV (1956), 144–155; Kenneth Lockridge, "Land, Population, and the Evolution of New England Society, 1630–1790," *Past & Present,* 39 (1968), 62–80; Pierre Léon, *Economies et sociétés pré-industrielles 1650–1780* II (Paris, 1970), II, 330–346. On the loss of control over tools, Paul Mantoux, *The Industrial Revolution in the Eighteenth Century* (London, 1961, rev. ed.), 64–65.

deed stimulated, by increased demand for agricultural products, and since the new rotation techniques then introduced tended to be labor-intensive or to require at least temporary increases in labor demand for hedging, etc., the newly created agricultural wage earners could find employment easily in the countryside—so they did not *have to* flock to the cities.[16] But they had become wage earners, nevertheless, and this was perceived as lower status.

A different facet of social mobility, namely migration, was also characteristically affected by proto-industrialization. One economic change in this phase was the increased interaction between agriculture and manufacturing in the countryside. The divergence which has been observed between the areas of subsistence farming and those of commercial agriculture gave rise to increased efficiency, and not only through the normal effects of division of labor and specialization. The subsistence farming areas exported labor, their surplus resource, to the commercial farming areas. As demand for labor in farming was highly seasonal, only a small fraction of the laborers hired for the summer were needed for the rest of the year on the commercial farms. It was easiest for commercial farms to hire workers for only a few weeks when there existed nearby an area which could export them. The growth of cottage industry in subsistence farming areas, by promoting the settlement in some areas of a dense population, helped the development of commercial farming. The development of rural industry near an area with seasonal agricultural labor needs made it unnecessary to use the gangs of migrant laborers that annually descended from the hills, mountains, or poor lands of Europe to the rich fertile plains.[17] One could instead tap the large local supplies by way of short-distance migration.

Since there is a shortage of rigorous empirical studies of social mobility during this phase of industrialization, the picture I have been drawing of the relations between mobility and economic change remains hypothetical. The hypothesis can be summarized

16   Chambers, "Enclosure and Labour Supply in the Industrial Revolution," in E. L. Jones (ed.), *Agriculture and Economic Growth in England, 1650–1815* (London, 1967), 94–127.
17   Roger Béteille. "Les migrations saisonnières en France sous le Premier Empire. Essai de Synthèse," *Revue d'histoire moderne et contemporaine*, XVII (1970), 424–441; Mendels, "Industrialization and Population Pressure in Eighteenth-Century Flanders," unpub. diss. (University of Wisconsin, 1970), 109ff; Arthur Redford, *Labour Migration in England 1800–1850* (Manchester, 1964, rev. ed.), 3–6, 141–149; Abel Châtelain, "Les migrations temporaires françaises au XIXe siècle," *Annales de démographie historique, 1967* (Paris, 1967), 9–28.

in the statement that as work constantly alternated between agriculture and manufacturing, the peculiar sort of occupational
mobility which resulted had no parallel in terms of status mobility,
but proto-industrialization promoted increases in both upward
and downward status mobility from different causes. Finally, by
helping the settlement of labor close to where agriculture needed it
seasonally, it tended to reduce the need for the seasonal immigration of manpower from remote areas. Was proto-industrialization
in turn affected by prevailing modes of social mobility? Did
mobility facilitate the process of proto-industrialization?

Landes, Kemp, and Perkin have assigned a determining role
to social stratification and mobility.[18] At a general level it is argued that more flexible definitions of class and a higher degree of
mobility have facilitated the process of industrialization in England. Conversely, it is said that the comparative *ease* with which
successful French businessmen used their new wealth to climb up
and out of the business world partly explains French backwardness. The same role has been assigned to the existence of a very
large and open *hidalgo* class in Spain. Finally, when one considers
that mobility may have even declined in England during the crucial decades preceding its industrial revolution, it seems that the
argument that comparative ease of upward mobility into a
privileged, old-regime upper class facilitated economic progress
by providing achievement incentives is dubious at a general level.
What remains, however, is that England was a country where the
nobility had no legal definition or privileges, and where up and
down movements between the aristocracy and the merchant class
were comparatively frequent. The actual practice of primogeni-
ture among the upper levels of English society meant that the
younger sons of English nobles commonly had to work for a living. In France the nobility avoided division of the land as well, but
titles and such privileges as tax exemption were passed down even
to the non-heirs. Moreover the rules of *dérogeance* placed a strong
deterrent in the way of younger sons going into trade and industry
(except long distance trade, glass making and mining) since it
would entail a loss of highly valued status and privileges. The incentives to purchase an office in the Church, army, or bureaucracy

18   David Landes, *The Unbound Prometheus* (Cambridge, 1969); Tom Kemp, *Industrialization in Nineteenth-Century Europe* (London, 1969); Harold Perkin, *The Origins of Modern English Society, 1780–1880* (London, 1969).

were all the stronger, and this reduced the flow of skills and capital into trade and industry.[19]

We can see the results of these social values on the development of agriculture. The possession of a country estate was a prerequisite to social prestige, but to make it into a profitable possession by careful personal supervision would be less rewarding than engaging in "conspicuous consumption" in the neighboring town, in Paris, or in Versailles. This meant that the immediate aim and long run policy of many French landlords was to squeeze as much surplus from the peasantry as was possible, thus removing any incentive on the part of the latter to improve yields. The manner in which taxes were assessed in this period had the same depressing effect on the peasantry insofar as the burden of the *taille* (from which nobles, clergy, and many towns were exempt) was distributed by the villagers in accordance with apparent wealth. The tax system, in other words, added its effects to the value system by reinforcing the strict compartmentalization of French society.[20] These differences between French and English society first appeared long before the beginnings of industrialization. Their persistence in the eighteenth century is the result of political forces, so that it would be fair to say that these differences played the role of an exogenous variable in the process of economic change.

Many of the characteristics of proto-industrialization (such as the continued importance of rural industries) did not disappear with the end of this phase and the beginning of the next. Nevertheless, it is comparatively easy to locate the coming of the second phase of industrialization, for the defining novelty of that new phase was the introduction of the factory system and the new industrial organization which it entailed.[21] In the phase of industrial history which preceded the introduction of the factory system, the

19 Lawrence Stone, "Social Mobility in England, 1500–1700," *Past & Present*, 33 (1966), 16–55; Alexis de Tocqueville (ed. J.-P. Mayer), *L'ancien régime et la Révolution* (Paris, 1964); Landes, *Prometheus*, 67, 129; Habakkuk, "England," in Albert Goodwin (ed.), *The European Nobility in the Eighteenth Century* (New York, 1967, rev. ed.), 1–21; Joan Thirsk, "Younger Sons in the Seventeenth Century," *History*, LIV (1969), 358–377; R. B. Grassby, "Social Status and Commercial Enterprise under Louis XIV," *Economic History Review*, XIV (1961), 19–38.
20 Tocqueville, *L'ancien régime*, 170, 209.
21 For a discussion of the processes which led to the Industrial Revolution and the manner in which proto-industrialization paved the way for further changes, see Mendels, "Proto-industrialization," 241–247.

growing number of households engaged in industrial work had not yet become fully specialized. Typically, agriculture and industry had complemented each other on each farm, and the family household along with its servants remained the focus of production and consumption as well as the fundamental unit of decision-making in family life. The creation of full-time, centralized, and specialized employment now caused disturbances in the household. Specialization and division of labor first meant the end of the traditional alternation of tasks between agriculture and industry. It also meant the separation of the workplace from home, and, sooner or later, the separation of family members during their working hours. To the extent that factory work demanded more attentiveness than dexterity or strength, a large fraction of the factory labor force could be constituted by children.[22]

Whether the introduction of the factory system facilitated upward social mobility is part of a larger debate, with an extensive literature, on the social consequences of the Industrial Revolution. First, that wages were often higher in factories than in the domestic system does not prove much. Rents and food prices were higher in the cities, and income from factory work could not be supplemented as easily with other sources as could rural domestic work with wages earned from harvest work or from the produce of one's own plot. Moreover, the wages had to be higher in the factories to compensate workers for the drudgery of coordinated and disciplined tasks. For this seems to have been the most detestable part of factory work: the regularity and monotony involved in it. From the means that had to be used in the early days by the factory masters, it appears that this kind of industrial organization was most undesirable for the workers. There are cases when the recruitment of the labor force was achieved through the penitentiary system.[23]

Second, the mechanization of a given industrial process naturally meant severe downward pressure on the earnings of those industrial workers who were eventually replaced or displaced by it. Since the factory system was not introduced in all in-

22 Neil J. Smelser, *Social Change in the Industrial Revolution* (Chicago, 1959), 180–312.
23 Sidney Pollard, *The Genesis of Modern Management* (Baltimore, 1965, 2d ed.), 189–231; the penitentiary in Ghent, Belgium, was turned over to textile manufacturers after the end of the eighteenth century. See also Roger Portal, "Serfs in the Urals Iron Foundries in the Eighteenth Century," in Val Lorwin (ed.), *Labor and Working Conditions in Modern Europe* (New York, 1967), 17–30.

dustries or processes at the same time and pace, not all categories of workers were affected in this manner at the same time either. The story of the shifting relations between the status and earnings of spinners and weavers, as spinning and weaving were modernized in a piecemeal fashion, has often been told.[24] This phenomenon was repeated in several industries during this phase.

Third, the separation of the family in different places of employment could result in the disintegration of the authority of the head of household, especially if his wife or children could earn a wage in the factory that could match or surpass his own. This was the case for the cotton handloom weavers during their period of decline. Nevertheless, it must also be recalled that the early textile factories sometimes hired entire families and, in such cases, the relative position of family members was maintained.[25]

Fourth, a large part of the first generation of factory workers was made up not of déclassé skilled artisans but of rural landless laborers. Was it downward mobility for the landless son of a small Irish peasant to end up in the factory after some years spent as summer harvest labor and in casual winter work?[26] It is therefore impossible to generalize on the balance of forces which led to upward or downward status mobility for the working class in this complex, revolutionary phase of industrialization. Specific groups experienced gains or losses in their status and income due to economic and technological forces which varied according to time, place, and occupation.

However, more can be said about other types of mobility. The rise of the factory system was accompanied by rapid urbanization and the growth of such new industrial centers as Barmen, Roubaix, and Manchester. Older cities also grew through the immigration of wage laborers, servants, craftsmen, and unskilled industrial workers. Furthermore, somewhat more definite statements can be made in this phase about status mobility for the middle and high levels of society. Skilled artisans as well as shopkeepers were then most favorably affected by the prevailing economic trends. This was a phase when skilled artisans were needed among

24 Mantoux, *Industrial Revolution*, 189–310; Landes, *Prometheus*, 84–87.
25 Smelser, *Social Change*, 188.
26 See Thernstrom, "Notes on the Historical Study of Social Mobility," *Comparative Studies in History and Society*, X (1968), 166, 168; Eric E. Lampard, "The Social Impact of the Industrial Revolution," in Melvin Kranzberg and C. W. Pursell, Jr. (eds.), *Technology in Western Civilization* (New York, 1967), I, 315–316.

the factory labor force in supervisory positions and for the non-repetitive tasks of maintaining and repairing tools and machinery. Few skilled artisans were yet replaced and downgraded by machine work in these early years. Those who were downgraded were among the unskilled ones, whose tasks had begun to be simulated by the still simple machines.[27] There were, moreover, numerous artisans during this phase who could enter the managerial or entrepreneurial ranks in their own lifetime. It was an age of unprecedented opportunities for those already endowed with skills, capital, or entrepreneurship. And the amounts of skill and capital needed were still such that they could be accumulated by individuals over a few years.[28]

Social mobility patterns, in turn, had an effect on the possibilities of industrialization under the factory system. The French "land reform" of the revolutionary period provides a good example of such mechanisms when it is compared with the effect of the German land reforms of the first half of the nineteenth century. The French land reform reinforced the control of the peasantry over the land it cultivated. This can be set against the disappearance of the peasantry in England and Germany. Here, peasants were finally able to gain personal freedom, but had to purchase it by surrendering a certain fraction of the land over which they previously had control. For many it meant descent into the ranks of the landless; whatever land remained in their hands was insufficient for sustenance, and they were likely to sell it in order to move to the city or to areas where rural wage labor was in demand. Meanwhile, those who were initially better off were able to consolidate and augment their holdings by purchasing at low prices the land that fell on the market in this manner.[29] Here is an example of the exogenous and causal effect of mobility patterns on industrialization for there is no doubt that the paths taken by "land

27 There are exceptions, like the wool croppers. See E. P. Thompson, *The Making of the English Working Class* (New York, 1966, 2d ed.), 521–533.
28 Herbert G. Gutman, "The Reality of the Rags-to-Riches 'Myth': The Case of the Paterson, New Jersey, Locomotive, Iron, and Machinery Manufacturers, 1830–1880," *Nineteenth-Century Cities,* 98–125; Eric J. Hobsbawm, *The Age of Revolution* (New York, 1964), 218–237.
29 Kemp, *Industrialization,* 81–118; Werner Conze, "Agrarian Reform in Central Europe," in G. S. Métraux and François Crouzet (eds.), *The Nineteenth-Century World* (New York, 1963), 86–103. Wolfgang Köllmann, "Les mouvements migratoires pendant la période d'industrialisation de la Rhénanie-Westphalie," *Annales de Démographie Historique, 1971* (Paris, 1972), 91–120.

reform" in France and Germany resulted more from political struggles than from previous industrialization. The effects of these struggles on the pace at which factory industrialization proceeded must have been important. The French peasantry was not pushed as strongly into the labor market, agricultural or industrial, as it would have been otherwise. Many of the French peasants, however, did not hold enough land to subsist on agriculture alone, so they complemented their incomes with the product of their rural manufacturing. As long as they stayed on the land and drew some income from it, their manufacturing wage rate, actual or implicit, could remain lower than the subsistence wage rate of urban workers who had no such complement. This helped to slow down the pace of factory-industrialization in France. Furthermore, the effect of the land reforms was not solely felt through the supply of labor: the poor but solidly established peasantry did not provide the modern industrial sector with a mass market for its products. It was not only that much was produced locally, but also that patterns of demand among the peasantry must have been less favorable for the growth of mass-produced consumer goods than would be the case among an urban population.[30]

The next phase (or type) of industrialization to consider is one where producers' goods are predominant in output or employment, or in shaping the growth of a particular locality. This phase, which can also be called the age of steel, was characterized by the rise of heavy industry as the leading sector. Advanced countries of Western Europe entered into it during the second half of the nineteenth century, although its chronological as well as conceptual borders with the previous phase are blurred. It must have induced a number of important changes in the processes of social mobility.

First, the development of heavy industry considerably increased fixed capital requirements over the previous phase. The more complex machinery also demanded much higher levels of technical skills among broad sections of the labor force; perhaps among the operators, but surely among those who designed and maintained them. As such industries now benefited from economies of scale, the advantage passed to the big industrial concerns whose administrations in turn created an unprecedented de-

30 Landes, *Prometheus*, 127–138, 187–192.

mand for white-collar employees. The considerable progress of engineering had an impact on the countryside as well as the cities. It was in this period that certain technical problems involved in attempting to mechanize the traditional industries were finally solved, as, for example, in wool combing. This determined the progressive but now irreversible decline of a number of handicrafts which had hitherto been protected from technological unemployment by their intricate nature. The demise of these last remnants of the old manufacturing system had a great impact. The disappearance of handicrafts from the countryside and the continued expansion of factory employment opportunities sharply increased the pace of rural depopulation. As this was also a phase when railroads were being built, large-scale population movements were being facilitated. But they created serious shortages in the countryside—the big farms could no longer rely on the summer work of the former peasant-craftsmen, who were now emigrating permanently. Mechanical reapers and other labor-saving machinery had to be introduced to replace them. I have selected the characteristics of this phase which strike the eye for their novelty. One must keep in mind that the continuing development of cities did also help the number and prosperity of shopkeepers as well as those in the building trades and other small-scale enterprises, all of which continued quantitatively to be of great importance in national economies.[31]

Thus, on the one hand, in view of the much increased capital requirements of new factories, this was no longer the age of individual entrepreneurs. Spectacular rises in business were more likely to need the mustering of scattered sources of capital in joint-stock companies or through the intermediation of financial institutions. Both the corporation and the bank were at the source of the creation of a large class of professional and clerical white-collar employees. As the capital accumulation necessary for in-

31 Philippe Pinchemel, *Structures sociales et dépopulation rurale dans les campagnes picardes de 1836 à 1936* (Paris, 1957), 106–120; John Saville, *Rural Depopulation in England and Wales, 1850–1950* (London, 1957), 20–30. E. J. T. Collins, "Labour Supply and Demand in European Agriculture, in E. L. Jones and S. J. Woolf (eds.), *Agrarian Change and Economic Development* (London, 1969), 61–94; Paul M. Hohenberg, "Change in Rural France in the Period of Industrialization, 1830–1914," *Journal of Economic History*, XXXII (1972), 227–231; T. J. Markovitch, "The Dominant Sectors of French Industry," in Rondo Cameron (ed.), with the assistance of F. Mendels and J. Ward, *Essays in French Economic History* (Homewood, Ill., 1970), 237–240.

dustrial success reached beyond the means of individuals, it is not surprising that a certain closing of opportunities for individual advancement through industrial or commercial success has been observed.[32] It resulted also from the rising technical complexity of most sectors of the economy which manifested itself among the managerial ranks of industry and in the development of large bureaucracies. On the other hand, there were enough areas left to small-scale enterprise; once more, it is hard on a priori grounds to make any general prediction.

A crucial novelty of this age with respect to the optimum path for social advancement was the importance of formal education. In the first, revolutionary phase of the Industrial Revolution in England, there initially had been a decline in literacy but jobs were being created which did not need literacy. The rising literacy of the 1830s may well have "led merely to a decline in mobility because the new jobs were not such as to absorb the literate in any case, in contrast, for example, to the creation of the vast clerk class at the end of the nineteenth century."[33] Indeed it is in this phase of industrialization that primary education first became a prerequisite for employment in a large section of the labor force, among the skilled factory workers as well as the growing army of white-collar workers. On the one hand, education opened up new avenues for social ascent because large corporations had a growing need for engineers, draftsmen, accountants, lawyers, etc. More generally, formal education facilitated inter-generational status improvements by opening rewarding careers to graduates of educational institutions whose entrance requirements were becoming, at least formally, blind to family origins. On the other hand, the bureaucratization of economic activity must have modified mobility patterns by curbing intra-generational mobility. Formal education acquired during youth, if it led to a recognized diploma, would place the laureate at the bottom of a hierarchical scale which

32 Perkin, *Modern English Society*, 424–428; Charlotte Erickson, *British Industrialists: Steel and Hosiery, 1850–1950* (Cambridge, 1959), 12, 56, 93, 129, cited in Perkin, *Modern English Society*, 425; Irene D. Neu and Frances W. Gregory, "The American Industrial Elite in the 1870s: Their Social Origins," in William Miller (ed.), *Men in Business* (New York, 1962), 193–211.

33 M. Sanderson, "Literacy and Social Mobility in the Industrial Revolution in England," *Past & Present*, 56 (1972), 102; Carlo M. Cipolla, *Literacy and Development in the West* (Baltimore, 1969), 62–99; Lenore O'Boyle, "The Problem of an Excess of Educated Men in Western Europe, 1800–1850," *Journal of Modern History*, XLII (1970), 471–495.

he would ascend with seniority. Formal education acquired at an early stage now strongly determined the life pattern of income and promotion for an increasing number of people.[34]

Cross-national comparisons, once more, show that social institutions could have had important effects on patterns of industrialization. The English economy experienced some setbacks in this period while the German and American economies were pulling ahead. Landes has assigned a large share of responsibility for English retardation to an educational system which failed to provide the economy with the needed skills, contrary to the German case. The English continued to rely much longer on the acquisition of skills by individuals through experience and on recruitment by patronage. The more rigid and authoritarian style of social interaction and stratification which prevailed in Germany nonetheless led to the creation of a schooling system and pattern of recruitment more favorable for rapid economic expansion. And yet it could hardly be said that it was previous backwardness in England which had in any sense prepared the way by bringing with it a schooling system of the German type. The creation of this school system can be traced back to the late eighteenth century. It must be ranked as an independent and exogenous event with largely unanticipated effects. The remarkable fluidity of English social stratification in the first two phases of industrialization undoubtedly contributed to the flourishing of industrial enterprise through individual initiatives. But this kind of mobility was no longer sufficient to promote industrial development under the economic conditions prevailing in this phase of industrialization.[35]

The last phase of industrial history began when the movement toward urban-industrial concentration was reversed in the late nineteenth century in Europe as well as in America. The rise of new sources of energy, petroleum and electricity, and the perfecting of the internal combustion engine contributed to a modification of the balance of costs and benefits of urban-industrial concentration at nodal points. The automobile and truck allowed a new flexibility not afforded by the railroad system. The use of electricity in industry also slowed down the trend toward

34 Hobsbawm, *The Age of Revolution*, 229.
35 Landes, *Prometheus*, 339ff, 348; O'Boyle, "An Excess of Educated Men," 485. See Margaret Scotford-Morton, "Some English and French Notions of Democracy in Education," *Archives Européennes de Sociologie*, VIII (1967), 152–161.

concentration which the steam engine had imparted.[36] The decentralization of industry was thus accompanied by the suburbanization of cities. Most of the economic forces which determined patterns of social mobility in the previous phase continued to operate in this new one as well. What had been said about the importance of education continued to be true. But the declining benefits of concentration could have been linked to new patterns of mobility. As the new industries, employing the largest proportion of highly skilled workers and employees, settled in the suburbs or the countryside (e.g., Princeton and Hightstown, New Jersey), rapid economic growth modified the social structure of the city itself. Upward mobility was accompanied by emigration from the city. The service industries, the banks, and the headquarters of many national corporations first remained in the center of the city, but the emergence of a new technology of communications rapidly diminished the advantages of central location for them as well.

The centrifugal forces characteristic of this phase also meant that countries where such forces were not given free rein, or where others counteracted them strongly, experienced economic difficulties. It is true that postwar French growth has been rapid, but one may justly wonder how much more rapid it would have been if a number of customs and institutions had not prevented the decentralization of the secondary and tertiary sectors instead of promoting the continued growth of Paris and its suburbs.[37] It has been a part of the national tradition of government and social life of that country for a long time that almost every initiative flows from the capital, leaving little power in the hands of localities. One result has been that migration to Paris has been a necessary means of upward social mobility. Whereas in another phase of industrialization this was a force promoting modernization (but it did not operate strongly then in France because of a peculiar rural social structure), its perpetuation in the contemporary world is an anachronistic force which causes a great misallocation of resources.

36 William N. Parker, "Economic Development in Historical Perspective," in Nathan Rosenberg (ed.), *The Economics of Technological Change,* (Baltimore, 1971), 137–147; Alexander Gerschenkron, "City Economies—Then and Now," in Oscar Handlin and John Burchard (eds.), *The Historian and the City* (Cambridge, Mass., 1963), 46–72; Eric Lampard, "The History of Cities in the Economically Advanced Areas," *Economic Development and Cultural Change,* III (1955), 124–126.
37 J. F. Gravier, *Paris et le désert français* (Paris, 1947); Tocqueville, *Ancien Régime,* 98–158.

This is an example of the persistence of a social pattern through several phases of industrialization, pointing to the need to consider national styles of social stratification and mobility as independent variables, not only as variables determined by economic development. Crozier's analyses of French society show how certain permanent traits in the national tradition of group or class interactions have affected the manner in which change and innovation could be introduced in that country throughout its modern history.[38] He argues that, on the one hand, there have been high barriers to mobility and communication between any levels of French society, class to class, profession to profession, or stratum to stratum within an occupation. On the other hand, there has been a high degree of egalitarianism within each of these levels, and much esprit de corps and camaraderie which make it possible to balance the strong centralizing tendencies. These characteristics and their multiple ramifications compose what he calls the "bureaucratic" system of social organization, entailing a certain pattern of social mobility and also explaining certain peculiarities of French economic history. The responsibility to innovate is left in the hands of the centralized authority of the state or the remote central headquarters of the company, at any rate not in the hands of those who are most directly affected by the innovation. The latter resist innovation which would disturb the social equilibrium prevailing at their level by leading to the promotion of some and the demotion of others. Although this style of social organization does not deter inventiveness, it does not provide a fertile ground for its practical application and therefore tends to prevent continuous change. When innovations are adopted by the force of blatant necessity, they are introduced from above, in a radical and sudden manner, and with considerable delays. An example would be the introduction of the railroad in France, postponed for several years by conflicts among vested interests until the legislature finally passed a law in 1842 outlining in a grand master plan the whole French network and the relations between the state and private enterprise.[39]

38 Michel Crozier, *Le phénomène bureaucratique* (Paris, 1971, 2d ed.), 247–347. For related aspects of French social structure, see Edmond Goblot, *La barrière et le niveau* (Paris, 1967, 2d ed.), 1–40; Jesse R. Pitts, "Continuity and Change in Bourgeois France," in Stanley Hoffmann et al., *In Search of France* (Cambridge, Mass., 1963), 235–304.
39 Arthur L. Dunham, *La révolution industrielle en France (1815–1848)* (Paris, 1953), 41–72.

What can an economic historian offer to those who undertake monographic studies or syntheses of social mobility during industrialization? Not much in terms of specific predictions. First, social mobility patterns are not unilaterally determined by what happens in industry or in the economy; on the contrary, the two mutually affect each other. Second, the interactions between mobility and economic change vary according to the type or phase in which a given local, regional, or national economy finds itself. Third, various kinds of mobility in a given period result from a number of economic changes, not all of which operate in the same direction. On theoretical and a priori grounds alone, therefore, there is little that can be said. Even for pre-industrial societies, which, in contrast, seem simpler to understand, predictions on the course of mobility can be made only for such particular economic and social structures that very few societies satisfy the conditions under which a model of mobility can be constructed at all. Only empirical research can reveal the course of mobility during industrialization in a given time and place.

On the other hand, an economic historian can certainly offer insights into some of the causative links which have operated in specific contexts, as I have done, for instance, for the phase of proto-industrialization. Focusing on the growth, persistence, transformations, and ultimate demise of rural (and urban) artisans reminds one that much is lost by assuming that industrialization is a linear process, and that comparing the two end points of that process should yield insights into social structure and mobility during the period examined. And yet, even though there is abundant information available on the artisan industries, modern economic historians themselves have failed to give them the place they deserve in abstract models and generalizations. Thus, students of mobility should not be blamed first if they experience difficulties in relating their findings to the dominant paradigms of economic history. A systematic and analytical economic history of artisan industries would be one step in bridging a gap.

William H. Sewell, Jr.

Social Mobility in a Nineteenth-Century European City: Some Findings and Implications

Recent international research on social mobility has found that rates of intergenerational upward mobility from manual to non-manual occupations are remarkably similar in nearly all industrialized countries—at least since World War II. This similarity of social mobility patterns has led Lipset and Bendix to conclude that a relatively high and uniform rate of social mobility is "determined by the occupational structure" of advanced industrial societies, and that any "differences in national value systems" have relatively little impact on mobility patterns in such societies. Although I am not convinced that differences in value systems are as unimportant as Lipset and Bendix claim, most of their data seem to support these generalizations. A parallel conclusion emerges from the more recent and more sophisticated analysis of American social mobility patterns by Blau and Duncan. They found that varying patterns of occupational mobility of different groups in the population can nearly always be explained by the groups' competitive advantages and disadvantages in the labor market, and that such factors as discrimination or differences in values rarely have much influence. (The great exception is American Blacks, who as a result of discrimination, have attainments far below what would be predicted on the basis of their qualifications.) Thus, both at the level of Lipset and Bendix's gross international comparisons, and at the level of Blau and Duncan's refined internal analysis, social mobility in contemporary industrial societies appears to be primarily a function of objective and impersonal economic and social forces, with differences in values having little, if any, impact.[1]

William H. Sewell, Jr. is a member of the School of Social Science at the Institute for Advanced Study, Princeton.

Earlier versions of this article were presented at the American Sociological Association Meetings in 1971 and at the Mathematical Social Science Board conference on International Comparisons of Social Mobility in Past Societies in 1972. The research has been supported by the Division of the Social Sciences of the University of Chicago and by National Science Foundation Grants GS-31730X and GS-32200.

1 Seymour Martin Lipset and Reinhard Bendix, *Social Mobility in Industrial Society* (Berkeley, 1959), 55, 73. Peter M. Blau and Otis Dudley Duncan, *The American Occupational Structure* (New York, 1967), esp. 207–241.

But this conclusion is based on evidence from a very short time-span. In advanced industrial societies it may be true that high rates of social mobility are "determined by the occupational structure," and that values have very little effect on mobility patterns. But was this true for earlier stages of industrialization? My research on nineteenth-century Marseille suggests that it was not. During the early stages of industrialization in Marseille, rates of upward mobility from non-manual to manual occupations were not nearly as high as in contemporary industrial societies, and disparate values held by different categories of the population appear to have had a profound effect on social mobility patterns. Marseille is only one city, and no conclusive generalizations can be based on a single case. But if Marseille was at all typical of nineteenth-century European cities, the apparently automatic generation of high mobility rates so characteristic of contemporary Western industrial societies may be a very recent development.

All of my figures on social mobility are based on an analysis of Marseille's marriage registers (*actes de marriage*) for the years 1846 and 1851. (Data for the two years are combined and treated as a single unit.) French marriage registers are an extraordinarily rich source of data. When a couple married, each spouse was required to give his or her name, age, place of birth, address, and occupation, and his or her father's name and occupation. All this information was duly recorded on a marriage certificate which was then signed by each spouse (if they could sign their names) and by four witnesses, each of whom also gave his age, occupation, and address. Measures of intergenerational occupational mobility can thus be obtained by simply comparing the occupation of the groom to that of his father. It should be noted, however, that the marriage registers can also be used to investigate a number of other important problems, including intermarriage, migration, labor recruitment, residence patterns, literacy, and friendship patterns.[2]

Marriage registers do not provide a perfectly representative sample of the population. It is essentially a sample of the young adult population, with no children and relatively few older adults included. (The median age at marriage was 30 for men and 25 for

2   The marriage registers for nineteenth-century Marseille can be found in series 201E in the Archives départementales de Bouches-du-Rhône.

women.) Furthermore, it leaves out men and women who remained unmarried, as well as residents of the city whose marriages
were celebrated elsewhere. Nevertheless, the sample obtained
from the marriage registers gives us a reasonably accurate picture
of the young adult population, and can provide us with satisfactory information if used with sufficient care. There were,
moreover, 2,559 marriages in Marseille in these two years, giving
us enough cases to make fairly reliable estimates.

Marriage register data do present one serious methodological
problem for a study of occupational mobility. As is true for many
official French documents of the nineteenth century, most men
working in small-scale handicraft industry failed to indicate
whether they were employers or employees; they simply designated themselves as *cordonniers* or *boulangers* rather than as *fabricants
cordonniers* or *ouvriers boulangers*. According to the best available estimate, the ratio of workers to employers in Marseille's handicraft
trades was about 5.2 to 1 in the period from which our sample was
drawn.[3] But in our sample, only thirty men designated themselves
as employers in small handicraft trades, as against 978 whose titles
indicate without further specification that they worked in such
trades. Assuming that all of the latter were workers, we would get
a clearly impossible worker to employer ratio of 33 to 1. This
means that over one hundred of the men in our sample whose
status as worker or employer is not designated were probably employers.

Being unable to determine which of these men were employers is especially unfortunate in a study of social mobility; it
means that a substantial amount of mobility between the status of
worker and that of employer will escape our scrutiny. Since the
reporting of the husband's father's occupation suffers from this
same problem, we are left with several different types of errors in
calculating mobility rates. If we work on the assumption that all
the indeterminate cases were workers, the following types of errors will result. (1) Some men whose fathers were workers but
who themselves became small employers will be incorrectly
counted as experiencing no upward mobility. (2) Some workers
whose fathers were small employers will be incorrectly counted as
experiencing no downward mobility. (3) Some men with white

3 Enquête sur le travail industriel et agricole, Archives nationale: C947.

collar occupations whose fathers were small employers will be incorrectly counted as upwardly mobile workers' sons. (4) Some small employers whose fathers were in white collar occupations will be incorrectly counted as downwardly mobile. There is no way of knowing a priori whether the combined effects of these measurement errors will be to inflate or to deflate the amount of mobility actually occurring.

There is, however, one alternative to assuming that all indeterminate cases were workers. Instead, one can assume that the husbands who actually identified themselves as small employers are typical of the remaining unidentified small employers, and, similarly, that the fathers who were identified as small employers are typical of the small employer fathers who remained unidentified. On the basis of this assumption one can generate a modified mobility matrix that corrects for the errors of classification by removing an appropriate number of cases from the skilled worker category and placing them in the small business category. It is quite possible that the men actually identified as small employers differed significantly from the small employers not specifically identified as such. But applying this correction to our mobility figures should give us some indication of the scale and the direction of the errors introduced by the initial misclassifications. In fact, the differences between the corrected and uncorrected figures are generally so small as to be negligible. For the sake of simplicity, therefore, I will always cite the *uncorrected* figures in the text of this article, but I will give both corrected and uncorrected figures in the tables.

By the middle of the nineteenth century, Marseille was a city of just under 200,000, the second largest city in France, a major provincial administrative center, and the fifth largest port in the world in terms of the quantity of cargoes unloaded onto its docks. In a country where urbanization and economic growth were generally occurring at a rather leisurely pace, Marseille nearly doubled in population from 1821 to 1851 (from 109,000 to 196,000), and experienced rapid growth in both the commercial and industrial sectors of the economy in the same years.[4] It was, in short, a so-

4 For a more detailed description of the social and economic setting of Marseille, see Sewell, "The Structure of the Working Class of Marseille in the Middle of the Nineteenth Century," unpub. Ph.D. diss. (University of California, Berkeley, 1971).

cially and economically diverse city which was undergoing rapid economic and demographic expansion—all of which should have been conducive to relatively high rates of social mobility. Opportunities for upward social mobility were further enhanced by the demographic situation in Marseille. Because the native population barely managed to reproduce itself, relying for expansion on migrants who generally came from lower socioeconomic backgrounds, there were never enough young men from non-manual family backgrounds to fill all the available non-manual positions. Furthermore, not all young men from non-manual occupational backgrounds managed to secure non-manual positions themselves. In our sample, fully 36 percent of the men whose fathers held non-manual positions had fallen into the manual category—the vast majority into the skilled trades. This substantial volume of downward mobility, which was at least as high as in most modern industrial societies, further increased the availability of

Table 1 Inter-Generational Mobility into Non-Manual Occupations

A. UNCORRECTED

| | FATHER'S OCCUPATION | | | | |
	(1) Agri- culture	(2) Maritime, Service	(3) Unskilled Worker	(4) Skilled Worker	(5) Total Workers (2 + 3 + 4)
Total no. of sons	513	172	242	849	1263
Sons with non-manual occupations	91	20	18	116	154
% upwardly mobile	18%	12%	7%	14%	13%

B. CORRECTED

| | FATHER'S OCCUPATION | | | | |
	(1)	(2)	(3)	(4)	(5)
Total no. of sons	513	172	242	771	1185
Sons with non-manual occupations	99	24	18	121	163
% upwardly mobile	19%	14%	7%	15%	14%

non-manual positions for ambitious men from farther down the social hierarchy.[5]

In these circumstances it is surprising how few men from working-class backgrounds had attained non-manual positions by the time they got married. Among sons of unskilled and semi-skilled workers only 18 out of 242, or 7 percent, had non-manual jobs, and among sons of skilled workers the rate was only 116 out of 849 or 14 percent. For the entire population of working-class origin, the rate of mobility into non-manual occupations was 13 percent, or about half to a third the rate that obtains in most contemporary industrial societies. In short, despite the relatively favorable demographic and economic circumstances, upward mobility from working-class to non-manual occupations was far lower in mid-nineteenth-century Marseille than in modern industrialized societies.

But if the rate of mobility into non-manual occupations was surprisingly low for sons of workers, it was surprisingly high for sons of peasants. Of the 513 peasants' sons who got married in Marseille in 1846 and 1851, ninety-one of them, or 18 percent, held non-manual occupational positions. Their rate of mobility into non-manual occupations was thus substantially higher than that of workers' sons. How can this rather surprising contrast between workers' sons and peasants' sons be explained? Were peasants' sons in mid-nineteenth-century Marseille more highly qualified for non-manual occupations than workers' sons? Judging from the limited evidence at hand, they were not.

The possession of literacy is obviously a crucial qualification for nearly all non-manual occupations, and in this respect sons of peasants were, on the average, clearly less qualified than sons of workers. Only 67 percent of the peasants' sons who married in Marseille in 1846 were able to sign their names on their marriage certificates, a literacy rate slightly above the 64 percent for unskilled workers' sons, but well below the 84 percent that obtained for skilled workers' sons, and substantially below the combined rate of 79 percent for all workers' sons.[6] If the average level of

5 The corrected figure for downward mobility is 28%. The most comprehensive set of figures on social mobility in contemporary societies is in S. M. Miller, "Comparative Social Mobility: A Trend Report and Bibliography," *Current Sociology*, IX (1960).
6 The corrected figures for literacy are very slightly lower, 83% for skilled workers and 78% for all workers.

qualification, as measured by literacy rates, had been the sole determinant of rates of mobility into non-manual occupations, peasants' sons should have found themselves in non-manual occupations only slightly more frequently than sons of unskilled workers, considerably less frequently than sons of skilled workers, and
somewhat less frequently than all workers' sons. Instead, peasants'
sons bested all categories of workers' sons by margins ranging
from 30 percent for skilled workers' sons to over 250 percent for
unskilled workers' sons.

One further possibility presents itself: perhaps those peasants'
sons who found non-manual positions in Marseille were not simple rustics driven from the countryside by poverty, but second or
third sons of prosperous landowning peasants who arrived in
Marseille with at least a smattering of education and perhaps with
a small amount of capital as well. If so, this might explain the
overall difference between sons of peasants and sons of workers.
This possibility can be tested by separating the peasants' sons who
married in Marseille in 1846 and 1851 into those whose fathers
were and were not proprietors of their land. As we should expect,
the proprietors' sons were considerably more likely to find non-
manual occupations than non-proprietors' sons: fully 32 percent of
the former, as against 16 percent of the latter, held non-manual
positions at the time of their marriage. But the 16 percent rate of
the sons of non-proprietors was still above the 14 percent attained
by skilled workers' sons, and was more than double the rate of unskilled workers' sons. Furthermore, the sons of both proprietors
and non-proprietors had lower literacy rates than workers' sons:
75 percent and 65 percent, respectively.

The conclusion, thus, seems inescapable: the remarkable success of peasants' sons in obtaining non-manual occupations cannot
be accounted for by competitive advantages in the labor market,
nor can the equally remarkable failure of workers' sons to do so be
explained by competitive disadvantages. It therefore follows that
many workers' sons must have either abstained from the competition for non-manual positions or entered it only half-heartedly,
voluntarily leaving most of the prizes to the more eager peasants'
sons. We seem to be confronted, in short, with a difference of
preferences, of values.

It is clear that many workers did not actively seek non-
manual occupations, even though the likelihood of successfully

finding such positions was reasonably high. Instead, they chose to
remain in the working-class occupational world. How can this
choice be explained? I believe it can be explained, at least in large
part, by the survival of a traditional corporative world-view
among the working-class of the city. Although the corporative
regime was formally abolished during the French Revolution,
there is a good deal of evidence that French workers, both in Marseille and elsewhere, retained a corporate mentality and continued
to use corporate forms in their labor organizations well into the
nineteenth century.[7] A worker still tended to see his trade as a solidary community governed by its own traditional rituals and sanc-
tions, and he felt his status in society and many of his social obligations to be defined by membership in such a community. To the
extent that this view of society remained in force among Marseille's workers in the middle of the nineteenth century, it should
have both intensified a young man's self-identification as a worker
and made bourgeois occupations, which lacked the corporative
forms, the powerful labor organizations, and the sense of solidarity of the working-class trades, seem unattractive. It should,
consequently, have caused workers' sons to seek jobs in working-class trades and to ignore opportunities in non-manual occupations.

Peasants' sons, by contrast, had no reason to prefer working-
class trades. Indeed, if there is any truth in the standard portrait
of the French peasant mentality—with its pronounced individualism and its obsession for private property—the *petite bourgeoisie*
should have been more congenial than the highly organized, solidary, and corporate world of the working class. But in addition to
this affinity between peasant and *petit bourgeois* values, the peasant
had also been affected by a process of uprooting. A peasant's son
who took up residence in Marseille had already decided to abandon his ancestral occupation, while a worker's son, even if he had
left his native town or village, could still seek a position in his
father's trade or in a similar working-class trade. When the peas-

7 Jean Vial, *Le coutume chapelière, histoire du mouvement ovrière dans la chapellerie* (Paris,
1941); Paul Chauvet, *Les ouvriers du livre en France de 1798 à la constitution de la fédération du
livre* (Paris, 1959); Joan W. Scott, *The Glassworkers of Carmaux* (Cambridge, Mass., 1974),
esp. 19–52. For Marseille, see Sewell, "Social Change and the Rise of Working-Class Politics in Nineteenth-Century Marseille," *Past & Present*, 65 (1974), esp. 81–82, 91–92, and
104–105.

ant's son entered the urban labor market, there was no "natural" place for him to look. He was therefore responsive to opportunities of all kinds, and especially to opportunities in non-manual occupations, where the rewards in pay, prestige, and possibilities for advancement were greatest. Thus, peasants' sons may have been responsive to opportunities in non-manual occupations at least in part because they had been so thoroughly uprooted in the process of migrating to the city.

If uprooting were one of the factors that led peasants to have high rates of mobility into non-manual occupations, we might reasonably expect that migration had similar effects on men from working-class backgrounds. To be sure, a worker's son who moved to Marseille from a small town or village might retain many of his family's values regarding occupations, but in moving to the city he loosened or broke his ties with the social institutions that reinforced his childhood values—his family, his peers, his church, and his native community. The migrant's escape from the familiar web of social relations, together with the cultural shock that was bound to result from migration, should have had the effect of eroding his commitment to and his identification with his ancestral occupation. Hence, migrants from working-class backgrounds should have been more responsive to opportunities for non-manual occupational positions than native-born workers' sons, who never escaped from their families' value assumptions or from the web of social relations that reinforced those assumptions.

Our data generally support this argument about the effects of migration. Immigrants from Italy, who made up about a quarter of all migrants from working-class backgrounds, had a much lower rate of mobility into non-manual occupations than native workers' sons (3 percent against 9 percent), but French-born workers' sons who migrated to Marseille had a rate twice as high as that of native workers' sons—20 percent as against 9 percent. These same differences held both for sons of skilled workers and for sons of unskilled workers. Among skilled workers' sons the rates of mobility into non-manual occupations were 5 percent for immigrants from Italy, 10 percent for natives of Marseille, and 20 percent for French-born migrants. Among unskilled workers' sons the rates were 2 percent for immigrants from Italy, 5 percent for natives, and 14 percent for French-born migrants.

Table 2 Inter-Generational Mobility into Non-Manual Occupations, Natives and Migrants

I. NATIVES OF MARSEILLE
A. UNCORRECTED

	FATHER'S OCCUPATION				
	(1) Agri- culture	(2) Maritime, Service	(3) Unskilled Worker	(4) Skilled Worker	(5) Total Workers (2 + 3 + 4)
Total no. of sons	60	108	93	432	633
Sons with non-manual occupations	4	9	5	42	56
% upwardly mobile	7%	8%	5%	10%	9%

B. CORRECTED

	(1)	(2)	(3)	(4)	(5)
Total no. of sons	60	108	93	386	587
Sons with non-manual occupations	8	13	5	36	54
% upwardly mobile	13%	12%	5%	9%	9%

II. FRENCH-BORN MIGRANTS
A. UNCORRECTED

	(1)	(2)	(3)	(4)	(5)
Total no. of sons	362	42	83	355	480
Sons with non-manual occupations	80	11	12	71	94
% upwardly mobile	22%	26%	14%	20%	20%

B. CORRECTED

	(1)	(2)	(3)	(4)	(5)
Total no. of sons	362	42	83	325	450
Sons with non-manual occupations	84	11	12	71	94
% upwardly mobile	23%	26%	14%	22%	21%

Table 2 (cont.)

III. ITALIAN–BORN MIGRANTS
    A. UNCORRECTED

	FATHER'S OCCUPATION				
	(1) Agri- culture	(2) Maritime, Service	(3) Unskilled Worker	(4) Skilled Worker	(5) Total Workers (2 + 3 + 4)
Total no. of sons	91	22	66	60	148
Sons with non-manual occupations	7	0	1	3	4
% upwardly mobile	8%	0%	2%	5%	3%

    B. CORRECTED

	(1)	(2)	(3)	(4)	(5)
Total no. of sons	91	22	66	60	148
Sons with non-manual occupations	7	0	1	6	7
% upwardly mobile	8%	0%	2%	10%	5%

These results seem to indicate that migration increased the likelihood of upward mobility, except in those cases where the migrants suffered from crushing disadvantages in the labor market. Thus, workers' sons who migrated to Marseille from elsewhere in France had higher rates of upward mobility than natives, while foreign-born workers' sons had very low rates. The foreign-born were mostly Italians, who were frequently illiterate, who were in any case ignorant of the French language, and whose values and work habits had been formed in an economically backward country. And in addition to these more-or-less objective handicaps, they were also subjected to widespread and open prejudice by the native population. It is possible that both Italian and French migrants were freed of their traditional ascriptive values regarding occupational choices by the experience of migration. But a combination of prejudice and lack of qualification kept the Italians from experiencing upward mobility, while the French migrants, unencumbered by such problems, attained upward mobility in a relatively high proportion of the cases.

The argument that high migrant mobility rates resulted from the effects of uprooting on values is also corroborated by evidence from other areas of social life. This evidence seems to show that uprooting affected a whole range of values and behavior patterns in the working class of mid-nineteenth-century Marseille. Thus, a massive study of the decline of religious practice in Marseille shows that "dechristianization" of the working class, which began at about the middle of the nineteenth century, advanced particularly rapidly among migrants to the city.[8] Secondly, French-born migrants made up the bulk of the militants in the democratic and socialist movement that grew up in Marseille after the Revolution of 1848, while natives either remained politically apathetic or supported traditional royalism.[9] Finally, an analysis of court records of Marseille from 1845 to 1847 reveals that French-born migrants were about three times as likely to be convicted of crimes as natives.[10] These findings suggest that migration liberated men from traditional value-constraints of all kinds, and made them more receptive to all kinds of modern ideas and behavior—to anticlericalism and to socialism, to competitive behavior in the labor market and to criminal behavior in the streets.

These findings about natives and migrants cast further doubt on the now much beleaguered concept of a "folk-urban continuum."[11] My findings hardly fit the assumption that city-dwellers are necessarily modern in outlook and behavior and that

8 F. L. Charpin, *Pratique religieuse et formation d'une grande ville* (Paris, 1964), 261–301.

9 Sewell, "La Classe ouvrière de Marseille sous la Seconde République; structure sociale et comportement politique," *Le mouvement social*, LXXVI (1971), 56–59, translated in Peter N. Stearns and Daniel J. Walkowitz (eds.), *Workers in the Industrial Revolution* (New Brunswick, N.J., 1974), 103–106; *idem*, "Social Change and the Rise of Working-Class Politics," 99–104.

10 Jugements du tribunal correctional de Marseille, Archives départementales des Bouches-du-Rhône, 403 U 52–57.

11 See Oscar Lewis, "Tepozlan Restudied: A Critique of the Folk-Urban Conceptualization of Social Change," and "Further Observations on the Folk-Urban Continuum and Urbanization with Special Reference to Mexico City," in *idem, Anthropological Essays* (New York, 1970); Philip M. Hauser, "Observations on the Urban-Folk and Urban-Rural Dichotomies as Forms of Western Ethnocentrism," in Philip M. Hauser and Leo F. Schnore (eds.), *The Study of Urbanization* (New York, 1965), 503–517; Francisco Benet, "Sociology Uncertain: The Ideology of the Rural-Urban Continuum," *Comparative Studies in Society and History*, VI (1963), 1–23.

the process of modernization can be described as an expansion of urban social patterns throughout the whole of society. In Marseille in the middle of the nineteenth century, native-born workers had "folk" traditions of their own that led them to behave in distinctly "non-modern" ways—traditions that kept them from acting like "rational" economic men in the labor market, that kept them from committing crimes, and that kept them from adopting new ideologies in politics and religion. This implies that at least in societies like those of Western Europe, where cities have long been part of the social landscape, modernization involved extensive transformations of a traditional *urban* social order, as well as of rural society.

The major conclusion of this paper is that social mobility patterns in mid-nineteenth-century Marseille differed in a number of respects from those of modern industrial societies. The most obvious difference is that the overall rate of upward mobility from working-class to non-manual occupations was much lower than in modern industrial societies. Indeed, the real difference between mid-nineteenth-century France and modern industrial societies may well be understated by our figures, since the modern figures are based on national samples while those for Marseille are based solely on one of the most dynamic and rapidly growing urban centers in the country. The case of Marseille therefore demonstrates that the early stages of industrialization did not necessarily produce the high rates of upward mobility that are characteristic of mature industrialism.

But this does not mean that all societies in the early stages of industrialization had similar social mobility patterns. Indeed, what evidence is available seems to indicate that American social mobility patterns were strikingly "modern" at a relatively early date. Thernstrom, who has done the best work on mobility in nineteenth-century America, has found that in 1890 41 percent of all Bostonians of working-class parentage had attained non-manual occupational positions—a figure that is far above Marseille's and that compares favorably with modern industrial societies.[12] The figures for Boston and Marseille are separated by

12 This figure is from Stephan Thernstrom, *The Other Bostonians: Poverty and Progress in the American Metropolis* (Cambridge, Mass., 1973), 86.

96 | WILLIAM H. SEWELL, JR.

some forty years, and it is not clear that either Boston or Marseille
was representative of the rest of America or of France. Nevertheless, the striking contrast between Marseille and Boston suggests a
significant amendment to Lipset and Bendix. One of the most important conclusions of *Social Mobility in Industrial Society* was that
American social mobility patterns were no more open than those
of other industrialized countries—contrary to received notions
about the unique fluidity of the American social structure. But the
comparison of Marseille and Boston implies that American society
may have been far more open than European societies in the
nineteenth century, and that the convergence found in studies carried out since World War II may be of recent origin.[13]

Another conclusion that arises from our data is that patterns
of social mobility in mid-nineteenth-century Marseille were by no
means automatically "determined by the occupational structure."
Differences in values had a significant impact on mobility patterns, reducing intergenerational upward mobility from
working-class to non-manual occupations to a level appreciably
below what would have obtained if workers' sons had chosen to
compete energetically for non-manual positions. It was adherence
to ascriptive values that caused workers' sons to enter non-manual
occupations in lower proportions than peasants' sons. Furthermore, native-born workers' sons seem to have had especially low
rates of upward mobility in part because their adherence to ascriptive values was especially strong.

However, the differences between Marseille and modern industrial societies may not be as great as they at first appear. It is
true that our findings about peasants' sons are in sharp contrast to
Blau and Duncan's findings about contemporary American farmers' sons. They find that farmers' sons in the urban labor market
are less likely to find non-manual jobs than workers' sons;
moreover, they find that the poorer performance of farmers' sons
can be explained by their low qualifications.[14] These findings are
the reverse of what we discovered in Marseille, where peasants'

13 Crew's study of social mobility in Bochum, Germany in 1900 shows rates of intergenerational mobility roughly similar to those of mid-nineteenth-century Marseille. In this one
German town, at least, mobility rates around the turn of the century were far lower than in
Thernstrom's Boston. David Crew, "Definitions of Modernity: Social Mobility in a German Town, 1880–1901," *Journal of Social History*, VII (1973), 60–62.
14 Blau and Duncan, *The American Occupational Structure*, 286–292.

sons did *better* than workers' sons, and did so in spite of their *lower* qualifications. It is also true that the patterns indicated by our data are very far from Lipset and Bendix's theoretical argument about social mobility, which stresses the imperatives inherent in a modern industrial economic order, and minimizes the impact of different systems of values. Nevertheless, one of the key findings on which we base our argument for the importance of values actually has a striking parallel in the studies reported by Lipset and Bendix. They point out in a long footnote that the United States is the only country for which data are available in which farmers' sons who leave agricultural employment are less likely to find non-manual positions than are workers' sons. They also present a number of speculations as to why this should be so—that rural-urban migration may be less selective in the United States, that in European countries rural people's education may be better than urban workers' education, and so on. In short, they argue that European farmers' sons who migrated to the cities must in some way have been better qualified than urban workers' sons, while the reverse was true in America.[15]

This is one possibility, and it could and should be tested empirically by methods similar to those used by Blau and Duncan in America. But until such research has been done, we cannot reject the possibility that the difference is accounted for by a difference in values—either that European farmers' sons have extraordinarily strong achievement values or that European workers' sons have relatively weak achievement values. This last possibility—that workers have values which make them prefer working-class occupations—is precisely what we have argued for mid-nineteenth-century Marseille. And given the strong class consciousness that prevails in most European countries, it is not entirely implausible that workers' sons may have some hesitations about entering non-manual occupations. But whatever the explanation may be, it is clear that Lipset and Bendix's arguments against the influence of values are by no means air-tight—at least so far as European countries are concerned.

Our limited data are obviously not sufficient to provide any decisive answers to the very complex question of the relationship between mobility and class consciousness, but they do suggest

15 Lipset and Bendix, *Social Mobility in Industrial Society,* 216–217.

some speculations. At first sight, our comparison between nineteenth-century Marseille and Boston would seem to restore the once axiomatic notion that high rates of social mobility have helped to preserve America from European-style class consciousness. After all, in Boston, where social mobility was high, no very significant class-conscious workingmen's movements ever developed; while Marseille, where social mobility was low, was and is a stronghold of socialism in France. But if our data seem to indicate a link between low social mobility and high class consciousness, the link they suggest is rather different from the one sociologists and historians usually assume. Most discussions of the problem have stressed the importance of blocked mobility aspirations in creating working-class consciousness. According to this formulation, the impossibility of individual betterment within the system led workers to band together in collective attacks against the system itself.

Although something of this mechanism may have operated in societies where socialism developed mass followings, our data for Marseille suggest an alternative mechanism. In Marseille the low levels of upward mobility from the working class seem to have been due in part to a voluntary abstention from the competition for non-manual jobs. After all, peasants' sons, whose qualifications were generally lower than workers' sons, managed to obtain non-manual occupations in 18 percent of the cases, a rate above that of workers' sons, and not much below the rates obtaining in some modern industrial societies. It appears that Marseille's workers were not driven to class consciousness by the impossibility of achieving upward mobility. Rather, they seem to have had low rates of mobility largely because they already had an embryonic form of class consciousness, because they were strongly committed to working-class occupations and regarded non-manual occupations as somehow alien and undesirable. Moreover, the continuing greater success of peasants' sons than workers' sons in modern European societies suggests that a similar mechanism may still be operating.

If this line of argument is accepted, it implies that one of the most important roots of European class consciousness may have been the corporate cultural tradition of the pre-industrial European working class. This tradition made working men feel that their destiny was linked to that of their fellow workers, and predisposed them to collective, rather than individualistic, ideologies and modes of social and political action. At the same time, it led men to stay in the working class rather than strive to enter the bourgeoisie, thereby maintaining stability of personnel and strengthening the continuity of working-class traditions. The corporate tradition was far from politically conscious class solidarity of the Marxian type, and the road that led from the relatively particularistic corporate consciousness to a broader and more inclusive working-class consciousness was long and sometimes tortuous. Nevertheless, many of the sentiments, symbols, and ideas that informed the class-conscious workers' movements of the later nineteenth and twentieth centuries probably had their origins in the peculiar corporate subculture of the pre-industrial European working class.

Similarly, the failure of class-conscious workers' movements to take hold in America probably owes as much to the absence of a pre-industrial tradition of artisan solidarity and distinctiveness as it does to the entraordinary fluidity of American society. It was particularly difficult to organize a working class whose membership was constantly changing as a result of both geographical and occupational mobility, just as the lack of mobility of the European working class made organizational tasks easier. But rates of mobility, as we have seen, are not themselves simple functions of the structure of opportunities: they are also affected by the values and social assumptions of the population, and in America these values and social assumptions accentuated the fluidity of society in general and the turnover of working-class personnel in particular. Thus, it was the American workers' individualistic cultural heritage, as much as the nature of the economic and social structure, that made them socially mobile and kept them from developing European-style class consciousness.

Michael R. Haines

Fertility, Nuptiality, and Occupation: A Study of Coal Mining Populations and Regions in England and Wales in the Mid-Nineteenth Century

Without question one of the important concomitants of modernization and modern economic growth is the structural change for the economy.[1] Clark's frequently cited model of economic change, for example, uses the share of labor force in the primary, secondary, and tertiary sectors to gauge the economic progress of a society.[2] In this context, the importance of geographical and occupational mobility appears central to the whole phenomenon of modernization:

> This shift in sectoral structure of the labor force, combined with the demographic trends and differentials in rates of natural increase, had vast consequences for conditions of life, institutions, and the prevailing views of the populations of developed countries that proved to be the dominant factor in changing the consumption structure, the social structure, and even the ideology of society.[3]

It is from this viewpoint that the significance of differential demographic behavior emerges. As the transition from high to low fertility and mortality levels accompanies modern economic growth, the pattern and speed of transition may depend partly on the occupational composition of the population.

Michael R. Haines is Assistant Professor of Economics and Program Associate, International Population Program, Cornell University, and author of several articles on economic demography.

I would like to express my thanks to the referee who made a careful reading of a preliminary draft of this paper. The research for this article was based, in part, on funds furnished by the Cornell University Western Societies Program and by NICHHD Grant No. R01-HD-07599. In the period since this paper was written, Professor Dov Friedlander of the Hebrew University brought to my attention a paper he has published on nineteenth-century English mining populations. It is encouraging to note that many of the conclusions are the same, although the data were largely different.

1   See Simon Kuznets, *Modern Economic Growth: Rate, Structure and Spread* (New Haven, 1966), 86–284; *idem, Economic Growth of Nations: Total Output and Production Structure* (Cambridge, Mass., 1971), 143–198, 249–302. Richard A. Easterlin, "Economic Growth: An Overview," in David L. Sills (ed.), *International Encyclopedia of the Social Sciences* (New York, 1968), VI, 468–474.
2   Colin Clark, *The Conditions of Economic Progress* (London, 1957; 3rd ed.).
3   Kuznets, *Economic Growth*, 258.

This paper will show that occupational fertility and nuptiality differentials existed historically in England and Wales and have remained through the modern era.[4] It will be argued that these differentials can be partly, even largely, explained by economic factors, although the general social and status "norms" (i.e., tastes in the economists' jargon) surrounding each occupation continue to play a role. The principal emphasis will be on one occupational group—coal miners—though other groups must be used for comparison.

There are several reasons for this emphasis on coal mining. First, coal mining in the nineteenth century, as today, was one of the most basic activities of the industrial revolution. Some have even labeled the nineteenth century the "Age of Coal."[5] Second, coal mining populations are often numerous and geographically highly concentrated. When demographic information on separate occupations is lacking, as it frequently is, then small areas containing high concentrations of a particular occupational group can be used in its stead. Third, coal miners have been observed to have relatively high fertility; for example, the United Nations states that "Miners have also been shown to be a highly fertile group in those censuses where information for them was tabulated separately."[6] Explaining this particular differential behavior, which has apparently persisted over time, should furnish clues as to the causes of general occupational fertility differentials.

England and Wales is also an appropriate area for study because of its early experience with industrialization and heavy dependence on coal mining. By 1851 35 percent of its population lived in urban areas of at least 20,000 inhabitants, over 49 percent of its labor force was in manufacturing, and over 3.3 percent of the total male labor force worked in mining.[7] Considerable material

4 United Nations, The Determinants and Consequences of Population Trends: New Findings On Interaction of Demographic, Economic, and Social Functions, (New York, 1973), I, 100–101.
5 M. Gillet (trans. by C. H. Kent), "The Coal Age and the Rise of Coalfields in the North and Pas-de-Calais," in F. Crouzet, W. H. Chaloner, and W. M. Stern (eds.), Essays in European Economic History, 1789–1914 (New York, 1969), 188–194, 201–202; David S. Landes, The Unbound Prometheus: Technological Change and Industrial Development in Western Europe From 1750 To The Present (Cambridge, 1969), 95–100; E. A. Wrigley, Industrial Growth and Population Change: A Regional Study of the Coalfield Areas of North-west Europe In The Later Nineteenth Century (Cambridge, 1961), 3–11.
6 United Nations, Determinants and Consequences of Population Trends (New York, 1953), 88.
7 Peter Mathias, The First Industrial Nation: An Economic History of Britain, 1870–1914 (New York, 1960), 243, 260; B. R. Mitchell and Phyllis Deane, Abstract of British Historical Statistics (Cambridge, 1962), 60.

exists from the censuses of 1911 and later which can shed light on the issues of occupational fertility differentials. For the mid-nineteenth century, sufficient demographic and labor force data are available for small geographic areas (i.e., registration districts) to permit some analysis of fertility and nuptiality within mining areas just prior to the decline in period fertility rates (c. the mid-1870s). Finally, a tradition of interest in occupation and social class in Britain dates from the work of Charles Booth in the nineteenth century.[8] This interest led to a limited literature on occupation and its social and demographic concomitants, including fertility and marriage, and to a heritage of statistical materials related to occupation and social class.

OCCUPATION, FERTILITY, AND MARRIAGE IN ENGLAND AND WALES AS A WHOLE   General occupational fertility differentials have been observed in both nineteenth and twentieth century England and Wales. The United Nations, surveying the literature in 1953, noted certain consistencies in the data for England and Wales as well as for a number of other countries.[9] As a rule, populations in agriculture, forestry, fisheries, mining, and some types of metallurgical work have had relatively large families; at the other extreme, professional and clerical workers have had relatively low fertility. In between, there is a general ranking from manual, blue-collar to nonmanual, white collar occupations. Table 1 presents data from the Census of Marriage and Fertility of 1911, a remarkable historical social document. As may be seen from the first panel, there was a general progression from the low fertility of high level professional and business occupations (Class I) to the high fertility of unskilled manual workers (Class V). Of special note were the relatively small families among textile workers

8 For a discussion of the application of historical data for historical and sociological purposes, see W. A. Armstrong, "The Use of Information on Occupation" in E. A. Wrigley (ed.), Nineteenth Century Society: Essays in the Use of Quantitative Methods in the Study of Social Data (Cambridge, 1972), 191–310. A major point of this article is that occupation is usable both as an industrial grouping for the study of the economic features of society and as a measure of social class or ranking. J. W. Innes, Class Fertility Differentials in England and Wales, 1876–1934 (Princeton, N.J., 1938); idem, "Class Birth Rates in England and Wales, 1921–1931," The Milbank Memorial Fund Quarterly, XIX (1941), 72–96; W. A. B. Hopkin and J. Hajnal, "Analysis of Births in England and Wales, 1939, by Father's Occupation," Population Studies, I (1947), 187–203, 275–300; T. H. C. Stevenson, "The Fertility of Various Social Classes in England and Wales from the Middle of the Nineteenth Century to 1911," Journal of the Royal Statistical Society, XXXVIII (1920), 401–444.
9 United Nations, Determinants and Consequences (1953), 87–88.

Table 1 Fertility & Child Mortality in Relation to Husband's Social Class & Occupation: England & Wales, 1911. (Children Ever-Born & Children Surviving Per 100 Couples)

CATEGORY	WIFE UNDER 45 AT CENSUS				
	CHILDREN BORN PER 100 COUPLES		CHILDREN SURVIVING PER 100 COUPLES		STAN-DARDIZED CHILD MOR-TALITY PER 1000 BORN
	ACTUAL	STANDARD-IZED	ACTUAL	STANDARD-IZED	
Total population	282	282	233	233	174
Total occupied	282	282	233	233	174
Total unoccupied	236	215	194	179	167
Social class I	190	213	168	187	123
II	241	250	206	212	150
(occupied only)					
III	279	278	232	231	167
IV	287	285	237	236	173
V	337	317	268	253	202
VI	238	247	191	197	203
VII	358	348	282	274	212
VIII	327	320	284	278	129
Selected occupations					
Coal miners (total)	360	349	283	274	213
Coal miners at the coal face	368	356	289	280	214
Iron & steel workers	354	336	274	262	222
Puddlers; rollers	357	340	275	262	229
Blast furnace workers	376	354	294	278	214
Builders' laborers	384	333	302	265	205
General laborers	370	330	293	263	203
Ship platers/ riveters	372	340	293	270	206
Glass manufacture	362	328	284	259	210
Agricultural laborers	330	323	285	279	135
Civil service officers & clerks	190	210	171	187	110
Indoor domestic servants	151	189	134	164	131
Farmers	276	283	248	254	104
Merchants	198	201	178	180	101
Cotton textile workers	232	242	182	190	218
Tailors	286	273	244	233	147
General shopkeepers	292	271	235	220	187

NOTE: The Standardization procedure for wives under age 45 involved taking the actual rates (of children ever-born per woman) in each category of wife's age of marriage cross-classified by duration of marriage for a particular occupation of husband and then multiplying each rate by the number of ever-married

WIFE OVER 45 AT CENSUS			ALL AGES OF WIFE			
CHILDREN BORN PER 100 COUPLES		CHILDREN SURVIVING PER 100 COUPLES	CHILDREN BORN PER 100 COUPLES		CHILDREN SURVIVING PER 100 COUPLES	SOCIAL CLASS
ACTUAL	STANDARD-IZED		ACTUAL	STANDARD-IZED		
487	487	368	353	353	280	—
489	487	372	350	353	278	—
465	489	334	445	310	322	—
365	389	294	249	274	210	I
435	451	341	311	319	255	II
504	489	382	350	351	279	III
498	492	379	356	357	283	IV
533	528	388	399	390	306	V
457	444	331	308	315	235	VI
626	585	445	423	430	321	VII
572	556	457	433	402	359	VIII
630	588	446	423	432	321	VII
652	604	462	427	442	325	VII
603	559	426	422	414	316	IV & V
622	571	434	436	420	322	V
625	578	451	442	432	336	V
536	540	384	435	405	329	V
542	548	396	441	406	335	V
614	555	442	432	415	330	III
600	537	429	426	401	323	IV
574	561	455	451	405	369	VIII
351	369	292	236	265	205	I
282	357	225	192	247	162	III
467	503	387	378	359	322	II
362	367	309	265	258	232	I
459	446	326	296	313	223	VI
496	484	379	355	346	288	III
467	469	339	361	340	276	II

women in each age/duration category for the total population of England and Wales. The marriage age categories used were 15–19, 20–24, 25–29, 30–34, and 35–44. The duration categories were 0–2, 2–5, 5–10, 10–15, 15–20, 20–25, and 25–30. The "expected" children ever-born were then summed and di-

Table 1 (Continued) Ratios to Total Population Averages (Total Population = 100)

CATEGORY	WIFE UNDER 45 AT CENSUS				
	CHILDREN BORN PER 100 COUPLES		CHILDREN SURVIVING PER 100 COUPLES		STAN-DARDIZED CHILD MOR-TALITY PER 1000 BORN
	ACTUAL	STANDARD-IZED	ACTUAL	STANDARD-IZED	
Total population	100	100	100	100	100
Total occupied	100	100	100	100	100
Total unoccupied	94	76	83	77	96
Social class I	67	76	72	80	71
II	85	89	88	91	86
(occupied only)					
III	99	99	100	99	96
IV	102	101	102	101	99
V	120	112	115	109	116
VI	84	88	82	85	117
VII	127	123	121	118	122
VIII	116	113	122	119	74
Selected occupations					
Coal miners (total)	128	124	121	118	122
Coal miners at the coal face	130	126	124	120	123
Iron & steel workers	126	119	118	112	128
Puddlers; rollers	127	121	118	112	132
Blast furnace workers	133	126	126	119	123
Builders' laborers	136	118	130	114	118
General laborers	131	117	126	113	117
Ship platers/ riveters	132	121	126	116	118
Glass manufacture	128	116	122	111	121
Agricultural laborers	117	115	122	120	78
Civil service officers & clerks	67	74	73	80	63

vided by the total number of married women for all marriage ages and durations at the census who were below age 45. This procedure was repeated for surviving children to women aged under 45. Standardized child mortality per 1000 born was then calculated as:

$$\frac{\left(\begin{array}{c}\text{Standardized Children Ever Born}\\ \text{per 100 couples}\end{array}\right) - \left(\begin{array}{c}\text{Standardized Children Surviving}\\ \text{per 100 couples}\end{array}\right)}{\left(\begin{array}{c}\text{Standardized Children Ever Born}\\ \text{per 100 couples}\end{array}\right)} \times 1000$$

For wives over age 45 at the census, children ever born per 100 couples was standardized only for age of marriage since duration was much less important for older women. (Standardizations for duration and age of marriage were done for the eight social classes and little difference appeared between those standardizations for age only). Children surviving per 100 couples was not standardized since child mortality for older women was greatly influenced by factors external to the family and therefore had

Table 1 (Continued) Ratios to Total Population Averages (Total Population = 100)

WIFE OVER 45 AT CENSUS			ALL AGES OF WIFE			
CHILDREN BORN PER 100 COUPLES		CHILDREN SURVIVING PER 100 COUPLES	CHILDREN BORN PER 100 COUPLES		CHILDREN SURVIVING PER 100 COUPLES	SOCIAL CLASS
ACTUAL	STANDARDIZED		ACTUAL	STANDARDIZED		
100	100	100	100	100	100	—
100	100	101	99	100	99	—
95	100	91	126	88	115	—
75	80	80	71	78	75	I
89	93	93	88	90	91	II
103	100	104	99	99	100	III
102	101	103	101	101	101	IV
109	108	105	113	110	109	V
94	91	90	87	89	84	VI
129	120	121	120	122	115	VII
117	114	124	123	114	128	VIII
129	121	121	120	122	115	VII
134	124	126	121	125	116	VII
124	115	116	120	117	113	IV & V
128	117	118	124	119	115	V
128	119	123	125	122	120	V
110	111	104	123	115	118	V
111	112	108	125	115	120	V
126	114	120	122	118	118	III
123	110	117	121	114	115	IV
119	115	124	128	115	132	VIII
72	76	79	67	75	73	I

much less significance for fertility. Thus, standardized child mortality per 1000 born could not be computed for women over 45.

The biases involved in choosing the total national population of married females of different marriage ages and durations as the standard population are evident and were noted by the compilers of the census (lxxx–lxxxii).

Social classes may be roughly categorized as follows:

    I: high skill level and high income professional and business occupations (e.g., scientists, artists, lawyers, physicians, managers, high level civil servants).

    II: lower skill and income professional and business occupations (e.g. small shopkeepers, agricultural employers and less skilled professional, scientific and artistic workers)

    III: skilled manual laborers

    IV: semi-skilled manual laborers

Table 1 (Continued) Ratios to Total Population Averages (Total Population = 100)

CATEGORY	WIFE UNDER 45 AT CENSUS				
	CHILDREN BORN PER 100 COUPLES		CHILDREN SURVIVING PER 100 COUPLES		STAN-DARDIZED CHILD MOR-TALITY PER 1000 BORN
	ACTUAL	STANDARD-IZED	ACTUAL	STANDARD-IZED	
Indoor domestic servants	54	67	58	70	75
Farmers	98	100	106	109	60
Merchants	70	71	76	77	58
Cotton textile workers	82	86	78	82	125
Tailors	101	97	105	100	84
General shopkeepers	104	96	101	94	107

V: unskilled manual laborers
VI: textile workers
VII: miners
VIII: agricultural laborers

(Class VI) and the large families among coal miners (Class VII) and agricultural laborers (Class VIII). These differentials held true both for women above and below age forty-five and for total children born and children surviving.

Since different socioeconomic groups in the population experienced differing patterns of age at marriage and duration of marriage, the rates in Table 1 were also standardized to the age and duration pattern of the female population as a whole.[10] The fertility differentials nonetheless persisted, although they were narrowed, after compensating for the earlier average age at marriage and longer average marital duration among the working classes. The same was also true for average surviving children.

More detailed breakdowns of completed fertility by date of marriage indicate that those differentials not only persisted over time but widened from a least the 1850s. Table 2 presents some evidence on this. Married females of completed fertility (i.e., over age forty-five by 1911) were tabulated by date of marriage and social class and then the rates were standardized for age of marriage

10 For an explanation procedure of the standardization techniques, see the note to Table 1. For women above age 45 standardization was only for the age of marriage and no standardization was done for surviving children.

FERTILITY AND NUPTIALITY | 109

Table 1 (Continued) Ratios to Total Population Averages (Total Population = 100)

WIFE OVER 45 AT CENSUS			ALL AGES OF WIFE			
CHILDREN BORN PER 100 COUPLES		CHILDREN SURVIVING PER 100 COUPLES	CHILDREN BORN PER 100 COUPLES		CHILDREN SURVIVING PER 100 COUPLES	SOCIAL CLASS
ACTUAL	STANDARDIZED		ACTUAL	STANDARDIZED		
58	73	61	54	70	58	III
96	103	105	107	102	115	II
74	75	84	75	73	83	I
94	92	89	84	89	80	VI
102	99	103	101	98	103	III
96	96	92	102	96	99	II

SOURCE: England and Wales, Registrar General, *Census of England and Wales: 1911*, XIII, "Fertility of Marriage," Part II (London: H.M.S.O., 1923), Table XLVIII.

within each group. For higher socioeconomic groups (I and II) completed fertility was declining relative to the national average while that of unskilled, manual workers (V) was rising relative to the average, which itself was declining for successive marriage cohorts. Completed fertility among miners' and agricultural laborers' families (Groups VII and VIII) rose sharply relative to the national average. The rates of decline of children ever-born for marriage cohorts after 1851 were greatest among the highest social classes and smallest among the lower groups. Completed fertility declined from the marriage cohort of 1852/61 to that of 1882/86 at an average annual rate of 1.21 percent and 1.08 percent per annum respectively for social classes I and II but only by 0.51 percent per annum for social class V and by 0.32 percent and 0.47 percent per annum respectively for coal miners' and agricultural laborers' wives. The national decline was 0.69 percent. The lower panel of Table 2 shows that a similar divergence was taking place for effective fertility (i.e., surviving children). Thus, during the fertility decline in late nineteenth-century Britain, class differentials widened as the lower socioeconomic groups, and especially coal miners, lagged behind the national average.[11]

11 This feature of the fertility decline was noted by Innes, *Class Fertility Differentials*, 41-52.

Table 2 Completed and Effective Fertility per 100 Wives By Social Class and Marriage Cohort. Wives over Age 45 at Census, 1911. Rates Standardized for Marriage Age. Total Rates Standardized for Class Composition.

DATE OF MARRIAGE	I	II[a]	III	IV	V	VI	VII	VIII	TOTAL	TOTAL OCCUPIED POPULATION
				CHILDREN BORN PER 100 COUPLES						
1851 and earlier	605[c]	728	681	740[c]	698[c]	*	*	746	697	700
1852–61	625	700	707	700	718	654	759	738	690	701
1862–71	593	650	679	673	698	633	760	702	662	673
1872–81	497	567	615	616	652	567	717	667	605	611
1882–86[b]	422	493	556	562	609	513	684	632	551	554
				PERCENT OF NATIONAL AVERAGE						
1851 and earlier	86	104	98	106	100	*	*	107	100	100
1852–61	91	101	102	101	104	95	110	107	100	102
1862–71	90	98	103	102	105	96	115	106	100	102
1872–81	82	94	102	102	108	94	119	110	100	101
1882–86[b]	76	89	101	102	111	93	124	115	100	100
				ANNUAL PERCENTAGE DECREASE						
1852–61 to 1862–71	0.52	0.74	0.40	0.39	0.28	0.33	+0.01	0.50	0.41	0.41
1862–71 to 1872–81	1.77	1.37	0.99	0.92	0.68	1.10	0.58	0.51	0.90	0.97
1872–81 to 1882–86	2.18	1.86	1.34	1.22	0.91	1.33	0.63	0.72	1.25	1.30

Table 2 Completed and Effective Fertility per 100 Wives By Social Class and Marriage Cohort. Wives over Age 45 at Census, 1911. Rates Standardized for Marriage Age. Total Rates Standardized for Class Composition.

DATE OF MARRIAGE	I	II[a]	III	IV	V	VI	VII	VIII	TOTAL	TOTAL OCCUPIED POPULATION
	CHILDREN SURVIVING PER 100 COUPLES									
1851 and earlier	378[c]	452	420	464[c]	405[c]	*	*	490	432	436
1852–61	433	492	471	472	466	436	465	527	464	478
1862–71	440	479	481	482	480	423	505	535	473	482
1872–81	393	438	460	464	470	406	502	534	454	458
1882–86[b]	345	393	430	434	451	379	497	521	425	428
	PERCENT OF NATIONAL AVERAGE									
1851 and earlier	88	105	97	107	94	*	*	113	100	101
1852–61	93	106	102	102	100	94	100	114	100	103
1862–71	93	101	102	102	101	89	107	113	100	102
1872–81	86	96	101	102	104	89	111	118	100	101
1882–86	81	92	101	102	106	89	117	123	100	101

a Includes only wives of occupied husbands.

b Includes a few women not quite age 45 in 1911 (i.e., wives married at ages 15-19 in 1881–86).

c Based on fewer than 100 cases.

* = Fewer than 10 cases available.

SOURCE: J. W. Innes, *Class Fertility Trends in England and Wales, 1876-1934* (Princeton, 1938), 42-43; England and Wales, Registrar General, *Census of England and Wales, 1911*, XIII, "Fertility of Marriage," II (London, 1923), Table XLIV.

Returning to Table 1, selected detailed occupations also suggest a ranking similar to social class; but certain occupations, especially coal mining, were notable. For wives over forty-five in 1911, children ever-born per 100 couples where husband's occupation was in coal mining was 630 (and 652 for workers at the coal face). This was 129 percent (and 134 percent) of the national average, and ranked miners' wives first among all occupational groups, closely followed by wives of blast furnace workers, iron puddlers and rollers, ship platers and riveters, iron miners (not shown), and glass workers. In contrast, wives of higher-level civil service officers and clerks were only 72 percent of the national average, wives of indoor domestic servants only 58 percent, wives of merchants only 74 percent, and wives of cotton textile workers only 94 percent. Adjusting for infant mortality (i.e., ever-born children surviving), fertility for miners' wives dropped to 446 for women aged forty-five and over (and 462 for wives of workers at the coal face). For this measure of "effective fertility," coal miners dropped slightly behind agricultural laborers (but not farmers), blast furnace workers, puddlers and rollers, ship platers and riveters, shipyard workers, some construction laborers, and some general laborers. When these rates were standardized by the age structure of marriage for the female population of England and Wales aged forty-five and over, the first rank of coal mining populations was regained and the rates became 123 percent (and 125 percent) of the national average. It is notable that many of the industrial occupations with high fertility had locational and economic characteristics similar to coal mining. For women under forty-five at the 1911 Census (and hence with incomplete fertility), whose fertility had been standardized to the age at marriage and the duration of marriage characteristic of all women under forty-five in England and Wales in 1911, the ranking remained roughly the same. Coal miners were second only to blast furnace workers and agricultural laborers. For children surviving and standardized for age of marriage and marital duration (a calculation not performed in the census for women over forty-five), miners' wives were only behind wives of agricultural laborers, blast furnace workers, and iron miners (not shown). Wives of workers at the coal face were still first, however, despite the relatively high child mortality among the mining population. Child mortality, standardized for duration of marriage and age at marriage of woman, was among the highest for coal mining families, 122 percent of the national average, but this was compensated by high total fertility.[12] The same was true for most of the other occupations with extremely high total fertility. The overall effect of differentials in child mortality was to cause some slight convergence toward the national average for "effective" fertility, but the effect was minimal and often altered by standardization procedures.[13]

Descriptive evidence for the nineteenth century conveys the same impression. For example, Redford remarked in his pioneering work on labor migration in England in the first half of the nineteenth century:

> In general, the evidence for any strong influx of labor into coal mining is not plentiful. A large part of the supply of new labour required by the expansion of the industry probably came from the natural increase of a *notoriously prolific section of the population*. To contemporary observers the coal mining population afforded 'an example of the principle of population in full vigour, in the absence of external influence, and (hitherto) of internal checks. Pitmen must be bred to their work from childhood . . . their numbers cannot be recruited from any other class . . . the increase of the pit population solely from internal sources has in consequence been such that . . . one hundred and twenty-five families attached to a single colliery were capable of annually supplying twenty to twenty-five youths fit for hewers.'[14]

It is notable that similar features are observable in the mid-twentieth century. In the Census of England and Wales of 1951, the mean number of children ever-born per woman aged 45 to 49

12   See note to Table 1.

13   It is important to note that the Census of 1911 presents only surviving married women with surviving spouses. If their marital fertility were systematically different from those who did not survive, a bias is introduced. Of course, couples who do not make it through child-bearing without one or both partners dying *will* have lower fertility, in general, because of the interruption of the marriage. The question is what their completed fertility would have been. Also couples having completed child-bearing but not surviving to 1911 might have been different from those who did survive. Innes and T. H. C. Stevenson, the man who conducted the 1911 Census of Marriage and Fertility, both argued that no important bias was introduced by inclusion only of surviving married women with surviving spouses. (See Innes, *Class Fertility Differentials*, 22–24; *Census of England and Wales, 1911*, XIII, xciv.) Counter arguments are advanced by R. R. Kuczynski, *The Measurement of Population Growth* (London, 1935), 95–96.

14   P. L. C. Report, 1834, Appendix A, Part I, No. 5, 130; in Arthur Redford, *Labour Migration in England, 1806–1850*, (Manchester, 1964; 2nd ed.), 56–57. [Emphasis added].

was 2.60 children for women whose husbands were in mining and quarrying. (See Table 3.) Only 14 percent of these couples were childless, compared to a national average for children ever-born to women 45 to 49 of 2.01 and a proportion childless of .208. Thus completed fertility of miners' wives was 130 percent of the national level and still 106 percent when standardized for age at marriage and socioeconomic composition.[15] Miners' wives ranked first among all industrial/occupational classifications for unstandardized mean number of children ever-born and still first when standardized only for age at marriage. The rank dropped to fourth (among thirteen industrial/occupational classifications) when fertility was standardized both for age at marriage and socioeconomic composition. The completed fertility of wives of semi-skilled and especially skilled workers (i.e., mostly workers at the coal face) was high relative to all other socioeconomic groups in the mining and quarrying industry. Since these workers made up the bulk of those in the industry, standardizing to the national socioeconomic composition, with its much lower share of skilled and semi-skilled workers, would tend to lower the relative standardized fertility in mining and quarrying.[16]

Marriage practices were also related to occupation. Mean age at first marriage for both males and females appears to have been among the lowest in miners' families and in mining regions. In a special study conducted in 1884–85 by the Registrar General, miners and their wives had the lowest mean age at first marriage (24.06 and 22.46 respectively) among all nine occupational groups

15 Great Britain, General Register Office, *Census: 1951, England and Wales,* lviii, 178, 208. Standardization for socioeconomic groups involved standardization of rates for the individual socioeconomic groups within an industrial classification to the national socioeconomic group composition. The thirteen socioeconomic groups were farmers; agricultural workers; higher administrative, professional and managerial; other administrative, professional and managerial; shopkeepers (including proprietors and managers of wholesale businesses); clerical workers; shop assistants; personal service; foremen; skilled workers; semi-skilled workers; unskilled workers; armed forces.
16 This fact was noted in the census, "The high fertility of the mining group as a whole was evidently due to the exceptionally large families of those actually employed as miners (i.e., skilled and semi-skilled), while the unskilled workers attached to the industry . . . had slightly smaller families than the average of [unskilled workers]." *Ibid.,* lxix. The share of skilled and semi-skilled workers in this sample of married couples was 84.18% for mining and quarrying as compared with 46.12% for all occupational/industrial categories.

studied. The rankings by occupational groups for age of marriage was similar to the ranking by marital fertility.[17]

Coale's index of proportion married (I_m)[18] was significantly higher in an 1861 sample of sixty-one coal mining registration districts than in a random sample of 125 registration districts. The same was true for 1871. (See Table 5). In 1861, the highest proportion of persons married at ages 15 to 24 was found in Durham, a county heavily populated with coal miners. In 1834, the Poor Law Commissioners stated that "miners assumed the most important office of manhood at the earliest age at which nature and passion prompted."[19] The census of 1911 noted that "[e]arly marriage is known as a matter of common experience to increase in frequency down the social scale."[20] It was noted that only 7 percent of middle-class husbands and one third of their wives were married before age twenty-five while for coal miners, those proportions were 57 percent and 75 percent for their wives.[21] For the occupational/social class groupings in between the gradation was regular. This differential marriage pattern has persisted,

17   The listing is as follows:

OCCUPATIONS	MEAN AGE AT FIRST MARRIAGE	
	MALES	FEMALES
Miners	24.06	22.46
Textile Hands	24.38	23.43
Shoemakers, Tailors	24.92	24.31
Artisans	25.35	23.70
Labourers	25.56	23.66
Commercial Clerks	26.25	24.43
Shopkeepers, Shopmen	26.67	24.22
Farmers and Sons	29.23	26.91
Professional and Independent Class	31.22	26.40

SOURCE: England and Wales, Registrar General, *Forty Ninth Annual Report* (1886), viii.

18   For a definition see Ansley J. Coale, "Factors Associated with the Development of Low Fertility: An Historic Summary," in United Nations, *World Population Conference: 1965* (New York, 1967), II, 205-209.

19   *British Parliamentary Papers* (1834), XXXVII, 125. Quoted in Margaret Hewitt, *Wives and Mothers in Victorian England* (London, 1958), 40-41.

20   Great Britain, "Fertility Tables," *Census: 1951, England and Wales* (London, 1959), xlvii.

21   Great Britain, *Census of England and Wales, 1911*, XIII, xvi.

Table 3 Mean Family Size and Proportions Infertile by Industry Group of Husband: England and Wales, 1951 (Women Aged 45–49 at Census. All Marriage Ages Combined. Once Married Women with Husband Present.)

INDUSTRY GROUP	(CHILDREN EVER-BORN) MEAN FAMILY SIZE			PROPORTION INFERTILE		
		STANDARDIZED FOR MARRIAGE			STANDARDIZED FOR MARRIAGE	
	UNSTAN-DARDIZED	AGE	AGE AND SOCIO-ECONOMIC GROUP	UNSTAN-DARDIZED	AGE	AGE AND SOCIO-ECONOMIC GROUP
1. Agriculture, horticulture and forestry	2.25	2.31	2.25	0.19	0.18	0.19
2. Mining & quarrying	2.60	2.37	2.13	0.14	0.17	0.18
3. Metal manufacture	2.33	2.23	2.15	0.17	0.18	0.19
4. Engineering & vehicles	1.97	1.99	1.99	0.21	0.21	0.20
5. Textiles	1.74	1.77	1.75	0.25	0.24	0.24
6. Clothing	1.69	1.73	1.81	0.24	0.23	0.22
7. Food, drink & tobacco	2.01	1.99	1.99	0.19	0.20	0.20
8. Other manufacturing industries & utilities	2.00	1.99	1.95	0.20	0.20	0.21
9. Buildings & construction	2.34	2.29	2.25	0.17	0.18	0.19
10. Transport & fishing	2.13	2.07	2.01	0.18	0.19	0.20
11. Distributive trades	1.72	1.77	1.97	0.23	0.22	0.22
12. Professional services	1.65	1.81	1.91	0.24	0.21	0.21
13. Other services	1.83	1.87	1.93	0.23	0.22	0.22

Table 3 Continued

	RATIOS TO TOTAL POPULATION (PERCENT)					
1. Agriculture, horticulture and forestry	112	115	112	94	88	94
2. Mining & quarrying	130	118	106	68	82	87
3. Metal manufacture	116	111	107	81	89	92
4. Engineering & vehicles	98	99	99	101	101	100
5. Textiles	87	88	87	120	118	116
6. Clothing	84	86	90	116	112	108
7. Food, drink & tobacco	100	99	99	95	97	97
8. Other manufacturing industries & utilities	100	99	97	98	100	101
9. Buildings & construction	117	114	112	85	89	92
10. Transport & fishing	106	103	100	89	95	98
11. Distributive trades	85	88	98	113	110	105
12. Professional services	82	90	95	120	103	101
13. Other services	91	93	96	111	107	105

SOURCE: Great Britain, General Register Office, *Census: 1951, England and Wales*, "Fertility Report" (London: HMSO, 1959), 207–210.

especially among mining populations. Among women aged 45 to 49 at the time of the 1951 census, the highest proportion married by age twenty-five was among wives of men in mining and quarrying (64 percent). The lowest proportion was among wives of professionals (38 percent), with other industries distributed in between.[22]

THE MODEL   The explanatory model proposed here focuses on the major factors in marriage and fertility decisions as they relate to mining populations. It is important to consider both marriage and marital fertility, since total fertility is the result of both and since both are affected by many common factors.[23] Modified, this model can be applied more generally to other occupational groups but in this instance focuses on coal miners because of their observed high fertility and early marriage customs. (What is said here regarding coal miners is also essentially true for other populations in mining and metallurgy.)

It is argued here that the higher marital fertility and earlier and more extensive marriage of coal mining populations is a product of the interaction of life style (as embodied in tastes and costs) and potential income outlook.[24] By its very nature, coal mining is not especially centered (at least initially) in large cities or established urban centers. Urban agglomerations do grow up around mines or mining centers, but not of the genre of great administrative, commercial, cultural, and market centers. In the early stages of development the population of these mining centers is often drawn from a rural environment. The hypothesis, then is that these persons, who were socialized (i.e., whose tastes were formed) in a rural life-style, maintained these tastes for a desired mix of goods and children in their new situation while experiencing the expanded income outlook and opportunities of industrial wage earners in a rapidly growing sector. In many cases the new miners experienced a cost situation intermediate between rural and

22 Great Britain, "Fertility Tables," *Census: 1951*, xvi–xviii.
23 Nothing is said in this section concerning illegitimate fertility since it was not too important in England and Wales at this time. It should be possible, however, to modify the model to discuss wife's occupation only and therefore illegitimate fertility.
24 A similar approach to the economics of fertility is taken by Richard A. Easterlin. See his "Towards a Socio-economic Theory of Fertility," in S. J. Behrman, et. al., *Fertility and Family Planning: A World View* (Ann Arbor, 1969), 127–156. Also *idem*, "The Economics and Sociology of Fertility: A Synthesis" (1973), mimeo.

urban and were able to supplement their money incomes with income-in-kind from produce raised on small garden plots and farms. The quasi-rural setting and the relative lack of opportunities for female employment outside the home (which characterized most mining areas) reinforced this latter phenomenon. Although the view of mining communities as quasi-rural is not as appropriate for nineteenth century Britain as it was earlier (or for other countries), the social isolation of mining communities nevertheless helped perpetuate these norms longer and caused them to follow general social norms much more slowly.

A generally good standard of living is evidence that miners enjoyed relatively high incomes. With respect to nineteenth century English miners "most authorities agree that miners enjoyed a relatively high standard of living" and that "against a background of ill-planned industrial conurbation the houses of many miners seemed well-ordered, healthy and clean."[25] Mining wages were generally high and above the national average. Miners also often received free cottages and free coal.[26] Evidence presented by Bowley shows that the average money wages of miners were among the highest in the nineteenth century.[27] The wages of printers, skilled iron workers, and sometimes building craftsmen were at times higher, but those of sailors, agricultural workers, and woolen and cotton textile workers were lower. Laborers' wages were always lower. Finally, these higher wages often accrued to miners at an early age (relative to farmers and professionals), thus encouraging earlier marriage and longer exposure to the peak child bearing period.

Another relevant aspect of coal mining is the comparative absence of female employment outside the home. In Britain, particularly, female and child labor underground was forbidden after Lord Shaftesbury's Act of 1842. Further, because of their location, mines often created male employment opportunities distant from factories or shops which employed women. For England and Wales in 1871, the mean proportion of females aged twenty and

25   Brian Lewis, *Coal Mining in the Eighteenth and Nineteenth Centuries* (London, 1971), 38, 107. He quotes from Louis L. Simonin, *Underground Life or Mines and Miners* (London, 1868).
26   A. L. Bowley, *Wages in the United Kingdom in the Nineteenth Century* (Cambridge, 1900), 96, 101.
27   Bowley, *Wages*, 96–109, 130–133, esp. Appendix I, Table II, 133.

over employed outside the home (in sixty-three registration districts with a significant proportion of the male labor force in coal mining) was 24.5 percent as opposed to 30.1 percent for a random sample of 125 registration districts. (See Table 5) These means were significantly different at a .001 level of probability. At the same date there was a –0.50 zero order correlation between the percentage of adult male employment in mining and minerals and the percentage of adult females employed outside the home within the mining districts.[28] For England in the early twentieth century the high fertility of mining districts relative to textile districts has been attributed to differential employment opportunities for women. "In mining districts there are practically no avenues of employment open to women outside the home, whereas in textile districts the bulk of the work is carried on by women."[29] Women are not usually employed in mining, and in the absence of employment elsewhere (in textiles, for example), would be available for work on garden plots or small farms or in domestic handicrafts, activities more compatible with child rearing. Or they simply would not work at all. Hence fewer available employment opportunities for women might simultaneously encourage earlier marriage and higher marital fertility.

As for the impact of employment on marital fertility, following the reason of Mincer, it can be argued that the contribution of a wife's income to family income has two aspects: a price effect and an income effect.[30] The decision of a wife to enter the labor force outside the home thus should have both a positive influence on fertility (i.e., the income effect), since her income should allow more children, and a negative influence (i.e., the price effect) since it now becomes more expensive and difficult to have young children with the mother working outside the home. Mincer found that where most work for women is outside the home (as in the

28 This correlation was significantly different from zero at a .001 level of probability, assuming normally distributed parent populations.
29 Enid Charles and Pearl Moshinsky, "Differential Fertility in England and Wales During the Past Two Decades," in Lancelot Hogben (ed.), *Political Arithmetic* (New York, 1938), 143. Cited in Samuel H. Preston, "Female Employment Policy and Fertility," in Robert Parke, Jr. and Charles Westoff (eds.), *Aspects of Population Growth Policy,* (Washington, D.C., 1972), VI, 380. See also Margaret Hewitt, *Wives and Mothers,* 40–41, 57.
30 Jacob Mincer, "Market Prices, Opportunity Costs and Income Effects," in Carl F. Christ (ed.), *Measurement in Economics: Studies in Mathematical Economics and Econometrics in Honor of Yehuda Grunfeld* (Stanford, 1963), 67–82.

population he studied for the United States in the 1950s), the negative price effect should dominate. That is, higher female labor force participation outside the home should lead to lower fertility. But where there is considerable employment opportunity in agriculture or in domestic handicraft industry, the income effect should dominate because the wife, staying home, can both work and rear her children. (In this case, the opportunity cost of the wife's time in employment outside the home, and hence the 'cost' of a child, should be lower). That female labor force participation outside the home has a negative effect on marital fertility has been confirmed by a number of authors.[31] It has also been found that a woman's participation in domestic handicraft industry is compatible with child-rearing and thus favorable to higher fertility.[32]

As far as female work and marriage are concerned, there is some contemporary evidence that greater female employment opportunities tend to lower proportions married at younger ages (i.e. 20 to 24).[33] Hewitt demonstrates that this was also the case in mid-

31 Kingsley Davis, "Population Policy: Will Current Programs Succeed?," *Science,* CLVIII (1967), 738; Preston, "Female Employment Policy and Fertility," 375–393; Glen G. Cain, *Married Women in the Labor Force: An Economic Analysis* (Chicago, 1966); Glen G. Cain and Adriana Weininger, "Economic Determinants of Fertility: Results from Cross-Sectional Data," *Demography,* X (1973), 205–233; James A. Sweet, "Family Composition and Labor Force Activity of American Wives," *Demography,* VII (1970), 195–209; John Kasarda, "Economic Structure and Fertility: A Comparative Analysis," *Demography,* VIII (1971), 307–317.

For England during this period it has been established by Margaret Hewitt. "[T]he diminution of fertility was common to all married women occupied away from the home. . . . [T]he lower fertility of the mother employed away from home was, in part at least, the almost inevitable result of the conflict between motherhood and the claims of her job." Hewitt, *Wives and Mothers,* 93. The evidence is not always favorable to the hypothesis of a negative relation of fertility and female employment, however, once a number of other variables are controlled. See Geraldine B. Terry, "Rival Explanations in the Work-Fertility Relationship," *Population Studies,* XXIX (1975), 191–206. The argument is also generally made for the relation between female employment and fertility for countries which have already experienced fertility decline. There is evidence that those arguments do operate in higher fertility, less developed societies, particularly in urban areas. See Sidney Goldstein, "The Influence of Labour Force Participation and Education on Fertility in Thailand," *Population Studies,* XXVI (1972), 419–436. The findings of Kasarda also include analysis of a large number of less developed countries. The findings for less developed, high fertility countries are not as uniform as those for developed, lower fertility countries. See J. M. Stycos and Robert H. Weller, "Female Working Roles and Fertility," *Demography,* IV (1967), 210–217.

32 A. J. Jaffe and K. Azumi, "The Birth Rate and Cottage Industries in Underdeveloped Countries," *Economic Development and Cultural Change,* IX (1960), 52–63.

33 Samuel H. Preston and Alan J. Richards, "The Influence of Women's Work Opportunities on Marriage Rates," *Demography,* XII (1975), 209–222.

nineteenth-century Britain, particularly in industrial areas.[34] The other side of this situation is that a paucity of female employment opportunities would lead to earlier marriage. The same factors which acted to increase marital fertility for miners' wives also produced earlier marriage and less celibacy among mining populations.

Another aspect of the marriage issue is the sex ratio (number of males per 100 females) in the peak marriage and childbearing ages. Coal mining, being largely a male employment, attracts disproportionate numbers of young adult males when the industry is expanding. This is a reflection of the differentials in male/female employment opportunity and migration. For 1871, for example, the average sex ratio for the age group 20 to 29 was 107 for the sample of mining districts but only 94 for the random sample of districts. The zero-order correlations between this sex ratio and Im were 0.73 and 0.50 for the two samples. The partial correlations were 0.52 and 0.45 respectively. The factor of heavily male employment often coincided with a relative scarcity of extra-household female employment and hence the tendency towards earlier and more extensive female marriage because the effect of imbalanced sex ratios would be augmented by low levels of female employment opportunity. The zero order correlations between the sex ratio (for ages 20 to 29) and percentage of adult females employed outside the home was -0.70 for the mining sample and -0.46 for the random sample. The sex ratio thus interacts with both nuptiality and marital fertility (inasmuch as it reflects lack of female employment opportunity). The strong relation of the sex ratio to female marriage has been noted by Wrigley for the coal mining areas of northwest continental Europe.[35] As will be seen below, the sex ratio is indeed a good predictor of both fertility and nuptiality.

The cost and utility of children must also be considered. Although it has been mentioned that child labor underground was prohibited in 1842, children could still work above ground. Further, education was not compulsory until 1876, and even then only up to age twelve.[36] Further, besides a "consumption" utility

---

34 Hewitt, *Wives and Mothers*, 35–47.
35 Wrigley, *Industrial Growth and Population Change*, 142–145.
36 G. D. H. Cole and Raymond Postgate, *The British Common People: 1746–1946* (London, 1961), 361–364.

and productive utility attached to a child of any given birth order, it has been argued that there is also a social security motive attached to children.[37] Thus, expecting relatively short working lives at peak efficiency, it should not be surprising that miners "discounted" their futures more heavily by marrying earlier and providing more children to care for them in old age. (This motive would obviously be weaker where an effective social insurance system was operating, but this was not the case in mid-nineteenth-century Britain.)

In sum, it is hypothesized that coal mining (and some similar occupations like iron puddling) involved a particular combination of income/earnings life cycle, related female labor force participation, and child costs which favored higher fertility and earlier and more extensive marriage. In addition, the migration patterns and less urban characteristics of mining areas lead to costs, tastes, and marriage patterns conducive to larger families. Finally, higher morbidity and debility among miners and higher mortality among their children also favored earlier marriage and more births both to insure the target family size and to help provide for old age and infirmity among the parents.

AN ANALYSIS OF THE CENSUSES OF 1851, 1861, AND 1871   Earlier it was stated that data from small, more homogeneous geographical areas are a partial substitute for detailed demographic information tabulated by occupation. The censuses of 1851, 1861, and 1871 were used to construct samples of registration districts, the smallest unit for which reasonable age/sex, occupational, and vital data were available. The census of 1841 lacked occupational data and sufficient accompanying vital statistics. The censuses of 1881 and later lacked occupational data for registration districts. The sample was thus restricted to 1851–71, which, unfortunately, precedes the period of fertility decline. For each census two samples were taken. One consisted of all districts (sixty-one) with more than 10 percent of the male population aged twenty and over in coal mining employment in 1861. A random sample of 125 districts was also taken at each census date. The reason for taking a separate sample of mining districts is that areas with a significant propor-

37 Harvey Leibenstein, *Economic Backwardness and Economic Growth* (New York, 1957), 163.

tion in mining constitute a rare or special occurrence. It is thus appropriate to sample completely this group of special districts in order to make some comparisons with the national sample. In particular, it is interesting to see whether the same relations held *within* the whole group of mining districts as for the national sample. Ten or more percent of males aged twenty and over in mining was the criterion for selecting the mining districts. This was hardly a homogeneous mining population in many cases, but it does allow scrutiny of some of the characteristics of mining *areas*. It must be remembered, however, that a test of the hypotheses advanced above can only imperfectly be studied using data for small, albeit more homogeneous, geographical areas.

Table 4 provides information on the variables used. The principal sources were, as indicated, the censuses of 1841 through 1871 and the *Annual Reports of the Registrar General* from 1841 through 1872. Most of the data were accepted without correction except birth statistics. Following the work of Glass and Teitelbaum, births were adjusted for each district on the basis of the correction factor for its county.[38] The exception was births used in computing infant mortality rates, since infant deaths as well as births were probably underreported. Although several adjustments were tried to correct for underreporting of infant deaths,[39] it was felt safest simply to divide uncorrected infant deaths by uncorrected live births to obtain the infant mortality rate.

The dependent variables used were Coale's indices of overall fertility (I_f), marital fertility (I_g), and proportions married (I_m). These indices are really a form of indirect standardization of birth rates using the highest observed fertility schedule, that of married Hutterite women in the United States in the 1920s, as the standard schedule.[40] In addition, the index of illegitimate fertility (I_h) was also calculated. For the computation of Ig, Im, and Ih, population by age, sex, and marital status is required. This was not available

38 D. V. Glass, "A Note on the Underregistration of Births in Britain in the Nineteenth Century," *Population Studies*, V, (1951), 70–88; Michael S. Teitelbaum, "Birth Underregistration in the Constituent Counties of England and Wales: 1841–1910," *Population Studies*, XXVIII (1974), 329–343.
39 Several assumptions about the share of unreported births which were also unreported infant deaths were considered. All were arbitrary and some led to strange results. Some correlations between child and infant mortality were tried but were also not encouraging.
40 See note 18.

Table 4 Regression Variables for Selected Districts in England and Wales: 1851, 1861, 1871

I_f	Index of Overall Fertility[a] (1851, 1861, 1871)
I_g	Index of Marital Fertility[a] (1861, 1871)
I_m	Index of Proportions Married[a] (1861, 1871)
I_h	Index of Illegitimate Fertility (1861, 1871)
MFR	General Marital Fertility Ratio (legitimate births per 1000 married women 15–59) (1851)
MM	(a) Percent of Males 20+ in Mining and Metallurgy (1851, 1861) (b) Percent of Males 20+ in Minerals Employment (1871)
FOH	Percent of Females 20+ Employed Outside the Home[b] (1851, 1861, 1871)
PE	Percent of Males 20+ in Primary Employment (farming and animal husbandry) (1851, 1861, 1871)
IMR	Infant Mortality Rate (infant deaths per 1000 livebirths per annum) (1848–50, 1858–60, 1868–70).
URB	Percent of Population in Principal Towns (1851, 1861, 1871)
RNM	Rate of Residual Net Migration in the Previous Decade (Per 1000 per annum) (1841–50, 1851–60, 1861–70)
SXR	Sex Ratio (Males 20–29 per 100 Females 20–29) (1851, 1861, 1871)

For the rates I_f, I_g, I_h, and MFR, births are taken as three year averages around the central date. For IMR, births and infant deaths are lagged two years.

SOURCE: Registrar General, *Census of 1841, 1851, 1861, and 1871: England and Wales*, passim. Registrar General, *Annual Reports of the Registrar General, 1841 through 1872*, passim.

Births were adjusted by county level adjustment figures furnished by Michael Teitelbaum. See his, "Birth Under-Registration in the Constituent Countries of England and Wales: 1841–1910," *Population Studies*, XXVIII (1974), 329–343.

a For definitions of I_f, I_g, and I_m see Ansley J. Coale, "Factors Associated With the Development of Low Fertility: An Historic Summary," United Nations, *World Population Conference: 1965*, (New York: 1967), II, 205–209.

b Females employed outside the home for 1851 and 1861 was arrived at by taking the total female population aged 20 and over and subtracting women classified as keeping house, pensioners, agricultural workers, and certain selected occupations (for 1851 and 1861 only) which could be identified as in the home (such as keeping a store or tavern in the home, or being a washerwoman), or for which a woman was identified as the wife of an occupied male (such as a butcher's wife or an innkeeper's wife). There was little basis for discriminating domestic handicraft industry. For 1871, females employed outside the home is total female population 20+ less pensioners, women classed as keeping house, and women in agricultural employment.

in 1851 and so the General Marital Fertility Ratio (MFR) was computed as a substitute for I_g.

Among the independent variables, it should be noted that the average infant mortality rate is lagged three years to account for the fact that fertility is expected to adjust to infant mortality with a lag of two to four years.[41] Some labor force structure variables (percentage of adult males in mining and metallurgy, of adult males in primary employment, and of adult females employed outside the home) are included, as well as some additional demographic variables (percentage of population in principal towns, rate of net migration in the previous decade, and the sex ratio for ages 20 to 29).

Means of the variables from Table 4 for the two samples for the three dates are given in Table 5. In addition, tests were made of the statistical significance of the differences of the means of each variable between the samples.[42] This table confirms a number of notions about mining areas relative to the national sample of districts. First, the mining areas had, at all three dates, significantly higher overall fertility, marital fertility, proportions married, and even illegitimate fertility. Second, the mining areas, although less agricultural than the national sample, still had a substantial proportion of the male labor force in agriculture (PE). Third, extra household female labor force participation (FOH) was significantly lower at all three dates in the mining areas. Fourth, the degree of urbanization (URB) was initially lower than that in the national sample (1851) but moved to being more urban by 1871. Fifth, the mining areas consistently showed much less net out-migration than the national sample, pointing to greater economic opportunity.[43] Finally, the sex ratio, as expected, was much higher in the mining areas, reflecting differential in-migration of males. Thus mining areas could be characterized as having higher marital fertility, higher levels of nuptiality, higher infant mortality, higher sex ratios, more in-migration, and lower levels

41   T. Paul Schultz, "An Economic Model of Family Planning and Fertility," *Journal of Political Economy*, LXXVII (1969), 160–161.

42   The test is strictly a test of differences of means from two independently distributed populations. The assumption of independence is not completely held since several districts appear in both samples. It is only a modest number (14 in 1851 and 1861 and 9 in 1871) and their removal from the random sample actually *increases* the differences and reduces the variances, thus making the differences even more significant.

43   Positive RNM indicates net out-migration.

Table 5 Mean Values of Regression Variables

VARIABLE	1851 MINING SAMPLE	1851 RANDOM SAMPLE	1851 SIGNIFI-CANCE[a] OF DIFFERENCE	1861 MINING SAMPLE	1861 RANDOM SAMPLE	1861 SIGNIFI-CANCE[a] OF DIFFERENCE	1871 MINING SAMPLE	1871 RANDOM SAMPLE	1871 SIGNIFI-CANCE OF DIFFERENCE
I_f	.422	.364	***	.433	.369	***	.452	.378	***
I_g	—	—	***	.716	.683	***	.738	.698	***
MFR (per 1000)	266.8	245.6	***	—	—	***	—	—	***
I_m	—	—		.563	.502	***	.576	.507	***
I_h	—	—		.069	.054	***	.066	.050	***
MM (percent)	20.7	2.2	***	24.5	3.1	***	39.9	12.5	***
PE (percent)	21.1	41.2	***	18.6	39.3	***	13.4	32.6	***
FOH (percent)	21.7	26.5	***	22.3	26.3	***	24.5	30.1	***
IMR (per 1000 live births)	150.6	137.3	***	149.7	137.5	***	154.3	135.6	***
URB (percent)	22.4	28.6	*	27.3	27.0	—	40.0	31.0	**
RNM (per 1000 population)	-0.28	18.7	***	1.17	5.92	***	0.79	5.68	***
SXR (per 100)	105.2	93.6	***	101.4	92.3	***	107.2	94.0	***

a   Based on a test of significance of the difference of two means drawn from independently distributed populations.

*** Significant at a 1 percent level.

** Significant at a 5 percent level.

* Significant at a 10 percent level.

— Not significant at a 10 percent level.

For definitions of variables and sources, see Table 4.

of extra-household female employment relative to the national sample. In addition, there was much more homogeneity among the mining areas with respect to their fertility and nuptiality. The coefficients of variability[44] were consistently smaller for the mining sample, indicating less dispersion around the higher means.

Ordinary least squares (OLS) regressions were applied to both the mining sample and the random sample at all three census dates, although only the results for the random sample are reported. The various fertility and nuptiality variables were taken in turn as independent variables. Two alternative specifications of each equation were tried, one excluding and one including the sex ratio.[45]

The results for the random sample are reported in Table 6. The coefficients in parentheses are those not significant at least at a 10 percent level. Also presented are the adjusted R-squared values and F-ratios. The results confirm some prior expectations about the effects of the designated independent variables on fertility and nuptiality, at least for areas. The proportion of males in mining and metallurgy (MM) was, when significant, positively related to fertility and marriage. In other words, controlling for the effects of the other variables, the marginal effect of a larger proportion of miners in the population was to increase both marital fertility and proportions married in an area.[46] For the percentage of adult males in primary employment (PE), it appears again, when significant, that a higher proportion of persons in farming and animal husbandry would lead to higher fertility, mostly via higher marital fertility.

It was earlier hypothesized that extra-household female employment (FOH) would result in lower fertility and marriage. Those coefficients in Table 6 which were significant were indeed negative but a substantial proportion of all coefficients (in 10 out

44 Sample standard deviation divided by the mean.
45 The reason for this result was the high degree of correlation between the SXR and FOH, which tended to increase the standard errors of both coefficients and reduce significance levels for FOH. It was desirable to see how FOH performed in the absence of SXR.
46 A question may arise as to why the proportion of adult males employed in mining and metallurgy is included at all on the right hand side of the regression equation. The answer is that it is of interest to see what effect varying *proportions* of miners and metal workers in the labor force have on fertility and marriage. It is also important to control for those varying proportions in the labor force when examining the effects of other social, demographic, and economic variables.

Table 6 · OLS Regression Equations: Random Sample of 125 Registration Districts: England & Wales, 1851, 1861, 1871. Overall Fertility, Marital Fertility & Nuptiality.

DEPENDENT VARIABLES	CON-STANT	MM	PE	FOH	IMR	URB	RNM	SXR	R^2_{adj}	F-RATIO
A) 1851										
I_f	.2742	.0030	.0006	(−.0004)	.0005	−.0006	−.0009	NI	.413	15.516
I_f	.1364	.0025	.0007	(.0002)	.0004	−.0003	−.0008	.0014	.504	18.972
MFR	241.3	.6962	(.0955)	(.0359)	(−.0419)	−.3003	−.6436	NI	.254	8.020
MFR	211.6	(.5825)	(.1001)	(.1655)	(−.0595)	−.2537	−.6254	.2968	.263	7.330
B) 1861										
I_f	.2958	.0037	.0010	−.0009	.0004	−.0002	−.0005	NI	.451	18.007
I_f	.2272	.0033	.0006	(−.0004)	.0003	−.0002	(.0004)	.0008	.544	22.135
I_g	.6821	.0030	.0011	(−.0003)	−.0002	(−.0002)	(−.0005)	NI	.396	14.577
I_g	.6484	.0028	.0006	(−.0000)	−.0003	(−.0002)	(−.0001)	.0004	.415	13.562
I_m	.4289	.0025	.0003	−.0011	.0007	(−.0002)	(−.0004)	NI	.248	7.821
I_m	.3618	.0021	(−.0001)	−.0007	.0006	(−.0002)	(.0005)	.0008	.319	9.301
C) 1871										
I_f	.3085	.0008	.0007	.0018	.0007	(.0001)	(−.0006)	NI	.204	6.313
I_f	.1105	.0007	.0011	(−.0006)	.0007	(.0002)	(−.0002)	.0015	.348	10.461
I_g	.6510	.0018	.0014	(.0005)	−.0003	(.0003)	(−.0005)	NI	.197	6.065
I_g	.6160	.0018	.0015	(.0007)	−.0003	.0003	−.0004	(.0003)	.197	5.338
I_m	.4986	(−.0006)	(−.0007)	−.0031	.0010	(−.0001)	(−.0004)	NI	.250	7.871
I_m	.2524	(−.0009)	(.0002)	−.0015	.0011	(−.0001)	(.0000)	.0018	.392	12.398

Figures in parentheses are coefficients not significant at least at the 10 percent level (using a one tailed test).

NI = not included

n = 125

For a definition of variables, see Table 4.

of 16 equations) were insignificant.[47] It is notable, however, that *both* marriage and marital fertility were negatively associated with this variable. Related to this is the closely (and negatively) inter-correlated variable of the sex ratio (SXR) for young adults (aged 20 to 29). This variable was strongly and positively associated with overall fertility, marital fertility, and marriage. Both female employment and the sex ratio often reflect the simultaneous effect of differential male employment opportunity, and so interact. In those equations in which both variables were present, the sex ratio generally performed much better than female employment, perhaps indicating a stronger association of fertility and marriage with sex imbalances among young adults than with actual employment of females. The mechanisms through which the sex ratio acted were both higher marital fertility and higher proportions married. The effect on marital fertility was, however, weaker—as indicated by the lower coefficients in the Ig and MFR equations which even became insignificant in 1871.

Of the other independent variables considered, the lagged infant mortality rate (IMR) was positively related to overall fertility and proportions married. The latter relationship is rather puzzling. It might have been the case that people married earlier in response to a higher recognized environmental risk of infant death, but it is more likely that a high level of infant mortality was caused by a low age of marriage. Since infant mortality is higher for young women relative to those in their mid-twenties[48] and since a high Im usually implies higher proportions married below age twenty-five, there might be some basis for a positive relation between proportions married and infant mortality. The relation of infant mortality to marital fertility was, when significant, negative, which is very puzzling since this relation would presumably have been most strongly positive. It would seem more logical that marital fertility would adjust, even in a regime of natural fertility, to high infant mortality. But such, apparently, was not the case in mid-nineteenth-century Britain.

The urbanization variable had a negative effect on overall and marital fertility in 1851 and 1861 and on marriage as well in 1871.

47 A nonlinear specification of the OLS equations resulted in much better performance of this variable, with 14 of 16 coefficients significant, suggesting nonlinearity in this variable.
48 United Nations, *The Determinants and Consequences of Population Trends* (New York, 1974; rev. ed.), I, 127.

The relationship appeared to weaken over time and even turned positive for marital fertility in 1871. It is possible that newer norms increased female labor force participation, and rising child costs associated with urbanization initially operated to depress fertility and marriage but that this altered over time. Perhaps by 1871 a greater proportion of urban population in a district reflected a greater economic opportunity.

The rate of net migration (RNM) was mostly insignificant after 1851 with the significant coefficients showing negative signs (i.e., the expected ones). A higher degree of out-migration would thus be associated with lower fertility and marriage because high net out-migration can be a proxy for poor economic opportunities which should tend to depress both fertility and marriage. It was, however, generally a weak variable.

Overall, the above equations provide some support for several of the hypotheses advanced regarding factors specific to mining *areas* which might tend to promote fertility and marriage. A higher proportion of males in mining and metallurgy was associated with higher levels of fertility and marriage in an area. A higher sex ratio, more infant mortality, and a lower level of extra-household female employment were features characteristic of mining areas relative to the national average of districts and all tended to increase fertility and nuptiality. For 1851, in addition, the fact that mining districts were relatively less urban exercized a positive influence on marriage and fertility. By 1871, when the mining districts had become more urban, the effects of urbanization had become insignificant. These results are supported by the regressions run for the mining samples.

In general, the two sets of equations (from the mining and the random samples) were rather similar at the three dates in terms of the direction and often the significance of the coefficients. The levels of the coefficients were usually different and a few coefficients, like the proportion of males in mining and metallurgy and in primary employment, showed noticeable differences. It is of some interest, then, that many of the same overall relationships held both for the national district sample and for the special subset of the mining districts.

The overall equations were modestly successful in explaining overall variation, as measured by the R-squared values adjusted for degrees of freedom. The group of socioeconomic and demographic variables used explained between 20 and 50 percent of overall variation in marriage and fertility for the random sample (and up to 70 percent for the mining sample). The R-squared values and the F-ratios (measuring the joint significance of all the variables) tended to become higher in both samples for overall fertility and proportions married, as opposed to marital fertility. This was most dramatic for the mining sample where the R-squared values rose for overall fertility between 1851 and 1871 and for proportions married between 1861 and 1871 but fell for marital fertility between 1851 and 1871. The equations for marital fertility in the 1871 mining equations actually had insignificant F-statistics, indicating that the independent variables lacked any significant explanatory power. Since $I_f \cong I_g \cdot I_m$, it is clear that for both samples, variation in marriage, rather than marital fertility, became increasingly important in accounting for variation in overall fertility. This is confirmed by the coefficients of variability which were lower for marital fertility than for overall fertility or the index of proportions married and also declined over time for marital fertility but not for the other measures.[49] Although there *were* differences in marital fertility, and although the *level* of marital fertility was significantly higher in the mining areas (see Table 5), control of overall period fertility for areas was still largely through marriage. Viewed from another perspective, it appears that on the very eve of the decline in marital fertility in Britain (dated from the 1870s), marital fertility was becoming increasingly *less* important in explaining variations in overall fertility. The socioeconomic and demographic factors which might be expected to influence fertility control within marriage, instead of becoming more important, were becoming less so. This certainly presents a challenging issue whose resolution depends, in part, on work done for the period after 1870–72.

It should be said that a number of estimation problems surround the application of ordinary least squares with a simple linear

49 The coefficients of variability (standard deviation divided by the mean) were:

	I_f		I_g/MFR		I_m	
	MINING	R.S.	MINING	R.S.	MINING	R.S.
1851	.108	.140	.077	.109	—	—
1861	.116	.142	.061	.077	.099	.114
1871	.109	.142	.050	.064	.101	.132

specification in this case. First, it is not clear that the relationship has been properly specified. To assess the importance of this problem, a nonlinear specification was estimated.[50] The form selected tried to account for expected nonlinearities especially in percentage variables which are upper and lower bounded. The transformed equations gave slightly higher adjusted R-squared values and one variable, female employment outside the home (FOH), became significant (with the correct sign) in almost all cases. Otherwise there were few differences, indicating that a simple linear approximation was quite good, except for female employment. A further type of specification error arises if important independent variables are missing. If these missing variables are in any way correlated with the regressors in the equation, then biased coefficients and erroneous significance tests may result.[51] The problem is serious, but there is no way to correct for it. The only answer is to bear in mind the qualification that not all desired variables could be included. A third problem which arises is multi-collinearity between the independent variables. This is a problem of experimental design and is tolerable as long as the t-values are not lowered a great deal. One instance was the high correlation between the sex ratio (SXR) and extra-household female employment (FOH). The inclusion of SXR usually caused FOH to become insignificant, so equations were specified both with and without SXR to examine the significance of FOH.

Finally, there is a serious problem with simultaneous equation bias for at least two independent variables, female employment and infant mortality.[52] As an example, low fertility may be a cause as well as an effect of high extra-household female employment. That is, women may be in the labor force *because* they have few children as well as the reverse. Similarly, high fertility may be a cause as well as an effect of high infant mortality because higher order births experience higher mortality.[53] The result of such a situation is biased coefficients, which may lead to erroneous

---

50 The functional form estimated was $\ell n \ I_f = \beta_1 + \beta_2/MM + \beta_3/PE + \beta_4/FOH$ $\beta_5 IMR + \beta_6/URB + \beta_7 RNM + \beta_8 SXR + E$ where $\ell n \ I_f$ is the natural logarithm of I_f, β_1 is the constant, β_i for $i = 2 - 8$ are the coefficients and E is the error term. A small positive number (.5%) was added to MM, PR, FOH, and URB to avoid division by zero.

51 J. Johnston, *Econometric Methods* (New York, 1972; 2nd ed.), 168–169.

52 *Ibid.*, 341–352.

53 Joe D. Wray, "Population Pressure on Families: Family Size and Child Spacing," in National Academy of Sciences, *Rapid Population Growth* (Baltimore, 1971), 409–418.

t-statistics. The solution is to specify and estimate a simultaneous equations system. This was done for 1861 and 1871 for both samples using two stage least squares (TSLS). The system was estimated in the following form.[54]

$$I_f = f(MM, PE, FOH, IMR, RNM, SXR)$$
$$FOH = g(I_f, URB, SXR)$$
$$IMR = h(I_f, MED)$$

where MED is medical personnel per 10,000 population.

The results (not presented) generally indicate that the coefficients of female employment and infant mortality estimated by OLS were downwardly biased, thus causing them to be rejected too often as insignificant. The problem with TSLS equations is that t-statistics are usually lowered by using this procedure (i.e., the estimates have higher standard errors) and that t-statistics, F-ratios, and R-squared values do not have the same interpretation as for OLS (except for very large samples). The results of OLS estimates for relatively small samples may be biased but are often efficient (i.e., have small standard errors). Given the fact that TSLS reveals that OLS downwardly biases both female employment and infant mortality, it appears that the OLS estimates are reasonable and that these coefficients may simply be found insignificant too often. This is encouraging from the standpoint of the original model.

CONCLUSIONS   Looking at historical differences in fertility and marriage among different occupational groups in England and Wales and concentrating on coal mining populations, we found that coal miners have had higher fertility and earlier and more extensive marriage than most other occupational groups. These differentials existed in the nineteenth century and persisted into the twentieth. A comparison of a sample of mining areas with a random sample of districts for 1851, 1861, and 1871 revealed higher average overall fertility, marital fertility, and proportions married in the mining areas than in the random sample.

It was hypothesized that a number of factors favorable to fertility acted on mining populations. Those include males reaching

54 It should be noted that urbanization is now specified as affecting fertility through female employment and not as acting directly. Here URB is the instrumental variable necessary to estimate FOH. The same is true for MED.

peak earning capacity at a relatively early age, relatively low child costs in mining areas, frequent lack of employment opportunities for women, higher infant mortality, high adult male debility and morbidity, and a taste and cost structure more rural than urban in the earlier stages of development. These factors combined to create earlier and more extensive marriage for both males and females in mining and in mining areas and also higher marital fertility. Net in-migration selective of males in many mining areas led to sex ratios further favoring earlier and more extensive marriage for females. Analysis of the mining and random samples yielded support for the hypotheses concerning female employment, infant mortality, the sex ratio, and urbanization for mining areas.[55]

The period under consideration preceded the decline in period fertility rates (after the mid-1870s), and there is some evidence for areas at this time that marriage differentials were much more important in explaining fertility differentials. This was particularly true for the mining districts by 1871, which may indicate that marriage longer remained more important in controlling fertility in more distinctly working class areas. There was virtually no change in period fertility measures and proportions married over this period. Further, there was little evidence of structural change with respect to the determinants of fertility and marriage in the mining areas. Joint F- tests for the mining equations of 1851 relative to 1861, and 1861 relative to 1871, were insignificant even at a 5 percent level.[56] The same tests for the random sample did indicate significant differences in the coefficients over time, however. The later fertility decline among mining populations might be connected to this lag in structural change, although work with individual data must be carried out.

This paper demonstrated the existence and long term persistence of differences in fertility between mining populations and other socioeconomic/occupational groups. There were, however, important changes over time. Marriage was a major explanation

---

55 No support was found for the adult morbidity hypothesis, using a test assuming that adult morbidity debility was correlated with adult mortality; but there were problems with this assumption and with the test which still leaves this hypothesis a viable one.

56 For a description of this test of significance between two different sets of regression coefficients see Gregory Chow, "Tests of Equality Between Sets of Coefficients in Two Linear Regressions," Econometrica, XXVIII (1960), 591–605.

of fertility differences across regions prior to the fertility decline. On the other hand, marital fertility differentials were the important factor during and after the fertility decline for occupational groups, since the differentials remained after standardizing for age at marriage and marital duration. Differences in marriage patterns were detectable in 1911 and 1951, however. The model described above is general enough to apply to both periods.

The model used in this paper could easily be generalized and applied to other occupational groups. It is not unique to mining populations, although some of the factors affecting fertility and marriage might receive different emphasis. The finding that marriage was more important than marital fertility in explaining differences among regions seems in itself to reflect the general phenomena of the "Western European marriage pattern" and control of overall fertility through marriage observable in early nineteenth century Western Europe.[57]

57 John Hajnal, "European Marriage Patterns in Perspective," in D. V. Glass and D. E. C. Eversley (eds.), *Population in History* (London, 1965), 101–143.

Jon Amsden and Stephen Brier

Coal Miners on Strike:
The Transformation of Strike Demands
and the Formation of a National Union

This study employs previously unused data on strikes in American coal mines in order to analyze the development of the coal industry and the emergence of a national union of mine workers. The data we have used are drawn from the Third and Tenth Annual Reports of the U.S. Commissioner of Labor.[1] These reports give detailed observations of virtually every strike which took place in all major U.S. industries between 1881 and 1894. The years for which the data are available span a particularly important period for the development of the coal industry and for the emergence of a national trade union organization among the miners.

Two major approaches presently dominate strike analysis: that of the economist and that of the social historian.[2] These con-

Jon Amsden teaches in the University of California Los Angeles Extension Program. Stephen Brier is a Ph.D. candidate in History at the University of California at Los Angeles. His participation in the research and writing of this article was supported by a U.S. Department of Labor Manpower Administration Doctoral Dissertation Grant.

The authors would like to thank Lutz K. Berkner, J. H. M. Laslett, John Mineka, David Montgomery, Alexander Saxton, and Paul Worthman for reading an earlier draft of this article and for invaluable substantive and methodological suggestions. They would also like to thank Pamela Brier for her research in the trade journals of the coal industry and for editorial assistance.

1 Third Annual Report of the Commissioner of Labor, *Strikes and Lockouts* (Washington, D.C., 1887); Tenth Annual Report of the Commissioner of Labor, *Strikes and Lockouts* (Washington, D.C., 1896). The method of reporting strikes is discussed in the preface to each of these volumes and in John I. Griffin, *Strikes: A Study in Quantitative Economics* (New York, 1939). For our study we made a complete enumeration of all coal strikes (1,410 in number) in the 1881–1894 period, for which we recorded some of the characteristics involved: year, cause or object, and union involvement. The results of this tally are presented in Figs. 1, 2, 3, and 4. To make more detailed comparisons we drew a sample of 280 strikes in coal using a systematic random sampling technique, for which we recorded information in all observational categories included in the Annual Reports. Results based on the sample are recorded in Figs. 5 and 6 and Table 3.

2 For general studies by economists see K. G. J. C. Knowles, *Strikes —A Study in Industrial Conflict: With Special Reference to British Experience Between 1911 and 1947* (Oxford, 1952); R. Goetz-Giery, *Le Mouvement des Greves en France* (Paris, 1965); Griffin, *Strikes*. For the most recent attempts by social historians see Peter N. Stearns, "Measuring the Evolution of Strike Movements," *International Review of Social History*, XIX (1974), 1–27; Edward Shorter and Charles Tilly, *Strikes in France: 1830–1968* (Cambridge, Mass., 1974).

trasting approaches raise major questions regarding the theory and
methodology of strike analysis which must be resolved before our
own analysis can be developed. Many theoretical problems arise
because of the way in which the economic motives and political
impact of strike activity are so closely bound together. Strikes represent an important index of social conflict either on the economic
or on the political level, and sometimes on both levels at once. The
economic effects of strike action are first felt by the employer (and
in some cases are sought by him) and then by the community at
large as the workers interrupt their regular pattern of labor and re-
fuse to produce. In the furtherance of their aims workers also in-
flict economic hardship on themselves. The political consequences
of strike activity find expression in the heightened class consciousness of the workers. This increased class consciousness results
from their concerted action against the employer and often from a
direct confrontation with the power of the state.

A meaningful approach to strike analysis in historical writing
therefore necessitates an awareness of both the economic and political aspects of strike activity. For this study we analyze strikes in a
single industry over a relatively short but crucially important
period of time. In the first section of the paper we develop our in-
terpretative framework by describing the evolution of the industry and the points of conflict between mine workers and operators
as a prelude to the presentation of our findings concerning strike
activity. We argue that strikes in coal mining between 1881 and
1894 reflected both the changing economic position of coal in a
burgeoning capitalist economy and the quality of the mine worker's life in and around the pits. The coal industry in this period
showed all of the tensions created by the vast expansion of production, the emergence of a national market, and incessant competition and consolidation of ownership and control. The stringent
financial constraints faced by most coal operators formed the
boundaries for their daily confrontation with mine workers. The
grievances of the latter grew out of a particular occupational structure and network of rules and practices which governed the work
process and the system of payment.

Our theory of strike activity is based in part on these aspects
of class struggle in the coal industry. The necessity of constant
conflict with the employers over a broad range of work and related problems, we contend, resulted in the creation of a trade

union organization which did not rest exclusively on the narrow base of craft skill. This organizational form represented an advance in working-class consciousness and is reflected in the changes in the form and content of miners' strikes.

George Bernard Shaw is reputed to have remarked that if you could take an infinite number of economists and place them end to end you would never arrive at a conclusion. This maxim seems particularly appropriate to economists who have studied the movement of strikes in the United States.[3] The economists' basic premise has been that the strike represents a measurable aspect of *homo economicus* conducting his daily affairs. Beyond this basic underlying assumption, however, economists have generally failed to agree on a comprehensive theory of strike activity, differing over the way in which the economic imperative is expressed in strike behavior. Some economists have maintained that workers tend to strike as economic conditions worsen in order to express protest against the worsening of their material condition. Others have argued that workers will go on strike when times are good as a reflection of their rising economic expectations.

It is not, however, simply the conflicting assumptions of economists over the basic motivation of strikes which limits the utility of their theory of strike action. Rather, disagreement among economists over theories of the strike centers on what they view as two related propositions: (1) a logical and demonstrable conception that workers are motivated to strike by the desire for economic gain or by the need to protect themselves from economic loss; and (2) the much more questionable assertion that strike activity is therefore always and everywhere related in some simple and direct way to movements in the level of business activity, i.e., the "business cycle."

As far as the first assertion is concerned, it would be foolish to

---

3 For a good summary of strike statistics see: Florence Peterson, *Strikes in the United States: 1880–1936,* U.S. Bureau of Labor Statistics Bulletin 651 (Washington, D.C., 1937). For the economists' conflicting views of economic causation of strike activity see: Ernest H. Jurkat and Dorothy B. Jurkat, "Economic Function of Strikes," *Industrial and Labor Relations Review,* II (1949), 371–382; Albert Rees, "Industrial Conflict and Business Fluctuations," *Journal of Political Economy,* LX (1952), 371–382; Andrew R. Weintraub, "Prosperity Versus Strikes, An Empirical Approach," *Industrial and Labor Relations Review*, XIX (1965–66), 231–238.

deny that, as Griffin put it, the strike moves in the material plane.[4] Clearly, economic considerations bound the possibilities of the strike both for the worker and for his employer. This was certainly true of strikes by nineteenth-century American coal miners. Throughout the period we have studied every business downturn was accompanied by wage cuts imposed by the coal operators, and every renewal of business activity gave rise to aggressive strike action by the miners as they attempted to regain their former positions and even, if possible, to put themselves materially ahead. The problem here, as we will show, is that there also was a proportion of strikes not easily attributable to these causes. In these cases economic imperative provides a necessary but not sufficient element of explanation.

The difficulty with the economists' general view comes when they move from the correct observation that strike activity is bounded by and to a certain extent the result of economic realities to the more questionable proposition that the pattern of strike activity is in some systematic way linked to the business cycle. The way out of this difficulty becomes clear when the question is raised as a historical rather than as a logical one. In the case of the American experience it would seem that the workers react differently from one period to the next.[5] When the coal industry alone is considered, however, even this seemingly simple historical statement is confounded. In the following section we present evidence which indicates that, when all types of strikes in the coal industry are taken together, both the "increasing misery" and "rising expectations" hypotheses are confirmed at different periods of time.

Views of strike behavior put forward by the social historians are both more complex and more subtle. This is not surprising as historians tend to be interested in a much broader range of social and political phenomena of which they take strike activity to be the reflection.[6]

4 Griffin, *Strikes*, 19.
5 *Ibid.*, 192–193. See also Alvin H. Hansen, "Cycles of Strikes," *American Economic Review*, XI (1921), 616–621.
6 Charles Tilly and Edward Shorter, for example, have been concerned to advance a political interpretation of the patterns of strike activity in France, in addition to making invaluable methodological contributions to the study of strikes: "Les Vagues des Greves en France," *Annales* (1973), 857–887; "The Shape of Strikes in France," *Comparative Studies in History and Society*, XLII (1971), 60–85. In *Strikes in France*, Tilly and Shorter have used the

For example, Stearns proposes the use of qualitative variables, in this case strike demands, as a tool for the analysis of changes in working-class life.[7] Following some of the theoretical and methodological directions suggested by the earlier work of Tilly and Shorter, Stearns has developed an interesting model of strike behavior. In order to develop this model, Stearns has combined two notions, namely that strikes can be seen to undergo structural changes over time and that there is a political content to certain forms of mass popular action.

The strike has evolved, Stearns argues, and consequently it ought to be possible to measure this evolution. Although not attempting any such measurement himself, Stearns nevertheless has expressed reservations concerning the meaningfulness of measuring only variables such as duration, frequency, and man-days lost.[8] In so doing he points to an important shortcoming of much of the current literature on strikes, namely that there has not been sufficient investigation of the evolution of the demands of strikers over time. Although we agree with Stearns about the importance of analyzing strike demands, we have serious reservations concerning his development of a "protest-sophistication" model of strikes.

Stearns begins his study by introducing what could be called the "protest analysis" of mass public action. The protest analysis grows from and is especially concerned with the political aims and organization of the pre-industrial crowd and has been debated over the last few years by writers on European social history.[9] In "Measuring the Evolution of the Strike," Stearns takes the step of conceptually joining forms of protest such as the bread riot to that of the industrial labor dispute. "We know," he says, "that strikes

---

more standard parameters of strike experience (e.g. size, frequency, and duration) to argue that the cyclical movement of strikes was related to the rhythms of French political life rather than to changes in economic conditions.

7   Stearns, "Measuring the Strike," 17.
8   *Ibid.*, 17.
9   George Rudé, *The Crowd in History: A Study of Popular Disturbances in France and England, 1730-1848* (New York, 1964). Eric Hobsbawm, *Labouring Men* (London, 1971), 5–22; E. P. Thompson, "The Moral Economy of the English Crowd in the 18th Century," *Past & Present*, 50 (1971), 76–136, represent the most important European studies. Pauline Maier, "Popular Uprisings and Civil Authority in Eighteenth-Century America," *William and Mary Quarterly*, XXVII (1970), 3–35, makes an important contribution to the debate from the American perspective.

142 | JON AMSDEN AND STEPHEN BRIER

replace riots as the main form of direct action protest in the advanced industrial countries, but we know little about this major
aspect of workers' lives." So abrupt a marriage between the riot
and the strike is mistaken, and even if the two forms of popular action were seen to keep company at an earlier stage, we contend
that the radical difference in their natures soon led them to a part-
ing of the ways.

We would maintain that the bulk of the difficulties created by
the use of a protest model in strike analysis flows from the notion
of protest itself. If hanging the baker from a street-lamp or sending the recruiting sergeant away in a hail of offal are what is meant
by protest, then the term is inapplicable to the largest proportion
of strikes which can be studied—either with the assistance of
statistical methods or without. The protest of the pre-industrial
crowd is best viewed as a historically specific and reactive form of
economic and political communication. It may or may not be followed by organized and coherent activity toward specific ends. A
strike, however, must be carried through as a concerted and conscious effort by the workers involved: to articulate demands, to
keep out strikebreakers, to organize strike relief, to plan mass action, and, finally, to decide when to go back to work. This kind of
coherent and sustained activity sharply distinguishes the strike
from the explosive and generally short-lived actions of the pre-
industrial crowd.

Tilly and Shorter have gone far towards discrediting what
they call the "frustration-aggression model" of strike behavior
with the use of quantitative evidence.[10] We would add that the
closely allied protest model is also faulty on theoretical grounds.
The protest model incorrectly postulates that from one historical
period to another there is some invariant quantum of protest
which merely assumes a different form of expression, according to
time and circumstance. An analysis of the strike should not view
that phenomenon as merely another form through which "the
people" express ever present discontent. The strike, rather, is a
form of conscious action which emerges with industrialism
and which expresses a new complex of class relationships in
society.

10   Shorter and Tilly, *Strikes in France*, 336–340.

It should be obvious that the sustained efforts necessary to keep a strike on its feet in the face of economic hardship and (on occasions) the repressive power of the state, indicate the vast distances that separate strike action from the reactive agitation of the crowd. Stearns is obviously aware of this, and he argues that the observable differences between strike and crowd activity can be accounted for by the fact that workers become progressively "sophisticated" in the strike demands that they raise. The meaning of the term sophistication as used by Stearns is widely inclusive of a variety of strike characteristics. He offers no precise notion of what sophistication means, and carefully limits himself to tentative definitions. Within this loose framework, however, Stearns does construct a model of the increasing sophistication of strike demands.

Stearns ranks the causes of strikes as follows, in order of increasing sophistication: defensive wage strikes; what he calls personal issue strikes (such as for readmission of a discharged worker or the firing of a foreman); defensive working conditions and intermediate wages and hours strikes (for example to regain wages lost to inflation and hence not "genuinely offensive"); genuinely offensive wage strikes which demonstrate what Stearns calls a "real attachment to material progress"; reduction of hours strikes; and finally, union and solidarity strikes (which are sophisticated only "on occasions").[11]

Although one could engage in criticism of Stearns' hierarchical ordering, for the purpose of this discussion we will simply concentrate on Stearns' ranking of personal issue strikes. Stearns insists on placing these strikes near the bottom of his scale of sophistication and this seems to us to be incorrect. We would argue that it is unlikely that an entire mine or workshop would ever go out over the question of someone's "personal" characteristics, whether these be congenial (in the case of a fellow worker) or the reverse (in the case of a supervisor). Larger issues are certainly involved. Rather, strikes for the readmission of a worker who has been fired challenge the entire order of productive relations in the coal pit as much as those over the form and method of payments, hours, or the quality of working conditions. In addition, strikes

11   Stearns, "Measuring the Strike," 24.

for the rehiring of a discharged worker often are at the same time strikes about organization in the formal sense. As we know from our own research, the discharged worker was often fired in the first place for his role in organizing his fellows against the company.[12] We would assert that what Stearns calls personal issue strikes should be considered as a form of labor force solidarity in a particular establishment and not as a form of reactive protest to which, on occasion, the workers are given.

By relating his sophistication model to a number of cases of strike behavior from the European experience, Stearns concludes that sophistication is reflected in a whole range of increasingly pragmatic improvements in tactics which will enable strikers not so much to win their objectives as to optimize their position, having taken the realities of their situation into account. Thus, for Stearns, the strikers' sophistication consists in: learning to "save themselves for more solid efforts"; developing a sense of "timing"; arriving at an "ability and willingness to negotiate"; conducting strikes of "shorter duration"; and, in general, coming to ". . . a recognition of what one has to do to maximize strike success. . . ."[13] When the strike can assume these sophisticated characteristics, Stearns claims, the protest of strikers becomes "modernized" as the strikers' tactics and demands become more pragmatic.

Stearns' theory of pragmatic strike action is of interest to the historian of strikes in the United States because it can be joined conceptually to the traditional interpretation of the American trade union movement developed by Commons and Perlman and which is continued today in the works of Grob and Taft.[14] A

12   *Ibid.*, 18–19. Our evidence suggests a rather different picture. The *Engineering and Mining Journal (EMJ)* carried reports of a number of strikes called in support of discharged union members and checkweighmen. For example, a report from Pennsylvania in 1890 noted that 4,000 Connellsville, Pa., coke workers and miners struck because of the discharge of a Hungarian fellow worker. Although ethnic ties were admittedly strong in the American working class, we cannot believe that 4,000 workers went out on strike simply because of the amenable personal characteristics of one Hungarian miner. See "Coal Trade Review," *EMJ* (Nov. 8, 1890), 558.
13   Stearns, "Measuring the Strike," 24.
14   John R. Commons, Selig Perlman, *et al., History of Labour in the United States* (New York, 1918), 2 v.; Gerald Grob, *Workers and Utopia: A Study in Ideological Conflict in the American Labor Movement 1865-1900* (Chicago, 1969); Philip Taft, *The American Federation of Labor in the Time of Gompers* (New York, 1957).

theory such as Stearns' which links the evolution of strike demands to workers' pragmatic "attachment to material progress" has the same theoretical underpinnings as the celebration of "job conscious" business unionism. Although we cannot engage in extensive examination of the questions raised by the traditional interpretation of American labor history, we can, however, point to general problems in the theory, at least with respect to its application to the miners' experience. Those who write in the Commons' tradition have succeeded in imposing a false dichotomy between working-class political action and the practical defensive work carried on by the trade union. The traditional view of American labor history presents these two aspects of workers' self-organization as opposed and warring impulses within the labor movement of the 1880s and 1890s. The history of the coal miners is also often read in this light.[15] We do not agree with this interpretation. We would suggest instead that the political and economic aspects of the miners' struggle remained inextricably bound throughout the period we have studied.

Our data will show that mine workers moved steadily away from reactive and defensive conflict throughout the period from 1881 to 1894 and, at the same time, increasingly employed the strike tactic as union members or at the behest of union organizations. The efforts of coal miners during this period were directed toward building a national industrial trade union for both defensive and offensive purposes. The analysis presented in this paper suggests that the miners' resolve was reflected in the changing pattern of coal strikes, and that neither the notion of conformity with the business cycle nor the notion of modernized protest is sufficient to account for this distinctive pattern of strike activity in the coal industry.

In 1888 the *Engineering and Mining Journal* (the principal trade paper in the industry) editorialized that, "the industrial condition of the country is more accurately measured by the consumption of coal than by any other item." The railroads, directly and indirectly, were the biggest consumers of bituminous coal in the late

---

15   See, for example, Grob, *Workers and Utopia*, 60–137. Commons, *History*, II, 487. See also Norman Ware, *The Labor Movement in the United States 1860–1895* (Gloucester, Mass., 1959), 213–217.

nineteenth century. Of the 71.7 million tons of bituminous coal consumed in 1885, 42 percent was burned in railroad locomotives, 13 percent was used for coke (largely destined for steel production), and the remainder went into various industrial and domestic uses.[16]

The figures in Table 1 reflect the incessant growth of an intensely competitive national market for coal during the 1880s and 1890s in which local differentials in price and production began systematically to disappear. The emergence of the national market and intense competition during this period ultimately gave rise to the creation of larger and larger economic units in the industry.

Table 1   Production and Average Value of Bituminous and Anthracite Coal, 1880–1895

	BITUMINOUS			ANTHRACITE		
YEAR	ANNUAL U.S. PRODUCTION (1,000 NET TONS)	% CHANGE FROM PREVIOUS YEAR	AVERAGE VALUE PER TON AT MINE	ANNUAL U.S. PRODUCTION (1,000 NET TONS)	% CHANGE FROM PREVIOUS YEAR	AVERAGE VALUE PER TON AT MINE
1880	50,757		$1.25	28,650		$1.47
1881	51,945	+2.1%	1.12	31,920	+11.5%	2.01
1882	58,917	+13.5	1.12	35,121	+10.0	2.01
1883	64,860	+10.2	1.07	38,457	+9.4	2.01
1884	71,737	+10.5	.94	37,157	−3.1	1.79
1885	71,773	0	1.13	38,336	+3.0	2.00
1886	74,645	+4.0	1.05	39,035	+1.8	1.95
1887	88,562	+18.8	1.11	42,088	+7.9	2.01
1888	102,040	+15.1	1.00	46,620	+10.7	1.91
1889	95,685	−6.2	.99	45,547	−2.4	1.44
1890	111,302	+16.3	.99	46,469	+2.0	1.43
1891	117,901	+5.9	.99	50,665	+9.3	1.46
1892	126,857	+7.6	.99	52,473	+3.6	1.57
1893	128,385	+1.2	.96	53,968	+2.9	1.59
1894	118,820	−7.5	.91	51,921	−3.9	1.51
1895	135,118	+13.7	.86	57,999	+11.7	1.41

SOURCE: *Historical Statistics of Minerals in the United States* (Resources for the Future, Inc., Washington D.C., 1960), 8, 9, 11, 12.

16 "The Industrial Condition, Past and Present," *EMJ* (Sep. 1, 1888), 168. See also "The Labor Movement and Its Significance," *EMJ* (Apr. 1, 1882), 166. Sam H. Schurr, *et al.*, *Energy in the American Economy 1850–1975* (Baltimore, 1960), 67–68.

The situation resulted, on the one hand, from the increased size and economic hegemony of the railroads and, on the other, from the persistant expansion of new coalfields and the consolidation of the ownership and marketing of coal output.[17]

The development of the rail empires led to economic consolidation in three ways: (1) by uniting producers and retailers throughout the country with an improved transportation network, thus undercutting the competitive advantage enjoyed by the smaller operator in the local market; (2) by making possible the application of economic power against the smaller operator whose profit rates and production levels were effectively decided by the railroad companies upon whom the operators were dependent for haulage; and (3) by creating marketing agreements and pooling schemes dominated by the railroads.[18]

The consolidation of the coal industry was also driven forward by factors outside the direct control of the railroads. What would later be called the "overdevelopment" of coal production caused operators to engage in intense competition during the upswing of the business cycle and to band together for mutual protection in periods of decline.[19] Whatever the impetus for consoli-

---

17 William Graebner, "Great Expectations: The Search for Order in Bituminous Coal, 1890–1917," *Business History Review*, XLVIII (1973), 49–72, tends to underestimate the importance of the pre-1900 movement toward consolidation. It also overestimates the ability of operators to cut production costs.

18 As early as 1883 the Ohio Bureau of Labor Statistics (B.L.S.) reported that: "In all of the prominent markets [Ohio coals] meet the coals of other States, and they can maintain themselves only by a sharp and constant competition with the product of the mines of Pennsylvania, West Virginia, Kentucky, Indiana and Illinois." Ohio B.L.S., *Seventh Annual Report* (Columbus, 1884), 295. For a discussion of the growth of the national market for coal during the late 1880s see the following *EMJ* reports: "General Mining News" (Jan. 26, 1889), 96; "General Mining News" (Mar. 16, 1889), 263; "Coal Trade Review" (Dec. 24, 1892), 620. The *EMJ* Special Chicago Correspondent reported in 1893 that the railroads were ". . . acting a double part in that they are advancing their rates to secure more revenues and trying to pound the operator down on his prices at the mines. . . ." "Coal Trade Review," *EMJ* (June 24, 1893), 596. See also "General Mining News—Indiana," *EMJ* (July 6, 1889), 13. For railroad domination of Hocking Valley coal marketing see Ohio B.L.S., *12th Annual Report* (Columbus, 1889), 206; "Coal Trade Review-Chicago," *EMJ* (Nov. 26, 1892), 525. For the Missouri-Pacific Railroad's ownership and control of coal lands in Missouri see "Railroad Companies as Coal Miners," *EMJ* (July 27, 1889), 73. See Joseph T. Lambie, *From Mine to Market The History of Coal Transportation on the Norfolk and Western Railway* (New York, 1954), 1–133 *passim* on the Norfolk and Western's control of the rich southern West Virginia coal fields.

19 By the end of the 1880s, for example, the H.C. Frick Co. either owned or controlled the marketing of the vast coke oven output in the Connellsville, Pa., field. See "General

dation in any particular case, the effect on mine workers was the same: consolidation gave the forces ranged against the miners a degree of concentration and coordination never previously achieved.

Business depressions were a recurrent phenomenon in this period. A long run of falling prices following the financial panic of 1873 resulted in a sharp contraction of economic activity and a severe depression lasting to 1878. The following year marked the beginning of a short but intense period of expanded industrial activity in which prices and wages also rose. The reversal of this trend came in 1882, when another contraction of business activity led to a general depression. The decline lasted into early 1886, reaching its low point in 1884–85 when an estimated 7.5 percent of all U.S. factories and mines were idled.[20]

The widespread labor agitation and social upheaval which took place in 1886 occurred in the context of a reviving economy. The events of that year brought about a heightened awareness of class issues among American workers, an awareness expressed in an aggressive and widespread strike wave.[21] As we show, 1886 also constitutes a turning point in the pattern of coal miners' struggles with the operators.

Between 1886 and 1890 total existing rail mileage was increased by an estimated 30 percent following financial reorganization in the industry. In the same period, production of pig iron and steel rose 62 percent. The production of coal paralleled railroad growth and steel production in every year save 1889. In that year the first decline in annual coal output since 1874 resulted from a series of factors internal to the industry, although business remained healthy in other sectors of the American economy. A

Mining News-Pennsylvania," *EMJ* (Jan. 11, 1890), 72; "Coal Trade Review," *EMJ* (July 13, 1889), 37. The Western Pennsylvania Bituminous Combination and Syndicate is discussed in "General Mining News-Pennsylvania," *EMJ* (Feb. 9, 1889), 148. On creation of a general Seaboard Marketing Association see *EMJ* (Feb. 21, 1891), 246; (Nov. 12, 1892), 476.

20 "Statistics of Manufacturing Industries," *EMJ* (Aug. 2, 1890), 120. United States Commissioner of Labor, *First Annual Report Industrial Depressions* (Washington, D.C., 1886), 65.

21 George McNeill, *The Labor Movement: The Problem of Today* (New York, 1887), 170. McNeill, a prominent member of the Knights of Labor, characterized the strike wave of 1886 as a "contagion" which "spread from one end of the country to the other." Also see *EMJ* editorial, "The Labor Question," (Apr. 24, 1886), 298.

short depression in the United States then followed in 1890, but good harvests led to a brief recovery in late 1891. A gradual decline in prices and monetary instability began in 1892 which eventually culminated in the panic and subsequent depression of 1893–1896.[22]

Figure 1, which shows the yearly incidence of strikes from 1881–1894, suggests the absence of a simple and direct correlation of coal mining strikes with the general movement of the business cycle. The number of strikes between 1882 and 1884 decreases relatively so that if the mine workers experienced increasing misery during the depression of those years, they did not respond by employing the strike weapon. The next period of relative decline in strike activity between 1886 and 1888 occurs in the midst of general economic prosperity and expansion. If in 1888 mine workers had rising expectations resulting from the business upswing, they did not at that time try to increase their share of the growing national income by striking as frequently as they had two years earlier. It should be recognized, however, that two of the relative peaks of strike activity (1886 and 1891) came at moments of economic recovery. These facts, taken together, suggest that it is not possible to make a direct correlation between strike activity in the coal industry and the level of general business prosperity.

We propose to overcome the difficulties inherent in the narrow economic interpretation of coal strikes by looking more closely at strike demands. The analysis of strike demands, however, necessitates an understanding of the techniques of mining and the organization of production in the industry. As many of the strikes which took place in our period were not only occasioned by wage issues but also by questions of control of the productive relations in the pit, it is necessary to precede an analysis of the causes of strikes with a certain amount of description of the mining process.

Throughout the 1880s and 1890s the "practical miner" who dug the coal from the seam's vertical "face" dominated the coal industry's occupational structure. The pit work force generally was divided between surface and underground workers. Under-

22   W. Jett Lauck, *The Causes of the Panic of 1893* (New York, 1907), 6, 72–86; "The Coal Trade in 1889," *EMJ* (Jan. 4, 1890), 19–21; "Coal Trade Review-Bituminous," *EMJ* (July 12, 1890), 60; (Dec. 13, 1890), 702.

Fig. 1 Number of Coal Strikes,[a] 1881–1894

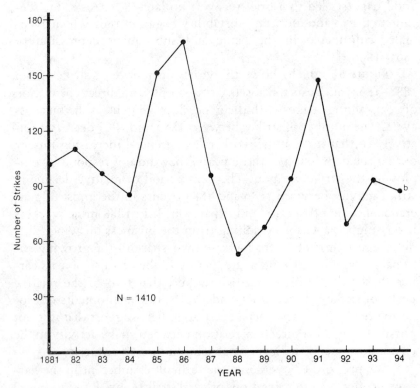

a   Lockouts are not included in these figures because of their relative insignificance in the coal industry. In the 1881–1886 period a total of 11 lockouts occurred in all mining industries, including metals. In the 1887–1894 period there were a total of 16 lockouts in the coal and coke industries.

b   The number of strikes in 1894 includes strikes recorded in the Commissioner of Labor's *Report* between January 1 and June 30 only.

ground workers averaged between 85 and 90 percent of the total number of workers. The miner worked with an assistant or "buddy" in his own individual "room" at the coal face. The miner's basic work at the coal face consisted of making an undercut with a hand pick at the bottom of the coal seam, drilling the holes for the introduction of blasting powder, and firing the shot. The force of the explosion broke off several tons of coal, in pieces of varying size, and the miner and his helper then loaded the coal with shovels onto mine cars. The pace of the work and the methods employed were decided upon by the miner. Miners also determined the length of their own working day. Face workers generally came to work when they pleased and went home when they were ready.[23] The face teams were supported by a small force of auxiliary workers which included blacksmiths, carpenters, ventilation workers, and hoisting engineers (all working on the surface). Working underground in addition to the face teams were coal car drivers, timbermen, track layers, and "trappers" (who watched and regulated the ventilation doors). The support workers were usually hired directly by the coal operator and paid a daily wage, whereas the miners were paid on a tonnage rate for coal sent to the surface.

Despite the large number of different occupations in the industry, coal mining in the late nineteenth century was almost wholly the domain of the coal miner and his helper.[24] Table 2, adapted from the 1890 Census, indicates the extent of the miner's domination; it was a dominance which was to have important consequences for the form that trade union organization would take among the mine workers.

The miner's commanding position in the occupational hierarchy was reinforced by a contracting system in which each miner was permanently assigned his place or "room" in a particular pit. The miner usually hired and paid his helper.[25]

Because of the ways in which miners functioned as individual contractors under this system, and because of the relatively high degree of autonomy that they enjoyed in their normal day-to-day work activities, one might be tempted to ascribe to them the sort of craft exclusiveness and preoccupation with job control that characterized other skilled workers in the nineteenth century.[26]

23   Oscar Cartlidge, *Fifty Years of Coal Mining* (Charleston, West Virginia, 1937), 18. For an excellent discussion of the reasons for this phenomenon in a later period see Carter Goodrich, *The Miner's Freedom* (Boston, 1925), 5–100.
24   Geoffrey Bauman, in an analysis of 62 western Pennsylvania mines, indicates that face workers represented, on the average, 82% of the total work force. This figure conforms to the census data presented in Table 2 above. See Bauman, "Coal Miners: From Craftsmen to Industrial Workers" (University of Pittsburgh, 1974), unpub. paper, Table I.
25   The Ohio B.L.S. reported that the mining process made the miner ". . . in some sense a contractor. He is his own master, can come and go at his own will and is largely independent of dictation as to the manner in which he shall do work." *Seventh Report*, 292, 305.
26   An argument about the iron puddler's craft control in the nineteenth-century steel industry is developed by David Montgomery, "Trade Union Practice and Syndicalist Thought" (University of Pittsburgh, 1973), unpub. paper.

Table 2 Structure of the Bituminous[a] Coal Mining Labor Force, by State

STATE	TOTAL NUMBER OF COAL MINE WORKERS (1889)	UNDERGROUND WORKERS/TOTAL COAL MINE WORKERS (%)	MINERS[b]/TOTAL COAL MINE WORKERS (%)	MINERS[b]/TOTAL UNDERGROUND WORKERS (%)	UNDERGROUND SUPERVISORS/ UNDERGROUND WORKERS (%)
Pennsylvania (bitum.)	53,132	90.6	75.5	83.3	1.3
(Allegheny Cty.)	(9,314)	(90.2)	(80.4)	(89.1)	(1.0)
(Westmoreland Cty.)	(8,962)	(90.2)	(73.5)	(81.5)	(1.4)
Ohio	19,343	89.4	76.2	85.2	1.3
West Virginia	9,778	84.1	65.1	77.4	1.4
Alabama	6,864	85.2	59.9	70.3	1.2
Tennessee	4,031	85.9	63.0	73.3	1.6
Maryland	3,702	91.3	72.6	79.5	.7
Illinois	23,934	89.2	64.3	72.1	1.4
Indiana	6,448	89.7	73.5	81.9	2.3
Iowa	9,244	88.4	71.3	80.6	1.7
Colorado	94,904	83.5	69.1	82.7	1.1

SOURCE: U.S. Census Office, *11th Census* (1890), *Report on the Mineral Industries in the United States* (Washington D.C., G.P.O., 1892), 349–350. The data included in the *11th Census* is for the 1889 fiscal year.

a States listed represent the major geological coal seams in the United States: Appalachian, Central, Western, and Rocky Mountain. Anthracite was not included in this table because the size and structure of the labor force, as well as methods of production and geographical concentration are markedly different from bituminous coal production.

b The term "miner," as used by the Census, denotes a mine worker engaged in removing coal from the seam. The miners' helpers were aggregated with other underground workers, such as trappers, tracklayers, etc., in a "laborers" category. If the miners' helpers could be aggregated with miners, the face workers' domination of the occupational structure would be even more marked.

Several factors, however, militated against the creation of craft consciousness among coal miners. The most important of these factors probably was the miners' numerical weight in the industry's occupational structure. Craft exclusiveness in other industries developed out of the needs of a relatively small craft group to protect its work skills and methods from managerial encroachment and from the technological dilution which usually followed. In the iron and steel industry, for example, the rationalization and mechanization in the 1890s resulted in opposition by skilled craft workers to the loss of their strategic position in the productive process.[27] Nineteenth-century coal miners, however, hardly felt the pressures engendered by mechanization or rationalization through supervision. The number of confrontations between miners and operators over these issues was minimal and miners did not articulate an ideology of craft control over production as, for example, did the iron puddlers.

Table 2 suggests the relatively minor role played by managerial supervision in coal mining in 1890. Mechanization of production to 1894 was halting at best, the transfer of skill from miner to machine not occurring until well into the twentieth century. The first form of power equipment to be introduced was the mechanical undercutter operated initially with compressed air and later with electric power. By 1891 only 6.6 percent of U.S. coal output had been undercut by machine, although the incidence of mechanical undercutting in certain geographical regions was higher than the national average would suggest. The southern Illinois field and the Hocking Valley in Ohio, for example, had both experienced the sharp impact of the coal undercutter by the mid-1880s. By 1888 three fifths of the coal produced in southern Illinois for the St. Louis market had been undercut by machine. Similarly, in the Hocking Valley machines had almost totally replaced the pick by the mid-1890s.[28]

27 Craft workers were also particularly concerned to keep their skills from being diffused among the significantly larger body of unskilled workers who were potential competitors. Coal miners, to the contrary, entertained few illusions about the exclusive nature of their skills or their ability to keep those skills solely in their own possession. Montgomery, "Trade Union Practice," 6; Ohio B.L.S., *Seventh Report*, 294, 297; David Brody, *Steelworkers in America: The Non-Union Era* (New York, 1969), 1–79.

28 See United States Geological Survey, *Mineral Resources of the United States* (Washington, D.C., 1900), 309, for machine production figures for the 1891–1900 period. Total national machine production increased from 6.6% in 1891 to 25.2% in 1900. Also see "Coal

A number of factors impeded the early introduction of mining machinery in most places. For one thing the narrow headings and crooked passageways of the older coal workings made the operation of new machinery difficult. More important, however, was the resistance of the miners themselves, who consistently fought hard to blunt the economizing power of the machines by insisting that machine miners, runners, and pick miners be paid at comparable rates. Installation of the coal undercutter was initiated in the 1880s more for its "moral effect" in combatting the organization of pick miners than for its value as an "expense reducer."[29] A prominent coal operator, writing in the mid-1890s, argued that the machine was introduced

> . . . not so much for its saving in direct cost as for the indirect economy in having to control a fewer number of men for the same output. It is a weapon with which to meet organized skilled labor and their unreasonable demands. . . . As the machine does the mining, the proportion of skilled labor is largely reduced, and the result is found in less belligerence and conflict; a sufficient inducement though the direct costs be the same.[30]

It was only in exceptional circumstances—where the potential short-term economies were sufficiently great—that the operators undertook the introduction of coal undercutters. In the Hocking Valley, where the seams were ten feet thick, introduction of the undercutter had a great profit potential. This motivated the operators to prepare a careful campaign to introduce the machine

---

Cutters in the Pan-Handle Field," *EMJ* (Sep. 29, 1883), 201; (Nov. 5, 1892) 435; Arthur E. Suffern, *Conciliation and Arbitration in the Coal Industry of America* (Boston, 1915), 47.

29 See the remarks of Ohio Miners' President John McBride as quoted in Christopher Evans, *The History of the United Mine Workers of America from the Year 1880 to 1890* (Indianapolis, 1918), I, 104; II, 165; "American Coal Mining Machines," *EMJ* (Aug. 25, 1888), 146.

30 William N. Page, "The Economics of Coal Mining," *The Mineral Industry: Statistical Supplement of the Engineering and Mining Journal*, III (New York, 1894), 151. It was estimated that if 10 Harrison coal undercutters were used in a southern Illinois mine, the cost of production would average 43.6¢ per ton, while the hand miner would be paid approximately 50¢ per ton. Since the initial outlay for 10 machines would average about $20,000, a 7¢ per ton savings did not necessarily warrant much haste in converting to machinery. "American Coal Mining Machines," *EMJ* (Aug. 25, 1888), 146.

in 1884, deliberately forcing the miners to engage in a bitter and violent strike shortly thereafter.[31]

One explanation for the relative absence of craft exclusiveness among miners can be found in their pragmatic awareness of the need to control the potential power of certain categories of day workers (drivers being the most important example). Such workers could throw the vast majority of miners out of work by undertaking independent strike action. Throughout the 1880s various groups of day workers refused on occasions to support strike demands put forward by the "tonnage" men while at the same time being prepared to shut down the entire operation in support of their own demands.[32] Although coal miners and their leaders initially were ambivalent about permitting other categories of mine workers to join their organization, by 1890, with the founding of the United Mine Workers of America, they had come to accept the need for inclusive trade union forms in order to wage coordinated struggles.[33] As we will suggest later in the discussion, the need to wage strikes over the general and inclusive demands of all grades of mine workers had, by this time, raised the industrial form of union organization to the level of basic necessity.

31 An excellent account of the strike is reported in "Labor and Wages," *EMJ* (Sep. 6, 1884), 162: "Some three months ago, the coal company determined to make the issue with its men and work its mines by improved processes, let it cost what it might. . . . The first move was to empty the mines. For this purpose, a reduction was ordered of from 70 to 60 cents a ton for mining. The result was as anticipated. The miners, drivers, and every body else went out on a strike. . . . The mines cleared, the company at once put in the new machinery and set it safe in position before the move was understood by the strikers. Then green men were taken to the mines on special trains, guarded by Pinkerton police armed with Winchester rifles. . . ." Following this series of events in Hocking Valley, a bitter and prolonged strike ensued. See also McNeill, *Labor Movement*, 261–262.

32 John H. M. Laslett, *Labor and the Left* (New York, 1970), 207. In 1891, for example, 191 striking drivers shut down the coal pits in the Nanticoke, Pa., area, thus throwing 2,300 mine workers off the job. Third Annual Report, *Strikes and Lockouts*, 492–495. The *National Labor Tribune* on Mar. 13, 1886, published a letter from a Hocking Valley miner who claimed that miners ". . . have little sympathy [for drivers] as they are a porcine breed, i.e. free turners, and you cannot persuade them to change a single bristle."

33 There is some indication that the face workers' participation in the eight-hour struggles of May, 1891, was motivated by a desire to demonstrate their solidarity with the day men. The strategy of the face workers suggests both the broad organizational base of the early national union and the highly developed political ideology of the nineteenth-century miners, especially as 75,000 skilled mine workers were willing to undertake what in essence was a sympathy strike in support of their fellow workers. See "General Mining News-Pennsylvania," *EMJ* (Apr. 25, 1891), 503.

We have said that, during our period of study, questions involving the pace, the methods of labor, and the length of the working day were decided by the individual miner, and his control over these matters generally went unchallenged by the operators. What then were the sources of conflict between the operators and the miners? Not surprisingly, questions of remuneration predominated. The number and range of disputes under this heading, however, varied greatly. The wealth of contentious questions between worker and employer derived in large part from the particular economic pressures to which the coal operator was being subjected. The individual operator increasingly was obliged to meet competition in a national market. Second, labor costs, representing an astonishingly high proportion of total costs, generally could not be reduced through intensified managerial supervision or by the replacement of man by machine.[34] The coal operators, unable to reduce their rather high labor costs, had only limited means by which they could directly extract increased amounts of surplus value from the miners' labor. They were impelled, therefore, to rely on a wide variety of methods through which the mine workers contributed indirectly to the company's profits.

Writing about the period of the 1880s and 1890s, Suffern listed the various forms of "audacious robbery" to which the miners were subject. Competition and overproduction, Suffern held, caused the operators to engage in the following illicit practices: shortweighing; the abuse of the "dockage" system (where the miners were penalized for slate and clay sent up with the coal); abuse of the coal screening system (by which the large "lump" coal was separated from the less desirable "slack"); nonpayment of the miners for so-called "deadwork" (which included all sorts of necessary maintenance); gouging through the company store; the coercion and exploitation associated with company housing; and, finally, a number of different abuses in payment systems

---

34 Our analysis of cost figures gathered by the U.S. Census in 1886 and 1892 from nearly 150 individual coal operators indicates that the cost of the miner's labor alone, excluding auxiliary workers, office staff, supervisors, etc., was on the average 65% of total production costs per ton of coal. Total labor cost, as a component of total production costs, averaged almost 90%. See Commissioner of Labor, *First Annual Report,* 100–103; *The Mineral Industry,* I, 80–81.

(e.g., payment in "scrip," irregular payment, and payment at long intervals.)[35]

Coal screens allegedly were introduced by the operators in order to separate the larger and more marketable pieces of coal from the smaller pieces or slack. As it happened the operators were able to sell the smaller pieces anyway, often as coking coal, and sometimes as "nut" coal which had a good domestic market. Since the miner received no payment whatsoever for this slack, it came to represent virtually pure profit for his employer. Accordingly, the operators often responded to competitive pressures (as well as to their own greedy impulses) by increasing the gauge of the coal screen when they could get away with it. Miners in Ohio estimated that every increase of one quarter of an inch over the standard one inch gauge cost them 10 percent of their output.[36]

In mines where screens were not introduced, coal operators often maximized profits by refusing to weigh the mine workers' daily output. Miners testified that they might be forced to load a "one-ton" coal car with as much as 3,500 or 4,000 pounds of coal. Since underpayment for tonnage was endemic, the disputed amount of the miners' daily output in many pits often provided the first occasion for organization. The principal object of such efforts was the employment of a checkweighman (paid for by the miners). In mining operations where no checkweighman existed, miners might be cheated by as much as 50 percent of their output.[37]

The company store, known to the mine workers as the "pluck me," commonly enjoyed a monopoly position either because the miners were strongly pressured to trade there or because there were no other stores in the area. The store represented an important source of profit for the company, one which could yield

35   Suffern, *Conciliation and Arbitration*, 24–29.
36   Tables in *The Mineral Industry*, I, 80–81, indicate that for the U.S. as a whole, coal operators averaged 15.1¢ per ton for slack coal derived from screening. Ohio B.L.S., *Seventh Report*, 290–311, includes a "Report of a Committee Appointed by the Governor to Inquire into the System of Screening Coal." See also Ohio B.L.S., *Eighth Annual Report* (1884), 269–271; Suffern, *Conciliation and Arbitration*, 26.
37   The practice of loading 3-ton coal cars for a flat rate of 75¢ was common in the southern West Virginia field during this period. See letter to West Virginia Governor William MacCorkle from the Executive Committee of U.M.W. Pocahontas District No. 25, Apr. 25, 1895. The letter is contained in MacCorkle Papers, West Virginia State Archives, Charleston, West Virginia. Suffern, *Conciliation and Arbitration*, 253.

as much as 15 percent return on capital invested. In some instances the operation of the company store was the only thing that kept a company in the black during a bad year. One operator, while admitting that the "pluck-me" was a "dishonest imposition," argued that it was employed "largely as a means of reduction where the organized miners would resist an open and honest reduction in wages." He concluded by saying that the abolition of the company store ". . . would take from capital one of the best means for reconciling labor to necessary reductions, by reducing its cost of living at the same time."[38]

The method and form of payment also were contentious questions during the 1880s and 1890s. Payment in company paper or "scrip" had as its principal aim forcing the miner to use the company store. In addition it probably helped the operator to solve his cash flow problems. That the operator had such problems is illustrated by the fact that during periods of economic decline some operators were willing to offer their workers a choice of either a wage reduction *or* the acceptance of payment on a monthly basis.[39]

Given this multiplicity of indirect means by which operators were able to reduce the miners' pay, the control exercised by face workers at the point of production provided an insufficient basis from which to fight back against these abuses. This fact impelled all categories of mine workers toward a common struggle against the employers.[40]

It is our main contention that the pattern of strike activity which developed during the period of our study reflected the drive to build a national industrial organization. When these strikes are

38 "Cost of Mining and Coking in Connelsville, Pa.," *EMJ* (Oct. 13, 1888), 300. Page, *Mineral Industry*, III, 150, quotes a leading coal operator's conclusion that "In many instances the books will show a loss on mining, with sufficient profits on [house] rents and store to make the business satisfactory to the operator." A similar point is made by W. P. Tams, *The Smokeless Coal Fields of West Virginia* (Morgantown, West Virginia, 1963), 25. U.M.W. *Journal* editorials, Feb. 15 and Mar. 8, 1894.
39 "Coal Trade Review-Bituminous," *EMJ* (Sep. 9, 1893), 275; "General Mining News-Ohio," *EMJ* (Oct. 7, 1893), 397. It has been estimated that the various forms of profit maximization through "audacious robbery" could conceivably add an estimated 25% to the gross profits of the coal operator. S. M. Lindsay, "Company Stores in the Pennsylvania Mining District," *Annals of the American Academy of Political and Social Science*, VII (1896), 162–164.
40 See the preamble to the Constitution of the National Progressive Union quoted in Evans, *History of the U.M.W.*, I, 403.

separated and classified by the nature of the specific demands put forward this pattern emerges clearly.

As is obvious from Figure 2, strikes concerning organization and conditions demonstrate a very different development from those undertaken to secure wage increases ("offensive wage strikes") and those undertaken to resist pay cuts ("defensive wage strikes"). It will be noted that the lines which describe the incidence of the latter two types of strikes move against one another during most periods. In a period of depression (e.g., 1883–84) these curves move apart, and then, as the economy turns into a period of prosperity (1886–1890) there is a "scissors-effect" as they reverse position. Thus, offensive and defensive wage strikes

Fig. 2   Strike Causes, 1881–1894 (as percentage of total annual strikes)

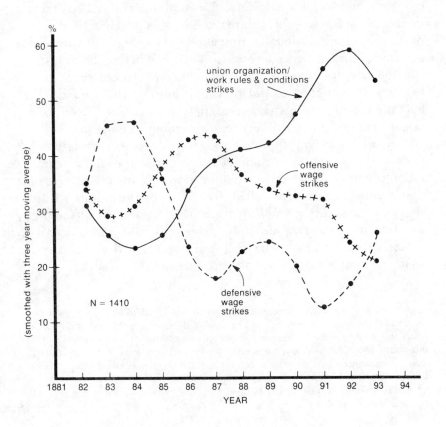

are best seen as immediate and short-term responses to direct economic pressures.[41]

In sharp contrast to this scissors-like progress is the line describing strikes over organization and conditions. This curve seems to follow a logic of its own. We contend that these strikes reflected the struggle to order productive relations in the industry. We constructed the productive relations category by amalgamating three basic types of strike causes: 1) those over work rules and conditions including questions of the form and regularity of payment and the conditions of life in the mining community; 2) those involving questions of union organization and worker solidarity; and 3) those over the employment of particular workers, including strikes to rehire a victimized worker and strikes to fire an obnoxious foreman.[42] We have regarded these types of strikes as efforts to reorder productive relations because in each case they represented an attempt to confront directly the coal operators' economic and social control in and around the mines. The dramatic increase in these strikes shown in Figure 2 is a direct reflection of the miners' increasing determination to challenge this control in a period of intensified consolidation and conflict in the industry. The increase in strikes to reorder productive relations represented the whole complex of relationships among the miners, the operators, and nationwide economic forces out of which a national union of mine workers was beginning to emerge.

As the following figure shows, the miners increasingly confronted the operators as trade unionists, or at the call of a trade union organization. Figure 3 demonstrates the steady increase in the number of strikes called by labor organizations, which suggests the steady growth of the miners' awareness of the need for a formal organization upon which to base strike activity. Union-called strikes in the coal industry reached a majority in 1886 and attained a peak of 70 percent in 1891.

41 This view is supported when the distribution of offensive and defensive wage strikes is considered with respect to seasonality. The seasonal differential is reflected in the way in which the causes of wages strikes are distributed throughout the year. Our results indicate that nearly 70% of defensive wage strikes occurred during summer months (Mar. through Aug.) when higher winter wage rates were cut back. During winter months (Sep. through Feb.), nearly 60% of the offensive wage strikes occurred.
42 Our data indicate that strikes in these three categories increased at the same rate throughout the period of our study.

Fig. 3   Strikes Called by Unions, 1881–1894

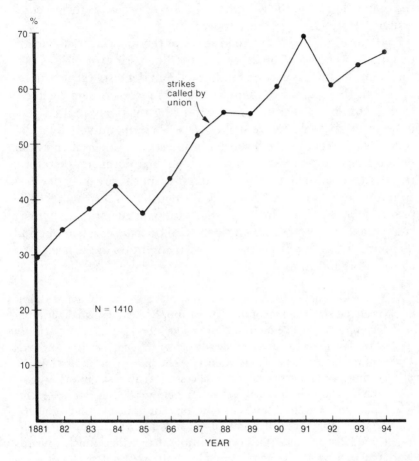

The miners' efforts to build a national union were prolonged both by the economic vicissitudes which characterized the times and by organizational competition among the early labor organizations in the industry. The initial attempts to organize nationally after the Civil War were smashed during the depression of 1873–1878. At the beginning of the 1880s "secret" local assemblies of the Knights of Labor had replaced "open" miners' unions in many localities. Many of the Knights' local assemblies in the coal districts consisted almost entirely of mine workers and functioned as local trade unions.[43] In this way they simultaneously propagated the political ideas of the Knights of Labor and acted as the practical centers of organized strike activity.

Before 1886 strikes were local, or at the most district-wide in extent. In many coal fields during the depression of 1882–1885, for example, miners carried out limited and defensive strikes in response to the operators' attempts to cut wages as orders declined. Our data indicate that in addition to being relatively limited geographically these defensive strikes were of comparatively long duration (54 percent of the defensive wage strikes undertaken in our period lasted one month or more).[44] For many miners, therefore, the idea of a national union came to represent the prospect of overcoming the isolation and defeat of the lengthy local struggles. The preamble to the Constitution of the National Federation of Miners and Mine Laborers, written near the end of this depression period (September 1885), reflects the miners' recognition of the need for a national organization.

> As miners and mine laborers, our troubles are everywhere of a similar character. The inexorable law of supply and demand determines the point where our interests unite. The increased shipping facilities of the last few years have made all coal-producing districts competitors in the markets of this country. This has led to indiscriminate cutting of market prices and unnecessary reductions in our wages, which for some time have been far below a living rate. . . . Our failure to act in concert when contesting for principles and rights has brought about the demoralization and degradation of our craft. Local, district and State organizations have done much towards ameliorating the condition of our craft in the past, but to-day neither district nor State unions can regulate the markets to which their coal is shipped. . . . Hence, while approving of local organizations, whether secret or open in character, we are convinced that by federating under one general head our powers for good would be increased and a speedy betterment of our common condition fol-

---

43 Andrew Roy, *History of the Coal Miners in the United States* (Columbus, 1903), 174–75; Ware, *Labor Movement*, 160, 211; Evans, *History of the U.M.W.*, I, 94; McNeill, *Labor Movement*, 251. The "official" organ of coal miners from the late 1870s until the publication of the U.M.W. *Journal* in 1891 was the *National Labor Tribune*, published in Pittsburgh.
44 This contrasts with strikes over working conditions and union organization, 60% of which lasted fewer than 14 days.

low. In a federation of all lodges and branches of miners' unions lies our only hope.[45]

The economic upswing that began in 1886 provided the miners with the opportunity to fight for their aims. They did so by undertaking offensive pay strikes to restore wage rates that had been forced down during the depression and by undertaking numerous strikes over work rules and conditions and union organization (strikes over these matters during the 1885–86 period exceeded those during 1883–84 by 75 percent). The National Trades Assembly #135 of the Knights of Labor was established in May 1886 as an organizational rival to the more open trade unionism of the National Federation. By this point the mine workers had developed two national organizations with which to wage offensive struggles against the operators.[46]

The standard view of these two organizations has stressed the vigorous and sometimes even bitter competition between them. The organizational rivalry which did exist, however, was considerably less important than the traditional view suggests. More significant than the occasional fistfight on the pitbank between members of the rival organizations was the fact that the National Federation and NTA #135 were committed to similar programs. Both sought to build up powerful district and state organizations, both preferred arbitration and conciliation despite an increasing reliance on strike action, and both undertook extensive political and legislative action to secure gains for mine workers.[47]

The traditional interpretation of the American labor movement has tended to counterpose pragmatic job action and third party political agitation in describing the rivalry between the Knights of Labor and the other labor organizations of the period. As far as the two major mine workers' organizations in the 1880s were concerned, however, political and strike action certainly were not opposed strategies. On the contrary, miners in both NTA #135 and the National Federation frequently challenged the operators' political power through vigorous efforts to secure legis-

45 Quoted in McNeill, *Labor Movement*, 254.
46 See *Proceedings* of the General Assembly of the Knights of Labor, 1888, 45; Ware, *Labor Movement*, 161–230.
47 Evans, *History of the U.M.W.*, I, 189; Ware, *Labor Movement*, 118.

lation to guarantee fair and frequent payment and regular safety inspection of mines and equipment. Furthermore, legislative campaigns and strike action were frequently tied together when miners walked out to insure the enforcement of state mining laws. The direct local challenge to the operator's control, the fight to build a national union of mine workers, and the campaign to pass and to enforce protective state legislation were, therefore, inextricably bound together in the miners' struggles.[48]

There is evidence to suggest the existence of legislative and organizational cooperation between the NTA #135 and the National Federation after 1887. For example, the common desire to employ arbitration and conciliation mechanisms led these organizations to attempt to cooperate in joint-scale agreements between 1887 and 1889 in the Central Competitive Field. Moreover, rank and file demands to disregard the antagonisms engendered in the early 1880s pressured the leaders of the two organizations to overcome their differences. These contacts and pressures would eventually culminate in the merger of NTA #135 with the National Federation (renamed the National Progressive Union in 1889) to form the United Mine Workers of America in January 1890. The creation of the UMW represented the final amalgamation of the organizational and political orientations present in its antecedents.[49]

At the time of its founding the UMW could claim only 17,000 "paid up" members out of the total labor force in bituminous mining of nearly 200,000 workers. Nevertheless, large numbers of miners were influenced by the national organization whether or not they were actually members. By the end of our period (1894) the UMW could call for a series of massive strikes

---

48 "General Mining News-Iowa," *EMJ* (Sept. 19, 1891), 341; Evans, *History of the U.M.W.*, I, 245–247; Katherine Harvey, *The Best Dressed Miners* (Ithaca, 1969), 207–277, 321–338. See the following *EMJ* articles: "General Mining News," (Aug. 15, 1891), 203; (Sept. 5, 1891), 277; (Nov. 18, 1893), 529; (Dec. 9, 1893), 600.

49 Evans, *History of the U.M.W.*, I, 224–229. The *National Labor Tribune* reported a number of attempts throughout 1887 and 1888 to reconcile the NTA #135 and the National Federation. The National Progressive Union had been formed in December, 1888, from the merger of the National Federation and a major portion of NTA #135. Evans, *History of the U.M.W.*, I, 395–410; Roy, *History of Coal Miners*, 268–273. The official name of the UMW, "United Mine Workers of America, composed of NTA #135, the Knights of Labor, and the National Progressive Union, affiliated with the American Federation of Labor," reflected the nature of the merger.

Fig. 4   Productive Relations Strikes, 1881–1894 (comparing union and non-union establishments)

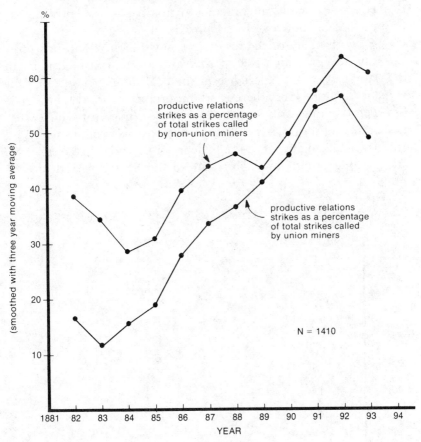

productive relations
strikes as a percentage
of total strikes called
by non-union miners

productive relations
strikes as a percentage
of total strikes called
by union miners

N = 1410

(smoothed with three year moving average)

YEAR

across the country to defend wage levels and bring out 125,000 miners, although only 13,000 were members of the union at the time.[50] The union was clearly influential beyond the confines of its formal membership.

Figure 4 indicates that both union and non-union miners increasingly utilized the strike to reorder productive relations in the pits. This suggests the possibility that trade union consciousness preceded rather than followed formal organization. Once the

50   These estimates are made by Roy, *History of Coal Miners*, 287, 325–330; Ware, *Labor Movement*, 221.

union became established, however, miners were better able to carry on strikes once they had begun, to extend the strike to more than a single establishment, and to involve consistently higher proportions of the work force in each pit.

As with many of the results presented earlier, Figure 5 indicates the way in which 1886 marks an important turning point in the nature of strike experience in the coal mining industry. Our evidence indicates that there is an important qualitative difference between the long strikes of the early 1880s (many of which were desperate and unsuccessful struggles against pay cuts imposed by employers during the 1882–1885 depression) and the strikes of relatively long duration which occurred during the period of eco-

Fig. 5 Mean Duration of Union and Non-Union Strikes, 1881–1894

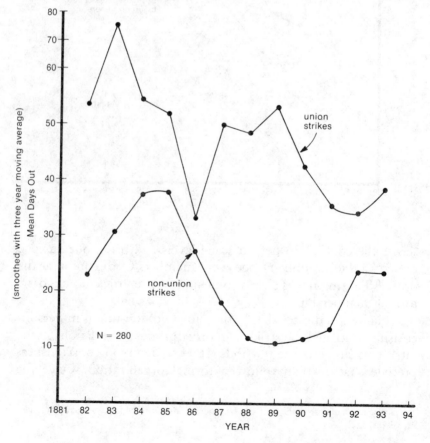

nomic upswing following 1886. As Figure 5 dramatically demonstrates it was the unionized miners who were able to mount strikes
of longer than average duration.[51] After 1886 it can be seen that
the curves representing the mean duration of union and non-union
strikes move apart, suggesting that the unionized mine workers
were able to take advantage of the prosperity of the late 1880s to
press their demands on employers with strikes of greater duration.
Non-union miners appear much less able to do this as indicated by
the strike duration figures recorded on the lower line of Figure 5.

Another indication of the growing aggressiveness of coal
strikes in the late 1880s and early 1890s is suggested by our figures

Fig. 6 Scatter Diagram of Multi-establishment Strikes, 1881–1894
(multi-establishment strikes = >2 establishments involved)

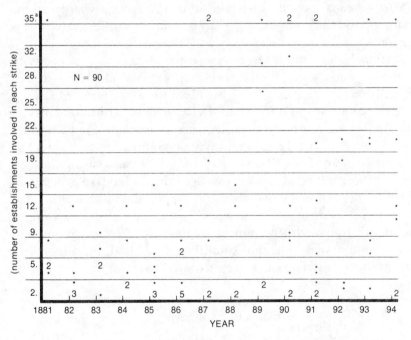

a   To make the graph more comprehensible we have recoded strikes involving 35 establishments or more into a single category (35). Ten strikes fall into this category ranging
from 47 to 225 establishments. All but one of the ten occurred after 1886.

51   See page 608 and note 44 above. The sharp decrease in the mean duration of strikes
called by unions in 1886 probably is attributable to the intense social and political upheaval
which characterized that year.

for the number of mining establishments affected by a particular strike. An increasing ability to mount multi-establishment strikes demonstrates the mine workers' ability to carry out strikes over greater geographical areas. Our results indicate that between 1881 and 1894 two-thirds of all multi-establishment strikes in coal were called by unions. Further, although 42 percent of all union-called strikes were multi-establishment in scope, only 20.4 percent of non-union strikes extended beyond a single pit.

When the growth in the number of mining operations involved in multi-establishment strikes is considered over time, a marked upward trend is noticeable. The mine workers' increased ability to undertake multi-establishment strikes after the mid-1880s is related positively to the crucial role played by the national union: more than half of the strikes called by trade unions between 1886 and 1894 were multi-establishment in scope, whereas in the same period only 17 percent of all non-union strikes were of this character.

Finally, in addition to the usual parameters of strike activity (duration and geographical dispersion), we have adapted an idea of Griffin's to create a measure which will show the impact of union organization on the miners' ability to achieve strike solidarity.[52] To do this we compared the categories of "strikers" and "number of employees" (i.e., total employment figures for each mine) as the basis of an index of solidarity for strikes in coal mining. By taking those who had actively involved themselves as a proportion of the entire mine work force (as opposed to those who had merely been "thrown out of work"), we developed a measure of solidarity by which to compare the experience of the union and non-union miners. The index numbers listed in Table 3 represent the number of strikers as a proportion of the total number of employees:

$$\frac{\text{strikers}}{\text{total employees}} = \text{level of solidarity}$$

Solidarity increases as the index number approaches 1.00.

As Table 3 indicates, unionized miners consistently were able to involve a higher percentage of the mine work force in their

---

52 Griffin compared the two categories of "strikers" and "employees thrown out of work by strikes" for all American industries between 1881 and 1905. See *Strikes*, 209–210.

Table 3 Index of Strike Solidarity

	UNION CALLED STRIKES		NON–UNION STRIKES	
YEAR	INDEX OF SOLIDARITY[a]	STANDARD DEVIATION[b]	INDEX OF SOLIDARITY[a]	STANDARD DEVIATION[b]
1881	.946	.076	.833	.251
1882	.893	.097	.789	.305
1883	.920	.091	.711	.384
1884	.965	.085	.809	.324
1885	.801	.224	.736	.332
1886	.867	.119	.793	.310
1887	.825	.265	.590	.320
1888	.912	.101	.682	.299
1889	.816	.178	.614	.349
1890	.883	.113	.873	.130
1891	.810	.252	.589	.384
1892	.846	.077	.641	.373
1893	.848	.146	.757	.200
1894	.905	.097	.636	.397
mean	.863[c]	.169	.731[c]	.316

a   mean solidarity index for all sample strikes = .795
b   mean standard deviation for all sample strikes = .264
c   analysis of variance F Test = 18.0824, T Test = 4.2523

strikes. We would attribute this fact to the ability of the miners' unions to mount strikes which involved a greater number of the occupational categories in each pit. It will also be noted that there is significantly less variation from the norm among the union-called strikes (i.e., standard deviations are much lower), indicating the fewer number of cases which did not conform to the general pattern among union-called strikes.

Our data have suggested a consistent relationship between the growth and impact of trade unionism among the American mine workers between 1881 and 1894 and the pattern of strikes in the coal industry during the same period. We have contended that the evolution of the strike in coal is reflected in the changing pattern of strike demands in which strikes over the reordering of productive relations in mining increase as a proportion of the total despite the fluctuations in business activity which characterized the times. In response to the attempts of coal operators to enhance their economic control over their employees, coal miners increasingly relied on strike activity which had as its object not only the elimination of immediate grievances but also the creation and extension of a permanent institution of self defense.

The ability of formal trade union organization to increase the impact and solidarity of the strike was an important lesson carried by mine workers through the severe depression that followed the defeat of the 1894 strike. Even though their union was nearly destroyed, formally speaking, between 1894 and 1896, mine workers were able and willing to rally to the UMW's strike call with the economic upturn of 1897.[53] That year marked the beginning of a string of strike victories for the UMW which would ultimately make it the largest and one of the most militant of all American trade unions before World War I. It was in the formative years between 1881 and 1894, however, that the miners transformed the strike into an aggressive and more broadly class-conscious tactic in their struggle to reorder the productive relationships which obtained within individual coal pits and in the industry as a whole.

53   At the 1896 convention of the union, Secretary Patrick McBryde reported that the organization's debt for 1895 was $3000. Evans, *History of the U.M.W.*, II, 413. See also letter from Samuel Gompers to UMW Secretary-Treasurer Pearce, Oct. 29, 1896 in Gompers Letterbooks, Library of Congress, XVI, #401.

Stephan Thernstrom and Peter R. Knights

Men in Motion: Some Data and Speculations about Urban Population Mobility in Nineteenth-Century America

Americans have long been a restless, migratory people, a fact which has left a deep impression on our national folklore if not yet on the writing of American history. Though it had earlier antecedents, the faith in spatial mobility as the key to virtue and success came into full flower in the nineteenth century. With an open continent beckoning, it was natural that mobility and opportunity were linked in the popular mind with the West and the frontier. But the supply of virgin land, though vast, was not limitless. As early as 1852, brooding about the future, the Superintendent of the U.S. Census saw trouble ahead:

> The roving tendency of our people is incident to the peculiar condition of their country, and each succeeding Census will prove that it is diminishing. When the fertile plains of the West shall have been filled up, and men of scanty means cannot by a mere change of location acquire a homestead, the inhabitants of each State will become comparatively stationary. . . .[1]

Cities, many feared, were serpents in Eden, ensnaring, enfeebling, and corrupting their inhabitants. They pinned a man down and drained him of the vital energies that he needed to pull up stakes and move on to the greener pastures that lay ahead. Well after urbanization and industrialization had transformed agrarian America, a residue of these suspicions remained. To many the city seemed a closed, confining,

Stephan Thernstrom is Professor of History and Associate at the Institute for Government and Public Affairs at the University of California, Los Angeles. He is the author of *Poverty and Progress: Social Mobility in a 19th Century City* (Cambridge, Mass., 1964) and co-editor, with Richard Sennett, of *Nineteenth-Century Cities: Essays in the New Urban History* (New Haven, 1969).

Peter R. Knights is Assistant Professor of Journalism at the University of Illinois, Urbana/Champaign. He is the author of articles on the newspaper industry and on population mobility. He is currently engaged in projects on the economic history of the United States daily newspaper industry, 1866–1900, and a social analysis of the political leadership of Boston since 1830. His book, *The Plain People of Boston, 1830–1860*, will be published by Oxford University Press in 1971.

This essay will also appear in Tamara K. Hareven, (ed.), *Anonymous Americans* (forthcoming).

1 U.S. Census Office, 7th Census (1850), *Report of the Superintendent of the Census for December 1, 1852* (Washington, 1853), 15.

static environment. And certain areas of the city—"slums," "ghettos"—were especially confining. Poor people were permanently trapped there, unable to escape from a degrading environment. An observer of New York's appalling Hell's Kitchen on the eve of World War I summed it up in a vivid metaphor. The district, he declared, was a giant "spider's web": "of those who come to it, very few . . . ever leave."[2]

At the level of popular thought, migration was understood to be a major determinant of the shape of the American social order, and urbanization was viewed as problematical because it seemed to restrict the spatial mobility of city-dwellers, or at least of poor city-dwellers. This is surely an issue worth exploring, but few historians have seen fit to do so. How volatile in fact was the population of the United States in the nineteenth century? Were city-dwellers notably less migratory than farmers, poor people than rich, immigrants than natives? How was movement through space related to economic opportunity? Were the slums and ghettos of the era indeed giant spider webs which entrapped the unfortunate?

Until quite recently, the only available systematic studies of population mobility in nineteenth-century America dealt with frontier communities.[3] It is clear that the population of such communities was extraordinarily restless and footloose. A number of scholarly efforts to test Frederick Jackson Turner's frontier thesis have yielded similar conclusions on this point.[4] Barely a quarter of the farm operators to be found in 1860 in the five Kansas townships examined by James C. Malin

2   Russell Sage Foundation, *West Side Studies* (New York, 1914), I, 8.
3   The most conspicuous exception to this claim is Adna F. Weber's classic volume on *The Growth of Cities in the Nineteenth Century* (New York, 1899; Cornell University Press reprint, 1963), a bold pioneering venture which regrettably fell upon barren ground and was little known until the resurgence of interest in urban studies and quantitative historical analysis that has taken place in the past few years.
4   James C. Malin, "The Turnover of Farm Population in Kansas," *Kansas Historical Quarterly*, IV (1935), 339–372; Merle Curti, *et al.*, *The Making of an American Community: A Case Study of Democracy in a Frontier County* (Stanford, 1959), 68; Mildred Throne, "A Population Study of an Iowa County in 1850," *Iowa Journal of History*, LVII (1959), 305–330; Peter J. Coleman, "Restless Grant County: Americans on the Move," *Wisconsin Magazine of History*, XLVI (Autumn, 1962), 16–20. Unless otherwise specified, all persistence figures given in the present paper are for employed adult males. It should be noted that persistence estimates cannot be directly translated into true out-migration rates. A 25 per cent persistence rate for a decade does not necessarily mean that 75 per cent of the population moved out of the community in the interval; some individuals disappeared because of death. Taking death into account, however, does not drastically alter the figures for a population with a normal age distribution, as will be evident from the detailed discussion below of out-migration from Boston in the 1880s, based on calculations which separate deaths from true out-migration.

in his pioneering 1935 inquiry could be located there a mere ten years later. In Trempealeau County, Wisconsin, the comparable figure for all employed males was nearly identical—25 per cent for 1860–1870, and 29 per cent for 1870–1880. Likewise, a mere 30 per cent of the male labor force enumerated by the census-taker in Wapello County, Iowa, in 1850 was there to greet his successor a decade later. Over a slightly longer interval—from 1880 to 1895—only 22 per cent of the households in five townships of Grant County, Wisconsin, remained. Clearly the agricultural communities of the West in the latter half of the century were not, in the simple demographic sense, stable "island communities" with a large core of permanent residents.[5] They were more like busy railroad stations, into which many travelers poured but in which few stopped for long.

But what of the cities of the era? Critics of the Turner thesis long ago challenged the identification of mobility with the frontier, and demonstrated that, important as the westward movement was in our national history, a far larger migratory stream moved eastward and city-ward. It was the burgeoning cities which provided the safety valve for the surplus rural population, and for the bulk of the European immigrants who came in such large numbers from the late 1840s on.[6]

That general point was effectively argued by Turner's critics and soon was widely accepted. But, perhaps because these critics failed to advance a compelling general theory of the American city that could stimulate and guide empirical research in the way that the frontier thesis did, or perhaps because of professional reluctance to tackle a subject which demanded the mastery of masses of quantitative data, the matter was left there.[7] The capacity of the emerging cities to draw in new

5 Robert Wiebe, *The Search for Order, 1877–1920* (New York, 1967).
6 Fred A. Shannon, "A Post Mortem on the Labor-Safety-Valve Theory," *Agricultural History*, XIX (1945), 31–37.
7 The most influential effort to advance an "urban" interpretation of American history comparable to the frontier theory, Arthur Schlesinger Sr.'s "The City in American History," *Mississippi Valley Historical Review*, XXVII (1940), 43–46, was considerably less rich in provocative, testable propositions. Its inadequacies were exposed in William Diamond's thoughtful essay, "On the Dangers of an Urban Interpretation of History," in Eric F. Goldman (ed.), *Historiography and Urbanization* (Baltimore, 1941), 67–108. It was already clear from census state-of-birth data, analyzed in Weber's *The Growth of Cities*, Harvey S. Perloff, *et al.*, *Regions, Resources and Economic Growth* (Baltimore, 1960), and Simon Kuznets, Dorothy S. Thomas, Everett S. Lee, *et al.*, *Population Redistribution and Economic Growth: United States, 1870–1950* (Philadelphia, 1957, 1960, 1964), 3v., that substantial numbers of Americans moved from state to state and region to region in the course of their lives, but this evidence gave little hint of what would be disclosed by microscopic examination of population movements in particular cities.

migrants was recognized, but there was no effort to trace migratory currents beyond the initial point of entry into the city. The result of this failure was a partial and distorted view of the process of migration and of the dynamics of urban growth. What was only the first step in a complex process—the initial move from country to city—was taken for the whole, and the fluidity of the urban population was grossly underestimated. Cities were thought to grow like brickpiles. Throw fifty bricks on the pile and it grows correspondingly larger; if 50,000 migrants enter Chicago in a given decade, the Chicago population would increase by 50,000. Net population changes from census to census were thus taken to be an adequate measure of the volume of inmigration. But this assumes, of course, that migration was a one-way, one-step process, and that all 50,000 of the newcomers *stayed* in Chicago. This was far from the case. Migration *out of* nineteenth-century cities took place on a massive scale. Most American communities of the era grew rapidly, but net population changes from census to census, though often dramatic, pale into insignificance by comparison with the actual gross volume of in and out movement. A number of recent investigations, which we shall review here, indicate that the composition of the urban population was far more fluid than has been suspected. Understanding this crucial fact will give us new insights into the nature of the urbanization process, and will dispel some common misconceptions concerning immigrant and working-class "ghettos" in the nineteenth-century city.

One of us, the senior author, first gained some hint of the remarkable fluidity of the nineteenth-century urban population in the course of an effort to plot the career patterns of common laborers living in Newburyport, Massachusetts, between 1850 and 1880.[8] Newburyport, it soon became clear, was no more a permanent resting place for these men than Trempealeau County and other frontier communities had been for their inhabitants. Nor was the volatility of the city's population confined to the largely Irish unskilled workers; less than a fifth of all the families listed in the local city directory of 1849 were to be found in the community thirty years later. Rochester, New York, had an even less stable population in this period; only 20 per cent of its 1849 residents could be traced in the city ten years later.[9]

8 Stephan Thernstrom, *Poverty and Progress: Social Mobility in a 19th Century City* (Cambridge, Mass., 1964), 96, 168.
9 Blake McKelvey, *Rochester, The Flower City, 1855–1890* (Cambridge, Mass., 1949), 3.

But this evidence was far from decisive. Newburyport, after all, was a way station in the orbit of a major metropolis, and Rochester was a stepping-stone to the West. These might have been special cases. And there were particular grounds for wondering if major cities were not notably more stable in population than smaller places, for it was the Bostons, Philadelphias, and New Yorks of America that were the sites of the classic big-city ghettos. There, one might still expect to find a settled population, trapped in misery, huddled together in some kind of "culture of poverty."

Recent work, however, makes it appear that these doubts are unfounded and indicates that not only the rural population but the urban population too was extraordinarily volatile in nineteenth-century America. Newburyport and Rochester were not atypical of smaller cities in the period as a result of the former's proximity to a major metropolis and the latter's location along a well-worn path to the West. Poughkeepsie, New York, fits neither category, and yet only 30 per cent of its 1850 residents were still living there ten years later.[10] Northampton, Massachusetts, had a rather more stable population, but, even so, little more than half (53 per cent) of its inhabitants at mid-century were present to be counted by the time of the Census of 1860.[11] Atlanta, Georgia, a city of 22,000 in 1870, ranked between Poughkeepsie and Northampton in stability; 43 per cent of its white residents remained in the community from 1870 to 1880.[12] There was some variation from city to city, obviously, but even in the most stable small or medium size community which has as yet been examined approximately half of the population was transient within a relatively brief span of years.

What of the really big cities of the era, the cities which we might naturally assume were the end of the road for the drifters who passed through smaller places like Newburyport, Northampton, and Poughkeepsie? Only one—Boston—has as yet been studied systematically, but if it was at all typical then the great metropolitan centers were not

10 Computed from data in Clyde Griffen, "Workers Divided: The Effect of Craft and Ethnic Differences in Poughkeepsie, New York, 1850–1880," in Stephan Thernstrom and Richard Sennett (eds.), *Nineteenth-Century Cities: Essays in the New Urban History* (New Haven, 1969), 49–97.

11 Robert Doherty, "Industrialization and Social Change: Northampton, Massachusetts, 1800–1860" (unpub. paper for the Yale Conference on 19th Century Cities, November, 1968).

12 Computed from data in Richard J. Hopkins, "Occupational and Geographic Mobility in Atlanta, 1870–1890," *Journal of Southern History*, XXXIV (1968), 200–213.

notably more stable in population composition. One would expect, of course, to find somewhat higher persistence rates and lower out–migration rates in a sprawling metropolis, simply because it is possible to move farther—both physically and socially—and still remain within its boundaries. All other things being equal, the probability of out–migration decreases as the area of the unit examined increases.[13] Large cities should display higher persistence rates than smaller cities, and the rate for any one community should increase as the city grows.

With this caveat in mind, the Boston figures indicate that the city's population was remarkably volatile. The city's total population grew from 61,000 in 1830 to 178,000 in 1860; the decade persistence rates for heads of households in this period were 44 per cent for 1830–1840, 49 per cent for 1840–1850, and 39 per cent for 1850–1860.[14] If unmarried males had been included in the samples, the figures would doubtless be even lower. Again we have a community in which a distinct minority of men remained in the city long enough to be counted by two successive census-takers.

By 1880 the Boston population had climbed to 363,000, by 1890 to 448,000, and the physical boundaries of the city had been much enlarged through the annexation in the 1860s and 1870s of such towns as Roxbury, Dorchester, and Charlestown. Much of the short-distance movement which previously would have been classified as out–migration now was intra-city movement, and the persistence rate rose accordingly. But it was still only 64 per cent for all adult males for 1880–1890, 45 per cent for unmarried men, and 53 per cent for blue-collar workers aged twenty to twenty-nine in 1880.[15]

13 Otis Dudley Duncan, et al., Statistical Geography (Glencoe, 1961), 34.
14 Peter R. Knights, "Population Turnover, Persistence, and Residential Mobility in Boston, 1830–1860," in Thernstrom and Sennett, Nineteenth-Century Cities, 272.
15 All Boston data, unless otherwise indicated, were gathered by the authors in the course of research for forthcoming studies. The junior author is preparing a demographic and social study of the city in the antebellum period, based on samples of 385 heads of households from each of the four censuses, 1830–1860. Sample members were traced through city directories, 1830–1860, city assessor's books, 1830, 1840, 1850, and 1860, and the state registration system, 1841–1910. The senior author is completing an analysis of migration and social mobility in Boston, 1880–1968. The figures drawn from this research pertain to 1982 adult males randomly selected from the manuscript schedules of the U.S. Census of 1880. Sample members were traced in the city directories and assessor's valuation books for 1890. One peculiarity of the sampling procedure could have biased the persistence figures for 1880–1890, but apparently did not. By 1890 Boston, was a large city, and one that contained a good many people with extremely common names; there were 122 John Smiths living there, and no less than 235 John Murphys. It would have been quite impossible to determine if a particular John Murphy from the

A different measure of persistence and turnover yields a more dramatic indication of the volatility of the Boston population. Instead of asking what fraction of the residents present at the start of a decade were still there at its end, we may ask about movement from year to year. Here the decennial census is of no value, and we must turn to another source—the annual city directory. Virtually all nineteenth-century American cities had regularly published directories by the time they had reached a population of 30,000 or so. Printed by private firms and sold largely to businessmen, they were prepared from a careful canvas of each house in the community and supplied a relatively accurate listing of the population.[16] The Boston directories provided a

---

1880 sample was still living in the community ten years later or not. Accordingly, men with common names were excluded from the samples. Comparison of the characteristics of the sample with those of the entire population of the city revealed that this produced some under-representation of men with Irish names, most of whom were blue-collar workers. But the overall occupational distribution of the sample was representative of the city, and Irish workers were not more volatile than other workers, so their under-representation did not distort the estimates. A full discussion and defense of the sampling procedure will appear in the senior author's forthcoming book.

16 For a discussion of the usefulness of city directories in urban studies, and some consideration of their reliability, see Peter R. Knights, "City Directories as Aids to Ante-Bellum Urban Studies: A Research Note," *Historical Methods Newsletter*, II (September 1969), 1–10. The directories did not provide a perfectly accurate enumeration of the population. Perfection has not been attained even in the U.S. Census of our own day; see the critical papers by Jacob S. Siegel, "Completeness of Coverage of the Nonwhite Population in the 1960 Census and Current Estimates, and Some Implications," in David M. Heer (ed.), *Social Statistics and the City* (Cambridge, Mass., 1968), 13–54; Leon Pritzker and N. D. Rothwell, "Procedural Difficulties in Taking Past Censuses in Predominantly Negro, Puerto Rican, and Mexican Areas," *ibid.*, 55–79; Jacob S. Siegel and Melvin Zelnik, "An Evaluation of Coverage in the 1960 Census of Population by Techniques of Demographic Analysis and by Composite Methods," *ibid.*, 132–173. The directory canvassing procedure in Boston, however, compared favorably with that employed in the census of the period. The greatest weakness of the city directories was not that they were biased against low-status residents *per se*, as has often been assumed, but rather that they were biased against very recent migrants, tending not to include them until they had passed some time in the city and seemed relatively settled. After careful comparisons of directory listings with other sources, the junior author has concluded that the operating rule in the antebellum period was to include individuals only after they had lived in the city for two years. To the extent that this bias prevailed, however, it strengthens rather than weakens the argument of this paper. A fully accurate enumeration of every individual living in the community, including casual laborers just passing through, would disclose an even more volatile population. In addition it should be noted that even a perfectly accurate and comprehensive set of city directories would underestimate the actual volatility of the population, for a canvas in May 1880 and in May 1881 would miss individuals who migrated into the city in June 1880 and left before the May 1881 canvas. A not inconsiderable fraction of the population may have fallen into this category. All in all, it seems likely that the estimates given here err in the conservative direction.

convenient, if crude, measure of annual population turnover for the city, in the form of tables noting the number of names expunged from the preceding year's directory in making up the current one.[17] One of the first of these tables appeared in the directory for 1836, and it disclosed that fully 24 per cent of the individuals and business firms listed in the directory for 1835 could no longer be located by the canvasser. Lest it be thought that 1835–1836 was an exceptional year, illustrative figures for selected years in the rest of the century are given in Table 1.

Table 1   Percentage of Listings in Preceding Year's Boston City Directory Dropped in Preparation of Current Directory

1840–19	1865[a]–24	1885–20
1845–25	1870–24	1890–21
1850–25	1875–25	1895–19
1855–26	1880–18	1900–21

a   This information was not provided in the directories for 1859–1863.

As this makes clear, the rate of annual out–migration from Boston, at least by this crude index, was remarkably high, and surprisingly uniform.

The measure is imperfect in a number of ways, however, and it seemed worthwhile to refine these calculations for at least one decade, that of the 1880s. There are two principal flaws in using the number of listings dropped from the directory as a measure of migration out of the city. First, some names were dropped from the directories because of death. Second, the directories listed not only individual household heads but other employed adults not heads of families and also business

17   The Boston directories also tabulated the total number of names newly added to each annual directory down to 1922. These computations of listings added and dropped from year to year made possible the analysis offered in this section of our paper. We believe that our results are interesting enough to justify testing for other cities, but are distressed to report that the job may prove more difficult elsewhere, because the practice of tabulating total listings added and dropped was apparently not a common one. We have examined 1850 and 1860 directories for twenty-one cities, including Albany, Baltimore, Buffalo, Chicago, Cincinnati, Detroit, New Orleans, New York, Philadelphia, and San Francisco, and have not found similar information in summary form. Perhaps the practice was followed later in some of these cities, or in other communities, but it may be that considerably more arduous sampling and tracing procedures will have to be followed by other investigators.

firms; with the rate of business mortality notoriously high for small marginal enterprises, there is the possibility that the estimated out–migration rate would be seriously exaggerated. These two distorting influences have been reduced or eliminated by the procedure followed in Table 2. From the U.S. Censuses of 1880 and 1890 and the Massachu-

Table 2 Annual Out-Migration Rates for Boston Families, 1880, 1885, 1890

	1880	1885	1890
1. Number of households, by census count	72,763	80,207	89,716
2. Number of listings dropped from directory	27,938	32,507	39,885
3. Ratio of directory listings to households	1.967	2.088	2.175
4. Estimated families dropped (2 ÷ 3)	14,201	15,570	18,336
5. Deaths of household heads[a]	2,527	3,050	3,363
6. Families migrating from Boston (4 − 5)	11,674	12,520	14,973
7. Per cent of families disappearing because of death (5 ÷ 1)	3.5	3.8	3.8
8. Per cent of families migrating from the city (6 ÷ 1)	16.0	15.6	16.7

a This figure is the total of adult male deaths in the city, as given in the reports of the City Registrar, plus one-sixth of the adult female deaths, to allow for female-headed households.

setts State Census of 1885 we discovered the total number of families living in the city at those dates. Dividing the number of households by the number of listings in the directories of 1880, 1885, and 1890 supplied the ratio of households to total listings, a figure fluctuating from 1.967 to 2.175. Because many households contained more than one employed adult, and because some individuals were in business for themselves and hence double-counted, once at their residence and once at their place of business, there were roughly twice as many listings as households in the city. It is necessary, therefore, to divide the number of listings dropped by the ratio of total directory listings to total households, to arrive at an estimate of the number of families actually dropped from the directories. (This assumes roughly similar turnover rates for household heads, employed persons who were not heads of households, and business firms—a source of possible error, but not, we believe, of a magnitude to call into question our chief findings.) To find out how many of the disappearing families did so because of death is simple, and we are left with an estimate of how many actually left the city for other destinations. In each of the three years something under 4 per cent of the households in Boston were deleted from the city directories due to death; in each a high and a similar proportion—16.0 per cent, 15.6 per cent, and 16.7 per cent—moved away from the city altogether. This is a somewhat lower estimate than the 18 per cent, 20 per cent, and 21 per cent figures yielded by the cruder method of dividing listings dropped by total listings, but it still indicates that one Bostonian in seven moved out of the city over as short a period as 365 days.

(Some readers may find it difficult to reconcile this estimated annual out–migration rate of 16 per cent with our earlier report that 64 per cent of the adult males in Boston in 1880 were still in the city in 1890. If 16 per cent of the population left the city each year, it would seem, the ten-year out–migration rate would be 160 per cent. But one cannot extrapolate annual migration rates in this fashion. Sixteen per cent of the 1880 residents of Boston had left the city by the time a year had elapsed; about 16 per cent of the 1881 residents of Boston probably had likewise left the city by 1882. It does not follow that 32 per cent of the 1880 group had disappeared by 1882, for many of those in the departing 16 per cent of the 1881 group had not been living in Boston in 1880. It would be possible, indeed, for a community to have a 16 per cent annual out–migration rate and a 16 per cent decadal out–migration rate as well, with all out–migration after the first year being migration by recent newcomers. A stable population core of 84 per cent, that is to say, could exist alongside a highly volatile, migratory segment which turned over completely each year.[18] Fortunately, we have measures both of annual and of longer-term population flows through the city, for there is no accurate way of translating the one into the other.)

With annual departure rates at this high level, how did the population of Boston grow at all, as it did by 24 per cent between 1880 and 1890? Partly through natural increase—the excess of births over deaths —but largely through continuing in–migration at an even higher level. It is tempting to assume that if a city's population increases by 85,638 in

18 For evidence that recent migrants into communities are also those most likely to depart from it in the near future, and hence of the inappropriateness of extrapolating annual out-migration rates over a longer period, see Sidney Goldstein, *Patterns of Mobility, 1910–1950: The Norristown Study* (Philadelphia, 1958), 207ff.

a decade, as Boston's did in that interval, subtracting the gain attributable to natural increase—approximately 20,500 in this instance—will yield a residual which is a valid estimate of the number of migrants who came to the city during the decade. It appears that in the 1880s 65,179 newcomers entered Boston, swelling its population to 448,000 by 1890. The new migrants, therefore, comprised a mere 14.5 per cent of the 1890 total (65,179 ÷ 448,000), suggesting that Boston was a city with an overwhelming preponderance of relatively settled long-term residents.

In fact, however, the vital statistics or residual method employed in this calculation is highly misleading. It is a poor measure even of the population change attributable to *net* migration,[19] and, in any event, it is not net migration but gross migration which is relevant to the question of how settled a city's population actually was. Analysis of the volume of in-migration and out-migration on an *annual* basis provides a far different, and far more revealing, estimate of the composition of the Boston population. It indicates that the proportion of the city's 1890 residents who had moved into Boston in the preceding decade was not 14.5 per cent but fully one third, and that the stream of in-migration into the community during the decade was more than *twelve times* as large as the net in-migration estimate would suggest. Nearly 800,000 people moved into Boston between 1880 and 1890 to produce the net migration increase of 65,179.

These startling, indeed hardly credible, conclusions may be substantiated as follows. The Boston population grew from 363,000 to 448,000 between 1880 and 1890; the number of listings in the Boston city directories increased from 143,140 to 195,149. (There were fewer listings than persons, of course, because the directories excluded dependent women and children.) The "listings added" and "listings

19 The method yields estimates of net migration which are much too low, because it credits all of the vital events occurring during the interval in question to the population resident there at the start of the interval. That is, all of the births and deaths taking place in Boston in the 1880s are removed from the 1890 population total, and only the remaining surplus is attributed to net migration. This ignores the fact that some of these births and deaths were the result of in-migration during the decade. Families who entered the city after the Census of 1880 produced children; in-migration also brought in persons who died before 1890. But these two influences were not of the same magnitude, for newcomers were disproportionately concentrated in the procreative age brackets, in which death rates were low. Via complex estimating procedures unnecessary to describe here, we calculate that a minimum of 27.7 per cent of the births in Boston between 1880 and 1890 were attributable to new migrants, but only 6.7 per cent of the deaths, which means that the true net migration figure was at least 26,000 higher than the residual method would indicate.

dropped" totals given in the annual directories allow us to determine, with the aid of some further data, how large a volume of gross population movement into and out of the city was required to produce the net increase of about 50,000 listings. As Table 3 indicates, the net increase of 50,000 occurred because no less than 398,995 listings were added to the directories in the decade, and just over 350,000 listings were dropped.

These raw figures must be adjusted, however, to provide true estimates of the migration flows to and from Boston. First we must attempt to eliminate the disturbing influence of business turnover by applying the ratio of directory listings to total households in the city to the listings added and listings dropped figures, to yield estimates of the number of families added and dropped. Applying these ratios, we learn that some 191,871 families were newly-listed in the directories at some point in the 1880s, and that 169,045 were dropped.

The families added and families dropped estimates need two further corrections to become valid measures of migration into and out of the city. Some of the new listings were caused not by the arrival of newcomers from outside the city but by young residents of the city reaching the age at which they were eligible for listing—twenty-one. Likewise, some of the names dropped disappeared from the directories because of death. The magnitude of these two influences can be estimated with data from the Censuses and the City Registrar's reports and their effect removed, and we are left with the final in- and out-migration estimates in Table 3.

During the 1880s, 157,974 families moved into Boston, more than twice the total number of families living there as of 1880. If the in-migrating households were of the same average size as those already in the city—namely five persons—this would mean that nearly 800,000 $(157,974 \times 5 = 789,870)$ individuals moved into Boston in this short period. But the net increase in the city's population over the decade that was attributable to migration was only *one-twelfth* of the total volume of in-migration $(789,870 \div 65,179)$, for tremendous numbers of people were also moving out of Boston in those years, 138,804 households or approximately 690,000 $(138,804 \times 5 = 694,020)$ individuals. Enormous though the stream of new arrivals was, it exceeded the total of individuals departing by only 14 per cent. The turnover of the Boston population in the decade, the total of families moving either in or out, was 296,778, a stunning *4.09 times* the total number of households in the city in 1880.

Table 3 Total In- and Out-migration and Population Turnover in Boston, 1880–1890

	1881–1885	1886–1890	DECADE TOTAL
1. Listings added	187,946	211,049	398,995
2. Listings dropped	161,755	189,774	351,529
3. Listings/household ratio[a]	2.029	2.131	2.079
4. Families added	92,698	99,015	191,871
5. Families dropped	79,780	89,033	169,045
6. Males reaching 21	16,388	17,509	33,897
7. Deaths of household heads	14,126	16,115	30,241
8. Families in-migrating (4−6)	76,310	81,506	157,974
9. Families out-migrating (5−7)	65,654	72,918	138,804
10. Population turnover (families)[b] (8+9)	141,964	154,424	296,778
11. Population turnover (individuals)[b]	709,820	772,120	1,483,890

a   These ratios differ slightly from those for 1880, 1885, and 1890 given in Table 2. The ratio used here for 1880–1885 is the mean of the 1880 and 1885 figures, and that for 1885–1890 is the mean of the 1885 and 1890 figures. The two five-year period totals fail to equal the decade totals in some instances because the three sets of figures were calculated using three different ratios with the ratios for the decade total equalling the mean of the two five-year ratios.
b   Population turnover is the sum of in- and out-migration. To estimate total turnover of individuals we multiplied the family turnover figures by five, since mean family size in Boston was 4.99 in 1880 and 5.00 in 1890. It is possible, of course, that migratory households were typically smaller than the mean, and indeed probable, since many were unmarried males. The staggering total individual turnover of 1,483,890, therefore, may be inflated. But the 296,778 family total is accurate, we believe, and we are certain from our analysis of persistence rates for married men with children that much of this turnover involved entire families, so that total individual turnover was at a minimum far above 296,778 for the decade, though possibly well below the 1,483,890 estimate.

The simple residual method of estimating net migration employed earlier indicated that less than 15 per cent of Boston's 1890 population was comprised of recent migrants to the community. In this respect, too, the net figures greatly underestimate the volatility of the Boston population. Two different and more satisfactory estimates reveal that the true proportion of recent newcomers in the population was more than twice that.

The first of these derives from an effort to trace in the 1890 city directory a sample of adult male Bostonians drawn from the 1880 U.S. Census, which disclosed that 64 per cent of them were still in the city in 1890; applying this persistence rate to the entire population would yield 232,217 people for 1890. In addition, there were children born in the city during the decade who were present to swell the population total in 1890. Through a calculation which utilized the total number of births in Boston during the decade, the number of deaths of children under ten, and an estimated out-migration rate for young children, we estimated that 47,059 of the 115,974 infants born in Boston in the 1880s were there to be counted by the census-taker in 1890.[20] Adding these

20 The 1890 population of Boston may be divided into three components: persons who had been living in the city since 1880 or earlier; individuals born in Boston since 1880 and still residing there in 1890; and migrants who had entered the community from elsewhere during the decade and remained there (the net total of in-migrants). The first of these components was estimated, through a persistence trace of 1880 residents, as 64 per cent of the 1880 population. The third could be gauged accurately if the second were known (1890 population minus the sum of 1880 persisters and surviving new-born children = net in-migration). Much depends, therefore, upon obtaining a valid estimate of the number of children born in Boston during the 1880s and remaining there in 1890; they are the key to a reasonably accurate estimate of net decadal in-migration to the city.

The unwary might conclude that the total number of births in Boston in the 1880s— 115,974—would be a satisfactory approximation of the size of this component of the population in 1890, but the true figure—47,059—was a mere 40 per cent of that. Many of the new-born died before 1890; many others moved away along with their parents. To estimate the magnitude of these two influences we made several assumptions. One was that the City Registrar's annual reports of births and deaths were accurate enough for our uses. Second, we assumed that 50 per cent of all deaths of children designated as "U.S.-born" were of children born in Boston. The State Censuses of 1885 and 1895 show that, of all U.S.-born persons residing in Boston, between 50 per cent and 60 per cent were born in Boston. We have used the lower figure as a conservative estimate of the corresponding proportion of children's deaths to assign to the category "born in Boston." Last, from our earlier analysis of changes in the city directory listings, we deduced an annual out-migration rate for 1880, 1885, and 1890 of about 16 per cent for Boston's families. For want of a better figure, we have applied this rate to children's cohorts in our estimate.

The method of producing the estimates was simple but tedious. For children born in Boston in 1880, we know the number of deaths of U.S.-born aged 1 year and under. For the years 1881–1884, we know the number of deaths of U.S.-born children aged 1 to 5, and for the years 1885–1889 we have the analogous figures for children aged 5 to 10. The mortality among the 1880 cohort through the decade would then be the sum of all deaths of Boston-born children (equal to half the native-born) in the following groups: for 1880, all aged under 1; for 1881, one-fifth of those aged 1 to 5; for 1882, one-fifth of those aged 1 to 5, etc., until 1885, when we shift to taking one-fifth of the deaths of children aged 5 to 10 years, continuing through to and including 1889. This produces for each year of the decade an estimate of the number of deaths of children born in Boston in 1880. The initial size of the cohort born in 1880 was 10,654; we then subtract the estimated deaths of Boston-born children in that year, 333, and 1,776, the estimated out-migration of one-sixth of the children. This leaves 8,545 as the size of the 1880 cohort at the start of 1881. Continuing the estimation process through to 1890 produces a residual for the 1880 cohort of 1,571. The procedure is then carried out for the 1881 cohort, starting with 1881 and going to 1890. When the residuals of all ten cohorts, 1880–1889, are summed, the total is 47,059.

children to the 232,217 persisters, we find that 279,276 of the 448,477 residents of Boston in 1890 had either been living in the city since 1880 or had been born there during the decade; the residual, 169,201, were migrants who had arrived in the 1880s and remained. That would mean that 37.7 per cent of the 1890 population of Boston was comprised of recent migrants.

Long after this estimate was first developed we stumbled upon some support for our argument from another quarter. To our surprise, we learned that the Massachusetts State Census of 1895 had inquired into length of residence in the state, though not in particular cities within it. These data were tabulated for Boston separately, and they indicated that 24.4 per cent of the city's population aged ten or more in 1895 had moved into the state since 1885.[21] What we want to know, however, is how many had moved into *Boston* during that interval, since residence in the state is not equivalent to residence in the city; a good many newcomers to Boston, after all, came from other parts of Massachusetts. To the 24.4 per cent of migrants from outside the state we would have to add some allowance for such intrastate migrants. No solid basis for an estimate of this migratory stream exists, but some clue may be gained from the fact that 8 per cent of the 1895 population of the city had been born in Massachusetts but outside of Boston. This figure is for the entire population, including young children who had had very little chance to migrate into the city; the proportion of intrastate migrants in the Boston population aged ten or more was doubtless significantly higher. There must, in addition, have been migrants born in other states or abroad who had moved into Massachusetts by 1885, but had only come to the city itself between 1886 and 1895. On the other hand, the 8 per cent figure pertains to individuals who moved to Boston at any time after their birth, and many must have done so more than ten years earlier. It is hard to believe that this last consideration was as potent as the influences biasing the estimate in the other direction, however, so that we would judge from this source that an absolute minimum of 32.4 per cent (24.4 per cent plus 8 per cent) and probably 35 to 40 per cent of the 1895 residents of Boston had moved into the community during the preceding decade, which fits nicely with the estimate for 1880–1890. Some guesswork could not be avoided in adjusting the figures from the 1895 State Census, but this second independent estimate increases our confidence in the first. A more

21 Massachusetts Bureau of Labor Statistics, *Census of the Commonwealth of Massachusetts, 1895. Volume II: Population and Social Statistics* (Boston, 1897), 333, 672, 790–791.

precise figure cannot be obtained, but it seems indisputable that about a third, and probably a little more, of the people living in Boston in 1890 had migrated into the community during the preceding decade.

Boston experienced only a modest population increase of 24 per cent between 1880 and 1890, and the commonly used vital statistics or residual method of estimating net migration makes it seem that the volume of migration to the community was similarly modest. Approximately 65,000 newcomers came into the city, and they comprised less than 15 per cent of its population at the end of the decade. But these undramatic conclusions are utterly erroneous. At least a third of the 1890 residents of Boston had come to the city within the past few years, and the total number of migrants who had entered the community at some point in the decade was not 65,000 but nearly 800,000, more than twice the total population of the city in 1880. Net population change in the city between 1880 and 1890 was on a modest scale, but only because two very powerful migratory currents flowing through the community nearly cancelled each other out, leaving only the small rivulet registered by the net figures.

Similar analyses of the changing Boston population from 1830 to 1890 reveal that the 1880s were by no means peculiar or deviant in this respect. The city grew from 61,000 to 448,000 over this sixty-year period, a net increase of 387,000. But the number of migrants entering Boston in those years was an amazing 3,325,000, eight and a half times the net population increase. It would take further spade work in other cities to be sure, but we strongly suspect that adding gross in-migration figures for New York, Philadelphia, Chicago, and hundreds of smaller cities would give a total far exceeding the total urban population of the United States, suggesting that the typical urban migrant went not to one city but to three or four (or perhaps a dozen) in the course of his wanderings.

Yet another revealing measure of the stability of the urban population may be gleaned from the city directories, for directory compilers normally indicated not only how many listings had been deleted in making up each new edition, but also how many households were still listed but at a new address within the city. Adding the proportion of names dropped and of listings with a change of address enables us to determine how many families were residentially stable in the sense that they lived at the same address for at least a year. Approximately 80 per cent of American families today remain in the same dwelling from one year to the next;[22] in Boston in the 1880s, Table 4 makes clear, hardly half did so. The annual residential stability rate ranged from a low of 40 per cent in 1882 to a high of 53 per cent in 1889, with 49 per cent the mean. Returning to the same dwelling after the passage of only 365 days, the city directory canvasser had less than a fifty-fifty chance of findings its former inhabitants living there. Not even in contemporary Los Angeles, supposedly the ultimate in residential instability, do people change their dwellings so frequently; only about a third of the population there moves annually.[23]

Table 4 Percentage of Listings Dropped, Changes of Address,
and Unchanged Listings in Boston, 1881–1890

YEAR	LISTINGS DROPPED FROM PRECEDING CITY DIRECTORY	LISTINGS WITH NEW BOSTON ADDRESS	LISTINGS RESI- DENTIALLY STABLE
1881	20	31	49
1882	21	39	40
1883	20	29	51
1884	21	29	50
1885	20	29	51
1886	20	30	50
1887	20	33	47
1888	20	34	46
1889	20	27	53
1890	20	29	51

It should be evident from all this that if Boston was at all typical of nineteenth-century American cities—and one would imagine that if it was a deviant case, it was deviant in having a *less* fluid and volatile population than more rapidly-growing cities like New York or Chicago —we must think about the process of past urban growth in quite a different way, with a heightened sense of the incredible fluidity of the urban as well as the rural population.

The typical city-dweller of nineteenth-century America had not been born in the city in which he resided, nor was he likely to live out

22 Donald J. Bogue, *The Population of the United States* (New York, 1959), 384.
23 U.S. Bureau of the Census, *Eighteenth Census of the United States: 1960, General Social and Economic Characteristics* (Washington, 1961), Vol. I, Part 6, California.

his entire life there. But if city-dwellers in general were a mobile breed, some city-dwellers were more mobile than others.

It is widely believed that immigrants and poor people were commonly clustered in ghettos in the nineteenth-century city, forming a permanent proletariat of sorts. An abundance of impressionistic evidence in support of this view may be gleaned from the literature of the era. Thus the testimony of Francis A. Walker in 1876:

> If we consider the population of the more squalid sections of any city, we can only conclude that . . . the more miserable men are, the less . . . likely they are to seek and find a better place in society and industry. Their poverty, their ignorance, their superstitious fears and, perhaps more than all, the apathy that comes with a broken spirit, bind them in their place and to their fate. *Such populations do not migrate; they abide in their lot; sinking lower in helplessness, hopelessness and squalor. . . .*[24]

Immigrants were thought especially vulnerable to entrapment:

> . . . with no small proportion of our vast foreign element, occupation is determined by a location that is accidental . . . these people are doing what they are doing because they are where they are. . . . There is a tendency at every harbor which lies at the debouche of a river, to the formation of a bar composed of mud and sand brought down by the current which yet has not the force to scour its channel clear out to deep water. And in much the same way, there is a tendency at every port of immigration to the accumulation, from the failure of the immigrating force, of large deposits of more or less helpless labor. . . .[25]

That there were indeed neighborhoods of the nineteenth-century city which at various points in time had large concentrations of particular ethnic and occupational groups cannot be denied (though their prevalence may have been exaggerated).[26] But computation of indices of residential concentration from aggregate data provides no valid basis for inferences about the experiences of individuals over time. Were the Irish of Boston in 1850 trapped in their ghettos? Plotting measures of residential concentration for the Irish in the city two or three decades later provides no answer, for we do not know that many of the individuals who comprised "the Irish of Boston in 1850" were in fact

24 Francis A. Walker, *The Wages Question: A Treatise on Wages and the Wages Class* (New York, 1876), 188. Italics added.
25 *Ibid.*, 181–183.
26 The leading study, though scanty on the nineteenth century, is Stanley Lieberson, *Ethnic Patterns in American Cities* (Glencoe, 1963). Cf. the excellent critique of the ghetto hypothesis by Sam B. Warner and Colin B. Burke, "Cultural Change and the Ghetto," *Journal of Contemporary History*, IV (1969), 173–187.

present to be counted as "the Irish of Boston in 1870." Direct tracing of individuals is necessary to deal with the question of how confining the ethnic or class ghettos of the city actually were.

Much more work needs to be done on these issues before we can speak with great assurance, but two tentative conclusions may be drawn from the evidence now available. One is that men on the lower rungs of the class ladder were less rooted, not more rooted, than their betters. Persistence rates for blue-collar workers were generally well below those for white-collar workers, with unskilled and semi-skilled laborers the least stable of all. Second, there seems to be little evidence of ethnic subcultures which exerted a sufficient hold over their members to yield unusually high persistence rates for the group. Indeed, there is some indication that ethnic minorities were more transient than WASPs of comparable economic status.

In support of the former proposition we might cite the following evidence. Seventy-six per cent of the upper white-collar workers (professionals and proprietors or managers of large enterprises) in Boston in 1880 remained in the city in 1890, as opposed to 68 per cent of the lower white-collar employees, 63 per cent of the skilled workers, and 59 per cent of the unskilled or semi-skilled. Of a sample of migrants to Boston from rural New England taken from the 1870 Census, 62 per cent of the upper white-collar, 50 per cent of the lower white-collar, 34 per cent of the skilled, and 32 per cent of the unskilled and semi-skilled workers persisted through the decade.[27] For second-generation Irish youths in Boston in the same years, the figures were 63 per cent for lower white-collar workers (there were no upper white-collar workers among them), 48 per cent for skilled, and 39 per cent for unskilled and semi-skilled employees. Comparable data for the white males of Atlanta between 1870 and 1880 show a persistence rate of 50 per cent for those in white-collar positions, but only 39 per cent for the skilled and 30 per cent for the unskilled or semi-skilled.[28] A full report on persistence by the broad occupational class in Poughkeepsie is not yet available, but the data for selected occupations look fully consistent with this pattern. Fifty-six per cent of the doctors in the city in 1850 were still there in 1860, 43 per cent of the lawyers, and 59 per cent of the merchants, as opposed to 25 per cent of the day laborers, 26 per cent of the gardeners, 17 per cent of the bakers, 35 per cent of the blacksmiths, 36 per cent of

27 Lester Lenoff, "Occupational Mobility Among Yankee Immigrants to Boston, 1870–1880" (unpub. seminar paper, Brandeis University, 1969).
28 Computed from Hopkins, "Occupational and Geographic Mobility."

the painters, and 36 per cent of the carpenters. Comparable figures for 1870–1880 are 59 per cent for doctors, 58 per cent for lawyers, and 45 per cent for merchants, as opposed to 30 per cent for laborers, 34 per cent for gardeners, 34 per cent for bakers, 40 per cent for blacksmiths, 41 per cent for painters, and 40 per cent for carpenters.[29]

As for the matter of ethnic ghettos, we have yet to find a city in which most members of any minority group remained for long in the community at all, much less within the confines of their particular neighborhood or neighborhoods. Close examination of the Fifth Ward of Providence, Rhode Island, the Irish ghetto of the city, reveals that only a quarter of its 1850 residents were still to be found in Providence in 1860, and the 1860–1870 persistence rate was little higher—31 per cent.[30] Only 21 per cent of the Irish in Poughkeepsie at mid-century survived for ten years in the community, 24 per cent of the English and Scottish immigrants, and 29 per cent of the Germans, as compared to 34 per cent of the native-born Americans.[31] The Irish laborers of Newburyport had lower persistence rates than their Yankee counterparts both for 1850–1860 and 1860–1870.[32] Some 40 per cent of the foreign-born residents of Atlanta in 1870 remained in the city in 1880, as opposed to 45 per cent of the native-born; by 1896, 18 per cent of the immigrants were still traceable, and 23 per cent of the natives.[33] In Boston earlier, from 1830 to 1860, native-born persons stayed in the city, on an average, two to three times as long as did foreign-born persons.

It would, however, be going too far to conclude, as these figures would suggest, that immigrants were notably *more* transient than natives in the nineteenth-century city. That seems to have been true around mid-century, when the first heavy migratory waves were breaking on American shores, but after a decade or two there seems to have been a settling-in process. The Irish laborers of Newburyport had a slightly higher persistence rate than the native-born in the 1870s.[34] Both the Irish and the Germans of Poughkeepsie were a little more rooted than the natives in that decade, though the English and Scottish remained

29 Griffen, "Workers Divided."
30 Robert Wheeler, "The Fifth-Ward Irish: Mobility at Mid-Century" (unpub. seminar paper, Brown University, 1967).
31 Griffen, "Workers Divided."
32 Data developed for, but not included in, Thernstrom, *Poverty and Progress*.
33 Computed from data in Hopkins, "Occupational and Geographic Mobility."
34 Unpublished data gathered in research for Thernstrom, *Poverty and Progress*.

more volatile.[35] In Boston in the 1880s there were no consistent ethnic differences in persistence once occupational level was held constant; first- and second-generation immigrants were somewhat more transient than old-stock Americans, but only because they were more heavily concentrated in lower-status occupations which had higher transiency rates generally. Still, the overriding fact to emphasize is that immigrants and their children were at least as transient as, and at some points more transient than, the American norm, which is to say that they were very transient indeed, so much so that the familiar image of the closed ghetto, sealed off from the rest of society, must be considerably revised.[36]

If the flow of migration *out of* the nineteenth-century American city was of such massive proportions—with a city of 363,000 inhabitants dispatching from it more than 690,000 out-migrants in the course of a decade—obviously it is important to inquire what happened to the typical transient after he left the city in which he was first observed. As far as we know, this question has never been explored systematically. This is hardly surprising, for there are no historical records which conveniently draw the necessary information together in one place.[37] Instead, the patient sifting of an awesome mass of materials

35 Griffen, "Workers Divided."

36 The closest thing to an exception to this proposition which has yet been discovered is the Negro community of Atlanta in the 1870s. Hopkins found blacks persisting more frequently than native whites or immigrants, notably more so when their disproportionate concentration in low-status occupations with generally low persistence rates was taken into account. Of the Negro unskilled or semi-skilled workers in Atlanta in 1870 46 per cent were still present ten years later, but only 25 per cent of the natives and 36 per cent of the immigrants; for skilled craftsmen the black figure was 77 per cent as opposed to 38 per cent for natives and 40 per cent for immigrants. Still, less than half of Negroes in the city remained there a decade, so that even this ghetto was far from closed. It is likely that the black population of Northern cities in this period was exceptionally volatile. Research in progress by Herbert G. Gutman and Laurence Glasco reveals that only 12 per cent of the Negroes living in Buffalo, New York, at the time of the state census of 1855 were still there in 1875. Of the adult Negro males recorded in Boston by the 1880 Census, little more than half (56 per cent) were to be found at the end of *one year*; Elizabeth H. Pleck, "The Black Family in Boston: 1880" (unpub. seminar paper, Brandeis University, 1969).

37 A partial exception, as yet unexploited by researchers, is found in the manuscript schedules of the U.S. Census for the State of Wisconsin in the 1850–1880 period, which apparently were indexed by W.P.A. workers in the 1930s. This should make it relatively easy to track down migrants from Wisconsin communities who moved elsewhere in the state. It is possible that similar indexes were prepared in other states as well, a question on which we seek further enlightenment. Another source which could be utilized to track

is required to obtain even a few clues about where the out–migrants went and what they did in their new places of residence.

A pilot effort in this direction carried out by the junior author utilized four principal sources to locate migrants who left Boston in the 1830–1860 period. After 1850, city directories began listing commuters' suburban residences, and cemetery records provided some information. More important was the state registration system for vital statistics established in 1841, which listed alphabetically all persons who died in the Commonwealth of Massachusetts. Finally, there were the manuscript schedules of the U.S. Census for 1850 and 1860; the schedules for 128 suburban cities and towns in the state were searched for sample members who disappeared from Boston in the antebellum years.

Three samples, totalling 1,155 individuals, were drawn from the Boston census schedules for 1830, 1840, and 1850. From 14 to 17 per cent of them died in the decade following the census, and 38 to 48 per cent were still to be found in Boston after ten years. Between 5 and 9 per cent were positively identified as having settled in other Massachusetts communities. From 31 to 38 per cent of each sample, therefore, was left unaccounted for at the decade's end and must be presumed to have left the state altogether.[38] (Some of those who left the state would, of course, have died by the decade's end; if their mortality rate was like that of sample members who stayed in Boston, about 30 per cent of each sample was alive and residing in another state by then.) That the great preponderance of migrants from Boston moved at a minimum more than 40 miles (the distance to the nearest state boundary) is startling in light of contemporary demographic studies which suggest that the bulk of migration today is in short-distance movement. This hints at the interesting possibility that migratory patterns in the mid-nineteenth century were fundamentally different from those later, that once people then had pulled up stakes at all—which, as we have already

down out-migrants is the manuscript school censuses of the state of Michigan; Sam B. Warner informs us that these indicate the projected destination of families moving out of each school district. Again there may be comparable materials for other states, now moldering in obscurity. The junior author plans extensive further research on the nature of out-imigration.

38 Some of these missing individuals may simply have been missed by the tracing process. This is particularly likely with out-migrants of Irish descent, since the Michael Murphys, John Rileys, etc. were nearly impossible to distinguish from each other in the sources. This difficulty was not of a magnitude, however, to throw into doubt the main conclusions of the analysis.

seen, they were far more likely to do than is the case today—they were also more likely to travel long distances to their new destinations, leap-frogging over all of the intervening territory. Possibly the lure of the West was involved here, a conjecture which finds some support in aggregated census data showing that migrants from several eastern, densely-populated states, including Massachusetts, were more likely to move to non-contiguous states in 1870 than they were later in the century.[39] We do not know with any certainty whether men who disappeared from Boston went to other cities or to rural areas—there were cities in the West, and there were rural areas even in heavily industrialized contiguous states—but it seems likely that the shift indicates that ever larger numbers of them moved to other cities as the century wore on.

Which types of people were most likely to leave antebellum Boston? There was a distinct tendency for migration to be economically selective. Well-to-do proprietors and professionals tended to be under-represented in the out-migration stream for most of the period, and unskilled and menial workers over-represented. Possession of property in the city discouraged migration from it, as Table 5 indicates. Men who were not assessed were from two to five more times as likely to leave Boston as to stay there; those who had a little property (under $200)

39 Kuznets et al., Population Redistribution, I, 249–298, presents a series of Census data for the states of residence, 1870–1950, of native whites born in each of the states and in the District of Columbia. They provide totals not only for those born in each state and still living in that state, but also for those residing in contiguous states and in all states other than that of birth. If the distances to which persons tended to move from their homes decreased as the nineteenth century went on, as we hypothesize, then we would expect a rise in the proportion of out-migrating individuals who had moved to contiguous states as opposed to states farther from their state of birth. When we calculate the proportion of persons born in a given state and residing in a contiguous state to persons born in that state and residing in all other states, for all states, 1870–1900, we find that the proportion rose consistently in sixteen states and fell consistently in nine. The states for which our conjecture was borne out were Arizona, Connecticut, Delaware, Maryland, Massachusetts, Montana, New Hampshire, New Jersey, New York, North Carolina, Oklahoma, Rhode Island, South Carolina, Texas, Vermont, and Wyoming. The nine states exhibiting a regular drop in the proportion were Alabama, Florida, Kentucky, Mississippi, Nebraska, New Mexico, Tennessee, Virginia, and Washington. It is interesting to note the number of eastern, relatively densely-populated states in the first group and the preponderance of southern and more sparsely-populated states in the second.
    Figures for analogous data for 1850 and 1860 are not available in tabulated form except for state-by-state totals. Accordingly, considerable manipulation of the 1850 and 1860 census results will be required before we shall be able to determine whether any of these trends were under way before 1870, and whether they remain consistent back that far. These calculations will be prosecuted, and the results reported in time.

were about as likely to stay as to leave up to 1850, and somewhat more likely to remain after that. Persons with holdings in the $200 to $1,000 range were from one-and-a-half to two times as apt to remain in Boston as to leave, and those with $1,000 to $10,000 in property were twice as likely to remain as to go in the 1830s, three times in the 1840s, but only four-fifths in the 1850s—a remarkable turnabout testifying to the strong middle-class movement to Boston's suburbs that began in the late 1840s. The wealthy, with over $10,000 in property, were from four to six times as likely to remain in Boston as to move away.

Table 5 Property Holdings of Persisting and Out-migrating Bostonians, 1830–1860, in Per Cent

SAMPLE AND CHARACTERISTIC	N	NOT ASSESSED		ASSESSMENT GROUP			
		MALE	FEMALE	UNDER $200	$200–$1,000	$1,001–$10,000	OVER $10,000
1830							
Persisting	163	9	15	30	20	19	8
Out-migrating	156	22	19	33	14	10	2
1840							
Persisting	183	5	8	31	21	27	9
Out-migrating	148	24	16	33	16	9	1
1850							
Persisting	145	17	7	44	12	8	12
Out-migrating	180	35	12	33	7	9	3

We may now ask where out-migrants from Boston went, and how they fared in their new destinations. Only 22 per cent of the sample members who disappeared from the city could later be identified as residents of other Massachusetts communities; nearly four-fifths of them, therefore, apparently left the state altogether. Migrants who could be traced elsewhere in Massachusetts were not a random slice of the entire migratory pool; they tended to be of higher occupational rank than transients moving out of the state, they were more likely to own property, and few of them were foreign-born. These traceable migrants moved relatively short distances within the state, with half of them in the 1830 sample and three-quarters of those in the 1840 and 1850 samples relocating within ten miles of downtown Boston.

The most interesting and important question to ask is whether migrants from the city found greater opportunities for personal advancement elsewhere, as popular folklore about Americans on the move and on the make would suggest. Our answer is severely limited, of course, because four-fifths of the migrants from Boston could not be traced, and that four-fifths included disproportionate numbers of laborers, immigrants, and men without property. It would be foolish to assume that their post-migration experience was necessarily like that of the select group of traceable migrants; there are good grounds for suspecting that it was not, and that many of these men continued to drift about as part of a floating proletariat. But it is noteworthy that the special group of migrants who could be located elsewhere in Massachusetts seems to have fared somewhat better than their counterparts who remained behind in Boston. Of the members of the 1850 sample who were still in Boston in 1860, one in five significantly increased his property holdings during the decade, about two-thirds remained at the same level, and about one-ninth suffered some loss. But of the out-migrants from the 1850 sample who were found in other communities, twice as many (or two-fifths) had accumulated additional property by 1860. Of the sample members who owned no property at all in 1850, 22 per cent of those who stayed in Boston, but 44 per cent of those who departed from the city, obtained a property stake during the decade. Although the migration stream from the city was on the whole selective of the least successful (Table 5), that portion of the stream which flowed into other nearby Massachusetts communities contained disproportionate numbers of men who had talent, ambition, ruthlessness, and whatever other traits brought economic success in mid-nineteenth-century America. We emphasize again that this group of traceable migrants was a rather small minority of all of the men who passed through Boston in the antebellum years, but for them at least American folklore about geographical mobility and success had some validity.

A number of tentative conclusions about urban population mobility in nineteenth-century America may be advanced on the basis of the evidence surveyed in this paper:

1. Very high rates of population mobility prevailed not only on the western frontier but on the urban frontier as well. Comparable studies for other countries will be needed to establish whether or not rates of spatial mobility in the United States were uniquely high, as

American legend would have it, but the absolute figures are certainly striking.[40]

2. The largest cities of the period seemingly had a somewhat more stable population than smaller communities in general, but only because it was possible to move a great deal and still remain within their boundaries. It is very doubtful that persistence rates within smaller units that comprised the metropolis—South Boston, let us say—were much higher than in cities of comparable area.

3. To estimate the fluidity of a city's population from *net* population changes is like assuming that the fraction of an iceberg projecting above the surface is the whole. Net figures register not the total flow of individuals into and out of the city, but only the magnitude of the difference between the two migratory streams.

4. While the United States might in many respects have been "a nation of loosely connected islands" as late as the 1870s, as Robert Wiebe argues, small islands in which face-to-face relationships predominated, there was a dizzying rate of population turnover well before that time in any community which has as yet been carefully studied. Possibly this movement was largely island-hopping, as it were, in which newcomers were attracted to communities and neighborhoods very much like those they left behind, but in any event it suggests that "interaction among these islands" in a simple demographic sense was far more common than Wiebe's otherwise persuasive synthesis indicates.

5. The concept of the closed ethnic or class ghetto clearly needs re-examination and empirical testing. Poor people, poor immigrants especially, may have been hopelessly entangled in the spider's web of poverty in many instances, but it is doubtful that many were permanently trapped in particular slum areas. A majority do not even seem to have remained within the confines of any one city for as long as ten years.

6. Long-distance or leapfrogging mobility seems to have been

---

40 There are fragments of valuable comparative evidence in Weber's *The Growth of Cities*, especially in Chapter IV, which Weber employed to attack the parochial notion that Americans were the only migratory people in the world. Probably he went too far in denying American uniqueness, as some of his own evidence suggests (see, for example, 259, 264, and 274). It is to be hoped that the research along these lines now going on in Europe will soon permit further exploration of this issue. For a taste of some promising work in progress in England, see E. A. Wrigley (ed.), *An Introduction to English Historical Demography* (London, 1966); D. V. Glass and D. E. C. Eversley, *Population in History: Essays in Historical Demography* (London, 1965); H. J. Dyos (ed.), *The Study of Urban History* (London, 1968). The paucity of information currently available, however, forced us to confine ourselves to the American scene in the present paper.

more common than short-distance movement in the antebellum period. There is some indication that in the late nineteenth century the pattern was shifting toward shorter moves, probably moves to nearby cities.

7. While migration out of contemporary cities is largely in response to the stimulus of superior economic opportunities elsewhere, with relatively well-educated and affluent individuals somewhat over-represented in the migratory stream, the incessant and massive movement of people out of the nineteenth-century city may have been largely of a different character. Certainly there were migrants from Boston who sought—and found—greater opportunity in their new destinations. But the men we were able to trace from antebellum Boston to their later residences held better jobs before they left, owned more property, and were more often of native American stock than the typical migrant. It is possible—though by no means certain—that the large majority of out-migrants who disappeared from our view altogether had a radically different experience, that they formed a class of permanent transients who continued to be buffeted about by the vicissitudes of the casual labor market. The likely political consequences of this state of affairs have been sketched elsewhere;[41] suffice it to say here that high rates of transiency for blue-collar workers presumably left them alienated but invisible and politically impotent, and minimized the likelihood of effective organized efforts to reshape capitalist society.

Any or all of these conclusions might, of course, be overturned or significantly modified by future research. The spectrum of cities which have been examined from a demographic perspective is still very narrow. Too much of the work done so far deals with eastern, indeed with New England, communities; the West and Midwest are conspicuously absent from the list, and the South is represented only by Atlanta. Smaller cities have attracted more attention than major metropolitan centers, because they are more easily studied, but convenience is no gauge of importance.[42] The knotty, but in principle not insoluble,

41 Thernstrom, "Working Class Social Mobility in Industrial America," in Melvin Richter (ed.), *Essays in Theory and History* (Cambridge, Mass., 1970).
42 Richard Sennett's *Families Against the City* (Cambridge, Mass., 1970), a study of a Chicago middle-class neighborhood in the late nineteenth century, is a significant exception. Some of the main findings are summarized in Sennett's essay, "Middle Class Families and Urban Violence," in Thernstrom and Sennett, *Nineteenth-Century Cities*. Work in this vein is beginning in Los Angeles; for a preliminary report, see Stephan Thernstrom, "The Growth of Los Angeles in Historical Perspective: Myth and Reality," Institute of Government and Public Affairs, University of California, Los Angeles, 1970 (mimeo.). There is a valuable study of "Residential Mobility in Omaha, 1880-1920," by Howard Chudacoff (unpub. Ph.D. thesis, University of Chicago, 1970).
2—J.I.H.

question of what happened to out-migrants after they left the city cries out for further systematic study. Much of the work that has been done is technically rather primitive, aimed at developing simple decadal persistence rates. Finer-grained analyses of population movements on an annual basis, using some of the methods we have employed in our discussion of Boston in the 1880s, may suggest that differences between cities were more significant than appears at present.

There is, however, unfinished business more important than further data gathering in other cities, or the development of more refined methods of estimating demographic parameters, important though we believe those tasks to be. Quantitative studies of grassroots social phenomena can help us to grasp basic social processes which left little imprint on conventional historical sources—newspapers, diaries, legislative debates, etc.—thus freeing us, to some extent, from our customary dependence upon materials reflecting the beliefs of the articulate classes who controlled the media of the era. But to trace out the implications of the startling demographic facts disclosed here we must fit our findings into the broad social context to which they pertain, and relate them to less readily measurable features of nineteenth-century urban life. Statistical analysis of historical data may be useful not so much for settling old questions as for posing new ones. If American city-dwellers were as restless and footloose as our evidence suggests, how was any cultural continuity—or even the appearance of it—maintained? A historian describing the Knights of Labor in its heyday, the 1880s, remarks that "so rapidly did its membership change" that "what appeared to be an organization . . . was in fact more like a procession."[43] Likewise, it might be said, American society in the period considered here was more like a procession than a stable social order. How did this social order cohere at all?

This is not the place to attempt an answer to that formidable question. We will content ourselves with two observations. One is that certain aspects of this seemingly unsettling, chaotic social process which kept so many Americans ever on the move were in fact stabilizing. For some—like the traceable out-migrants from antebellum Boston— migration brought economic success, and promoted confidence that the society rewarded men on the basis of merit. Others may not have been so fortunate, but the floating urban proletariat we believe to have

43 George W. Coleman, "Labor and the Labor Movement, 1860–1930," in A. B. Hart (ed.), *The Commonwealth History of Massachusetts* (Boston, 1933), V, 433.

existed was so transient as to prevent the growth of feelings of collective solidarity.[44] Poor people moved about so rapidly, indeed, that substantial numbers of them must have been legally disenfranchised by the electoral laws of many states, which required a year's residence in the state and six months in the city before voting.

A second observation is that, as Berthoff has suggested, many features of nineteenth-century American society are best understood as efforts to overcome or offset the "excessive" mobility of the era.[45] We are not sure that population mobility was "excessive," and are distressed that Berthoff made no effort to measure mobility systematically, but his speculations about the social consequences of mobility are provocative. Doubtless it is significant that it was precisely during the period which we have analyzed here that Americans became frantic joiners of voluntary associations, lacking as they did traditional ties to particular communities. It was an era in which loyalty to political party and interest in national elections (as indicated by voter turnout rates) were at a high point. Party, that is to say, may have been a substitute for community as a source of personal identity. Even the desperate assertions of communal loyalty of the period, like the Iowa picnics of contemporary California, testify not to the strength of surviving communal loyalties but to the felt lack of community.

Research of the kind reported here deepens our understanding of some key facets of nineteenth-century social history, and dispels some common misconceptions that derive from uncritical acceptance of literary evidence, but it cannot by itself resolve the larger issues which it raises. To do that will require both a sure grasp of the demographic facts and an ample measure of the knowledge that comes from a mastery of traditional historical sources.

---

44 For further discussion, see Thernstrom, "Working Class Social Mobility," and the works cited there.

45 Rowland Berthoff, "The American Social Order: A Conservative Hypothesis," *American Historical Review*, LXV (1960), 495–514. For further suggestive discussion of the consequences of population mobility, see George W. Pierson, "The Moving American," *Yale Review*, XLIV (1954), 99–112, though this paper too is marred by unsubstantiated, and in some cases mistaken, assumptions about the demographic facts.

Virginia Yans McLaughlin

Patterns of Work and Family Organization:
Buffalo's Italians
In their discussions of industrialization
and urbanization, some social scientists have described the family as
a dependent variable. Implicitly or explicitly, they view technical
and economic organization as the prime determinant of family organization.[1] Not surprisingly, power relationships within the family
are also frequently considered to be dependent upon economic roles
within the larger society. A common assumption, for example, is
that because the industrial city offers work opportunities to women,
they can become less reliant upon their husbands and fathers, especially
if the latter are unemployed. And so, the argument continues, female
employment outside the home encourages the decline of "traditional"
family relationships in which the chief power and control reside with
the male. In extreme cases, the unemployed male deserts his family
altogether and female-headed households result.

Not all social scientists, of course, agree with this interpretation.
Historians have a specific task in this dispute—to seek empirical evidence which will sustain or weaken generalizations concerning the
dependent and causal relationships between the family, urbanization,
and industrialization. As Goode put it, one of our difficulties is a
"simple lack of information about the past history of family systems
under varying conditions of urbanization and industrialization."[2]

In line with Goode's suggestion, this paper attempts to add to
our knowledge of family history by examining the relationship between female occupational patterns and family organization among
south Italians in Buffalo from about 1900 to 1930. It questions the
idea that the family should be viewed simply as a dependent variable

Virginia Yans McLaughlin is Assistant Professor of History at Princeton University.
She is revising her dissertation, "Like the Fingers of the Hand: The Family and Community Life of First-Generation Italian-Americans in Buffalo, New York," for publication. This paper was originally presented before the American Historical Association,
Boston, 1970. The author would like to thank Allen F. Davis and J. Stanley Lemons
for their criticisms.

1 For a discussion of the relationship between the family, urbanization, and industrialization, see William J. Goode, *The Family* (Englewood Cliffs, N.J., 1964), 110;
Sidney M. Greenfield, "Industrialization and the Family in Sociological Theory,"
American Journal of Sociology, LXVII (1961), 312–314.
2 William J. Goode, "The Process of Role Bargaining in the Impact of Urbanization
and Industrialization on Family Systems," *Current Sociology*, XII (1963–64), 1.

by demonstrating that female assumption of new economic functions did not necessarily alter family power arrangements or disrupt the "traditional" family.

Any historian attempting to deal with working-class families immediately confronts the problem of documentation. Until recently, scholars have relied upon the reports of reformers and social workers for evidence concerning "the inarticulate." Thus, we have viewed working-class history through a filter of middle-class values. In order to overcome this problem, as well as the scarcity of literary sources concerning the family, historians have increasingly relied upon manuscript censuses and other statistical data. Much, but not all, of the argument presented in this paper is based upon such evidence, and I should caution the reader concerning its limitations. With the help of census materials, we can inform ourselves about the percentage of husbandless families, of unemployed males, and of employed wives. On the basis of these formal indices, inferences can be drawn regarding possible power relationships within the family. Statistics concerning household organization, however, cannot tell us to what degree traditional arrangements were being strained without actually being eliminated, nor can they describe the quality and "normal" tensions of family life. The picture that emerges tends to be static: If the family were broken, we can assume conflicts occurred. But if a family remained together, we cannot conversely assume that it did so free of tension. This is a problem, especially with relatively stable groups such as Buffalo's south Italians, who did not exhibit extreme family pathology in the process of becoming assimilated into American society. Statistics simply do not permit absolute conclusions concerning conflict and change among Italian families remaining together. But female occupational arrangements can tell something about family power alignments. Buffalo's south Italians favored conservative female employment patterns, patterns which usually kept women working at home or under relatives' supervision despite possibilities of better pay and opportunities elsewhere. These occupational styles, it will be argued, are a strong indication that patriarchal control continued.

An examination of south Italian families within the context of one city, Buffalo, makes one thing abundantly clear. The usual question—"What is the impact of 'urban-industrial life' upon the family?" —is much too general, too imprecise. The class and ethnic identity of the families in question, as well as the type of city and range of industrial development existing in the communities under consideration, must be specified because each can play a critical part in determining the family's relationship to the social order. First, in some cases, ethnic background and associated cultural ideals had an important impact upon the way immigrant families responded to their new environment. Buffalo's south Italian women, for example, expressed, and acted upon, a decided preference for occupations which permitted minimal strain upon their traditional familial arrangements. In this way, Old World family values could continue to operate effectively even within an advanced industrial city such as Buffalo. Other options were available, and other ethnic groups took them. This clearly suggests that south Italian values played an important part in determining family work patterns; in other words, the family acted as an independent variable. Some may wish to argue that immigrant family values, not the family itself, were the prime determinant here. Such an argument makes a strict distinction between the family as a formal structure and the system of values, norms, rights, and obligations associated with it. Although such a distinction is useful in some cases, in this paper values and organization are considered together as parts of the family as a social institution.

In discussing the relationships between economic and familial organization, it should also be noted that actually available work opportunities define the perimeters of behavior. In a small city dominated by one industry, the relationships between family and economy should be relatively clear. In the early twentieth century, for example, Homestead, Pennsylvania was a typical steel mill town, offering work to men on a fairly regular basis. Women could find employment only occasionally. Therefore, the possibilities for varying family occupational patterns were obviously limited: In Homestead, the overwhelming majority of working-class families adopted the attitude that men should be the breadwinners and that women should contribute to the family economy through their housekeeping skills, and not by leaving the home to work.[3] In a cotton mill town, another type of one-industry city, we would expect to find women from needy families working; ethnic or cultural biases against female employment would probably be modified to meet the family's economic needs. In short, in one-industry towns, family occupational patterns would ultimately be determined by that industry regardless of cultural preferences. In larger, highly diversified manufacturing centers

3 Margaret F. Byington, "The Family in a Typical Mill Town," *American Journal of Sociology*, XIV (1909), 648–659.

such as Buffalo, a variety of economic opportunities for both men and women existed; despite the city's emphasis on heavy industry women could, and did, find work. In such cities, the relationship between occupational patterns and family organization was, as we shall see, correspondingly much more complex. The nature of work opportunities permitted freer expression of cultural preferences concerning women's work role, and Old World family values could operate easily despite the urban-industrial context.

Finally, it should be emphasized that the subjects being considered, south Italian immigrants, were "working-class." I use that term here to refer not only to their occupational status as an unskilled, frequently unemployed group, but also to their relatively stable life style and culture, much of which represented a survival from traditional European peasant life.[4] In such families, the occupational positions of husband and wife are frequently related to family structure. Hence, our original question regarding the family's status as a dependent or an independent variable is raised once again. Most social scientists argue that working-class and lower-class family structures are dependent upon occupational arrangements. They frequently cite unusual work patterns, for example, as a cause for family disorganization. The Moynihan report is a case in point. It stressed male employment difficulties in conjunction with more stable female employment as a key cause for male desertion and consequent female control of the family.[5] Some historians similarly suggest that disrupted preindustrial work patterns upset family stability among first-generation immigrants. The move to industrial America supposedly caused radical changes in the traditional male-dominated family economy and hence forced a restructuring in family roles and relationships.[6]

Although this model appears logical enough, it is not in agreement with historical fact. Buffalo's south Italians provide a fine example.

4 Herbert Gans, *The Urban Villagers: Group and Class in the Life of Italian-Americans* (Glencoe, 1962), 250, views working-class culture as a "continuation of European peasant culture." S. M. Miller and Frank Riessman, "The Working Class Subculture: A New View," *Social Problems*, IX (1961), 90, 95, correctly emphasize the distinction between working- and lower-class culture, a distinction of which the author is aware. Although white immigrants shared many of the hardships which today's urban poor experience, I think it is best to place them in the working-class category because of their traditional peasant background, much of which survived immigration.
5 Daniel P. Moynihan, "The Negro Family: The Case for National Action," in Lee Rainwater and William L. Yancey (eds.), *The Moynihan Report and the Politics of Controversy* (Cambridge, Mass., 1967), 41-124.
6 Oscar Handlin, *The Uprooted* (New York, 1951), 228ff., 239 takes this position.

Because tradition bestowed upon the mother great prestige, authority, and power (frequently including control of the household budget), south Italian peasant family organization was not purely patriarchal. Male superiority and paternal control, however, were the norm. To this degree at least, the south Italian family resembled the traditional peasant form described by Handlin in *The Uprooted*.[7] The New World's industrial work patterns, however, did not destroy it. Specifically, women leaving the home to work did not necessarily cause an erosion of male control. This was true throughout the decades under consideration, despite the existence of certain female prerogatives in south Italian familial culture which could have emerged during times of family crisis, such as periods of male unemployment.

In southern Italy economic functions and family functions were closely integrated. Tradition required Italian men, the majority of them poor peasants without farms of their own, to support their families; children contributed their work in the fields or at home; wives ran their households, and, from this area, most of their rights derived. But the basis for each person's status within the family was *not* purely economic. Thus, strong cultural traditions sustained male authority despite seasonal or year-round unemployment. Although wife and children worked outside the home at harvest time in Sicily and more often elsewhere, the father's domination over family affairs remained unchallenged. Apparently this "family constellation" was strong enough to endure periods of male unemployment in America when women worked.[8] Consequently, family disorganization among Italians (measured by male desertion and non-support, at least) remained relatively rare, and female-controlled families were unusual. This appears more remarkable given the existence of certain female privileges in south Italian culture.[9] The point is that male authority

7 *Ibid.*; Leonard Moss and Walter Thomson, "The South Italian Family: Literature and Observation," *Human Organization*, XVIII (1959), 38, quote an old Italian proverb testifying to the mother's importance: "If the father should die, the family would suffer; if the mother should die, the family ceases to exist." Although the two sources of authority were constantly clashing, the father was generally able to assert himself, "receiving his main support," according to Covello, "from the elevated status of the male in general." See Leonard Covello, "The Social Background of the Italo-American School Child: A Study of the Southern Italian Family Mores and Their Effect on the School Situation in Italy and America," unpub. Ph.D. thesis (New York University, 1944), 347.
8 Gans, *The Urban Villagers*, 240–241.
9 Covello, "Italo-American School Child," 328ff., 336, 378. See also Phyllis Williams, *South Italian Folkways in Europe and America* (New Haven, 1938), 76–77.

did not depend entirely upon fulfillment of economic obligations; therefore, when a woman co-opted the male's economic function in whole or in part by becoming a wage-earner, she did not necessarily obtain greater bargaining power and so tip the balance of family authority in her favor.

Despite a potentially disruptive work situation, Buffalo's Italian men performed exceedingly well as husbands and fathers. Until the 1920s brought slightly improved conditions, the majority worked in low-paying construction, railroad, and other seasonal outdoor occupations; most were unemployed six or more months a year. This condition was not peculiar only to Buffalo Italians. Outdoor laborers all over the nation faced similar difficulties.[10] Frequently, construction work drew Italians away from the city and their families. In addition, the immigration process itself had caused temporary separations for many. Buffalo Italians, then, endured two conditions commonly associated with family breakdown and female domination—irregular male employment and temporary absence of the father from the household[11] —but the proportion of husbandless or female-headed families among them remained surprisingly low. Calculations based upon the 1905 New York State manuscript census reveal that only 4 per cent of more than 2,000 first-generation families were headed by women with no spouse present.[12] And some of these were widows, not deserted wives. In 1908–09 Italians were the least likely Buffalo ethnic group to obtain welfare because of neglect or desertion by a family head. And, although the proportion applying for welfare had increased by the 1920s, the percentage giving desertion or non-support as their justification actually declined from 6 per cent in 1908 to 4 per cent in 1926.[13]

10 Amy Bernardy, "L'Emigrazione delle donne e dei fanciulli italiana," *Bolletino dell'Emigrazione* (1909), 17. Bernardy toured several eastern cities, including Buffalo, and noted the seasonal unemployment of Italian men. See also U.S. Department of Commerce, *Seasonal Operation in the Construction Industries: Summary of Report and Recommendations of a Committee of the President's Conference on Unemployment* (Washington, D.C., 1924).

11 Gans, *The Urban Villagers*, 240–241.

12 All figures cited are either from the New York State manuscript censuses of 1905 (Buffalo, 1905) and 1925 (unpublished census schedules) unless otherwise indicated. For a discussion of the accuracy of these censuses, see Virginia Yans McLaughlin, "Like the Fingers of the Hand: The Family and Community Life of First-Generation Italian-Americans in Buffalo, New York, 1880–1930," unpub. Ph.D. thesis. (State University of New York at Buffalo, 1970), 450–455. A 10 per cent sample check revealed that in no case did coding and key-punching errors exceed the reasonable range of 5 per cent in any one variable; in most cases it remained well below that figure.

13 The 1908–09 figures are from United States Senate, *Reports of the Immigration Commission*, XXXIV, 61st Cong., 3rd Sess., *Immigrants as Charity Seekers*, I (Washington,

These figures dispute the notion that male unemployment or contact with industrial city life disrupted immigrant working-class families; they also invite comparison with other urban groups who did not fare as well. How can the south Italian family's relative stability be explained? Undoubtedly inherited ethnic traditions supporting male authority helped, but let us look elsewhere before coming to definite conclusions. The answer resides, at least partially, in long-term female employment patterns, for they, and not male unemployment, distinguished Italians from less stable working-class families.

The south Italian family's traditional work patterns and economic roles were not seriously disturbed after immigration to a modern industrial city. Most important of all, women's work roles were adapted to the new industrial situation. This resulted to some extent from Buffalo's peculiar occupational structure. Unlike other upstate cities, heavy industry and transportation dominated its economy. The city offered comparatively little in the way of light industrial production for unskilled women. But it should be emphasized that even though alternatives were available, Italians *preferred* specific types of labor—occupations on the fringes of Buffalo's industrial structure—where customary family relationships could be and were effectively maintained. This preference helps to explain why Italian immigrant families remained stable. There was for them a period of transition, a time of adjustment, rather than rapid family disorganization or reorganization. Thus there was a lot of room in some late nineteenth- and early twentieth-century cities for immigrant families who wished to avoid a head-on collision with the new way of life. It was not simply a case of occupational arrangements determining family organization; cultural preferences also played a part in determining patterns of work. In short, traditional family values acted as an independent variable, and the occupational opportunities of industrial cities provided enough variation for individual families to find work arrangements appropriate for their cultural needs.

D.C., 1911), 137. The 1926 figures were computed by the author from City of Buffalo Department of Public Welfare, *Annual Report of the Bureau of Public Welfare for Fiscal Year Ending June 30, 1927* (Buffalo, 1927). The Charity Organization Society did not aid persons of the Jewish faith, and, therefore, they are not included in the 1907–08 figures. The author is well aware that welfare agency statistics do not necessarily give the most accurate picture of family life. Nevertheless, it is not necessary to rely upon these alone. Other sources confirm family stability among Italians. See McLaughlin, "Like the Fingers of the Hand," 121ff.

Let us first turn to the occupational patterns of Buffalo's first-generation Italian women in the period preceding World War I. In 1905, for example, less than 2 per cent of more than 2,000 wives reported to census-takers full-time employment which could have taken them from domestic concerns; some involved themselves in family enterprises which did not draw them permanently from the home or give them the status of independent wage earners. Only three women worked because their husbands were unemployed; only 1 per cent of the working women had children. Clearly, in 1905 Italian women did not sacrifice child-rearing responsibilities for work and no trend toward female assumption of the role of chief provider existed. Most women who contributed to the family budget in this year did so by providing housekeeping services to roomers and boarders residing with their families. Twelve per cent of all first-generation wives belonged to this category. The remaining 86 per cent reported no occupation at all, but we know that several hundred women engaged in part-time work as part of family groups. They did so most commonly as migrant laborers in northwestern New York's canneries and vineyards during the summer. A smaller number worked in Buffalo's domestic industries.

Italian women and girls rarely left their homes unsupervised by relatives or friends to work either as housekeepers or as factory laborers. Buffalo's Irish, Polish, Swedish, and German women commonly sought employment as domestics in middle-class homes, but jealous Italian men would not permit their wives to work under another man's roof, no matter how serious the family's economic circumstances. For example, efforts of various organizations in Buffalo and elsewhere to interest Italian women in such positions failed to erode this Mediterranean attitude toward female honor. The women themselves preferred employment which would not separate them from their families; even second-generation Italians failed to find service occupations as agreeable as did those of other ethnic groups.[14] Italian husbands and fathers apparently appreciated the dangers of female employment outside the home. A National Federation of Settlements survey, noting that Italian parents tended to be more careful than most

14 This was a common attitude among Italians all over the United States. See, for example, Williams, *South Italian Folkways*, 36; Bernardy, "L'Emigrazione," 8. For efforts to interest Italian women in domestic service, see "Uncle Sam's Debt to the Italians," Utica *Pensiero Italiano* (Sept. 26, 1914), which discusses an Italian baroness who attempted to work with organizations and individuals in several cities, including Buffalo, to place Italian women in such positions.

regarding their daughters' place of employment, cited parental concern for their children's morality as a reason.[15]

Buffalo Italians responded to economic need by removing male children from school and sending them to work so that the women could remain in a sheltered environment. The 1905 manuscript census reveals that sons and daughters under fifteen, for example, had an equal chance to remain in school. From the ages of fifteen to nineteen, they dropped out of school at the same rate—79 per cent of the sons and 82 per cent of the daughters left school or were not attending. But the sons generally entered the labor force, while the daughters remained at home. Boys withdrawn from school had to pay the price of restricted occupational mobility, which helps to explain the Italians' slow rise up the social ladder. Considerations of female honor restricted the girls' freedom and achievement. As a result, Italian women almost always worked within the confines of their homes or as part of a family group, especially before World War I. Most who labored did so only part-time or by the season. This continued to be true throughout the 1920s. If these occupational patterns are examined in detail, it becomes clear that they minimized strain upon the traditional family system.

An examination of the homework industry indicates that Italians were especially noted for their preference for this type of occupation, which also acted as a kind of shock absorber for other ethnic groups including, for example, Russians and Germans. There are a number of ways in which homework did not challenge Old World family organization. The mother's roles as arbiter of household organization and tasks and as disciplinarian and child-rearer were reinforced by her economic position as manager of the domestic undertaking, be it artificial flower-making, basting, or sewing. Because she still had not become, in the strict sense of the term, a wage-earner, she presented no clear threat to her husband's authority and power. The basic unit of homework industries continued to be just as it had been in the Old World—the family, not the individual. The seasonal nature of most homework industry meant that the wife and child were only sporadically occupied. Finally, and critically, the wife did not leave the home, and therefore did not abandon her important roles of childbearing and child-rearing. These two responsibilities clearly exceeded in importance any economic obligation, for homework wages were lower than

15 Robert A. Woods and Robert J. Kennedy, *Young Working Girls: A Summary of Evidence from Two Thousand Social Workers* (Boston, 1913), 59, 23.

those a woman could earn working full- or even part-time away from home. The similarity between the family as a working productive unit in preindustrial southern Italy and in America under the home-work system is striking.

Although some domestic manufacture existed in Buffalo and Italians worked in it, the women and their children earned better pay as migrant laborers on farms and processing sheds near Buffalo. The canneries, which also utilized the family as the basic work unit, permitted the same sort of easing of family members into a poten-tially disruptive work situation. Due to the immigrants' handling of the situation and the industry's special character, the Italian family was able to maintain its Old World complexion. Once again, although Italians preferred this kind of work, other ethnic groups in different parts of the nation engaged in it, probably for similar reasons.[16]

At first glance it seems surprising that conservative south Italian men would sometimes permit women and children to leave their Buffalo homes without husbands and fathers. The men sought and often obtained city construction jobs during the summer. South Italian mores, after all, required a husband to guard his wife with a jealous eye. In Italy, moreover, the wife who left home to work was viewed disapprovingly. But was going to the cannery really such a radical departure? In the first place, seasonal migration had not been an un-usual experience for south Italian families. Laborers frequently fol-lowed harvests throughout the *Mezzogiorno*. Second, though many fathers remained in Buffalo, some found employment with their families as harvesters or as canning factory mechanics.[17] Third, the women and children did not drift as separate family members into the labor mar-ket. They were recruited, lived, and worked as a family under the close scrutiny of the Italian-American community of migrant workers, many of whom were close associates, *paesani*, and kin. Fourth, as was the case in Italy, the seasonal income earned by wives and children who ventured into migrant labor camps was never understood as a replacement of the father's wages, as earlier figures on low desertion and non-support rates indicated, but as a supplement. The Italian father

16 Alexander Cance, "Immigrant Rural Communities," *The Survey*, XXV (1911), 588; United States Senate, *Reports of the Immigration Commission*, III, 61st Cong., 2nd Sess., *Immigrants in Industries, Recent Immigrants in Agriculture*, II (Washington, D.C., 1911), 489–490, 801.
17 Maria Maddalena de Rossi, "Le donne ed i fanciulli italiani a Buffalo e ad Albion," in Segretariato femminile per la tutela delle donne e dei fanciulli emigranti, *Relazione* (Rome, 1913), 14.

did not relinquish his obligation to support his family; likewise, he did not forfeit his control and authority over it. Finally, like the domestic industries, the migrant labor camp permitted close integration of living and working quarters and therefore did not separate the family's productive from its child-rearing capacities. Here a close integration of economic and family functions, similar to those which existed in Italy, prevailed. In short, the initiation of women into the factory system did not necessarily cause disruption of the traditional south Italian family.

The seasonal and part-time character of female employment patterns also prevented disruption. In the pre-World War I era, when Italian males were most likely to be chronically unemployed, their wives were also likely to be unemployed for at least as long. If women contributed to the family budget the year round, they generally did so by keeping boarders, an activity which did not contribute to their social or financial independence. Rarely did the Italian wife provide greater financial stability than her husband. Cultural tradition prevented her from taking the one suitable readily available job for unskilled women which would have guaranteed more steady employment than her husband—work as a maid or domestic. The contrast with black women who continue to depend upon this important source of income is striking. Equally striking are the contrasting attitudes between Italian and Polish families toward women entering the work world. Unfortunately, none of the evidence presented in the following pages allows for class distinctions between ethnic groups. (Because the overwhelming majority of both Italians and Poles were unskilled laborers, the difficulty is not a serious one.)

Buffalo's Polish women eagerly sought work in factories and as domestics.[18] According to a 1910 survey of 146 Buffalo firms employing almost 11,000 individuals of Polish background, two Polish women found employment in the city's manufacturing and industrial establishments for every eight Polish men. If *all* Italian women who worked in all occupations—excluding those in cannery work and those with boarders in their households—are considered, the ratio for 1905 was only one to twenty.[19] Even granting a higher proportion of Polish

18 United States Senate, *Recent Immigrants in Agriculture*, II, 491; John Daniels, "Polish Laborers and Their Needs," Buffalo *Express* (March 13, 1910), 7.
19 John Daniels, "Polish Wage Earners in Buffalo," Buffalo *Express* (March 6, 1910), 3, contains information on the Polish population. The Buffalo Italian data are based upon the New York State manuscript census for 1905.

women to men, these differences are significant. They were not peculiar to Buffalo alone. Butler, noting the relative unimportance of Italian women in Pittsburgh's industrial life, also emphasized cultural differences between Italian and Polish women. "The Polish women," she wrote in 1910, "have not the conservatism which keeps the Italian girl at home. They have not the same standard of close-knit family relations. There is a flexibility in their attitude toward life and toward their part in it." [20] In 1909 Tobenkin compared Chicago's Italian, Polish, Jewish, and Lithuanian girls and came to similar conclusions regarding the Italians' conservatism.[21] In New York City, Italian girls left domestic and personal service work to other ethnic groups and entered the factory. Still, they viewed factory work chiefly as an opportunity to learn a skill such as sewing, which they might keep up at home after marriage.[22]

During the war and pre-depression years when more Italian women began to leave their homes to work, Italian men were also more likely to be employed, or at least more likely to be earning higher incomes. Hence female employment did not represent a serious challenge to male authority at this time. Even after World War I female employment patterns had not changed radically, at least insofar as first-generation wives were concerned. An analysis of fifteen densely populated blocks in the Buffalo ward most heavily settled by Italians in 1925 indicated that although daughters had gone to work in silk factories, clothing trades, or offices, not one mother or wife in this district had left her home to work. Very few households in these blocks, moreover, contained boarders or lodgers, so the number of women contributing to family income in this way had actually declined.[23] Italian women continued to work in the canneries during the summer after the war, but, as I have argued, this work tended to sustain, not challenge, traditional family relationships.

Italians retained a cultural bias against female employment even among the second generation. A survey of all second-generation families in sixteen wards, once again including those most heavily populated by Italians, revealed that in 1925 only 12 per cent had working wives

20 Elizabeth Beardsley Butler, "The Working Women of Pittsburgh," *The Survey*, XXIII (1910), 573.
21 Elias Tobenkin, "The Immigrant Girl in Chicago," *The Survey*, XXIII (1909), 190.
22 Mary Van Kleeck, *Artificial Flower Makers* (New York, 1913), 32, 38.
23 New York State manuscript census, 1925.

(120 of 1,022). Moreover, these women were not forced to work because their spouses were unemployed or had deserted their families. Only one had no husband, and she may have been a widow. The remaining wives had employed husbands.[24] The evidence produced by the 1905 data and suggested by the 1925 samples is amply substantiated by other local and national sources.[25] In some cities, especially those with significant light industry, Italian women worked more often than they did in Buffalo, but even in these cases they tended to enter occupations which, like the canneries, assured the security and protection of working closely with fellow Italians or at least within Little Italy's confines.

Even if women entered factories in greater numbers, they could not have been the family's chief support. Italian female factory laborers, like most women in industry, tended to be irregularly employed. For example, in 1909 Odencrantz, known for her studies of women wage earners, found that one-half of a group of 1,000 New York City working girls held their jobs for less than six months, chiefly because most had seasonal occupations and their employers frequently discharged them.[26] Most of the light industries to which women flocked for employment, such as clothing, textiles, food, candy, and paper box manufacturing, responded to irregular seasonal demand. Employers in these trades could not afford to maintain a year-round labor force if they wished to maximize profits. The situation was worst in cities like Buffalo where heavy industry predominated.[27] Thus, even if other working-class

24 *Ibid.*, Wards 12–27. Second-generation families were defined here as a family with an Italian name in which both spouses were born in the United States, in which the wife was born in the United States and the husband in Italy, or in which the husband was born in the United States and the wife in Italy. In every case, of course, in which the wife was born in the United States, she could have been of either non-Italian or Italian descent.

25 The following support the description of female employment: For the pre-war period, the infrequency of Italian female employment outside of the home is observed in Walter Goodale, "Children of Sunny Italy," Buffalo *Express* (Oct. 15, 1915), 1. Post-war sources on Italian female employment include: H. E. Burber, *Industrial Analysis of Buffalo* (Buffalo, n.d.), no p.; Eleanor G. Coit, "An Industrial Study, Buffalo, New York" (unpub. paper, Business and Industrial Department, Young Women's Christian Association, 1922), 44; Young Women's Christian Association (Business and Industrial Department), "Further Data from the Industrial Study," *Buffalo Foundation Forum* (Nov., 1922), 12. For a national perspective, see Bernardy, "L'Emigrazione," 12, 50; Butler, "The Working Women of Pittsburgh," 571–572.

26 Louise Odencrantz, "The Irregularity of Employment of Women Factory Workers," *The Survey*, XXII (1909), 200.

27 Coit, "Industrial Study," 49; Business and Industrial Department, YWCA, "Some Facts Concerning Women in Buffalo Industries, A Study Bringing up to Date Certain

ethnics took a more open-minded approach toward female labor than did Buffalo's south Italians, the nature of work opportunities for unskilled females in early twentieth-century America made it possible, albeit difficult, for them to supplant their husbands as chief breadwinners.

Why was family disorganization minimal and why were female-headed families rare among Italian-Americans? First, Italians had strong cultural and historical traditions regarding their women's role which survived long after emigration. The male continued to dominate in spite of his own unemployment and despite the existence of certain matriarchal privileges within the south Italian family. The conservatism of female employment patterns is clear evidence for continuing male domination. Male unemployment, furthermore, was not an entirely new experience for this group of former peasants any more than it was for other agricultural laborers, and the Italians withstood it as well in America as they did in Italy. Once in the United States, the peculiar occupational patterns of Italian women permitted the traditional family system to survive. Rather than permit their wives to leave the home, men who needed money resigned themselves "rather painfully" to daughters working in factories. The general disposition toward women's work, however, remained one of disapproval.[28] This attitude persisted well into the 1920s, and it had a considerable influence upon second-generation families, which looked unfavorably upon female employment.

More Italian women entered the labor force after World War I, but generally these were daughters, not mothers. By contributing to the family income, they merely fulfilled the proper function of children, and hence represented no challenge to their fathers' prestige and control. In any case, because daughters and sons—not wives and mothers—left the home to work, the latter had little opportunity to enhance their bargaining power within the family by way of significant economic contributions.

Figures on the Employment of Women in 200 Industries" (unpub. paper, Buffalo, 1925), 6–7; Burber, *Industrial Analysis of Buffalo*. Each of the above indicate some of the major companies which employed women, most of which had highly seasonal employment cycles. Thomas W. Triller, "The History of the Development of the International Institute in Buffalo, New York," unpub. M.A. thesis (University of Buffalo School of Social Work, 1952), 4, quoting a report of Miss Ely (Nov. 1, 1919) to the International Institute for Women, notes that Buffalo's industry simply did not provide enough work for women.
28 Bernardy, "L'Emigrazione," 13.

Although Buffalo's Italians differed in some ways from other working-class groups, on the basis of their experience it is possible to offer a few speculations regarding the white working-class of late nineteenth- and early twentieth-century America. Single and unmarried sons and daughters, not wives and mothers, were the most likely candidates in these families to supplement the male head's earnings. Most were not occupied full-time or year-round. The white working-class male family head, though poor and unemployed, therefore probably found himself in a stronger familial position than does today's urban unemployed male, who is forced to depend upon his wife's wages. In the case of blacks, of course, wives and mothers supposedly assumed year-round employment or at least significantly more stable positions than their husbands and so challenged male control and authority within the family. Further studies of white working-class families, especially those in which wives worked year-round and husbands remained unemployed, and of ethnic groups with strong matriarchal tendencies, are required to determine the relative importance of ethnicity, the slavery heritage, and employment patterns. The findings of this paper, however, caution against assuming, as Moynihan and others have, that partial or total female control of the economic function necessarily predicts family power arrangements. Furthermore, before applying Moynihan's matriarchal model to the past, we should examine historical evidence to see if matriarchal families existed. As TenHouten suggests, conceptual muddling has caused many scholars to confuse matriarchies with female-headed families, a structure in which no male is present.[29]

In conclusion, contrary to general descriptions of European immigrant adjustment, Buffalo's Italians suffered no immediate or radical disruption in family life. Although the Italian family had its share of poverty and unemployment, it did not develop a characteristic frequently associated today with lower-class life—a female-headed family system. In fact, there is little evidence of family disorganization among Buffalo's Italians. This is not to suggest that these Italians and their contemporaries were superior or more adaptable than today's urban minorities. First-generation European immigrants entered an industrializing economy and responded to it with the equipment of a traditional peasant background. Their historical experience as a class was strikingly different from today's urban workers.

29 Warren TenHouten, "The Black Family Myth and Reality," *Psychiatry*, XXXIII (1970), 154.

We have moved throughout this discussion from the narrow focus of women's history to the broader realm of women, the family, and working-class culture. The seasonal, part-time, sporadic work patterns of wage-earning women stemmed partly from their sexual peculiarities, for most women dropped out of the labor market during the childbearing and child-rearing years. But the demands of a developing capitalist industrial economy for a cheap labor force which could be discharged periodically with a minimum of difficulty also explains their position. In this case the demands of employers and working-class cultural priorities coincided. The traditional, conservative character of this era's working-class culture advocated keeping women at home in order to avoid familial tensions, and in this manner worked toward providing the part-time labor force which employers sought.

We are now in a position to question clichés concerning the impact of industrialization and employment upon the family and woman's role. Probably no one generalization will hold for all women in all families everywhere. One can only plead for careful examination of women within the context of family life by class, ethnic group, region, city, and perhaps by religious background.

Daniel T. Rodgers

Tradition, Modernity, and the American Industrial Worker:

Reflections and Critique

Much of the current writing on labor history begins in complaint. The field, it is said, suffers from fossilization; its techniques are old-fashioned, its guiding questions archaic, and its institutional preoccupations downright myopic. There is a measure of truth to these charges, but it is a rapidly diminishing measure. Evident signs of change abound: a wholesale embrace of statistical techniques with often iconoclastic results; an egalitarian effort to recover working-class history from the bottom up and, in consequence, a flight from the study of trade unions or, at least, of conservative ones; and a new interest in the complex web of social and cultural relations too often overlooked by earlier generations of economics-trained scholars.

Labor history has been driven before the winds of the present in less obvious ways as well. One change, unheralded but far-reaching, has been the impact of the internationalization of the industrial revolution. It is a commonplace, though a momentous one, that the non-Western world has experienced a massive upheaval in economic habits in the twentieth century. As the factory and the supermarket, the ethics of Samuel Smiles, and the precepts of Henry Ford burst the boundaries of the West, the study of industrialization shifted as well, from past to present and from history to sociology. The result has been the emergence of new models and new vocabularies which, in turn, have begun to recast the axioms of Western labor history.

The mediators between the non-Western present and the Western past were a corps of industrial sociologists and social theorists who turned to the study of international industrialization after 1945, and their contributions ran in separate but complementary directions. The first was to heighten interest in the strains experienced by the first generation of workers to encounter industrialization head on. As Luddites, as Chartists, or as Wobblies, these uprooted workers have always occupied a conspicuous place

Daniel T. Rodgers is Assistant Professor of History at the University of Wisconsin, Madison.

in Western social history. But the concerns of the industrial sociologists who took up the study of non-Western work forces were less political than managerial, and they were above all interested in the more pervasive, work-place tied issue that they called labor commitment—the process by which new industrial employees adjusted deeply set rural loyalties and work habits to the disrupting demands of factory labor. It was a difficult process, the first studies suggested. In the early stages of industrialization, the labor force remained mentally rooted in the ways of the past; stability and efficiency were rare, the lure of wage incentives weak, and turnover and absenteeism high. Beneath the exterior of the industrializing community, as Kerr and his associates summarized the existing studies in 1960, there "is always latent protest, seething and simmering."[1]

Over the long run, however, Kerr and others predicted a steady increase in the commitment of new workers. In their confidence in the "logic of industrialization" their conclusions meshed with those of a group of more theoretical students of international development who began to describe the fundamental process at work in the non-Western world as something that they called "modernization." The term has since acquired an ample train of imprecisions and confusions. Yet the roots of the idea belong to the long-standing sociological vision of comprehending change by dichotomizing the processes of history. From Henry Sumner Maine's effort to show how the age of status gives way to the age of contract, the bipolar habit of mind has had a firm hold on the sociological imagination, and the modernization hypothesis is its latest and most sophisticated recrudescence.[2]

Essentially the modernization hypothesis proposes to understand the larger processes of industrialization as the irreversible transition from one ideal social type, "traditional" society, to its mirror opposite, "modernity." Traditional society, on the one

---

1 Clark Kerr, *et al., Industrialism and Industrial Man: The Problems of Labor and Management in Economic Growth* (Cambridge, Mass., 1960), 202, 166–181, 202–210; Wilbert E. Moore, *Industrialization and Labor: Social Aspects of Economic Development* (Ithaca, 1951); Wilbert E. Moore and Arnold S. Feldman (eds.), *Labor Commitment and Social Change in Developing Areas* (New York, 1960); Charles A. Myers, *Labor Problems in the Industrialization of India* (Cambridge, Mass., 1958), 36–54; Walter Elkan, *Migrants and Proletarians: Urban Labor in the Economic Development of Uganda* (London, 1960), 97–110.
2 For a perceptive treatment of this theme, see Philip Abrams, "The Sense of the Past and the Origins of Sociology," *Past & Present*, 55 (1972), 18–32.

hand, is closed and static, organized around tightly woven patterns of kinship and village relations, tied to a subsistence
economy, and committed to the worlds of the past and the un-
seen. Modern society, on the other hand, is socially and
technologically innovative, open to a high degree of mobility, and
highly rationalized; it is urban, industrial, and bureaucratic; and its
capstone is said to be a new social nature. Definitions of "industrial" or "modern" man differ somewhat from writer to writer,
but all are joined by the assumption that industrialized societies
produce a character type which internalizes the needs of an expan-
sive industrial economy. Mobile and ambitious, modern man has
nonetheless made his peace with the new forms of labor. In the industrial sociologists' terms, the worker in modern society is fully
committed, "dedicated to hard work, a high pace of work, and a
keen sense of individual responsibility for performance of assigned
norms and tasks." He is moved, Kerr and his associates write, not
by grudging acquiescence, but by "an ideology and an ethic."[3]

Taken together, the work of the modernization theorists and
the early students of new non-Western industrial employees
formed a two-sided story. Industrialization begins with a short
and turbulent period of uprooting; but, with time, resistance suc-
cumbs to the processes of acculturation and the result, ultimately,
is something approaching harmony and stasis. The grandchild of
the premodern peasant laborer adjusts to the time clock and the incentive wage; the primitive rebel is succeeded by the leader of a
wage-conscious trade union.

Incompletely, but unmistakably, the new labor history has
begun to echo this schema of generational shock and gradual acculturation. Led by Thompson, Gutman, Pollard, and Stearns,
labor historians have consciously turned the industrial
sociologists' questions of work habits and commitment to the first
generations of workers to enter the factories in the West, and the
results have been new and sensitive insights into what Gutman has
called "the painful process by which an old way of life was dis-
carded for a new one." Although Stearns would except the Ger-

3 Kerr, *Industrialism*, 43; Neil J. Smelser, "The Modernization of Social Relations," in
Myron Weiner (ed.), *Modernization: The Dynamics of Growth* (New York, 1966); Daniel
Lerner, *The Passing of Traditional Society: Modernizing the Middle East* (Glencoe, Ill., 1958);
Alex Inkeles and David H. Smith, *Becoming Modern: Individual Change in Six Developing
Countries* (Cambridge, Mass., 1974).

man peasant turned industrial laborer, the emphasis of these studies has been on the ways in which new industrial laborers stubbornly resisted the new work-forms, clinging to accustomed patterns of time, work, and social relations in the face of the factories' demands, refusing to respond to incentives in the ways the inventors of "economic man" predicted, and, on occasion, erupting in brief bursts of tradition-asserting protest. These were not necessarily the acts of conscious rebels, they stress, but of workers caught in the creases of time, whose habits and values, nurtured in pre-industrial cultures, could not but jar against the standards of work and discipline that industrialization demanded.[4]

Historians have not given comparable attention to the processes of acculturation. Yet there is a widespread assumption among these same writers that with time and generational change the initial tensions subsided, the worker was modernized, and the factory lessons were learned and accepted. Thompson, despite deep reservations about the literature of economic development, nonetheless agrees with its central premise, that the transition to "mature industrial society" entailed not only new disciplines and new incentives but "a new human nature upon which these incentives could bite effectively"—forged in England, he maintains, by the Methodist revivals. Stearns writes, to much the same end, that in Germany experienced industrial workers learned "the 'modern' idea of the wage" and made "the basic bargain industrialization requires" by accepting the new work forms in return for an increasing material standard of living. In yet another example, Dawley and Faler argue that the industrial revolution gave birth to a new, modern-minded person among the laboring classes of Europe and America, who gave up the traditionalist's casual work attitudes and raucous mores for a new ethic of self-control, self-denial, and self-improvement.[5] Frequently the acculturation as-

4 E. P. Thompson, "Time, Work-Discipline, and Industrial Capitalism," *Past & Present*, 38 (1967), 56–97; Herbert G. Gutman, "Work, Culture, and Society in Industrializing America, 1815–1919," *American Historical Review*, LXXVIII (1973), 531–587; Sidney Pollard, "Factory Discipline in the Industrial Revolution," *Economic History Review*, XVI (1963), 254–271; Peter N. Stearns, "Adaptation to Industrialization: German Workers as a Test Case," *Central European History*, III (1970), 303–331. The quotation is from Gutman, "The Worker's Search for Power: Labor in the Gilded Age," in H. Wayne Morgan (ed.), *The Gilded Age: A Reappraisal* (Syracuse, 1963), 40.
5 Thompson, "Time, Work-Discipline, and Industrial Capitalism," 57; Stearns, "Adaptation to Industrialization," 322, 323; Alan Dawley and Paul Faler, "Working-Class Cul-

sumption lurks more discreetly in the background, buried somewhere in the half-consciousness of historians, its presence marked by the currency of the terms "traditional," "premodern," and "modern" where "agrarian" and "industrial" once sufficed. The new terminology has created strange and not altogether compatible bedfellows. Above all, those who share the assumptions of initial shock and gradual accommodation are deeply divided as to the moral of the story—whether it should be read as tragedy or comedy, as the collapse of a viable working-class culture or the triumph of progress. But the tale itself has become an increasingly familiar part of contemporary scholarship.

Yet perhaps the story is wrong or, at best, oversimplified. In their quest for a coherent evolutionary order to labor history, it is possible that historians have exaggerated both the fractiousness of first-generation industrial workers and the docility of their descendants, just as it is possible that in accepting the concepts of "traditional" and "modern" man they have fallen too eagerly into formulations as mechanical as the "economic man" from which they were in pell-mell flight. Above all, it is possible that working-class cultures have been far too diverse and the ties between gross levels of economic development and working-class mores far too tenuous to fit the grand schemes half-consciously accepted. The confident grasp of the shape of the future which so strikingly marked studies in international development in the generation after the war has eroded sharply in recent years, and modernization theorists have become increasingly tentative about hypotheses that they boldly argued less than a decade ago. The uniform experience of newly industrializing work forces, the assumption of global convergence upon Western-style modernity, and the utility of the tradition-modernity polarity itself have all been seriously questioned by students of social change.[6]

ture and Politics in the Industrial Revolution: Sources of Loyalism and Rebellion," *Journal of Social History*, IX (1976), 466, 468. See also Bruce Laurie, " 'Nothing on Compulsion': Life Styles of Philadelphia Artisans, 1820–1850," *Labor History*, XV (1974), 337–366; and, for a broader application, Richard D. Brown, "Modernization and the Modern Personality in Early America, 1600–1865: A Sketch of a Synthesis," *Journal of Interdisciplinary History*, II (1972), 201–228.

6   Morris D. Morris, *The Emergence of an Industrial Labor Force in India: A Study of the Bombay Cotton Mills, 1854–1947* (Berkeley, 1965); Manning Nash, *Machine Age Maya: The Industrialization of a Guatemalan Community* (Menasha, Wisc., 1958); Clark Kerr, *et al.*, "Postscript to *Industrialism and Industrial Man*," *International Labour Review*, CIII (1971), 519–540;

In their interdisciplinary zeal it would be a shame for historians to leap unwittingly onto an outmoded bandwagon. What follows is an attempt to pose the hypothesis of initial entrenchment and progressive acculturation against what can be gleaned about the behavior of factory workers in the United States, focusing primarily on the years from 1865 to 1919 and, more briefly, on the modern years since World War II. The results are cautious and skeptical reflections. But if the historian pays his way in doubts and a sense of alternatives, perhaps we should not insist that he be taxed entirely in the hard coin of certainty.

Two matters are open to relatively little question: that industrialization in America, as elsewhere, required a major assault on the existing norms of time and labor, and that during the years of that attack the factories were the site of frequent contest and widespread friction. Given the highly uneven development of the American economy, the assault on the old work norms was far from uniform. But as the nineteenth century wore on and as manufacturers learned to count the monetary value of time with increasing precision, they turned an arsenal of new weapons— precise work rules and personnel departments, the steam whistle and locked factory gates, the time clock and, eventually, the efficiency expert's stop watch—against the irregular work rhythms of pre-industrial America. Nor were their efforts without result. A French labor delegate who toured the industrial states in the 1890s marveled that, "work in the American shops is altogether different from what it is in France. Nobody talks, nobody sings, the most rigorous silence reigns."[7] But accommodation to work rules such as these (as often as not enforced by heavy fines) was far commoner than internalization of the new standards, and the new model workers that the factory masters tried to forge—punctual,

S. N. Eisenstadt, *Tradition, Change, and Modernity* (New York, 1973), 3–21, 98–115; Joseph R. Gusfield, "Tradition and Modernity: Misplaced Polarities in the Study of Social Change," *American Journal of Sociology*, LXXII (1967), 351–362; Robert A. Nisbet, *Social Change and History: Aspects of the Western Theory of Development* (New York, 1969), 240–304; Reinhard Bendix, "Tradition and Modernity Reconsidered," *Comparative Studies in Society and History*, IX (1967), 292–346; Dean C. Tipps, "Modernization Theory and the Comparative Study of Societies: A Critical Perspective," *ibid.*, XV (1973), 199–226.
7 E. Levasseur (trans. Thomas S. Adams), *The American Workman* (Baltimore, 1900), 173–174.

efficient, sober, disciplined to the clock and the incentive wage
—were not easily made.

A part of the evidence lies in the vigorous complaints of the
manufacturers themselves. Suspect and inextricably tangled in
ample doses of prejudice, employers' laments of drunkenness
among their hands, irregular attendance, and general inefficiency
are nonetheless too numerous to dismiss out of hand. Another
part of the evidence is to be found in the persistent dream of
shorter working hours, which captured the imagination of all of
the period's labor organizations and runs through the rank and file
testimony preserved in the records of the state bureaus of labor
statistics as a constant challenge to the factory masters' aim of constant, untiring labor. Still more direct were the repeated contests
between the new standards of toil and shop-maintained work patterns which undercut them. Like so many of the essential facts of
social history, the outlines of these shop cultures are often hidden
and difficult to recover, although something of them can be sur-
mised from the rules factory supervisors felt compelled to make
explicit—against leaving one's place during working hours, for
example—and something more from the controversy over scientific management which came to a head just before World War I.
As far as employers were concerned, worker-maintained production quotas were the nub of the issue. Only a few skilled factory
workers at the height of their power—glass blowers, potters, iron
molders, and puddlers and rollers in the iron and steel mills—
maintained openly acknowledged output limits. But the Bureau of
Labor report on the subject in 1904 concluded that clandestine
shop-level output agreements were far more common than this,
and, if often short-lived, the mood behind them was clearly serious. In 1901, in one of the most dramatic examples of the period,
sheep and cattle butchers slowed down the lines of the Chicago
packing plants by some 30 percent until the new regime fell apart
in a disastrous strike. And where workers could not actually control the factory pace, they could at least intimidate the exceptionally fast worker, branding him with shop names—hog, boss's pet,
bell-horse, rusher, swift—which amounted to a string of
epithets.[8]

8   U.S. Commissioner of Labor, *Eleventh Special Report: Regulation and Restriction of Output*
(Washington, 1904), 18, 715.

Quantitative evidence, on the whole, confirms the clash of work norms within the factories, although some of its dimensions are exceedingly difficult to determine. Absenteeism is a case in point. Throughout the period, employers complained of irregular attendance and tried to curb the habit by stiff fines, occasionally equivalent to a day's pay or more, for unexcused absences and tardiness. But typical absence rates are another matter. Payroll records from three late-nineteenth-century industrial firms show that a quarter of the employees stayed out at least one day a week, although some of the lost days may have been due to a shortage of work at hand, often a chronic problem. Another way to count absences is in the number of "spare hands" kept to fill the places of absentees. In isolated country mills, where the practice was widely used, the spares might amount to 10 to 25 percent of a mill's total labor force, although again the figure inflates the actual voluntary absence rate, for the system worked in a vicious circle, forcing regular employees to stay home in order to give enough work to the spare hands to keep them from drifting elsewhere.[9] By the turn of the century in the industrial Northeast, factory managers had clearly succeeded in reducing absences far below the levels typical of nonfactory trades—to less than 4 percent according to a Massachusetts survey of 1904 compared with rates of up to 17 percent in the state's shop and building trades.[10] Nonetheless, between factories absence rates varied widely. In 1916, when labor shortages may have begun to drive industrial absence rates upward, the handful of reported figures ranged from 2 percent at the reorganized Ford plant to 11 percent in a set of South Carolina textile mills. During the war years, observers forced to generalize set-

H. M. Gitelman, "The Labor Force at Waltham Watch during the Civil War Era," *Journal of Economic History*, XXV (1965), 229; Thomas R. Navin, *The Whitin Machine Works since 1831: A Textile Machinery Company in an Industrial Village* (Cambridge, Mass., 1950), 68; Robert S. Smith, *Mill on the Dan: A History of Dan River Mills, 1882–1950* (Durham, N.C., 1960), 48; U.S. Senate, Committee on Education and Labor, *Report upon the Relations between Labor and Capital* (Washington, 1885), III, 207–208; August Kohn, *The Cotton Mills of South Carolina* (Charleston, S.C., 1907), 61–63; U.S. Bureau of Labor, *Report on Condition of Woman and Child Wage-Earners in the United States*, 61st Cong., 2 sess. (1910–1912), XVI, 154–155.

10 *Massachusetts Labor Bulletin*, 32 (1904), 210–215. A replication of the survey in August of that year, however, produced such astonishingly low figures (0.1% in Fall River, for example) that these rates should be treated with some skepticism.

tled on 6 percent as the goal for a well-run industrial plant.[11] But how often and by how much that figure had been exceeded in the preceding half century is a matter of impressions and guesswork.

But if the rate at which workers stayed away from the factories is obscure, the rate at which industrial employees moved between jobs in the early twentieth century is not. The picture it shows is of an astonishingly restless and mobile labor force. The median job tenure for industrial workers seems to have been slightly less than three years, and a sizeable fraction moved much faster, deserting their jobs after a matter of days or weeks. The result was a constant shuffling of men. To keep a work force of about 8,000 employees, for example, Armour in Chicago hired 8,000 workers during the course of 1914, and the pattern was repeated over and again in the early-twentieth-century factories. Larger turnover surveys concluded that about one-third of the employees of a typical factory held on to their jobs a year or less, and, because they moved so often, annual factory turnover in normal times was at least as high as the 100 percent reported at Armour. Turnover in the wool industry between 1907 and 1910 varied between 113 and 163 percent; in 1913–1914 a Bureau of Labor Statistics survey of sixty-eight manufacturing plants found an average yearly turnover of 115 percent, despite the current economic slump. At casually managed plants or regions troubled by labor shortages, the turnover rate ran still higher. It reached 176 percent in the Southern textile industry in 1907, 252 percent in a sample of Detroit factories in 1916, and the bewildering rate of 370 percent at Ford in 1913. As turnover investigators were forced to rely on plants concerned enough about the transiency problem to have collected their own data, the Bureau of Labor Statistics figure of 115 percent seems a cautious estimate.[12]

---

11 John S. Keir, "The Reduction of Absences and Lateness in Industry," *Annals of the American Academy of Political and Social Science,* LXXI (1917), 140–155; Paul H. Douglas, "Absenteeism in Labor," *Political Science Quarterly,* XXXIV (1919), 591–608; Emil Frankel, "Labor Absenteeism," *Journal of Political Economy,* XXIX (1921), 487–499; Boris Emmet, "Labor Turnover and Employment Policies of a Large Motor Vehicle Manufacturing Establishment," U.S. Bureau of Labor Statistics (hereafter USBLS), *Monthly Labor Review,* VII (1918), 846; J. D. Hackett, "Absentism: A Quantitative Study," *Management Engineering,* II (1922), 85.
12 U.S. Commission on Industrial Relations, *Final Report and Testimony,* 64th Cong., 1 sess. (1916), IV, 3507, 3510; U.S. Tariff Board, *Wool and Manufactures of Wool,* 62nd Cong., 2 sess. (1912), IV, 963, 983; Sumner H. Slichter, *The Turnover of Factory Labor* (New York,

Systematic turnover data do not extend back before the turn of the century, but it is likely that the overall pattern then was much the same. A knowledgeable observer of the Lowell textile industry reported in 1873 that most of the operatives left within four years, and, even at the model Pullman plant in 1894, 21 percent of the workforce had less than a year's tenure. Certainly employers were aware of the "nomadic system of employing men" and made strenuous efforts to escape it by offering bonuses for steady work, requiring labor passes certifying that the worker had left his last job with the permission of his employer, or, most frequently, demanding that those who left without adequate notice forfeit one or two weeks' back wages. Called upon to defend the last practice in the 1870s, a Massachusetts textile mill agent insisted that if a mill did not withhold wages it would simply wake up to find all of its hands gone by morning.[13]

It is easier to count the transients than to know why so many workers changed jobs so often. Prior to 1919, few companies distinguished between those who quit and those who were laid off or fired, and, even then, such categories are far from clear cut. Quitting was undoubtedly more pleasant than being fired or waiting for the layoff one sensed was imminent. Nevertheless, the best students of early-twentieth-century turnover were convinced that in normal times layoffs and discharges directly accounted for well under half and perhaps as little as one quarter of all job separations. Fluctuations in the turnover rate bear out their emphasis on the high proportion of voluntary quitters. Turnover was far higher in years of prosperity than in depression years when all who had jobs worked hard and anxiously to keep them; and throughout the course of the year turnover rose in spring and fell in winter in a cycle which apparently had more to do with wanderlust than with industrial conditions.

1919), 16–27, 34–35, 44–45; Paul F. Brissenden and Emil Frankel, *Labor Turnover in Industry* (New York, 1922), 50–51, 118–119. I have recalculated Brissenden and Frankel's aggregate figures throughout to eliminate the nonfactory trades from their sample.
13 Massachusetts Bureau of Statistics of Labor (hereafter MBLS), *Fourth Annual Report* (Boston, 1873), 281; Stanley Buder, *Pullman: An Experiment in Industrial Order and Community Planning, 1880–1930* (New York, 1967), 248, n. 2; Wisconsin Bureau of Labor and Industrial Statistics, *Third Biennial Report* (Madison, 1888), 111–115; Melton A. McLaurin, *Paternalism and Protest: Southern Cotton Mill Workers and Organized Labor, 1875–1905* (Westport, Conn., 1971), 32; MBLS, *Third Annual Report* (Boston, 1872), 376. Withholding wages also served, of course, as a strike preventative.

Attempts to probe still further into the reasons behind the high quit rates were not particularly successful. Skilled workmen sometimes defended moving about as a way to learn more than one branch of their increasingly specialized trades. Yet very few of those who quit claimed that they had a better job in hand, and, in most of the plants investigated, less than a third cited better opportunities as their grounds for leaving. The quitters were "dissatisfied," looking for something else to turn up, leaving town— in all, taking a vacation from factory discipline. No statistics more clearly show the restlessness of the industrial work force than this army of voluntary migrants (perhaps one worker in seven in the year 1913–1914, according to one careful estimate) continually on the run from—and to—industrial labor. But their grievances may not have been essentially different from those who stayed behind. A machinist at the federal arsenal at Watertown, unnoticed by history save for his participation in a strike against the introduction of scientific management, told investigators that the new regime threatened to make a man stick to his work "every second of the eight hours, and if there is any man who can do that I don't believe I ever saw him." Industrialization in post-Civil War America pressed repeatedly and not always successfully against sentiments like these and against recalcitrant human materials.[14]

To grant the restlessness of the industrializing work force, however, only begins to answer the essential questions. How close was the match between factory rebels and neophyte industrial workers? To what extent was the persistent conflict in the factories due to what Gutman has called the central problem of American labor history, the repeated clash of "premodern" patterns of behavior with the industrial setting?[15] Certainly large numbers of first-generation industrial workers toiled in the factories of post-Civil War America. And it is often not hard to trace

14 Brissenden, *Labor Turnover*, 94–96; Slichter, *Turnover*, 163–185; Anne Bezanson, *et al.*, "Four Years of Labor Mobility: A Study of Labor Turnover in a Group of Selected Plants in Philadelphia, 1921–24," *Annals*, CXIX (1925), supplement, 70–72; U.S. House of Representatives, Special Committee to Investigate the Taylor and Other Systems of Shop Management, *Hearings* (Washington, 1912), I, 453. The estimate of the number of floaters is W. S. Woytinsky's, adjusted to eliminate nonfactory workers from his base data: *Three Aspects of Labor Dynamics* (Washington, 1942), 27.
15 Gutman, "Work, Culture, and Society," 541, 543.

direct connections between the turbulence which bedeviled employers and these new workers' attempts to cling to custom and memory in the face of the new and strange demands of the factories. The army of industrial transients included its regiments of the classically semi-committed: French-Canadian and Maine mill hands who deserted the factories for their farms or fishing villages each summer in a regular cycle, Southerners who drifted back to the land with rising cotton prices or who practiced "summer farming," and immigrant workingmen retreating homeward, their dreams fulfilled or their energies exhausted. Factory absence rates, too, were clearly inflated by the pull of the past—by workers not yet broken from the rural prerogative of taking a day off at will to go fishing and by immigrants who struggled hard to keep Old World holiday schedules intact against the factory demands of regular attendance. Cigar makers, potters, and other one-time hand workers caught in the vise of change figured prominently in the complaints of drunkenness and disorder as their artisan ways jostled painfully against new standards of industrial discipline.

None of this can be dismissed, yet the matter will not rest here. Some of the apparent rebellion against industrial discipline was not rebellion at all, but accommodation to the constant turbulence of the industrializing economy. Whether seasonal or afflicted by unpredictable changes in demand, few industries escaped repeated cycles of boom and famine which, for the workers, meant that short time and layoffs followed hard on the heels of bouts of overtime and rush work. The experience had a deep impact on the industrial work force. "At one time they drive us like slaves, and at other times we have to beg for work," a Brooklyn worker charged in the 1880s, and the complaint runs as a constant thread through the reports of the bureaus of labor statistics and through immigrant letters.[16]

Had the ethos of industrialization been all of one piece, employers might have cushioned the destabilizing effects of these cycles on their workers. But the economics of cheap labor took

16 Marion C. Cahill, *Shorter Hours: A Study of the Movement since the Civil War* (New York, 1932), 42. On the irregularity of employment: Constance M. Green, *Holyoke, Massachusetts: A Case History of the Industrial Revolution in America* (New Haven, 1939), 76–77; David Brody, *Steelworkers in America: The Nonunion Era* (Cambridge, Mass., 1960), 39–40; W. Jett Lauck and Edgar Sydenstricker, *Conditions of Labor in American Industries: A Summarization of the Results of Recent Investigations* (New York, 1917), 74–100, 137–164.

precedence over the ideal of steady, clockwork toil, although the result was to undermine the factory masters' disciplining efforts. Irregular employment helped fuel the shorter-hours drive by turning workers' dreams to shorter but steadier hours of labor. It fostered clandestine slowdown agreements as employees struggled to stretch out the work at hand and stave off the layoff they knew was coming. Finally, unstable employment contributed to the high industrial turnover, throwing initially steady workers out of their jobs so often that motion became an ingrained habit. Economic conditions were at the root of these matters, not memory or culture. In the case of the most transient laborers restlessness slides paradoxically into functional integration, for these highly mobile and uncommitted workers, complained of by employers, provided what the factories sorely needed—a reserve army of workers able to iron out the fluctuations of an expanding economy.

The picture is made still more complex by the fact that, far from resisting the new demands, some first-generation industrial workers labored considerably harder than the norm. Weber, noting the phenomenon among sojourning laborers in Germany, concluded that "the simple fact of a change in residence is among the most effective means of intensifying labour. . . . The same Polish girl who at home was not to be shaken from her traditional laziness by any chance of earning money, however tempting, seems to change her entire nature and become capable of unlimited accomplishment when she is a migratory worker in a foreign country." In considerably cruder language, many American employers of immigrant workers agreed. A Chicago clothing contractor in the early twentieth century warned his forelady that he had no use for experienced help: "I got to pay them good wages and they make me less work, but these greenhorns, Italian people, Jewish people, all nationalities, they cannot speak English and they don't know where to go and they just came from the old country and I let them work hard, like the devil, and these I get for less wages."[17] Obviously not all immigrants worked exception-

---

17 Max Weber (trans. Talcott Parsons), *The Protestant Ethic and the Spirit of Capitalism* (New York, 1958), 191; anon., "Bricks without Straw," *Survey*, XXV (1910), 425. The point, of course, can be carried past the brink into caricature, as in Gerald Rosenblum, *Immigrant Workers: Their Impact on American Labor Radicalism* (New York, 1973).

ally hard, and fewer still changed their entire nature in the crossing. But the "greenhorns" were a conspicuous feature of industrializing America. Their experience suggests something of the
severe limits of the term traditional, certainly the danger of any
easy equation of non-industrial cultures with premodernity.
Moreover, it suggests that what shaped those who moved across
the boundaries of industrial society was neither culture nor economic conditions but the highly specific interaction of the two—
the ways in which expectation, memory, and habit met with the
force of circumstance. The process contained not one, but a wide
variety of potential outcomes.

The making of an exceptionally diligent workman out of a
European immigrant began with the fact that, although relatively
few immigrants in post-Civil War America brought industrial
habits with them, they were not, as a necessary consequence,
premodern—not the backward, fatalistic traditionalists described
by students of social change. Immigration historians have repeatedly testified to the importance of economic ambition in the
population movements which unsettled the continent in the late
nineteenth and early twentieth centuries. Often the emigrant had
been on the move before as a temporary laborer in Europe when
tales of success manufactured from the letters of those who had
left for America or from the example of the successful repatriate
turned his thoughts toward the United States. Most immigrants,
moreover, brought with them not only ambition but a faith in toil
itself. Even in southern Italy, for example, where the working
year might be half as long as in the United States, folk songs
warned that "lazy" girls would not find a husband. The confidence and expectations ran deep. A young Polish Catholic, determined to make his fortune in two or three years in America,
wrote an emigration assistance league that his priest had tried to
dissuade him from the journey, "show[ing] me the dangers, the
terrible work there which often costs one's life, and in general the
reasons why it is not worth leaving here." "But," the emigrant
concluded, "I was not persuaded."[18]

18 Phyllis H. Williams, *South Italian Folkways in Europe and America* (New Haven, 1938),
20; William I. Thomas and Florian Znaniecki, *The Polish Peasant in Europe and America* (Boston, 1919), III, 22.

Eagerness for success and willingness to work characterized large numbers of new immigrants. What happened next, it would appear, depended on highly particular circumstances. Some found "easy work" and wrote happily of the fact in letters home; others had their illusions stripped bare and reemigrated or became potential rebels; still others had the blow of adjustment cushioned by strong families or strong subcultures and effected a compromise with industrial expectations. But for the potential greenhorn the governing experience was the irregularity of work—the initial, painful shock of unemployment which led in turn to entrapment in a brutal round of temporary jobs.

Steiner, who emigrated from central Europe in the 1880s, may serve as an example for nameless others. Landing in New York City, he found his first job in the clothing industry, but the slack season soon dried up the work. He tried to eke out a living in other short-term jobs in a bakery, a feather-renovating shop, and a sausage factory, abandoned the city for harvest work, moved on to a Pittsburgh steel mill where his job ended in a layoff, worked in a coal mine until a strike halted production, tried a job in a South Bend plough factory until he became ill from the heat and the damp, moved on to a Chicago machine shop where he was fired for lecturing his fellow employees, and shuttled on through more harvest, mine, and factory work—all in the space of about two years.[19] Whether one went "on the tramp" like Steiner or scrambled for a foothold in the casual labor market of the city, the permanent job that the immigrant had so eagerly anticipated often eluded him. And the combination of extravagant hopes and the trauma of finding and keeping a job worked together to shatter village norms of toil, to undercut the props of tradition, and to confuse what was "proper" work and what was unacceptable drudgery.

The result was the ferocious energy observers repeatedly found in the American mills and sweatshops. Once a greenhorn was not always to remain a greenhorn. There is some evidence

19   Edward A. Steiner, *From Alien to Citizen: The Story of My Life in America* (New York, 1914), 53–208. For other examples of the immigrant's initial "tramping" period: Eli Ginzberg and Hyman Berman, *The American Worker in the Twentieth Century: A History through Autobiographies* (New York, 1963), 75–79; Charlotte Erickson, *Invisible Immigrants: The Adaptation of English and Scottish Immigrants in Nineteenth-Century America* (Coral Gables, Fla., 1972), 247–254.

that, with time, many such immigrants reassessed the bargain they had made with industrial society and grew as confident and stubborn as the more experienced workers around them.[20] If so, theirs was the mirror opposite of what is conventionally described as the modernizing experience; in any event, the greenhorns suggest how the combination of mobility, hope, and radically uncertain employment might produce far different results from those that formula implies.

The formula does not do much better with a second prominent group of first-generation industrial workers—the white farm and farm tenant families who took up work in the textile mills of the New South. Cultural and economic forces interacted here as well—not ambition and unstable employment but isolation together with changes in the ratio of labor supply and demand. Ultimately these combined to generate one of the most nomadic work forces in the country. But the process was not a straightforward one of challenge and resistance, for the restlessness of the southern mill hands took time to emerge and the habits which frustrated early-twentieth-century employers were not simply country ways carried into the factories.

The first part of that statement rests on inference from the thin and impressionistic evidence. Yet from an extensive series of manufacturers' comments on industrial conditions printed in the reports of the North Carolina Bureau of Labor Statistics from 1887 to 1908 it is possible to graph a curve of employers' complaints, and, even by the generous standards of the South, the level of criticism of the mill hands through the mid 1890s is strikingly low. Newly built mills seem generally to have found more applicants for work than they could employ, and the labor surplus gave manufacturers an enormous leeway to weed out the fractious from the tractable and orderly. This search for the most adaptable workers was a conscious policy, if the boasts of the southern mill men are to be believed, and it went on even within the mill families, drawing the women and children into the factories while many a potentially troublesome adult male was left to work only sporadically, at odd jobs outside the mills, or not at all. The mills

20 Rudolph J. Vecoli, "Chicago's Italians prior to World War I: A Study of Their Social and Economic Adjustment," unpub. Ph.D. diss. (University of Wisconsin, 1963), 435–440.

employed fifteen adult women for every ten adult men in 1870, seventeen women for every ten men in 1880, and, until the proportions finally equalized and reversed in the labor-short decade of the 1890s, the non-working father, or "cotton mill drone," was a common and functional feature of the southern mill villages. Even the most rigorous selectivity had its limits. Mill managers universally agreed that southern workers could not be induced to save their wages, and it is also clear that the general standards of efficiency were not always particularly high. Nevertheless, southern employers initially seem to have found more than enough workers capable of making the adjustment to industrial labor in ways that satisfied their expectations.[21] Even agricultural societies, it would appear, have their corps of the particularly flexible, not only the adventurous but the powerless, the dependent, and those with little reserves of resistance.

The mill building boom of the 1890s and the acute labor shortage which followed unsettled this early pattern. Complaints in North Carolina began to rise in the mid 1890s, grew increasingly shrill, and reached a peak in 1906–1907. Plants which once reported all hands stable and orderly began to deplore the growing restlessness "of late years," and by the early twentieth century wrote in despair that their hands were working only four days a week and left on the slightest pretext. The village drones were outlawed and forced into the mills throughout the southern states, and, if this proved a mixed blessing for the manufacturers, so did other tactics that they employed in their efforts to find sufficient workers to operate the new machinery. Wage increases seemed only to aggravate absenteeism, and raids on the labor forces of other mills simply encouraged transiency. By 1910, despite the easing of the most acute phase of the labor famine, the southern textile industry was no longer the same. Every mill claimed a core of steady, long term employees, but these rubbed shoulders with a turbulent army of floaters, variously estimated at 20 to 40 percent

21 Confirming evidence exists outside North Carolina: U.S. Senate, *Labor and Capital,* IV, 508–542, 582–597, 684–696, 721–756, 793–796; Broadus Mitchell, *The Rise of Cotton Mills in the South* (Baltimore, 1921), 176–209; McLaurin, *Paternalism and Protest,* 21, 55. On the sex ratio and sometimes very lax efficiency standards, see Elizabeth H. Davidson, *Child Labor Legislation in the Southern Textile States* (Chapel Hill, 1939), 8; North Carolina Bureau of Labor Statistics (hereafter NCBLS), *Tenth Annual Report* (Winston, 1897), 60–61; C. Vann Woodward, *Origins of the New South, 1877–1913* (Baton Rouge, 1951), 222–225.

of the work force—twice as mobile as northern textile workers, according to a study made in the early 1920s, and twice as prone to absenteeism.[22]

Undoubtedly the labor shortage had forced less adaptable rural folk into the industry, but the ways of the "floaters" were not simply more deeply set country work mores rattling against the confines of factory discipline. Only a fraction of the enormous turnover of the southern mill hands, for example, involved a return to farm work. Most of the job changing amounted to a restless movement from mill to mill; and it was greatest not in country mills but in the urban centers of the South and among workers who had drifted considerably farther from their pasts than a single step from the worn-out cotton fields. Southern landlords, moreover, fearful of mill habits, were not eager to take the textile workers back. Isolated and ostracized in the mill villages, the mill hands increasingly appeared to outsiders not as farm folk but as a separate people.[23]

These are threads of evidence, but what they seem to add up to is a process of cultural hybridization. Cut off from their pasts, southern workers built a half-new world of their own. That world could not escape the imprint of rural memory, particularly in its casual attitudes toward time and in its deep streak of fatalism. But the isolation of the southern workers and their ability to float on the tide of a labor-short economy transmuted the old into new forms—an apparently stable, quasi-industrial subculture, passed on to cotton mill children with the tricks of piecing threads and doffing spindles until the Great Depression shattered the economic conditions which had nurtured and supported it. Measured against

22 NCBLS, *Twelfth Annual Report* (Raleigh, 1899), 401; NCBLS, *Twentieth Annual Report* (Raleigh, 1906), 254, 261; NCBLS, *Twenty-second Annual Report* (Raleigh, 1908), 219–221; Kohn, *Cotton Mills of South Carolina*, 22, 60–66; U.S. Bureau of Labor, *Woman and Child Wage-Earners*, I, 126, 453; Smith, *Mill on the Dan*, 100–105; "Lost Time and Labor Turnover in Cotton Mills," U.S. Department of Labor, Women's Bureau, *Bulletin*, LII (1926), 39, 179. For indications of the extent of the "floating" population: Lois MacDonald, *Southern Mill Hands: A Study of Social and Economic Forces in Certain Textile Mill Villages* (New York, 1928), 49, 89, 124; Jennings J. Rhyne, *Some Southern Cotton Mill Workers and Their Villages* (Chapel Hill, 1930), 107; U.S. Bureau of Labor, *Woman and Child Wage-Earners*, I, 127.
23 *Ibid.*, XVII, 22; II, 585–587; U.S. Women's Bureau, "Lost Time and Labor Turnover," 191, 46; Kohn, *Cotton Mills of South Carolina*, 29; Liston Pope, *Millhands and Preachers: A Study of Gastonia* (New Haven, 1942), 67–69; John K. Morland, *Millways of Kent* (Chapel Hill, 1958).

the conventional story of shock, entrenchment, and gradual accommodation, the southern experience was an extensive detour.

Examples such as these should not minimize our sense of the toll industrialization exacted of those caught in the upheaval of work processes. All such workers faced a sharp break in habits and values and an enforced recasting of their sense of self and place in society. But since they came from widely different pasts into a far from uniform economy, the encounter with industrialization could not but be complex and multiform. The groups sketched here—uprooted and mobile Southerners, success-striving immigrants, workers who struggled to be rational in an irrational economy, and tradition-asserting rebels—do not exhaust the possibilities. Other groups of industrial newcomers spring quickly to mind, each worth careful and imaginative study: women workers of many backgrounds and cultures, black workers (including those who entered industrial work through the uncomfortable role of strikebreaker), Jewish workers carrying a culture no more peasant than it was industrial, artisans forced into factory labor, downwardly mobile children of white-collar families, or farm boys seeking their fortunes in the cities. In each case culture, expectation, and the particular economic circumstances of the encounter met in different ways, with different compromises, and with different outcomes. The mills had many doorways.

Can more be said for the premise of acculturation? Did industrial experience extended over several generations produce increasingly convergent accommodations and ultimately make a 'modern man" of the American factory worker?

For the years before 1919, second- and third-generation industrial workers are far less easy to identify in the factories than are newcomers. One reasonable place to look for acculturated workers, however, is among immigrants from the Lancashire towns where the Western industrial revolution began. Many such workers could be found in the late-nineteenth-century American factories, particularly in the New England textile mills where they filled the more skilled places, most conspicuously those of tending the complex and temperamental spinning mules used in the manufacture of fine grade yarn. But if the mill agents are to be believed, the Lancashire-raised mule spinners were as "rowdy, drinking, [and] unprincipled" a set of workingmen as existed in

America. The largest concentration of British textile workers collected in Fall River. By 1878 the city had already acquired a justified reputation as a second Manchester, and, through repeated contrast to Lowell, which was said to run placidly on the labor of its native-born, Irish, and French-Canadian workers, an equally wide reputation for industrial disorder. Part of the "rowdiness" with which the Fall River spinners were charged had more to do with their stubborn propensity to strike than with work habits. But the mule spinners not only challenged the economic power of the Fall River manufacturers but also flaunted industrial discipline, taking their holidays when they thought they needed them and rarely working full time even when the mills ran at full production.[24] Refractory as these habits were, they were neither preindustrial nor artisanal customs, for mule spinning by the 1870s had been a factory occupation in England for well over a generation, reached by a long apprenticeship from childhood at simpler mill tasks.[25] The Lancashire spinners were, to be sure, not typical second-generation workers but highly skilled factory aristocrats who built their quasi-industrial subculture on the rock of their indispensability. But their factory-nurtured, disorderly habits make it clear that industrial experience did not invariably result in acquiescence to the ideals of the new economic order.

It is perhaps unfair, however, to expect to find modern workers in the imperfectly rationalized economy of the late nineteenth and early twentieth centuries. If one turns instead to the years since 1945 the hypothesis appears more promising, for in the interim the behavior of factory workers has changed in important ways. Turnover in manufacturing began to decline in the 1920s, rose once more in the labor-short years of World War II, but has remained at levels half or less than the pre-World War I estimate in all but four years since 1950. And although the overall absence rate

---

24 Rowland T. Berthoff, *British Immigrants in Industrial America, 1790–1950* (Cambridge, Mass., 1953), 30–36; MBLS, *Report* (Boston, 1871), 469; MBLS, *Thirteenth Annual Report* (Boston, 1882), 194–415; Mosely Industrial Commission to the United States of America, *Reports of the Delegates* (London, 1903), 127; U.S. Industrial Commission, *Reports* (Washington, 1900–1902), XIV, 571.

25 Sydney J. Chapman, *The Lancashire Cotton Industry: A Study in Economic Development* (Manchester, 1904), 69–70, 216; Neil J. Smelser, *Social Change in the Industrial Revolution: An Application of Theory to the Lancashire Cotton Industry, 1770–1840* (London, 1959), 193–204. Robert Howard, for example, the Fall River spinners' most prominent spokesman, began his career at age eight as a piecer in a Cheshire silk mill.

in the factories still remains a matter of considerable guesswork, the 5 to 6 percent levels personnel managers in the early twentieth century thought normal are now sufficient to trigger considerable alarm. The closing of unrestricted immigration, the introduction of systematic personnel policies and industrial welfare programs in the 1920s, the searing experience of the Great Depression, and the incentives to stability built into the factories since the 1930s by union seniority rules, non-transferable pensions, and the requirements of unemployment compensation have all left their mark. Highly mobile and overtly restless workers still exist, but they are now most common outside the factories where statisticians rarely tread.[26]

But modernity is a matter of values as well as behavior, and, if some of the overt restlessness of industrial workers has been tamed, it remains far from clear that they have internalized the rules by which modern man is said to live. These rules are not merely matters of speculation, according to many social scientists, but can be proved to cohere in complex and empirically tested syndromes. Modern man is said to be a rationalist who believes in science, technology, and the inherent logic of things—convictions inculcated in part through exposure to the orderly and routine processes of the modern factory, according to Inkeles' findings. He is an inveterate optimist—an "activist"—who is convinced that societies and individuals shape their destinies, and who responds to the survey question, "Can an able, smart, industrious boy succeed against fate?" with the answer, "Yes." Modern man is an individualist—ambitious, hardworking, and possessed of a high esteem for efficiency and punctuality. He is flexible, open to change, and eager for new experiences—"empathetic," to use Lerner's term.[27]

26 Ewan Clague, "Long-Term Trends in Quit Rates," USBLS, *Employment and Earnings,* III (Dec. 1956), iii–ix; "Handbook of Labor Statistics, 1973," USBLS, *Bulletin* no. 1790 (1973), 124; USBLS, *Monthly Labor Review,* IC (April 1976), 76; Janice N. Hedges, "Absence from Work—A Look at Some National Data," *ibid.,* XCVI (July 1973), 24–30; "Absent Workers—A Spreading Worry," *U.S. News & World Report* (Nov. 27, 1972), 48–49.
27 Joseph A. Kahl, *The Measurement of Modernism: A Study of Values in Brazil and Mexico* (Austin, 1968), 3–44, 133–134; Inkeles and Smith, *Becoming Modern,* 15–35, 154–191; *idem,* "The OM Scale: A Comparative Socio-Psychological Measure of Individual Modernity," *Sociometry,* XXIX (1966), 364–365; Lerner, *Passing of Traditional Society,* 47–52. A comprehensive list of "modern" traits would be considerably longer and would include at the minimum an active interest in the mass media, a preference for urban life, and participation in organizations.

Not all of these characteristics have been tested against present-day American industrial workers, but some of those most directly related to work values have, and some of them fit. The bureaucratic labor union structure, which has everywhere pushed aside older, fraternal forms of workers' organizations, and the responsiveness of contemporary workers to incentive wage formulas both attest to the ascendancy of rationalistic attitudes in the working class. Not that union behavior is a perfect exercise in rationality or shop behavior in income maximization. Workers still test their wits against the time-study man and still set output limits on their work in a battle governed as much by custom and frustration as by careful estimation of the effects of output on the prevailing piece rates.[28] Nevertheless, fining is a far less common practice in contemporary factories than it once was, and few employers find it necessary, as Robert Owen did, to reward each day's performance with a visible, non-pecuniary badge of merit.

But other, central aspects of modernity simply do not apply to modern American industrial workers. The majority do not believe in the efficacy of striving up the occupational ladder against the pull of fate. Several studies of factory employees made in the decade after World War II failed to turn up more than one worker in three who admitted he would like to move out of the blue-collar ranks into a supervisory position, a foreman's job in most cases; at least as many workers told the interviewers they would not take a foreman's job if it were offered to them. Industrial workers do dream of success in other ways. In surprising numbers they harbor entrepreneurial hopes of a business of their own, or at least did so in recent years. Bendix and Lipset's study of Oakland, California, in 1949–50 found that two thirds of the blue-collar heads of families had at one time thought of going into business for themselves, a rate exceeded only by salesmen. Studies of the automobile industry in the late 1940s and early 1950s seemed to confirm their findings. Auto workers told interviewers of their hopes for a farm of their own, an auto repair shop, a gas station, or a "little" stationery store—where you can "give your own orders and not have to take them from anybody else." These are not newfangled dreams of rising to the top, however, but old ones of

---

28 Donald Roy, "Quota Restriction and Goldbricking in a Machine Shop," *American Journal of Sociology*, LVII (1952), 427–442.

getting out of the factory and the employee relationship, akin to
the Knights of Labor's hope to evade the wage system through the
cooperative workshop. And for the majority of factory workers
the optimism of modern man is undercut by the conviction that
neither the corporate ladder nor entrepreneurship holds much
chance at all.[29]

Finally, what of work itself? How committed are present-day
workers to the tasks industrial society provides them? A "work
ethic"—an abstract belief in the value of toil—is still strong among
industrial workers. From 1953 to 1973, a half dozen samples of
male factory employees and blue-collar men in general have been
asked whether, suddenly given a comfortable income, they would
continue to work. At least one half, and generally closer to two
thirds, said that they would keep working. The answer has the
force of tradition behind it. Struggling for status and respect in a
society which has at once honored work and demeaned the industrial laborer, American workers have repeatedly insisted on the
necessity and worth of manual toil. They once proudly called
themselves the "producing classes," the "horny-handed sons of
toil," the "knights of labor," the bedrock of the nation, and the
feelings behind such phrases have not yet been extinguished. This
same pride carries over into the unwillingness of laboring men to
demean the jobs they do. A majority of industrial workers—
skilled or unskilled, assembly-line workers or craftsmen—tell
interviewers they are "satisfied" with their jobs and find them "interesting." But the response tells much more about working-class
culture than of the satisfaction it is frequently presumed to measure. When the question is rephrased and respondents are given an
open choice, a majority of male industrial workers would exchange their jobs for something else, in numbers larger than most
of the rest of the population. In two surveys designed to probe
further the bonds blue-collar men have with their work, only a
tenth of those questioned talked about the intrinsic rewards of

29 *Fortune,* XXXV (May 1947), 10; Ely Chinoy, *Automobile Workers and the American
Dream* (Garden City, N.Y., 1955), 47–61, 82–95; Robert H. Guest, "Work Careers and
Aspirations of Automobile Workers," *American Sociological Review,* XIX (1954), 157–158,
162; Bennett M. Berger, *Working-Class Suburb: A Study of Auto Workers in Suburbia* (Berkeley, 1960), 17; Seymour M. Lipset and Reinhard Bendix, "Social Mobility and Occupational Career Patterns," *American Journal of Sociology,* LVII (1952), 502. For more recent
confirmation: Curt Tausky, "Occupational Mobility Interests," *Canadian Review of Sociology and Anthropology,* IV (1967), 246.

what they did; for the largest number of respondents—71 to 76 percent in the groups surveyed—what came first to mind about their jobs when they thought about quitting them was that they kept them busy and preserved them from the boredom of having nothing to do.[30]

Specific comparison of these responses with the moods of earlier generations of industrial workers remains an open and vexing question. Within it lie shifts in the styles and grounds of discontent at least as important as the persistent conflict itself. But experience with factory labor has not yet won over the inner minds of most of those who do it. In the midst of a society which, in structural terms, is fully modern, the ancient contest over norms and styles of work persists, not only where the latest arrivals—southern migrants and black and Spanish-speaking Americans—are most numerous but also throughout the contemporary factories.[31]

Nor has American society as a whole gone modern in quite the way that theorists of economic development predicted. Modernity is not only a highly class-bound phenomenon but it is time-bound, and in the West its peak may well be over. Certainly to historians familiar with the literature of Anglo-American Victorianism, modern man's faith in science, success, individualism, work, and progress is bound to have a suspiciously archaic ring. The sober-sided ambitions Kahl ascribes to modern man are barely distinguishable from those that Smiles preached to multitudes of nineteenth-century readers. As for Inkeles' conviction that machine civilization forms an effective school for orderly

30 Nancy C. Morse and Robert S. Weiss, "The Function and Meaning of Work and the Job," *American Sociological Review*, XX (1955), 196, 197; Tausky, "Occupational Mobility Interests," 246; William H. Form, "Auto Workers and Their Machines: A Study of Work, Factory, and Job Satisfaction in Four Countries," *Social Forces*, LII (1973), 5, 8–9; Harold L. Sheppard and Neal Q. Herrick, *Where Have All the Robots Gone? Worker Dissatisfaction in the '70s* (New York, 1972), 52, 74n; 1969–70 Survey of Working Conditions and 1972–73 Quality of Employment Survey, unpub. data made available by the Survey Research Center, Institute for Social Research, University of Michigan; Robert P. Quinn, *et al.*, *Job Satisfaction: Is There a Trend?* U.S. Department of Labor, Manpower Research Monograph no. 30 (Washington, 1974); Robert Blauner, "Work Satisfaction and Industrial Trends in Modern Society," in Walter Galenson and Seymour M. Lipset (eds.), *Labor and Trade Unionism* (New York, 1960); idem, *Alienation and Freedom: The Factory Worker and His Industry* (Chicago, 1964), 202; Harold L. Wilensky, "Varieties of Work Experience," in Henry Borow (ed.), *Man in a World at Work* (Boston, 1964), 136–137.

31 Cf. S. M. Miller and Frank Riessman, "Are Workers Middle Class?" *Dissent*, VIII (1961), 507–513; John H. Goldthorpe, *et al.*, "The Affluent Worker and the Thesis of *Embourgeoisement:* Some Preliminary Research Findings," *Sociology*, I (1967), 11–31.

habits and rational thought processes, this too was a nineteenth-century article of faith, reiterated most firmly when revolt from below seemed most imminent, and ultimately put in classical form by Veblen—although Veblen wisely thought that the virus of rationalism would infect the engineers and technocrats long before it reached the semiskilled machine operators.[32] One may not press the parallel between the moderns and the Victorians too far. The nineteenth-century middle class was not particularly empathetic, in Lerner's use of the term. Prophets of success and technological rationalism, moreover, are still abroad and prominent in the West. But the Norman Vincent Peales and the Buckminster Fullers have been forced to alter the nineteenth-century tune in telling ways not as yet comprehended by the fabricators of modernity scales. Perhaps America, unique in so many ways, is an exception to the pressures of modernity. But it is more likely that technology is not the potent determinant of culture that it is sometimes said to be and that, as a shaper of the men it needs, the industrial revolution has been overrated.

If the hypothesis of initial shock and gradual acculturation to the political economy of the factory is not the highway to the promised land and if the modernization hypothesis is suspect, what are the alternatives? Of first importance is a de-escalation of the levels of generalization. Tradition and modernity are too homogenizing of the intractable variety of both past and present to serve historians well. They may be of real help in distinguishing a hunting and gathering tribesman from a twentieth-century engineer, but for most historical questions the terms barely suffice at all. They carry their sway in part on the basis of their appeal to the obvious. No one would deny that in the millennium or so after the Middle Ages the West has changed from something like a collection of traditional societies to a society far more modern. Nor would anyone deny that the reflex of these changes has had an enormous impact on the non-Western world, transforming its traditions in ways past reversing. But the modernization hypothesis does not merely restate the evident—that medieval society broke down with momentous consequences. Behind the

---

32 Thorstein Veblen, *The Instinct of Workmanship and the State of the Industrial Arts* (New York, 1914), 299–355; *idem, The Theory of Business Enterprise* (New York, 1904), 312–313.

terms tradition and modernity lies a law of societal evolution, which carries with it implicit assumptions of historical linearity and of a determinate relationship between culture, personality, and gross levels of economic development. As long as workers use machines and the technology of work processes remains essentially additive, there will always be a degree of linearity to labor history. But workers are more than appendages to economic and work relationships, and it is possible to embrace the insights, the sensitivity, and the humanity of the newest labor history without also embracing its evolutionary framework.[33] Historians would do well to subject the current revival of evolutionism in the social sciences to critical scrutiny.

One can state the whole question differently: all men in all cultures are born premodern, with concepts of time and activity profoundly unsuited to the modern factory. Throughout much of childhood and through many adolescent subcultures, time still runs as irregularly as it ever did before the coming of the factory system. And the passage from childhood to industrial work remains as potentially long and difficult. How a working-class child makes that passage has much to do with the institutions and values which push and shape him until he finally stands at the factory gate. His play and rearing; the precepts taught him by elders, peers, and schools; the heroes (real and mythological) offered him for emulation; and the shape adolescence takes in his society—all of these factors hold important clues for labor historians. What did the nineteenth-century emergence of full-blown adventure stories for the young mean for the values that working-class boys would carry with them into adulthood? What was the experience of a child laborer besides abuse and exploitation? What have schools taught working-class children?

To think of labor history in these ways is to recognize that working-class cultures are not made once and set in motion but must be refashioned with each generation. Not only early life experiences matter but later stages of life as well—the shape of marriage, adulthood, old age, and work in specific times and cultures.

---

33 For example, Gareth S. Jones, "Working-Class Culture and Working-Class Politics in London, 1870–1900: Notes on the Remaking of a Working Class," *Journal of Social History,* VII (1974), 460–508; William H. Sewell, Jr., "Social Change and the Rise of Working-Class Politics in Nineteenth-Century Marseille," *Past & Present,* 65 (1974), 75–109.

The source materials for labor history of this kind are not easy to locate and to interpret, as the few tentative probes in this direction have found.[34] But within this material there are rich and original working-class histories waiting to be written.

The collateral advantages are many. Recasting labor history as collective working-class biography would greatly help to recover the varieties of subcultures within the working class, the continuities, reversions, and departures between working-class generations, and the strikingly different ways new workers have met the encounter with industrial labor. And if it helped to recover the variety of the past, it might also curb the long-standing habit among labor economists to see the present as in stasis. It might make it understandable why, in what are called fully industrialized societies—where the gulf between the child and the adult has been stretched wide and the winds of pleasure blow strongly—adjustment to the factory can still be an intensely difficult experience. It might remind us that, even in the West, industrialization remains a fact of the present.

34 John Demos, *A Little Commonwealth: Family Life in Plymouth Colony* (New York, 1970), 128–178; Joseph F. Kett, "Growing Up in Rural New England, 1800–1840," in Tamara K. Hareven (ed.), *Anonymous Americans: Explorations in Nineteenth-Century Social History* (Englewood Cliffs, N.J., 1971), 1–16.

Stuart M. Blumin

In Pursuit of the American City

Chicago: Growth of a Metropolis. By Harold M. Mayer and Richard C.
Wade, with Glen E. Holt (Chicago, University of Chicago Press, 1969)
510 pp. $30.00

The Private City: Philadelphia in Three Periods of Its Growth. By Sam
Bass Warner, Jr. (Philadelphia, University of Pennsylvania Press, 1968)
236 pp. $5.95

Although one hears often enough that the city has replaced the frontier
in the minds of American social historians, the urban past somehow
resists playing the central role that many would like to assign to it.
Frontier historians were never at a loss to explain how and why the
Western fringe of the American population was at its social, cultural,
and political center. So confident were they of the formative role of the
frontier that empirical research often seemed more of a formality than
a necessity. Urban historians seem to suffer from an opposite malady—
legions are at work on endless and often minute research projects, but
no grand framework of the American urban past and its impact on
American society and culture (and no Frederick Jackson Turner)
appears.

It now seems that urban history in America is destined to find its
place not through the inspired revelations of a Turner, but through an
extended search by many historians for a common set of concepts and
methods. It may be useful, therefore, to consider the two books being
reviewed here from this perspective. Harold M. Mayer and Richard C.
Wade's *Chicago: Growth of a Metropolis* is largely an experiment in just
such method-building. Sam Bass Warner's *The Private City: Philadelphia in Three Periods of Its Growth* is more complex, and will serve to
lead us beyond methodology. The two viewed together provide a
useful if not entirely complete picture of the present state of urban
history and suggest, by their omissions as much as by their substance,
ways in which the field can be advanced.

Stuart M. Blumin is Assistant Professor of History at the Massachusetts Institute of Tech-
nology. He is the author of "Mobility and Change in Ante Bellum Philadelphia," in
Stephan Thernstrom and Richard Sennett (eds.), *Nineteenth-Century Cities: Essays in the
New Urban History* (New Haven, 1969) and "The Historical Study of Vertical Mobility,"
Historical Methods Newsletter, I (Sept., 1969), 1–13.

Mayer and Wade's *Chicago* is a large, handsome, boxed volume containing over 1,000 pictures, fifty maps, and six narrative chapters, all dedicated to the task of explaining "*how* the city expanded and *why* it looks the way it does" (vii). As is evident from these proportions, the book is dominated by its photographs. Increasing this domination are the notes specific to each picture, the four panoramic fold-outs depicting Chicago in 1858, 1913, 1937 and 1969, and the fact that the text, occupying perhaps a fifth of the book, is little more than a supplement to the pictorial "narrative" of Chicago's growth. But of greater importance is the authors' stated intention "to use photography as evidence instead of mere illustration" (vii). This is presumably the point where the book passes from mere illustrated local history, interesting only to the Midwestern Christmas shopper, into serious historical scholarship. The panorama of 1858, for example, "is not simply a quaint view of a young town; it is a visual census of the city which tells us things that we cannot get easily or at all in other ways. For instance, the mixture of land uses . . . the scale and spatial relationships of the urban environment . . . the relationship of the city to the lake and to the surrounding countryside . . ." (viii).

These are, to be sure, important data. It may be added that pictures provide a coalescence of the city's parts that no other source seems capable of providing. In this book one can *see* congestion, the importance of business, the primacy of big business, the extremes of poverty and wealth, the unimportance of the church—all interacting to produce the human environment that analysis so often fails to invoke. But if the reader expects to find here a model of pictorial data analysis, he will be disappointed. Pictures do not become evidence, after all, until they become linked to some hypothetical structure, just as fingerprints do not become criminal evidence until a crime has been committed. Thus, while Mayer and Wade profess an interest in the causation of urban growth, they fail to develop the concepts and hypotheses which are necessary to turn narration into analysis and illustration into evidence.

There are two assertions in the text which do suggest the value of the visual data. First, the authors claim that many of the patterns of metropolitan life, particularly suburbanization, appeared almost at the beginning of the city's history. Second, they claim that Chicago's existence and growth reflected its role in the national and international economy—that it did not evolve out of regional development. The former issue is one that has evoked considerable interest among recent American historians; the latter is parallel to Henri Pirenne's controversial explanation of the rise of European commercial cities almost a millennium before Chicago was incorporated.[1] Both ideas can be approached at least in part by pictorial data. Yet, even in these two cases the authors do not marshal their abundant pictorial "evidence" for systematic analysis. The case for the unique value of the "visual census" to the urban social historian, therefore, remains to be made.

Warner's *The Private City* exemplifies a methodological approach to the city that already has a number of adherents—the analysis of quantitative social data. In order to describe the differentiation of the city's neighborhoods by occupations, rent levels, race, and ethnic groups, he employs the Teaubers' Index of Dissimilarity, using as his sources local tax lists and the manuscript schedules of the United States census. The latter source, used in conjunction with the census of manufactures, produces an interesting estimate of daily commutation patterns and of the separation of residence and work. Districts are further characterized by the proportions of different types of structures contained within them and by varying degrees of residential mobility and mass transit usage. All of these are imaginative and rather novel attempts to answer the same *general* questions approached photographically by Mayer and Wade: How did the physical structure of the city interact with the lives of its citizens? The two approaches beg comparison at this point, but to do so on the basis of two very different books would seem foolhardy. I, for one, find Warner's tables more illuminating than Mayer and Wade's photographs, but I am certainly not ready to claim that a single number is worth a thousand pictures.

The Private City is much more than an illustration of quantitative methodology. Unlike *Chicago*, Warner's book is primarily intended to convey a substantive thesis. Specifically, it attempts to explain the crisis of the twentieth-century American city as the logical consequence of a tradition he labels "privatism," a well-chosen term intended to convey what happens when individualism and materialism come up against problems which require collective action and the equitable distribution of scarce resources. As Warner notes, even the urban American was, and is, above all a self-oriented seeker of personal wealth. But, according to Warner, while the culture of individualism may have served agrarian America well enough, it went tragically awry in the city.

But not from the beginning. Warner structures his case by examining the effects of privatism in "three Philadelphias": The "Eighteenth-

1 (Trans. Frank D. Halsey), *Medieval Cities: Their Origins and the Revival of Trade* (Princeton, 1952).

Century Town" of 1770–1780, the "Big City" of 1830–1860, and the "Industrial Metropolis" of 1920–1930. In the first, the pre-industrial "walking-city" of 20,000 or so inhabitants, with its active street life, its family shops, and its citizens' meetings, privatism cost but little. The city's problems were few, its resources were fairly evenly distributed, and men had little control over one another. Privatism may have revealed considerable weakness during the inflation that accompanied the Revolution (when local control over international business proved futile), but it was not fully in conflict with urban problem-solving until the town gave way to the big city of 1830–1860. By then Philadelphia had acquired the problems of the modern city—violence, the distribution of municipal services, and the quality and distribution of education. But no longer was there a "citizenry" capable of or even interested in coming together to solve them. The process of seeking personal wealth had thrust the middle-class Philadelphian into the national marketplace (which only its merchant princes had heretofore experienced), the working-class Philadelphian into large shops and factories, and all Philadelphians into a large, featureless city which could no longer be traversed easily on foot or even fully comprehended. The single society of the streets was yielding to the countless, separate societies of the factory, the office, and the voluntary association. And into this vacuum stepped the political machine, which was, after all, but a variation of privatism. By the twentieth century, the division of the metropolis into distinct zones of affluence and poverty, commerce, manufacture, and residence destroyed any hope that this collection of private persons might have had of forming a community sufficiently powerful to solve its collective problems.

In *The Private City*, therefore, we have a perfect illustration of the merging of methodological and conceptual innovation that urban historians appear to be looking for. This is not to say, however, that the book itself is perfect. Despite its methodological sophistication, its empirical evidence is often more suggestive than conclusive. Despite its clearly stated theme, its narrative is at times too detailed (as in the discussion of political figures and of nativist riots), so that its relationship to privatism is almost lost amidst particulars, and at times not detailed enough (as in the discussion of ante bellum private associations), so that the theme is insufficiently developed. The book as a whole would be more effective, I think, if it dealt more evenly with "one Philadelphia" rather than with "three." But, if *The Private City* is not conclusive, it is highly suggestive, not only as to the way in which urban history can best be written, but also as to the more important matter concerning the roots of urban failure.

There are other ways, of course, in which both of these books represent current trends in urban historical research. I am struck by three such trends, each of which may be briefly stated. First, the tendency to focus on specific interests or issues seems to have inhibited a more general approach to the city as a social system, and as a sub-system within the larger national society. The city is most often treated as a backdrop for certain types of events or conditions, such as slavery, mobility, industrialization, and Progressivism, some of which are neither unique to nor uniquely affected by the city. *The Private City*, for example, is primarily a study of privatism *in* the city and secondarily a study of the city itself as a social system. This type of approach often produces valuable insights, but it cannot result in a fully articulated urban history, even when all such studies are added together. To a much greater degree than is presently the case, the city itself must be made the primary subject of urban history.

Second, the bulk of urban history has dealt thus far with large and middle-sized cities, almost to the exclusion, even for comparative purposes, of small cities, towns, and rural townships. The weakness, indeed the danger of this deficiency, is obvious—the ease with which observed phenomena can be attributed to urbanization whether or not they existed in smaller communities quite independently from urban growth. For example, it is often assumed that urbanization has had important effects on the size and structure of the household. Yet studies of the urban household seldom, if ever, offer empirical comparison with households in smaller towns or villages. This leads to an important qualification of the suggestion I made in the previous paragraph: In the process of focusing upon the city as a social system, historians of the city should also expand their operation outward to communities of all sizes and types.

Finally, and closely related to the above, historians of the city have given inadequate treatment to the ways in which the city has functioned as a component of larger regional or national social systems. Urbanization is, after all, a process by which parochialism gives way to cosmopolitanism, or, more negatively, a process by which the self-sufficient community becomes "eclipsed" by its participation in the "mass" society. Our very interest in urban history stems largely from the post-Turnerian recognition that the city played a major role in the shaping of American society and culture well before the closing of the frontier. Yet, by confining themselves to events in the city itself, urban historians have inadvertently built city walls which never existed in reality. This narrowness of scope has, more than anything else, kept urban historians from fulfilling their larger role as social historians. To actually fulfill this role, urban historians must not only deal more comprehensively with the city, they must also expand their vision to society as a whole.

Clyde Griffen

Public Opinion in Urban History

Town into City: Springfield, Massachusetts, and the Meaning of Community,
1840–1880. By Michael E. Frisch (Cambridge, Mass., Harvard University Press, 1972) 301 pp. $10.00

With fluent prose and clear organization, Frisch unfolds the inner logic of proposals, decisions, and rhetoric with which Springfield's leaders grappled with the problems of growth. True to the promise in his introduction, he emphasizes the conceptual implications of the details of urban biography. The result is a major contribution to our understanding of the process of urbanization in the United States, and especially of the evolution in ideas of public and private responsibility. Even if one remains unconvinced, as this reviewer does, that "the community" or "the people" in any inclusive sense participated in this intellectual journey, both the significance of that journey for the future governance of all American cities and the skill with which Frisch develops it make the book important reading for social historians.

Frisch defines his own approach to urban history partly through a discussion of the structural analysis urged by Eric Lampard and Samuel Hays. Thus, Hays' emphasis on looking behind urban reformers' perceptions and prescriptions to find the interests that they serve, and the social conflicts to which they respond, seems unnecessarily limiting to Frisch. In Springfield's story traditional leaders groped for solutions to community problems before they perceived any threat to their own leadership; indeed, the abstractions they adopted had the unexpected result of encouraging previously deferential groups to challenge their leadership. Frisch concludes that "the experience of sharing in and overseeing community growth could generate structural conflict as much as it reflected it" (248).

Although he interprets a wide range of social and economic phenomena with sensitivity, the intellectual dimension of his subject most interests Frisch. In part, this preference reflects his view of causation, his conviction that "the process of actually building a city and an urban community involved at its heart the dynamics of conceptual change.... In order for a new type of community to be produced,

Clyde Griffen is Associate Professor of History at Vassar College.

there had to be a new type of approach, and the evolution of progressively more abstract understandings both determined and grew out of
the perceptions, the understandings, and the responses that shaped
the city" (249).

But his affinity runs deeper, involving style as well as substance,
and suggests the influence of that tradition in the social sciences which
emphasizes the usefulness of ideal constructs in clarifying the messiness
of reality. The very neatness in Frisch's ordering of conceptual implications—the systematic way in which he develops the ideas of community and of public responsibility that he finds in municipal controversy—occasionally makes one wonder whether the conceptualization
may be dominating the evidence unduly rather than simply expressing
it. The "birth of a modern city-image" may be useful in explaining the
emergence of a grand style in public buildings but seems excessive or
superfluous for most architectural competition among rich men in their
residences or among churches during the Gilded Age (145–156).

Generally, this reviewer finds Frisch's interpretation of his evidence
persuasive, or more plausible, than alternative interpretations. The
largest part of his story, the extension by the old elite of their understanding of leadership and public interest, elicits only admiration. But
Frisch does not limit his conclusions to the elite or even to the articulate;
he argues that prior to the 1880s the rest of "the community" shared
their assumptions. His treatment of the vast majority is the least substantial, most questionable part of the book for reasons which should
have been made clear to the reader.

Little direct evidence can be found on the attitudes of most of the
inhabitants in Springfield or anywhere else before the age of pollsters.
When literary sources reveal little trustworthy evidence, historians turn
to inference. This has been especially true of the growing number of
social historians preoccupied with the experience of inarticulate
Americans. In an afterword to *Nineteenth-Century Cities*, Norman
Birnbaum, a sociologist, complained that the authors, who include
Frisch and this reviewer, "extrapolate from their findings concerning
external indexes of social position to hypothesized states of political
and social consciousness."[1] Birnbaum urged more use of qualitative
materials, such as contemporary observations, letters, and political dis-
course, but the problem cannot be dismissed so easily.

1   In Stephan Thernstrom and Richard Sennett (eds.), *Nineteenth-Century Cities* (New
Haven, 1969), 424.

In fact, newspapers, public records, and histories, biographies, and reminiscences written by contemporaries provide Frisch with his most direct evidence of public opinion. In the nineteenth century, however, all of these sources usually issued from the more prominent and articulate members of the community. It remains to be determined in each case how limited these sources were to reflections of the perspective and special concerns of an articulate minority, even when they claimed to represent the entire community. With the exception of a biographical compendium and two newspapers, Frisch does not discuss the biases of his sources. But one of the newspapers had a nation-wide reputation for independence and intelligent coverage so that the reader inclines to Frisch's belief that it reflected the drift of local opinion.

So long as the attitudes reported seem plausible and relatively simple, the tendency is not to question their generality. Why doubt the statement that "the community watched proudly" (82) as new business blocks rose in post-war Springfield? At most, the context suggests that "the community" here may be largely confined to those who identified themselves with the city. It may not include the more transient residents whom recent quantitative studies of other cities show to be both numerous and more common among poorer and less skilled workers.

Profound doubts do arise when agreement of the city's two newspapers appears as sole documentation for the assertion that "Springfield embraced, as it had resisted before, the implications of the 'true economy' argument. A general understanding emerged that necessity, even more than economy, was involved, that the community had a positive obligation to anticipate its future" (159). That the sophisticated understanding which brought about a more professional and efficient educational system, fire protection, and water supply had become general among the adult population of Springfield seems unlikely. Unskilled workers, factory operatives, and even artisans do not seem to have figured greatly in the shaping of municipal policy—not even as subjects of concern.

Frisch himself emphasizes the dominance of traditional and largely elite leadership during the years he studies, explaining the consensus that he finds in public opinion as a lingering pattern of deferential politics, and demonstrating this consensus by the absence of conflict along class lines in referenda and in elections. Only toward the end of his period and of the evolution in ideas which he describes does he believe that "others in the community responded, increasingly, by coveting the power that frightened them, their traditional deference eroded

by the very notions of public interest championed by the elite"
(245).

The difficulty with this interpretation, like so much of the discussion of popular attitudes by historians, is that it rests primarily on inferences which are as arguable as they are unsupported. Lack of challenge to elite leadership does not necessarily imply that the other inhabitants shared its perspective and opinions, nor does political challenge imply their rejection, apart from the issue of who should hold office. In the absence of direct evidence of workers' attitudes, one can argue plausibly that workers did not challenge elite leadership because they lacked the solidarity, confidence, and resources to do so. The very diversification of Springfield's economy, the small scale of its shops, and its ethnic differences did not favor common action by workingmen even if they were discontented.

Frisch does offer a variety of circumstantial evidence to suggest that workers saw no necessary conflict between the interests of labor and capital, that they affirmed traditional social relationships. He first removes the unskilled poor from consideration with the comment that they were "too unorganized and isolated to complain" (128). The reader does not learn what proportion of Springfield's labor force they comprised, but their very absence from discussion seems to attest that Frisch regards them as marginal to "the community" or to "the people of Springfield."

For more skilled workers Frisch claims, "Faith in mobility could be sustained by the new businesses and industries prospering on all sides, and meanwhile wages in Springfield were demonstrably higher and more secure than elsewhere in Massachusetts. . . . Workingmen enjoying this relative prosperity were still far from challenging the assumption that their well-being and the progress of local business, industry, and community growth were one of a piece" (128). These inferences from wage rates and the prosperity of city enterprises are reasonable, but they remain inferences. We still know too little about the frame of reference within which artisans and mill-hands, native and foreign-born, interpreted their experience to generalize quite so easily. The degree of satisfaction implied by Frisch's choice of language certainly invites questioning.

More persuasive evidence appears in the participation of workingmen in organizations with an inclusive and apparently "middle class" social outlook. Temperance activity in Springfield apparently conformed to Joseph Gusfield's analysis of it as "a sign of middle-class respectability and a symbol of egalitarianism" (36). The significance of the Workingmen's Association and the Sovereigns of Labor, both "dedicated to the older concept of the community of all producers," seems more ambiguous. Frisch does not specify the occupational composition sufficiently to indicate the distribution of manual workers of various kinds; more important, it remains unclear how far the more powerful Association affirmed "traditional relationships." The angry denunciations of privilege, corporate capital, and the wage system characteristic of a speaker like Wendell Phillips seem hard to reconcile with Frisch's assertion that "the more articulate workers simply did not feel complaint was appropriate or necessary" (128).

Frisch's view of community consensus relies most often, however, on the absence of political opposition along class lines as the elite redefined public responsibility. The issue here is the interpretation of political process. Despite "few real obstructions to those who wished to vote," only one-half of the native male adults and one-fifth of the foreign-born held the franchise in 1865 (126). Frisch does not trace levels of political participation over time but says that low turnouts were common "particularly among less well-established citizens" (40). Deference to elite leadership is explained partly by a consensus that the limited activities of local government concerned property owners primarily, a narrow understanding of the "public interest" which fostered indifference among other inhabitants. But Frisch's tone suggests a much more positive attitude among ordinary men toward elite leadership. His analysis is similar in spirit to the genial picture of respect accorded Virginia gentlemen by their social inferiors in Sydnor's *Gentlemen Freeholders* which Frisch cites as the classic study of deferential politics.[2] No direct illustration is offered of deferential attitudes in Springfield, but Sydnor's book suggests the problem of documentation: Its quotations on respect for gentlemen come from gentlemen and their friends.

One difficulty in evaluating the merits of "consensus" and "conflict" interpretations of American history prior to the twentieth century is this kind of bias in the literary sources. What was the balance between fear and respect, and intimidation and indifference, in the acquiescence of Springfield's workingmen in elite leadership? Frisch's emphasis seems more plausible than its opposite to this reviewer, but it is disquieting to

2 Charles Sydnor, *Gentlemen Freeholders: Political Practices in Washington's Virginia* (Chapel Hill, 1952).

find so little attention to the many, often subtle, ways by which the rich and powerful in America have inhibited their fellow citizens.

In his last chapter, Frisch talks about the erosion of deference among immigrants and workingmen, their realization that they could turn the elite's notions of public interest to their own benefit. The only direct evidence given for this new self-consciousness is the emergence of serious organizing in the skilled crafts and the founding by Edward and Charles Bellamy of the city's first working-class-oriented newspaper. No evidence appears for the content of that consciousness. The interesting argument that the less privileged asserted themselves in politics through the appropriation of ideas that the elite had formulated remains an undocumented assertion. Yet this argument seems central to Frisch's view of the importance for urban history in New England of the intellectual journey he has portrayed: "as the idea of public interest with which the businessmen consolidated their power became more abstract, it began to function less as a guideline to policy and more as a conceptual umbrella in the shade of which conflicting groups could struggle for power. A new framework for legitimized self-conscious interest-group conflict seemed to be emerging, a far cry from the consensual, anti-political tradition of New England community government" (246).

Town into City makes an important contribution to our understanding of how the premises of urban government and politics evolved. But its generalization about public opinion should be more circumscribed and the difficulty in interpreting that opinion more evident. Unless the growing number of community studies confront more directly and more openly the problems of analyzing the consciousness of the inarticulate, they will mislead readers and generate unproductive controversies over interpretations which have very slight foundations.

Gilbert Rozman

Urban Networks and Historical Stages Possibilities for comparing premodern cities are countless, but research strategies for guiding comparisons away from circuitous or dead-end paths are rare. In order to articulate a general strategy for research, a number of fundamental characteristics of urban systems should be considered. In comparative terms, the definition or what qualifies as a city, the sample number of cities, the historical period selected, the larger societal context, and the focus on particular aspects of the urban environment all merit attention. This article examines these elements of urban research separately and considers how they fit together in an overall strategy for using relatively limited data to measure settlement changes prior to modernization.

Studies centering on individual cities could match any two or more of the 50,000–80,000 administrative and marketing centers (central places) in existence around 1800, or of the successively smaller numbers of centers characteristic of earlier times.[1] Although concentration on single cities may, on occasion, offer intriguing glimpses of persistent patterns, it fails to provide a representative sample of settlements for a systematic approach. Within a particular society, the waxing and waning of individual cities normally testify more directly to local and regional competition than to possible commonalities with urban developments elsewhere.

A more broadly-based comparative orientation, which shifts attention away from the single city and toward the urban cluster, emerges from central place theory and from its rare premodern applications by Skinner and Russell.[2] Central place theory clas-

Gilbert Rozman is Associate Professor of Sociology at Princeton University.

1 For data on the number of central places in various countries see Rozman, *Urban Networks in Russia, 1750–1800, and Premodern Periodization* (Princeton, 1976), 245. Extrapolation from the relatively high population-to-market ratios in England, France, or China would indicate a total of as many as 70–80,000 central places throughout the world, but assumptions of less dense distributions elsewhere would reduce this total.

2 See Brian J. L. Berry and Allen Pred, *Central Place Studies: A Bibliography of Theory and Applications* (Philadelphia, 1961). Central place theory began in 1933 with Walter Christaller's deductive explanations for the size, number, and distribution of cities and received substantial empirical verification in the 1950s and 1960s in studies that confirmed the

sifies cities by size and function and examines regularities in the ensuing distributions. Drawing upon insights from central place theory, but focusing exclusively on the premodern era, the urban networks approach likewise relates data from one country on city populations and administrative and marketing functions to similar data from other countries. Applied originally to China, Japan, and the Russian empire, and briefly also to England and France, this approach charts an evolutionary course through the changing urban distributions before the nineteenth century.[3] In contrast to the inherently static assumptions about premodern urban features often implicit in studies preoccupied with questions of urban origin or with the identification of an all-embracing "pre-industrial" city type (inclusive of contemporary nonmodernized societies),[4] the urban networks approach draws on extensive evidence in support of independent and parallel transformations in clusters of cities.

Some critics have found this approach insufficiently theoret-

---

existence of regularities in distributions of cities by size, primarily within modern societies. The ways in which central place systems were changing in premodern societies became a focus of study in a series of articles by G. William Skinner, "Marketing and Social Structure in Rural China," *Journal of Asian Studies*, XXIV (1964-65), 3-43, 195-228, 363-399. Estimates of city-size distributions grouped by regions can be found in Josiah Cox Russell, *Medieval Regions and Their Cities* (Newton Abbot, Eng., 1972). And for successive rankings of the largest cities in the world, see Tertius Chandler and Gerald Fox, *3,000 Years of Urban Growth* (New York, 1974). More recently, Skinner has treated urban population data in his edited volume, *The City in Late Imperial China* (Stanford, 1977). Although Russell uses data narrowly and questionably, Chandler and Fox fail to use sources in languages essential for their task, and Skinner makes many inadequately supported claims for the precision of his data and the exclusive utility of his chosen framework, all focus instructively on large numbers of premodern cities.

3 The fullest application of the urban networks approach is found in Rozman, *Urban Networks in Russia*. Another application can be found in *idem, Urban Networks in Ch'ing China and Tokugawa Japan* (Princeton, 1973). The major sources for urban population data were eighteenth- and nineteenth-century Chinese local gazetteers, Russian archival records from 1782, French geographical dictionaries of 1726 and 1771, and numerous twentieth-century secondary sources on Japanese and English local urban histories. Using a common definition of urban (all residents of central places with a minimum of 3,000 persons and one half of the total number of inhabitants in administrative or intermediate marketing centers with fewer than 3,000 persons), I estimated the percentage of the national population as: 20-21% in England during the 1680s, 17-18% in Japan during more than 100 years in the eighteenth and nineteenth centuries, 16% in France during the 1760s, 8-9% in Russia during the 1780s, and 6-7% in China during the first half of the nineteenth century.

4 For both a brief review of the debate on urban origins and an attempt, poorly grounded in urban sources, to interpret varied information within the straitjacket of a single urban type, see Gideon Sjoberg, *The Pre-Industrial City* (New York, 1960), esp. 25-51.

ical.[5] Whatever the pros and cons may be of relying on a primarily inductive approach, the challenge before us is to consider its implications as a research strategy for comparing urban and related social change over long periods of history.

Explanations for parallel developments in societal evolution often acquire an urban cast. If the object is to generalize about elements of correspondence between stages of history in various countries, then the study of cities offers many advantages. Among the foci for comparisons ranging over many centuries are: 1) are these aspects present in large numbers of societies? 2) can the degree to which they are present in various societies be readily quantified? 3) can changes in the degree of their presence within a given society be readily quantified? and 4) is the degree of their presence likely to have powerful implications for other aspects of social structure? One phenomenon which precisely meets these criteria is urbanism. Premodern societies can be classified as pre-urban and as more or less urban.[6] Furthermore the degree of maturation of urban networks, as will be explained below, is likely to be an indication of many other characteristics of a society.

Social scientists interested in comparing societies have long been attracted to cities. Identifying urban places as the source of civilization, of capitalism, or of revolutionary opposition, Marx, Weber, and many who have kept alive their perspectives have examined similarities and differences in the history of cities. Their fascination with diverse forms of merchant organization and urban autonomy may have detracted interest from other urban phenomena which vary more directly as a function of stages of history defined in some consistent fashion, yet their ideas about social change emanating from cities have long guided comparative research.[7]

---

5 See Skinner, Review of Rozman, *Urban Networks in Ch'ing China and Tokugawa, Japan,* *The Journal of Asian Studies,* XXXV (1975), 131–134; Paul Wheatley, "Handle *sans* Blade: A Misappropriation of Central Place Theory," *The Journal of Interdisciplinary History,* VI (1976), 477–483.
6 A sequence of sociological concerns, evident in the writings of Marion J. Levy, Jr., e.g., *The Structure of Societies* (Princeton, 1952), starts with the common requisites for all societies and then compares relatively modernized with relatively nonmodernized societies. A next step down from these generalized interests is to focus on the main lines of variation among premodern societies. Probably the majority of studies that have at least implicitly classified stages of history according to urban criteria are oriented toward subdividing the long feudal era, as discussed by Karl Marx, within separate countries.
7 Max Weber stated his detailed views on urban history in *The City* (New York, 1958). For Karl Marx's scattered references to premodern cities, it is helpful to examine a number

Recent Soviet writings have somewhat revitalized the statement by Marx that the history of all societies is summarized in the movement of the contradictions between city and countryside.[8] Cities are portrayed as centers of production and commerce for a designated territory. Soviet authors argue that as evolutionary changes occur in what Marx labelled the forces of production and the relations of production, corresponding evolutionary changes occur in cities and in the relationship between cities and their hinterlands. Although these authors still have not systematically applied this concept of changing systems of cities to the stages of development of Russia or of any other society, they have kept alive the promise of an urban-centered view of premodern history through the repetition of their assertions even more than through the execution of their studies.

Although the vagueness of urban studies carried out under Marxist doctrine has long posed an obstacle to explicit comparisons of city systems,[9] the precision of central place theory is squandered by the groping accumulation of data which is inevitable in the use of premodern sources. Such data often benefit from some modification in customary methods, for instance via the simplification of rank-size orderings into a succession of levels defined by population size and/or functions. Bearing in mind that all we can expect is an approximation of reality through a device designed to compare conditions without showing them precisely, we consider how a research strategy emerges through a series of conscious choices among the main alternatives available in urban studies.

FUNDAMENTAL CHARACTERISTICS OF URBAN SYSTEMS

Urban Definition   In choosing a definition, there is a danger of unduly restricting the existence of this settlement type temporally or spatially, e.g., by requiring the presence of self-governing

---

of his writings. Some of these references are brought together in his *Selected Writings in Sociology and Social Philosophy* (New York, 1956), 105-124.

8 For instance, see Iu, R. Klokman, *Sotsial'no-ekonomicheskaia istoriia russkogo goroda* (Socioeconomic history of the Russian city) (Moscow, 1967).

9 This criticism applies particularly to Soviet and Chinese urban studies, as in the above-cited book by Klokman or in Fu I-ling, *Ming Ch'ing shih-tai shang-jen chi shang-yeh tzu-pen* (Merchants and merchant capital of the Ming and Ch'ing periods) (Peking, 1956).

organizations of merchants with substantial autonomy vis-a-vis authorities governing largely rural territories. Greater generality to longer periods of time and to more than a small number of countries can be obtained by a definition based either on population or on a combination of widely observed commercial and administrative functions. Selection of a standard definition (or definitions) for "urban" in all premodern countries is the first requirement facilitating comparisons.

Publications on premodern cities often accept a purely administrative definition, excluding all central places regardless of population and economic prosperity unless they ranked on the ladder of formally designated centers of government. Since there is no reason why the same criteria would have been applied in designating administrative centers from country to country or even in a single country over long stretches of time, such definitions, subject to the vagaries of decisions made by national leaders, do not provide comparability essential for general studies of cities.

I propose a definition of urban with two variants. Both variants define as urban all settlements at levels 1 to 5 (see the two sets of definitions of levels in Table 1) and as semi-urban all level-6 central places. And both variants exclude central places with only local marketing significance (level 7). The difference between the two is that variant I, based on the first set of definitions of the seven levels, can be used to determine how many cities and semi-urban places existed during all premodern periods regardless of the availability of population data: the definitions for variant II are premised on the availability of considerable population data and make possible more refined analysis. This second variant has only been applied to societies with a complete network of central places (in a large-scale society of perhaps thirty million or more people this requires the presence of central places at all seven levels. In less populous societies, with at least five million inhabitants, five or six levels are presumably sufficient owing to the smaller scale).

Using the first variant, all settlements designated as administrative centers and other places boasting commercial functions of some significance beyond the immediate local area qualify as full-fledged cities ranking at levels 1 to 5. Using variant II, all central places with populations in excess of 3,000 qualify as cities and intermediate marketing settlements with fewer than 3,000

Table 1 Definition of Seven Levels of Central Places

LEVEL	VARIANT I	VARIANT II
1	National administrative center	National administrative center and more populous than any level-3 city
2	Regional center or a capital of a decentralized state	Regional center and more populous than any level-3 city
3	Elevated administrative center or a major port linking a level-1 or -2 city to distant areas	Population: 30,000–299,999 and not classified at levels 1 or 2
4	Second lowest administrative center or a major regional port	Population: 10,000–29,999
5	Lowest administrative center	Population: 3,000–9,999
6	Intermediate marketing settlement	Population: fewer than 3,000 people and an intermediate marketing settlement
7	Standard marketing settlement	Population: fewer than 3,000 people and a standard marketing settlement or an administrative center without a periodic market

residents rank as semi-urban. With this second variant, it is possible to determine the percentage of the population urban in any area or any country where population data are sufficient. For the broadest comparisons of premodern countries the first set of definitions of the seven levels applies; in comparisons focused on societies with complete or potentially complete networks, the second set of definitions proves more useful. Obviously, the two must not be used interchangeably.

The application of the population-based definitions maps out the universe of places to be sampled. In the five countries chosen for detailed study at specified points in time ranging from the 1680s in England to the 1830s in China, there were some 1,900 cities and 7,500 to 8,000 level-6 settlements. Corresponding estimates for the entire world in 1800 (with a reduced input of 20–25 percent for less populous China) yield 3,000 to 3,500 cities and 10,000 to 15,000 level-6 places.

Should a higher minimum population be chosen to qualify as a city? For premodern societies, a cut-off of 100,000, 30,000, or 10,000 would be unnecessarily high. Most administrative centers did not reach even the lowest of these levels and many famous trading centers (perhaps doubling as administrative centers) also did not number as many as 10,000 residents. A definition requiring 10,000 residents (levels 1 to 4) would exclude all but eight English settlements and all but thirty-four Russian settlements, and it would cause a drop in the world-wide city total in the year 1800 to roughly 1,000 or 30 percent of the larger figure based on a minimum of 3,000 residents.

Using the first set of definitions not based on population to calculate the number of places with administrative or superior marketing functions yields essentially the same totals for 1800; somewhat smaller totals could be estimated for earlier periods. The number of cities in the world according to this variant probably ranged narrowly for some two thousand years between 2,500 and 3,500, although the number of places which exceeded 3,000 in population must have been rising gradually from an initial low of only a few hundred some two millennia earlier. Stability in the number of administrative centers obscures the slow but continuous growth in their average population. This stability of level-5 centers contrasts with the more volatile explosion of semi-urban (level-6) settlements from the time of their initial proliferation around 1000 A.D. until more than 10,000 existed by the year 1800.[10]

This definition of "urban" with two variants meets three basic requirements for use in wide-ranging comparisons of premodern societies. 1) It neither narrowly restricts the concept of city by country nor by historical period. 2) It reduces the impact of potentially idiosyncratic national designations of settlement types, such as the number of administrative centers. 3) It incorporates a cut-off point in terms of necessary functions or minimal population that eliminates the vast majority of central places in which agricultural occupations predominate, while still including a considerable number of settlements. This definition also contains two other unusual features which enhance its utility for handling imprecise premodern data. Through a division into two variants

10 Rozman, *Urban Networks in Ch'ing China and Tokugawa Japan*, ch. 1, describes the emergence of periodic markets and substantial marketing centers. China seems to have been the first country in which level-6 marketing centers proliferated.

it draws on both descriptive and statistical sources of information, expanding the range of historical coverage and the discriminatory power when data are available. Moreover, through a separate designation of semi-urban central places, it does not ignore the often notable presence of settlements with a mixture of substantial agricultural and non-agricultural functions. Like any definition, this one is arbitrary and the test of whether it should be preferred to possible alternatives lies in its application.

Sample Size   Choice of a sample poses another dilemma in urban research. How many cities and what types of cities should be represented in a particular comparison? In the absence of desired data on each of the hundreds and later thousands of cities in existence from century to century and decade to decade, the goal of increasing the generality of findings can best be realized by obtaining data on large numbers of cities in diverse areas of the world at varying times and at contrasting stages of societal development. East Asia, followed by Europe, South Asia, and the Near East, dominates in any comprehensive sample.

Cross-societal comparisons ideally should be based on representative sampling. To the extent that data are available, sampling should account for regional variations, change over time, and different types of settlements within the urban hierarchy. For many purposes it is desirable to hold certain characteristics common through the choice of countries with similar networks. Each of these sampling goals can be enhanced by refining the categories for classifying both cities and urban networks.

Three refinements substantially narrow the range of potentially useful choices in urban comparisons: the classification of cities into types; the division of countries into areas of integration; and the identification of stages in the maturation of urban networks. The hierarchical classification of cities into types—a cornerstone of central place studies—replaces an undifferentiated term referring to thousands of settlements, some as many as 300 times as populous as others, with specific categories designating separate parts of the total universe of cities. The designation of integrative areas divides national urban networks of widely differing size into comparable clusters of local and regional central places. And the periodization of successive urban stages demarcates similar landmarks in breaking the hundreds or thousands of years of each country's urban history into briefer segments.

Seven levels of central places have already been differentiated in the two variants of the urban definition noted in Table 1. Based on the second variant of the definitions of levels 1 to 5 referring primarily to population data, the distribution of cities at each level can be ascertained as a preliminary step toward sampling. At each successive level up the hierarchy of central places, the number of lower-level cities exceeds the number of places with more substantial functions.

Areas of integration within countries identify the territorial units to be sampled in comparisons of urban networks. Derived from central place theory, these areas refer to hinterlands of cities with a similar range and scale of functions. Area V is defined as the hinterland in which the local marketing or administrative functions of a city take precedence over corresponding functions centered in another city. There is, of course, no precise overlap between the local hinterland for a city operating as a central market and the designated territory of the city's administrative jurisdiction; nevertheless, in a rough manner, the two hinterlands can be joined for the purpose of generalizing. The world of 1800 can be considerably homogenized from a diverse list of hundreds of countries to several thousand relatively similar area V's. Centering on cities at levels 1 to 5, these areas characteristically comprise a population of 50,000–120,000, with the exception of China where the figure climbed rapidly in the century before 1840 to more than 250,000. Each area V supports one city, making this unit the hinterland for every city no matter what its size and regardless of how many level-7 and level-6 central places dot the area.

Area IV (defined, as in the case of each of the other areas, as the territory in which marketing or administrative functions appropriate to a city of this size take precedence over corresponding functions centered in any other city) is the hinterland for cities at levels 1 to 4, encompassing the smaller area V's associated with these cities as well as adjoining area V's of level-5 cities. The world of 1800 comprised many hundreds of these superior integrative units, usually centered on intermediate administrative centers such as a Russian *guberniia*, a Chinese prefecture (*fu*), or a

French province.[11] In comparisons focusing on areas V or IV, the scale of the society is irrelevant.

Countries with populations in the millions correspond to area III's. Within a very large country such as China, area III's centered on level-3 cities, but in a society the size of England the level-1 city operated without any supporting centers at levels 2 and 3. In the world of 1800 some 200 or so units of integration existed at this scale. Above at area II could be found only Japan and the largest European countries, spatially equivalent to any of nine or ten units of regional integration in China. Even larger in scale as the only indisputable area-I unit was the national urban network of China. Perhaps, the voluminous international contact centered in Western Europe warrants ignoring political boundaries in the search for an area I there as well.[12]

Choice of Historical Period   The approximately 5,000-year history of premodern cities poses the need for temporal divisions based on differences in urban patterns. Given the different dates when cities originated in various countries and variations in observed rates of change, no simple chronological classification would be satisfactory. This applies to any attempt to distinguish either a tenth-century city from a fifteenth-century city, or a city in a country with a 500-year urban history from a city in a country with a 1,000-year urban history. For a temporal classification the focus on national urban systems promises to be a truer reflection of changing patterns than the more haphazard choice of individual cities.

I have identified seven distinct stages of urban networks according to the number and pattern of levels of central places present. Similar to the choice of levels, the designation of stages of history is to some extent arbitrary; the stages could be defined in various ways, leading to an increase or decrease in the number chosen. Change is continuous; each stage that has been carefully studied can be further subdivided into sub-stages.

11 Urban comparisons of these units are virtually absent for premodern times, even in intra-societal studies.
12 For the notion that a single world system embraced Western Europe and beyond by the sixteenth century, see Immanuel Wallerstein, *The Modern World-System* (New York, 1974), 15–17. India lacked the integration to be an area I.

The initial stage of history, here called stage A, can be simply described as pre-urban. Although some differences in the distribution of activities within settlements in societies of this kind can often be identified, no single settlement had attracted a high degree of concentrated commercial or craft production.

Stage B marks the beginning of urban development. The first cities generally stood isolated from each other, loosely, if at all, integrated into any large territorial setting. These cities provided only weak control over the resources of the countryside.

The advance from stage B to stage C is signaled by the establishment of a hierarchy of urban centers. Only in stage C societies did a formal administrative hierarchy appear. The existence of two levels of cities facilitated the regular movement of goods and manpower from scattered areas in which lower level cities were found to a small number of higher level cities. Larger territories became integrated into one administrative system, improving the capacity to support populous cities.

Continued increase in centralization based on a hierarchy of administrative centers culminated in stage D societies. Indeed, because of the essentially administrative character of centralization, stage C could be bypassed altogether in those cases where proximity to a great empire at stage D proved infectious, or where conquest resulted. Heijō and Heian Japan and Kievan Russia appear to merit classification as stage D societies although they had only two administrative levels. Occupying relatively small territories as compared to Han China or the Roman Empire, they were able to achieve high degrees of centralization with fewer levels of cities. Heirs to long traditions of city building, the huge empires of Han China and Rome were divided into three levels of cities. Regardless of the number of levels present, societies at this stage sprouted great imperial capitals with hundreds of thousands of people and representing a substantial proportion of the total national urban population.

Also included in the stage D category are the periods of relative decentralizaton which seem in each case to have followed the heyday of the great empires. The number of levels of cities may have remained as before or, as in Western Europe, decreased. In most cases a single imperial center was replaced by several competing regional centers. Only in China did a sudden resurgence of centralization result in an extension of the stage D category when four levels of administrative cities coexisted in the early T'ang dynasty.

It is useful to distinguish stages A through D from the subsequent stages of premodern urban history. The principal force behind the maturation of the urban network in these early stages was administrative centralization. Commerce remained a secondary factor; it was almost entirely confined to closely regulated sections of administrative cities.

Stage E marks the beginning of what I label commercial centralization, although it should be remembered that advances in commerce furthered administrative control in some respects just as advances in the establishment of a hierarchy of administrative centers had previously benefitted commercial growth. The widespread appearance of periodic markets in settlements miles removed from administrative centers marked the onset of stage E societies. It is likely that life in most villages was significantly affected by the development of nearby markets making possible the regular buying and selling of goods.

Stage F societies had larger numbers of periodic marketing places, including a new level of intermediate marketing centers, level 6 in the first set of definitions. With the greater integration of local standard markets under more substantial intermediate markets, the flow of goods from villages to administrative centers could become more efficient and eventually be accelerated. Higher level administrative cities acquired correspondingly greater commercial activities as the centers of expanding networks of markets. As indicated in Table 2, stage F societies normally had five or six levels of central places.

Finally, stage G societies are those that had all seven levels of central places. The final level to be added in each of the three cases that I have studied closely was level 2. The existence of both level 1 and level 2 in a given society is a sign that separate regions support very large cities. In China, Japan, and Russia the shift of the national administrative center from the region with the major crossroads of domestic commerce (Nanking, Kyoto, and Moscow) to another region (Peking, Edo, and St. Petersburg) signaled that a national market was nearing realization and that the seven-level hierarchy was nearing completion.

Table 2   The Seven Stages of Premodern Urban Development

STAGE	NUMBER OF LEVELS PRESENT (LESS COMMON PATTERNS)	ACTUAL LEVELS PRESENT (LESS COMMON PATTERNS)	CHARACTERISTIC
A	zero	—	preurban
B	one	2	tribute city
C	two	1,5 or 2,5	state city
D	two, three or four (one)	1,4,5 or 2,4,5 or 2,3 or 2,3,5 or 1,3,4,5 or 2,3,4,5 (2 or 1,5 or 2,5)	imperial city
E	four or five (three)	1,3,5,7 or 1,3,4,5,7 (2,5,7 or 2,3,5,7)	standard marketing
F	five or six (four)	1,3,4,6,7 or 1,3,4,5,6,7 (2,5,6,7)	intermediate marketing
G	seven (five or six)	1,2,3,4,5,6,7 (1,3,4,5,6,7 or 1,4,5,6,7)	national marketing

We can now review the commercial centralization of premodern societies. Just as stages B, C, and D designate phases in the maturation of an essentially administrative hierarchy, stages E, F, and G refer to the maturation of a commercial hierarchy, even though many of the major commercial nexuses were found in cities which also had administrative functions. From the time standard periodic markets began appearing with the start of stage E until well after the beginning of stage G, the number of level-7 markets continued to proliferate. Correspondingly, after the emergence of level-6 central places from among level-7 centers, there was a persistent expansion of intermediate markets. In countries which did not have as many as four administrative levels, the missing levels were filled in during stage F. Zones of large-scale commercial interchange gradually widened to encompass level-5 cities—the lowest administrative centers—then level-4 cities, level-3 cities, and finally level-2 cities, signifying the inception of stage G.

Stages of history contribute immeasurably to the task of sampling the universe of premodern history. By multiplying the number of countries in the world by the number of stages B-G experienced in each country, we obtain a likely total of at least one thousand separate national urban networks. These can be differentiated by scale and by chronological period in the process of dividing them into units for comparison. The choice of large-scale stage G networks in China, England, France, Japan, and Russia represents but one possibility. In Table 3 the timing of the stages in these five countries is identified on the basis of my research.[13]

Societal Context   In considering the need for studying cities in interaction as well as individual cities, I have assumed that the proper unit of analysis is the society. Variations in other constituents of social structure, such as the individual city, largely reflect the more broadly encompassing differences between societies. Curiously, neglect of societal comparisons sets premodern urban studies apart from other social science fields and from modern studies. This narrowness is a principal factor in the disparate and noncumulative character of premodern urban studies.

A premodern society consists of from zero to about 1,400 cities (of 3,000-plus population) and up to 30,000 or more central places. Individuals in these settlements interact in some systematic fashion, thus justifying identification of them as an urban network. Subnetworks centering on level-5, level-4 and, if the scale of the society permits, level-3, or level-2 cities can be distinguished within the greater societal network. These are the integrative areas noted above. Intersocietal trade and migration may in some cases reach a sufficient scale to lessen the utility of treating a society's urban network as insular.

Just as priorities can be determined in the choice of social phenomena to study, so too can priorities be designated in the countries that merit greatest attention. The search for the ideal historical laboratories should pay close attention to societies which were relatively isolated from foreign influences, large enough to be highly self-contained, and successful in maintaining long, continuous histories. Isolation as measured in the low value of foreign trade compared to domestic commerce and the slight role of diffusion in structuring the urban network increases the visibility of spontaneous maturation based on purely internal conditions.

13   See Rozman, *Urban Networks in Russia*, 73–83.

Table 3 The Stages of Urban Development in Five Countries (estimated century when each stage was reached)

STAGE	CHINA	JAPAN	RUSSIA	ENGLAND	FRANCE
B	18th (B.C.)	7th	9th	2nd (B.C.)	2nd (B.C.)
C	8th (B.C.)	—	—	—	—
D	3rd (B.C.)	8th	11th	1st	1st
E	8th	13th	15th	10th	10th
F	11th	15th	16th	12th	12th
G	16th	17th	18th	16th–17th	16th–17th

Large-scale societies and countries with continuous patterns of urban development further expose the most basic elements in the independent but parallel changes in progress. To isolate these elements priority should go to countries that moved sequentially from stages A to G, remained quite separate from other countries, and reached a population by 1800 of tens or hundreds of millions. There will undoubtedly be little disagreement that China meets these conditions until the middle of the nineteenth century. Despite intense borrowing from China around the seventh century A.D., Japan also meets these conditions. Little of the actual social structure of Tokugawa Japan (1600–1868) can be explained in terms of Chinese precedents. There is more difficulty fitting Russia through the eighteenth century into this category; we are tempted to recall Peter the Great's widely noted Westernizing efforts. Yet, the case of Russia resembles that of Japan. Dramatic and conscious borrowing before the nineteenth century probably exerted little impact on the major contours of social structure that existed in the late stages of premodern development. In my opinion, the choice of these three populous countries, with continuous histories of more than 1,000 years each, offers the most unobscured view of all societies in world history of the independent development of complex social phenomena. These countries and perhaps a few others that are also well-documented and share the above conditions deserve the highest priority in the effort to generalize about societies.

In my work, I have added England and France to this list of three countries for purposes of comparative analysis. As Western European countries they lacked the isolation produced by the vast area or impregnable location of the others; nevertheless possessing well-documented, long, continuous histories, they expand the sample from which generalizations about periodization can be induced and against which they can be tested. After all, given the predominant scholarly concerns of the past, omission of Western European cases from a study of urban periodization would no better serve the purpose of generalizing about premodern cities than has the omission of China and Japan until now.

Among stage G societies, I would suggest an order of priority based on the scale of the urban network. First precedence should be given to China, the only case of which I am aware with 1,000 or more full-fledged cities. Second in importance are countries with roughly 200 to 400 cities, i.e. central places with a minimum of 3,000 population. Japan, France, the Russian Empire, and perhaps the Ottoman Empire, the Austro-Hungarian Empire, and separate regions of decentralized India would qualify. Together these areas roughly approximated the 30–33 percent of the world's population settled in late eighteenth- and early nineteenth-century China. Third in priority are the urban networks boasting about 50 to 150 cities. England, Korea, and Persia number among the 5–10 percent of the world's population with networks on this scale. Finally, lowest in priority are the networks of roughly 10, 20, or 30 cities.

What is striking about this list of national urban networks is the high proportion of cities located in a small number of countries. By examining China and several countries with networks of 200 to 400 cities at levels 1 to 5, over half of the world's cities can readily be included.

Aspects of Urban Life   There is little distinctive about urban studies per se; practically every behavior can take place in an urban setting. Indeed, only one fundamental concern gives this field a separate identity, i.e. its focus on settlement size as an independent variable. Among the variables frequently singled out by social scientists, such factors as nationality, ethnicity, age, sex, and social class are commonly credited with powerful implications for explaining variations in individual behavior and attitudes. Settlement size merits inclusion in a list of this sort. In many societies a sharp urban-rural dichotomy exists and elsewhere, with few exceptions, notable differences in life styles are also associated with the separate levels in an urban hierarchy. In choosing among the numerous alternatives for comparing cities, we should not lose sight of the importance of focusing on settlement size.

Each of the previous decisions among the possible alternatives in urban studies has implications for and requires justification in the determination of a useful focus for analyzing the selected cities. The decision regarding *what* qualifies as a city contributes to the theoretical objectives of the social sciences, not only by incorporating only a minimal number of widely present and clearly identifiable elements into the definition, but also by easing the task of classifying settlements by population or by functions that are likely to correspond relatively well to population.

The sampling decision that answers the question concerning *which* cities should be chosen supports social science objectives by ordering cities into five separate size categories and by grouping clusters of central places into integrated areas of five successive sizes within an urban network. Selection of six stages of urban history partially resolves the problem of *when* cities are comparable in basic respects. Finally, identification of priorities in the countries to be studied responds to the need to know *where* it is most useful to begin in order to obtain an unadulterated viewpoint of urban networks and a relatively complete picture of the world's cities. Given this focus on settlement sizes, we can now use the framework established through the above decisions to devise a new method for calculating rates of social change from century to century. Changing networks of cities offer one perspective on the evolution of societies.

Stages of History   Using the classification of all premodern central places into seven levels, we can study the histories of separate countries to determine which levels appeared from century to century. This is the approach that I have applied in differentiating stages A to G, an empirically observed sequence of seven stages from pre-urban to relatively complex networks comprising many levels of central places. With information on the duration of stages A to G in various countries, it becomes possible to measure the rate of maturation of societal urban networks. Countries exhibiting slow rates of change would spend disproportionately long periods at a given stage of urban development, while other countries would pass more rapidly from stage to stage. At the two extremes, we might expect to find the relatively static pre-urban society never passing on into stage B and the unusually dynamic country adding a new level in the urban hierarchy once every 100 or 200 years until, in a span of perhaps 1,000 years, a stage G society would emerge. If countries with rapid rates in one phase of the maturation process were to maintain similar rates in the transitions between other stages, then the search could be broadened to identify interdependencies in the overall pattern of urban development throughout premodern history.

From the time cities first originate in a region (stage B) until the realization of a full administratively-based network (stage D), how many centuries elapse? Depending on whether we treat the entire Mediterranean area as one region, the record amount of time can be as long as 3,000 or more years or perhaps the briefer 1,600 years in China. Countries on the periphery of vast stage D empires, such as Japan and Russia, could shorten this period to as little as 100 or 200 years.

From the onset of a stage D urban network to the initial proliferation of periodic markets characteristic of stage E societies, in the cases of China and the Mediterranean regions of the Roman Empire roughly 1,000 to 1,200 years elapsed, whereas Japan and Russia made the same transition in approximately 500 years.

From the time stage E patterns are established to the appearance of a stage G society, China's development again appears unduly slow, comprising about 800 years. Western European countries passed these landmarks in perhaps 600 to 700 years, Japan took about 400 years, and Russia required only about 250 years.

We observe at least four patterns of movement from stage to stage. First, the vast majority of world societies can be classified as having incomplete forward motion. They either remained pre-urban at stage A or became stalled at other stages short of stage G. Second, among societies that reached stage G, China's development was a gradual, grinding forward. Ahead of the rest of the world for perhaps as long as 1,500 years, China pushed relentlessly but gradually forward. Third, the pattern of Western European countries was intermediate in speed, not as slow as China except during the intervals to stage E. Fourth, the Japanese and Russian cases reveal a quicker path from stage to stage, although these countries did not overtake Western Europe.

Characteristics of one stage of urban development may survive in other stages. Thus a network weak at level 5 in stage D is likely to become strongly decentralized in stages E and perhaps F. Intermediate levels of central places are absent as level-7 and -6 settlements appear, reducing the capacity of central governments to control the new opportunities for mobilizing local resources.

If one looked only at individual cities, it would be difficult to obtain any general awareness of stages of history and rates of change. The rise and fall of particular cities may have no wider meaning since other cities may assume their abandoned functions. The gradual addition of new levels of urban networks is likely to have much greater significance for it represents a society-wide phenomenon involving both an increase in the overall number of cities and the concentration of a new range of urban functions. This concept of periodization involves a sequential movement through a series of distinct points or stages in development likely to have wide implications for other aspects of social structure.

In striving for a generalized approach to settlement size as a variable, the principal issue in addition to the analysis of rates of change is the analysis of the distribution of central places at each of the designated levels in the urban hierarchy.[14] The varying pyramidal shapes of a graphic representation of the number of central places at each level in the hierarchy convey a general image of the urban network.

The notion of an urban-rural dichotomy or continuum has meaning only where a noteworthy segment of the population resides in both urban and rural areas. With a breakdown into separate urban levels, this notion can be substantially refined. To the extent that such a pattern exists, it should be reflected in differentials between settlements in each pair of adjoining urban levels. The sharpest differentials, equivalent to the sum of the successive differentials between seven adjoining pairs, would prevail between level-1 cities and ordinary villages.

A first step in applying this approach is to find the shape of the urban pyramid in each society. In Figures 1 and 2, I ignore differences in the total number of central places in each of five

14 This subject is treated in Brian J. L. Berry, "Cities as Systems Within Systems of Cities," *Papers and Proceedings of the Regional Science Association*, XIII (1964), 147-163.

Fig. 1 Stage G Urban Networks

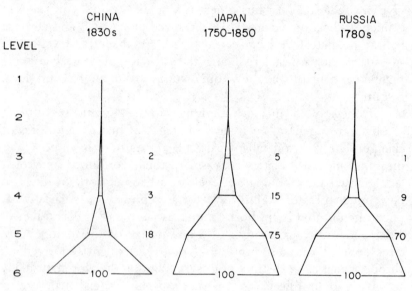

CHINA 1830s   JAPAN 1750-1850   RUSSIA 1780s

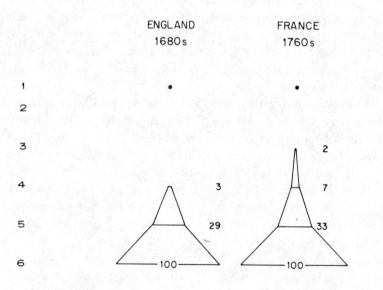

ENGLAND 1680s   FRANCE 1760s

Fig. 2 Stage G Urban Networks: Number of Settlements at Levels 1–5 relative to Number at Level 6

LEVEL

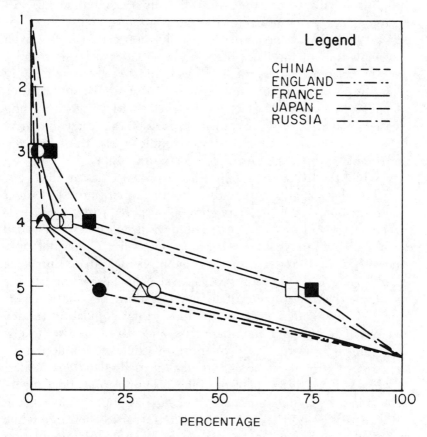

countries by treating the number of level-6 places as a constant base of 100. The figures for each country are approximations based on studies of their stage G urban networks region by region and province by province.[15]

The ratio of level 5 to level 6 in these five countries reveals three distinct patterns. In Japan and Russia the ratio reaches as high as 70:100 or 75:100. The number of cities of 3,000–10,000 population is not greatly surpassed by the number of semi-urban

15 Rozman, *Urban Networks in Russia,* 244–250, 245 for Figure I data.

centers of fewer than 3,000 inhabitants. The intermediate pattern found in England and France reveals a ratio of 29:100 or 33:100. Instead of two thirds or more cities at this higher level, the proportion falls below one third. Finally the Chinese ratio of 18:100 is barely one fourth of the ratios in Japan and Russia.

At higher levels no similarly neat division materializes. Given the small scale of England, the absence of cities at levels 2 and 3 and the relative scarcity of level 4 should not be assigned any wider importance. France and Japan are most similar in the ratios of level-4 to level-5 and of level-3 to level-4 settlements, but using a base of 100 for level 6 conveys an impression of greater similarity between France and Russia at these middle levels. Both England and France exhibit an incomplete network topped by a level-1 city while the other three countries maintain cities at all levels.

To what extent do these distributions of cities by settlement size contribute to our understanding of observed patterns of rural-urban dichotomies? As the one country alleged not to have had such a dichotomy in life styles or architecture, China not only brandishes the thinnest tip of the pyramid measured from level 5 or level 4 on a base of 100 at level 6 but also supports the smallest urban percentage of total population, i.e. about 6 percent.[16] Only about 3 percent of China's total population resided in cities of 30,000 or more inhabitants, and that figure rises to just 4 percent in cities of 10,000 or more. In contrast, London alone approached 10 percent of the population of England and Wales, whereas as many as 8–9 percent of Japan's population and 6–7 percent of France's population resided in cities as populous as 30,000. Only Russia is noted for a sharp rural-urban dichotomy while maintaining a meager figure of 2–3 percent of its total population in cities of 30,000 or more, although its overall urban figure of 8–9 percent exceeded the Chinese proportion.

Based on comparisons of both urban pyramids and rates of change characteristic of stage G urban networks in these five countries, I would tentatively posit three substages of this period in societal development immediately prior to contacts with the process of modernization. Substage G1 fits the Chinese data for roughly three centuries prior to 1850. It is distinguished by no

16 See F. W. Mote, "The Transformation of Nanking," in Skinner (ed.), *The City in Late Imperial China*, 101–153.

major change in either the shape of the urban pyramid or the percentage of population in cities. The number of level-7 central places continues to increase rapidly. Substage G2 generally fits the data for the other four countries during their first century as stage G societies. In each case a notable rise occurred in the percentage of population urban and the number of periodic markets increased, if at all, slowly. These generalizations need to be qualified somewhat for the Russian case, where the urban percentage did not double and the number of periodic markets appears to have grown at a faster pace as opposed to England and Japan. Substage G3 accompanied the second century of stage G development in these four societies that had experienced G2. The urban population was relatively stagnant and periodic markets declined in number. Referring to Japan, Smith labels this period one of rural-centered development.[17]

By looking more closely at the full urban pyramids in the four countries that reached G3, two basic distinctions become evident. On the one hand, England and France reveal a pattern of commercial centralization. This pattern consists of a small average population sustaining level-7 central places, a high ratio of level-6 to level-7 centers, a relatively small percentage of central places at level 5, and a large level-1 city relying heavily on commercial support. On the other hand, Japan and Russia reveal a pattern of administrative centralization. This pattern consists of a low number of level-7 centers per capita, a modest ratio of level-6 to level-7 centers, a high percentage of central places at level 5, and a circulating service nobility alternating in their residence between cities at levels 1 and 2 and local areas from which they drew their incomes. I would hypothesize that the first pattern is conducive to initiating modernization and the second pattern provides a good foundation for the modernization of a latecomer to the process.

My examination of urban pyramids has so far only provided a framework for describing the variables that relate to settlement size. Indeed, the urban networks approach has been used for designating historical stages, but not for measurements of the correlations between urban-based designations of stages and other

17 Thomas C. Smith, "Pre-modern Economic Growth: Japan and the West," *Past & Present*, 43 (1973), 127-160.

variables. Yet the obvious rationale for starting with this approach is the expectation that interrelationships between cities reflect in a relatively accurate way how societies become more complex.

What other indicators of societal evolution might vary as a function of changing stages of urban networks? I will divide this exploratory effort into five social science categories: human resources, patterns of settlement, organizational contexts, redistributive processes, and aspects of personal relationships.

1. Human Resources. For modern times, a number of demographic variables have occasionally been correlated with settlement size. In premodern times there is occasional reference to large cities with higher mortality rates and smaller average household size. It might therefore be worthwhile to examine the ways in which mortality varies directly and fertility and nuptiality inversely with urban size.

Overall national demographic trends may show some relationship to the stages of the urban network. Among the cases studied, stage G societies grew quite rapidly in population because of as yet poorly understood reasons. China, Japan, and Russia all experienced considerable natural increase for more than a century, resulting in a more than doubling of the national population. In the case of G3 societies, the earlier population expansion slowed sharply. A striking similarlity of G3 societies is that fertility appears to have fallen, owing to higher ages of marriage in Western Europe and to a variety of factors in Japan.[18]

Why should demographic rates reflect changing urban networks? First, peaks in mortality can be softened by expanding interregional exchange of agricultural products. The more mature the urban network, the greater is likely to be the commercialization and the coordinated national exchange of goods in the society. Second, although fertility remains at a high level in premodern societies, important differences in this variable also existed. The diffusion of urban consumption patterns and educational standards had at least regional significance; large cities and areas in close contact with them in G3 societies began to exhibit new appreciation for rising per capita incomes.

---

18 On Japan, see Susan B. Hanley, "Fertility, Mortality, and Life Expectancy in Premodern Japan," *Population Studies*, XXVIII (1974), 127–142; Robert Y. Eng and Thomas C. Smith, "Peasant Families and Population Control in Eighteenth-Century Japan," *Journal of Interdisciplinary History*, VI (1976), 417–445.

Comparisons of the various stages of development suggest the following regularities in stratification. In societies at stages B to D, the occupations associated with military, administrative, and ceremonial functions acquire exceptional importance. Then as societies move on to stages E, F, and G, merchants, artisans, and hired laborers comprise a greater percentage of the total population. These non-agricultural activities, whether full-time or measured by adding the full-time equivalents of part-time work, spread increasingly to rural areas in the late premodern stages. In G3 societies rural by-employments become especially widespread in the hinterlands of major cities. Thus movement from stage to stage is accompanied by an increasing number of persons freed from the routine of rural life.

Efforts to apply this approach also confirm that the occupational structure varies directly with settlement size. As we move up the hierarchy from level 7 to level 1, the percentage of the population in various nonagricultural occupations rises accordingly.

2. Patterns of Settlement. Not all aspects of settlement patterns are incorporated into the definitions of the various urban levels and therefore may, at least in theory, vary at random from the independent variable: stage of development of urban networks. If we use the first variant of the definitions of the seven levels, it is not true by definition that the percentage of the population in cities increases as a society proceeds from stage to stage. It should not, however, come as a surprise that the percentage of population urban in a given country appears to rise, or at least stay even, in the movement from stage to stage.

Rural setttlement patterns and other characteristics of rural living have not been much investigated from the perspective of societal evolution. I anticipate that stages in correspondence with the urban network stages will be found in this environment as well. As marketing areas become more complex and better integrated, the relation of the village to the outside presumably induces changes internal to the village.

From my initial study of three countries, I find evidence also that land use changes reveal distinct regularities. Highly ordered city plans during the stages of administrative centralization generally yield to more chaotic, dispersed growth by the time of stage G societies.

3. Organizational Contexts. In a number of organizations signs of evolutionary premodern development can be found. Most important for these societies is the transformation in family structure, marked by a decline in large kinship units. Also of major importance are changes in administrative bureaucracies and military organizations. The rise of large and relatively skilled civilian bureaucracies and of large standing armies can be noticed in stage G societies.

Intermediate between the small family and the national bureaucracies, a variety of organizational contexts can be identified. One of the few that has been considered in an evolutionary context is the guild, which at least one writer, taking a Marxist perspective, alleges has changed in a predictable historical fashion.[19]

4. Redistributive Processes. Variables such as marketing, migration, mobility, and taxation all bear close scrutiny in the context of changing urban networks. Although some facets of marketing are incorporated into the definitions of the urban levels, many others can be studied as possible dependent variables. For instance, the percentage of all goods produced that are traded may rise from stage to stage. Regularities in the places of origin of migrants might also be related to the urban networks approach. And after the concept of social mobility is broken down into various channels, such as mobility into and out of the merchant profession, I expect that both a division into levels of settlements and one into stages of history will have considerable utility.

5. Aspects of Personal Relationships. A set of continuous variables used to compare modernized and nonmodernized societies has relevance for comparisons of premodern societies as well. Relationships are likely to change during the course of premodern evolution in the direction of the prevalent patterns in modernized societies. For instance, the landlord-tenant, merchant-consumer, official-subject, and official-official relationships become more rational, universalistic, and functionally specific in some stage G societies examined.[20]

19 E. P. Stuzhina, "O kharaktere tsekhovoi organizatsii v Kitae v XVII - pervoi polovine XIX v" (On the character of guild organization in China in the seventeenth to the first half of the nineteenth centuries), *Problemy Vostokovedeniia*, I (1961), 35-53.
20 These relationships are considered in more detail in Cyril E. Black, et al., *The Modernization of Japan and Russia* (New York, 1975), 94-96.

These suggestions of areas worthy of examination through the application of the urban networks approach give some idea of the range of concerns that ought to be incorporated into a full treatment of historical stages. Even if the decisions associated with this approach are soon proven to be less heuristic than some other set of decisions, they will at least have focused attention on the questions that make it possible to realize social science objectives in studies of premodern cities. Above all, the identification of a common sequence of distinct stages in the evolution of networks of cities suggests that broad systems of periodization should be revived as a device for historical comparisons of societies.

Howard Spodek

From "Parasitic" to "Generative": The Transformation of Post-Colonial Cities in India

The bipolar concept of generative and parasitic cities, most explicitly expressed by Hoselitz, has penetrated the literature of pre-industrial cities. As Hoselitz describes it, the concept is economic: "A city will be designated as generative if its impact on economic growth is favorable, i.e., if its formation and continued existence and growth is one of the factors accountable for the economic development of the region or country in which it is located. A city will be considered as parasitic if it exerts an opposite impact."[1] Underlying this economic definition, however, remains an even more significant political question: For whose interests do the urban ruling groups work? Are the tax and investment policies of the urban elites designed to stimulate regional productivity—rural as well as urban—or, alternatively, to draw agricultural surpluses into the city for conspicuous consumption by a privileged few? At an even more basic level, the question of values is encountered: Do the urban elites wish primarily to promote economic expansion, or are control of retainers, land, and prestige—regardless of their effects on economic productivity—more significant goals? The initiation of urban industrialization invests cities with at least some generative functions, but in economically underdeveloped countries, the degree of this generativity is by no means resolved. Noting that the promise of employment lures enormous amounts of surplus labor to industrializing cities, McGee asks whether contemporary large Asian cities, even with industry, are "Catalysts or Cancers."[2]

In the history of the urbanization of Europe and North America, the problem of parasitism plays only a small role. For the most part, the generative role of cities predominates. As market places, cities elicited

Howard Spodek is Assistant Professor of History and Urban Studies at Temple University and the author of several articles on India.

Research for this paper was carried out under grants from the National Science Foundation and the Danforth Foundation.

1 Bert Hoselitz, "Generative and Parasitic Cities," *Economic Development and Cultural Change*, III (1954–55), 278–296, 279.
2 Terry McGee, "Catalysts or Cancers? The Role of Cities in Asian Society," in Leo Jakobson and Ved Prakash (eds.), *Urbanization and National Development* (Beverly Hills, 1971), 157–181.

SAURASHTRA, INDIA

Bhavnagar

Rajkot

Gondal

Junagadh

Jamnagar

INDIA

extensive cash cropping, for example, as early as the sixteenth century in England. As service centers, and communication and transportation points, they were crucial in the rapid development of the American West. Throughout northwestern Europe the "bourgeois revolution" ushered in a new age of generativity which promoted rural as well as urban development. Not that parasitism was unknown, but it did not compare with the experience of regions under foreign colonialism nor those in which the urban ruling classes devalued rural economic development.[3]

Such devaluation took a variety of forms. In many places, urban rulers chose the conquest of additional territory rather than the development of their own hinterlands as the better means of increasing agricultural holdings. In addition, many urban rulers taxed their rural areas heavily. A combination of high rural taxation which antagonized farmers and a policy of predatory militarism toward neighbors led rulers in western India, for example, to build their cities as remote fortresses for protection rather than as open market places for trade. A British officer observed, "The traditional policy of the state was to maintain inaccessibility. Forests, difficult passes, vile roads, thick jungles, were the bulwarks not only of the capital but of most of its towns and villages."[4] Thus, in at least some areas, the political system conflicted with economic incentives. In other areas—for example, in substantial regions of China on the eve of the Communist revolution—the urban elites allied themselves with a rural gentry which collected heavy rents while doing little to develop agriculture. Here, the urban elites did not act in a direct parasitic fashion, but they watched benignly as their rural allies did.[5] Finally, in cities fostered by colonial administration, local profits—rural as well as urban—were often soaked up in taxes and in the purchase of consumer goods produced in the colonial factories. Economically, this "drain" left no surplus for investment in development. The urban elites lost interest in the welfare of the countryside as they oriented themselves toward the metropolitan culture of the colonizers.

3   J. D. Chambers and G. E. Mingay, *The Agricultural Revolution 1750–1880* (New York, 1966); Alan Everitt, "The Marketing of Agricultural Produce," in Joan Thirsk (ed.), *The Agrarian History of England and Wales*, IV: *1500–1640* (Cambridge, 1967); Richard Wade, *The Urban Frontier* (Cambridge, Mass., 1959); Henri Pirenne, *The Medieval City* (Princeton, 1952).
4   George LeGrand Jacob, *Western India: Before and During the Mutinies* (London, 1872), 121.
5   Hsiao-tung Fei, *China's Gentry: Essays in Rural–Urban Relations* (Chicago, 1953).

In the long run, the cultural reorientation also inhibited rural development by devaluing its importance.[6]

For Asia, in particular, the question of the roles of cities has suffused recent political debate. The foremost leaders of the two largest countries of Asia have profoundly questioned the role of the city in economic development.[7] From 1927 onward, Mao Tse-tung shifted his headquarters and much of the thrust of his political revolution from the city to the countryside. Mao's spectacular agrarian revolution has, with apparent success, rechanneled urban political and economic power for the benefit of the countryside and thus modified the historic roles of urban and rural areas in China.

In India, Mahatma Gandhi's radically anti-urban message was published in *Hind Swaraj* or *Indian Home Rule* in 1909. Although Gandhi later recognized the importance of the urban–industrial economy to national political and economic development, his legacy to substantial segments of the Congress Party of India has been a strong ideological concern for village development, even at the expense of cities.[8] Both Gandhi and Mao were eager to reform parasitic cities into generative ones. Neither wished to destroy cities altogether, for they recognized that no city was solely parasitic; the problem was one of degree.

In light of the literature and the political-economic speculation on generative and parasitic cities, what now seems necessary is an examination of the transformation of a city or group of cities from parasitic functioning to generative. A historical study of such a transformation will enable us to escape from the bipolarity of the theoretical, heuristic model. It will facilitate an examination in greater detail of the actual functioning of cities and their elites in regional and national development at different periods of time.[9] The present essay provides such a case study of the Saurashtra peninsula of western India in modern times, and particularly since the attainment of national independence in 1947.

6 Cf. Clifford Geertz, *Islam Observed* (Chicago, 1971).
7 Rhoads Murphey, "City and Countryside as Ideological Issues: India and China," *Comparative Studies in Society and History*, XIV (1972), 250–267.
8 Mohandas Karamchand Gandhi, *Hind Swaraj or Indian Home Rule* (Ahmedabad, 1938); Howard Spodek, "On the Origins of Gandhi's Political Methodology: The Heritage of Kathiawad and Gujarat," *Journal of Asian Studies*, XXX (1971), 361–372; Sachin Chaudhuri, "Centralization and the Alternate Forms of Decentralization: A Key Issue," in Roy Turner (ed.), *India's Urban Future* (Bombay, 1962), 213–229.
9 Hoselitz called for just such study ("Generative," 291).

Table 1   Percentage of the Population of the Saurashtra Peninsula Living in
Urban Areas, with All-India Comparison, 1901–71

YEAR	TOTAL	ALL–INDIA	IN TOWNS OVER 20,000	ALL–INDIA IN TOWNS OVER 20,000	IN CITIES OVER 100,000	ALL–INDIA IN CITIES OVER 100,000
1901	26	11	10	5.5	—	2
1911	23	10	9	5	—	2
1921	24	11	9.5	6	—	3
1931	25	12	13.5	7	—	3
1941	28	14	16	9	3	5
1951	31	17	20	12	8	7
1961	31	18	22	14	9	9
1971	31	20	N.A.	16	10	10

SOURCES: *Census of India*, for appropriate years.

Under British rule, Saurashtra (previously called Kathiawad), was
a minor regional division of the Indian Empire. The 25,000 square mile
peninsula registered some two million people in the first national
census of 1872, and tripled to about six million by 1961. Throughout
the twentieth century it has shown significantly more urbanization than
India generally (Table 1). The British chose to sanction and increase
the powers of the local potentates and to rule the peninsula through
them. This policy of indirect rule carved the peninsula into some 200
semi-autonomous city-states. By Independence, seven of them, led by
Bhavnagar, Jamnagar, and Junagadh, had populations ranging from
100,000 to 700,000 and filled, together, about half of the land area.
This political fragmentation, coupled with idiosyncratic, indigenous
cultural patterns, made Saurashtra unique among Indian regions and
might raise some question of the usefulness of such a case study. For
many post-Independence political and economic developments, however, the individual state is the appropriate unit of examination. The
federal structure of government in the Indian Union has accommodated
regional differences by granting vast powers to the constituent states,
particularly in the field of agricultural reform. Although the study of a
single state may provide only a partial view of India's recent experience,
the individual states are, in fact, the level at which much significant
change is implemented.

PRE-BRITISH SAURASHTRA   The tradition of "parasitic" colonial cities dates back at least several hundred years in India. The leading historians of Mughal India (1526–1700s) have stressed the exploitative nature of the capitals of these pre-British rulers. Moreland, a high ranking British civil servant, for example, contrasted the producing, rural, agricultural classes with the urban "consuming classes."[10] If Moreland can be charged with a bias against the Mughals in order to contrast the improvements wrought by their British successors, the same charge cannot be brought against Irfan Habib of Aligarh Muslim University, the foremost contemporary historian of Mughal India. Habib argues that the high rates of land revenue—often reaching 50 percent of the gross crop—precipitated rural armed revolution. According to him, the ruling Mughals, their courtiers, and administrative personnel spent some two-thirds of this total land revenue on an economically unproductive military. (He estimates the military and its dependents at about 5 million people of a total population of perhaps 100 million.) An additional 10 percent of the revenue supported a professional class, and much of the balance went into conspicuous consumption. Although this yielded great cultural and aesthetic treasures, it did little to expand the economy.[11]

In Habib's view, two non-governmental groups—one predominantly urban, the other rural—had significant access to capital. The merchant class invested in commerce rather than industry or agriculture; this commerce, apparently, was most often in luxury trade. The local, rural, landholding elites, who also served as tax collectors under the Mughals, spent the 10–25 percent of the land produce which was their share largely on attracting and supporting retainers. They did not invest in increasing rural productivity.[12] Presumably control of retainers in the short run was more highly valued than an increase in productivity in the long.[13]

10 W. H. Moreland, *India at the Death of Akbar* (Delhi, 1962).
11 Irfan Habib, *The Agrarian System of Mughal India, 1556–1707* (Bombay, 1963). Habib stresses developmental aspects of the economy most explicitly in "Potentialities of Capitalistic Development in the Economy of Mughal India," *Journal of Economic History,* XXIX (1969), 32–73.
12 *Taccavi,* a temporary loan, was extended by government primarily in times of bad harvests to tide the peasants over, rather than as a stimulus to increased investment and productivity.
13 According to Walter Neale, "This system of values which puts preservation of status and achievement of power above direct acquisition of wealth continues to this day. The rational man, whether he wants respect, income, or to be obeyed, is not an economic

Habib overlooks yet another point which would further support his view of a parasitic ruling urban group. In pre-industrial economies, especially, a major force for economic modernization must be the reciprocal economic interaction of city and countryside.[14] Cities must stimulate agro-industries, the production and refining of commercial products from local agricultural commodities. City markets must help in the dissemination, if not in the invention, of new rural machinery and techniques. Otherwise agricultural potential remains unexploited and the energy of the farmers remains untapped. Mughal farmers, however, failed to adopt such available innovation as metal implements. Habib suggests that it was cheaper to employ added labor at the prevalent low wages than to innovate. But if, as he suggests, land was so plentiful as to be almost free of charge, could not newer technology be used to extend cultivation even as the economy provided full employment? The apparent conclusion is that the farmers were not permitted to retain adequate profits to purchase improved equipment. Mughal policies of high land revenues precluded farmers from investing in improved technology and acted rather to sustain a dual economy.

The recent revisionist argument by Naqvi for the productive contribution of the Mughal City finds the industries of the five cities studied producing largely consumer goods.[15] Such produce would serve the urban elites, but would do little to stimulate the further production of national wealth. Despite Naqvi's emphasis on the productive nature of the cities, consumer industries alone are not adequate to improve agriculture by promoting productive innovation.

Saurashtra came under Mughal suzerainty only briefly, but the other governments to which it was subjected often emulated Mughal policies of rural exploitation. The Marathas, who effectively claimed a share of Saurashtra's revenues during most of the eighteenth century, followed revenue policies which also drained capital away from the countryside and, indeed, shipped most of the revenue collections back to Maratha headquarters on the mainland. The Marathas did not exempt

---

man because economic sucess is not the primary road to the fulfillment of his aims." ("The Indian Peasant, the State and Economic Deveopment," *Land Economics*, XXXVIII (1962), 284.)

14 Cf. E. A. J. Johnson, *The Organization of Space in Developing Countries* (Cambridge, Mass., 1970); various articles in Raanan Weitz (ed.), *Rural Development in a Changing World* (Cambridge, Mass., 1971); Eric Lampard, "The History of Cities in the Economically Advanced Areas," *Economic Development and Cultural Change*, III (1955), 90–104.

15 Hameeda Khatoon Naqvi, *Urban Centres and Industries in Upper India 1556–1803* Bombay, 1968).

urban areas from collection, but because the fortress defenses of the Saurashtrian cities usually protected them from the Maratha armies, they often escaped payment.[16]

Local administration, in the hands of princes of Rajput castes, also inhibited economic growth in the countryside. Beginning about the eleventh century, Rajputs immigrated from northwest India into Saurashtra as a military caste intent upon seizing land to rule. As foreigners and as a group whose goal was control of land rather than economic improvement, they, too, were unconcerned with the necessity of rural investment. For example, of the half-dozen mines and metal refineries which various Rajput rulers operated, all seemed designed for the production of weapons rather than farm equipment. From the time of the alliance which the North Indian Rajputs made with the Mughal Emperor Akbar in the sixteenth century, Rajputs began to emulate Muslim court manners and policies of administration. In their policies of urbanization, in particular, the Rajputs sought to build, in miniature, along Mughal lines, and to establish an integrated cultural pattern for areas under Rajput sway. To build such centers—as the Mughals had demonstrated—required great exactions from the countryside. The Rajputs, like the Mughals, did not generally see the necessity for rural investment nor for the linking of rural productivity into a market nexus with urban nodes. Their capital cities carried on administrative functions characteristic of urban areas but in their lack of economic institutions they were more akin to rural areas: Fox has aptly dubbed them "rurban."[17]

Within Saurashtra the capital cities of most Rajput rulers (and of the Muslim ruler of Junagadh as well) followed this "rurban" pattern. Rulers built their capitals inland, generally neglecting trade. Early British accounts reported them as attempting to enlarge themselves primarily through conquest of neighboring regions rather than through internal development.[18] British accounts might be accused of bias and a desire to exalt the Pax Britannica, but the indigenous records reflect the same value system. The bardic narratives of pre-British Rajput rule, compiled by order of the rulers themselves, also stress military virtues

16 Alexander Kinloch Forbes, *Ras Mala* (London, 1878), 394–395.

17 Richard G. Fox, "Rajput Clans and Rurban Settlements in Northern India," in Richard G. Fox (ed.), *Urban India: Society, Space and Image* (Durham, N. C., 1970), 167–185.

18 Cf. the papers assembled in Bombay Presidency, Political Department, *Selection From the Records of the Bombay Government* (Bombay, 1856), XXXVII, XXXIX.

and pay little attention to the importance of economic development.[19]

Rajput rulers built cities to function as military fortresses and to exhibit their power and wealth. Their wish to remain sovereign within the narrow borders of their small states discouraged the external economic connections required for trade.

This overall pattern was, however, somewhat modified to allow some economic entrepreneurship in parts of Saurashtra. Millennia of oceangoing and coastal trade had linked the Saurashtra–Gujarat–Kutch coast with ports stretching from East Africa to Indonesia.[20] Although the trade to the East had ended centuries earlier, contacts with Africa, the Middle East, and along the west coast of India remained strong. Presumably the requirements of the Haj pilgrimage and the allure of trade profits sustained these contacts. The bulk of the traders at the time when the British arrived were Muslims.

The economic potential of this commerce enticed a few of the coastal Rajput rulers to abandon their reputed scorn for trade. The head of the Gohel Rajput clan, as the most remarkable example, re-evaluated his ancestors' position, and in 1723 removed his capital from the inland town of Sihor and built a new coastal capital, Bhavnagar. The coastal city was more defensible and at the same time opened the possibility for increased participation in trade. Bhavsinhji, the Gohel Rajput founder, invited merchants and administrators to immigrate and develop his port. Thereafter, Bhavnagar developed a tradition of support for commerce, trade, and cash cropping in the countryside. In 1800, as the British were beginning to seek Saurashtra's cotton, the state was already exporting cotton valued at Rs. 1,200,000.[21] Tod, the great chronicler of the Rajputs of western India, reported that around 1800 the port of Bhavnagar collected Rs. 700,000 yearly, making it the

19   *Shree Yaduvansh Prakaash* is one such volume of bardic tales. It tells of the Jadeja Rajputs of northwestern Saurashtra and was published in Jamnagar or Rajkot *c.* 1934. Cf. J. W. Watson's *Statistical Accounts* (Bombay, 1879–84), of five princely states of Saurashtra—Bhavnagar, Dhrangadhra, Junagadh, Nawanagar, and Porbandar. Their historical portions are based on bardic sources. Forbes' *Ras Mala* also derives its tales from bardic sources. A. M. Shah and R. G. Shroff, "The Vahivanca Barots of Gujarat: A Caste of Genealogists and Mythographers," in Milton Singer (ed.), *Traditional India; Structure and Change* (Philadelphia, 1959), stress the military orientation of the bardic literature.

20   The excavation of the ancient port of Lothal, dating about 3,000–3,500 years back to the Harappa period, indicates the antiquity of trade in the Gulf of Cambay region (Mortimer Wheeler, *The Civilizations of the Indian Valley and Beyond* [New York, 1966]).

21   Pamela Nightingale, *Trade and Empire in Western India, 1784–1806* (Cambridge, 1970), 187.

294 | HOWARD SPODEK

greatest source of revenue in the state. But Tod stressed the anomaly of
the Gohel clan among the Rajputs: "A Rajpoot emigrant chief from
the great desert of India in the capacity of merchant and ship owner,"
he wrote in 1818, "is a strange compound."[22]

UNDER BRITISH PARAMOUNTCY   The British arrived seeking cotton
in Saurashtra *c.* 1800, became the paramount ruling power by 1820,
and began active rule in the years immediately following the Indian
revolt of 1857–58. They viewed the Rajputs as impeding economic
growth and pointed specifically to their fortress towns as symbols of a
militaristic system which fragmented the countryside and an urban
ruling class which had little concern for enriching agriculture. This was
not true everywhere; Bhavnagar eagerly competed with the British
for control of trade in southeastern Saurashtra. But the dominant picture
transmitted by the British was one of war and parasitism.

The British in Saurashtra, as in India generally, introduced new
systems of economics which increased both parasitism and generativity.[23] By expanding trade and commerce, particularly in cotton,
they gave impetus to, and channels for, increased productivity. At the
initiative of the princes, a railway network of about 1,000 miles was
constructed. The traditional administrative castes, the *brahmins* and the
nagars, mastered new paradigms of rule, and the *bania* businessmen
formed wider connections with the international business community.[24] Many of the merchants and administrators began to press
for increased attention to agriculture, industry, and commerce. They
urged the rulers to equip their capitals with markets, transport networks, banks, and commercial intelligence facilities; they wanted increased commercialization of the countryside. By 1931, about 10
percent of the total population of Saurashtra, evidently dissatisfied
with its rate of progress, had emigrated from the peninsula to other
parts of India. About half of these emigrants chose to live in the
coastal cities of western India, primarily in Bombay.[25]

22   James Tod, *Travels in Western India* (London, 1839), 263.
23   Marx was among the first to describe this; see Shlomo Avineri (ed.), *Karl Marx on
Colonialism and Modernization* (Garden City, N.Y., 1969).
24   Gandhi, the son of a *diwan*, or chief minister, in the Saurashtrian state of Rajkot went
to London to law school because it had become apparent to his parents that if they were
to maintain their status in the administrative cadre, their son would need this new form
of education; traditional forms of education were no longer adequate (Mohandas
Karamchand Gandhi, *An Autobiography* [Boston, 1957]).
25   India, *Census of India, 1931, IX: Cities of the Bombay Presidency*, Pt. II (Bombay, 1933).

Even the more progressive of these groups, however, were concerned with the gross product of their states rather than with the distribution of the wealth by geographical sectors of the economy. In the 1920s, when Bhavnagar State first began an investigation of rural indebtedness, it found remarkable indebtedness in rural areas. Farmers needing money were obliged to pay moneylenders' rates of 25 percent since they could not mortgage their land as collateral; land was owned by the ruler and the actual cultivators were tenants-at-will under his jurisdiction.[26]

Farmers had little access to competitive money markets, government assistance, or a system of rural cooperative banks. The financial and marketing institutions headquartered in the cities failed to spread to the countryside. The increases in land value and crop production which had taken place were related to proximity to urban markets; villages not well linked with markets had, by comparison, stagnated. The isolation of farmers restricted the possibilities of further economic modernization.[27] Bhavnagar, a progressive state, took early interest in these economic problems of urban–rural linkage and acted to promote new rural institutions, such as cooperative agricultural banks and limited rural self-government.

Most rulers exhibited less concern. Indeed, the Pax Britannica, by protecting rulers from attack and insurrection, allowed the Rajput chiefs to ignore their village. To maintain himself, the Rajput prince had to win the support of the British adminstrators rather than that of the Indian subjects whom he ruled. Uprisings against the prince, formerly an alternative available to subjects to coerce changes in government policy, were precluded by British paramount power.[28]

Under the British, the local rulers continued their tradition of emulating the style of the paramount power and its court. Now, however, the court to be copied was European rather than Mughal. The princes of Saurashtra were educated in a special *Raj Kumar*, or prince's

---

26 Bhavnagar State, *Redemption of Agricultural Indebtedness in Bhavnagar State* (Bombay, 1934).

27 Bhavnagar State, *Some Important Papers Relating to the Revision Settlement of the Mahals of the Northern Division, Bhavnagar State* (Bhavnagar, 1936); idem, *Some Important Papers Relating to the Revision Settlement of the Mahals of the Southern Division, Bhavnagar State* (Bhavnagar, 1937), 2v.

28 Saurashtra's leading folklorist and chief literary spokesman of the nationalist movement in the 1920s and 1930s wrote four volumes of stories glorifying the pre-British rebels who periodically rose to confront injustices on the part of the rulers (Jhaverchand Meghani, *Sorathi Bahaarvatiyaa* [Ahmedabad, 1929]).

school, and later taken on chaperoned tours of England and the Continent in order to impress them with European values and styles. They were to model the court of St. James's as they had earlier modeled the court of Delhi. After coming to power at home, the princes spent huge sums of money on economically unproductive city- and monument-building.

Meanwhile, the historic feuding among the multitude of tiny states into which the peninsula was divided now moved from the battlefield to the market place. States often acted to restrict the trade advantages of one another, inhibiting the development of an inter-urban trade system. A well-integrated train network throughout the peninsula, begun in 1888, was disjointed in 1911 when states could not agree on the proper division of routes and profits. From that time onward, customs barriers and points of inspection interrupted travelers and goods on the trains of Saurashtra as they passed from one state's jurisdiction to the next. The road network was never well integrated, and customs barriers were also instituted here. When bus and truck travel began to spread after 1920, many states refused to recognize the vehicle licenses of their neighbors. "Each state had its own separate road transport system unconnected with those of other states." By 1948, interstate tariffs were netting the various states of Saurashtra about Rs. 4,500,000. Princely jealousies impeded the establishment of an integrated inter-city market system, a key to the development of a flourishing trade economy.[29]

Paralleling the desire to compete with their neighbors ran the wish to achieve internal self-sufficiency in food. Here, the traditional responsibility of the ruler to ensure an adequate food supply for his people collided with the new possibilities introduced by modern transportation. Although by the twentieth century a state could enter the exchange economy and thus engage primarily in cash cropping at home and purchase food abroad, few of the rulers encouraged this; many, indeed, prohibited the export of agricultural commodities until a certain level of food consumption was first ensured. The goal of internal self-sufficiency, though understandable, inhibited the villages from participation in wider markets.[30]

29 C. N. Vakil, D. T. Lakdawala, and M. B. Desai, *Economic Survey of Saurashtra* (Bombay, 1953), 323. See Jane Jacobs, *The Economy of Cities* (New York, 1970), on the necessity of integrated, inter-urban market networks for economic development.
30 The ruler of Kotda Sangani rightly felt that if his capital were integrated into a market network which included the nearby capitals of Gondal and Rajkot, his city would

British policies and British modification of historic local practices had mixed results. On the eve of Independence Saurashtra had in some ways a better infrastructure for economic development than many other parts of India: a transportation network which branched deeply into the countryside; a wide distribution of cities, as each major ruler had built himself a capital; extensive areas of cash cropping; a few internal examples, as those provided by Bhavnagar, of the possible efficiency of land reform, debt rationalization, rural cooperatives, and governments responsive to rural demands; and a favorable man–land ratio of perhaps 20 acres per farmer. On the other hand, the region was politically fragmented into literally hundreds of separate jurisdictions. Most of the rulers were oriented to values and traditions inappropriate to agricultural development and increased rural participation in state affairs. Traditional rulers and a substantial part of the peasantry had very limited horizons and were unconcerned with, and perhaps unaware of, the possibilities of economic development. The new independent government described the narrowness of the pre-Independence view-point, noting that people's aspirations had been limited indeed:

> In that little world, there was undoubtedly more misery but certain advantages, too. They were accustomed to see all that belonged to them before their naked eyes. If there were any debts to be paid, they knew what they were and what they meant. If there were assets, they knew how they were utilized whether for their betterment or for the individual aggrandizement of the Ruler. It was a feudal framework, but it was a paternal framework too in some respects.[31]

INDEPENDENCE   Independence brought major changes to Saurashtra, among them a transformation of the urban economy for the benefit of the rural areas, and a remarkable degree of increased interaction between urban and rural areas. Specific changes included an increase of factories, particularly factories in rural areas for processing agricultural products; a land reform program which gave Saurashtra the most egalitarian distribution of land of any state in India; a revised tax structure which

---

shrivel. From 1951 to 1961, Kotda Sangani town's population dropped from 4,219 to 4,194 though the district population grew by about 30 percent.

31   Government of Saurashtra, "Memorandum Presented by Government of Saurashtra to the Part B States (Special Assistance) Enquiry Committee, June, 1953" (unpub. report), 13.

shifted the burden from a primary reliance on rural taxpayers to primary reliance on urban payers; the peninsula-wide institution of *panchayati raj* or local, rural self-government, which called for the election of new governmental units and turned over to them significant amounts of the rural tax revenues; an increase of 23 percent in the area under cultivation, and an increase in cash cropping from some 40 percent of the overall farmed area to well over 60 percent. Within the cities, the government assisted the establishment of light industries and new urban groups embarked on entrepreneurial roles. As cities oriented themselves more and more toward industrialization, they concentrated on the production of equipment useful in increasing rural productivity. The cities which previously had been largely "parasitic" clearly became "generative."

The economic transformation of the cities was rooted in a peaceful political revolution. The end of colonialism was but one aspect of it: necessary, but not alone sufficient. In Saurashtra, the old indigenous elite was also replaced, though not entirely without violence. By the late 1930s it had become clear to the nationalist Congress as well as to the princes that with the fall of the British, the princes would also topple. The princes were so totally tied to British support, and so lacking in popular support, that they had no chance of playing both sides. Although the future clearly was with the nationalists, the princes of Saurashtra could not afford to desert to them so long as the British remained in power.

The old elite with its orientation to autocracy and conspicuous consumption was replaced by a new elite committed to an expansion of economic and political opportunity. This new elite came to power with an unusual sense of cohesion and mission, backed by a sweeping mandate. The Congress movement, reconstituted as a political party, ruled as an interim government after Independence and subsequently carried fifty-three of the fifty-seven seats in the first Saurashtra Legislative Assembly elections in 1952, the most decisive majority in India.[32]

Stemming from the home territory of Saurashtra-born Mahatma Gandhi, the newly elected government was particularly committed to his concern for rural India. The local party leader and first chief minister of the new state, Dhebar, asked rhetorically, "Can anyone consider with equanimity the picture of India technologically advanced

32 John R. Wood, "The Political Integration of British and Princely Gujarat," unpub. Ph.D. diss. (Columbia University, 1971), v, 21, 22.

in the urban sector and static in the rural sector?"[33] The new leadership was united by coming essentially from only three caste groupings: the *bania* businessmen, and the *brahmin* and *nagar* administrators. Indeed, all members of the first cabinet in the new state government were of these castes. Because these same castes had traditionally dominated urban business and professional life, the new leaders tempered the Gandhian concern for rural welfare with an equal appreciation for urban productivity and organizational potential. Also, they had strong ties to their caste-fellows who had preferred Bombay to Saurashtra and, through them, were linked to more cosmopolitan traditions. They went to work quickly to achieve the changes that they had espoused during a generation-long campaign of political opposition.

First, they merged the former states of the peninsula, integrating them into a single political state, the new United State of Saurashtra. Integration led at once to an opening of horizons, an end to city-states and to restrictions on internal transportation and trade, and, thus, paved the way to increasing market orientation. The former desire to maintain a high degree of self-sufficiency in food was abandoned. This policy had particularly affected the smaller states, which were now quick to shift to commercial agriculture. Compare, for instance, the shift in agriculture of the Rajkot taluka, comprised largely of the former Rajkot State, with that of the neighboring talukas of Dhoraji and Gondal, which had been part of the much larger, far more commercialized princely state of Gondal:

Table 2 Acreage Under Groundnut

YEAR	DHORAJI TALUKA	GONDAL TALUKA	RAJKOT TALUKA
1949–50	68,000	49,199	6,158
1950–51	115,771	80,826	5,430
1951–52	47,499	75,728	5,340
1952–53	38,382	74,525	32,355
1953–54	22,000	67,985	28,000
1954–55	70,000	111,038	53,509

SOURCE: Government of Saurashtra, Directorate of Statistics and Planning, *Estimates of Area and Yield of Principal Crops (1949–50 to 1954–55) Saurashtra* (Rajkot, 1955), 20.

33 U. N. Dhebar, "Role of Khadi and Village Industries," in Nawanagar Chamber of Commerce, Industrial Information Center, *Souvenir* (Jamnagar, 1965).

Gondal's ruler, Bhagvatsinhji, had early encouraged trade; Rajkot was more typical of the multitude of small states which had sought self-sufficiency under princely rule.

Many of the changes instituted by the new government cut at the heart of the urban–rural balance and linkage in the peninsula.

The new Congress government had come to power in Saurashtra with virtually no debts to landlord interests. Land reforms were quickly legislated and decisively enforced.[34] The Congress package of land reforms was designed to abolish the middlemen in agricultural taxation, to channel the agricultural revenues directly from the tiller to the state, and to secure land to the tiller. It also ended the crop-share system and replaced it with a cash system of revenue, bringing the villagers more directly into the market economy. It lessened the total burden of revenue both by a reduction in the land revenues and by the abolition of additional taxes which had plagued the tenants-at-will.

No time was wasted. "A proclamation on the 15th April, 1948, the date of the actual establishment of the United State of Saurashtra, conferred full occupancy rights upon the cultivators of *khalsa* land under direct authority of the prince without any payment, introducing cash assessment system of land revenue and abolishing *weth* or forced labor."[35] This *khalsa* land was considered to have been state land rather than the private possession of the prince. The new state therefore succeeded to jurisdiction over it and could distribute it as seemed fit. The princes, who had relinquished control over the states, and thus the land, were granted privy purses in return, consonant with the policy of the national government. Farmers who, in most states of Saurashtra, had had no tenure rights now became land owners.

On *girasdari* and *barkhalidari* land, the process was more complex. *Girasdars* held their land by virtue of historical control, usually by conquest; *barkhalidars* had been granted their land at some time in the past for services rendered to the ruler. Both categories paid nominal assessments to their states. These landholders argued that, unlike the princes, they actually lived in the countryside and often did at least some cultivation themselves; some parts of their land they let to tenants.

34 R. R. Mishra, *Effects of Land Reforms in Saurashtra* (Bombay, 1961) is a useful review of the entire land reform program in Saurashtra, replete with a survey of 64 sample villages to test the results of legislation in the field. I know of no similarly comprehensive account of land reforms in other areas of India. Unless otherwise noted, the description of land reform in Saurashtra is taken from this book.
35 Government of Saurashtra, *Memorandum Presented*, 14.

Girasdari and *barkhalidari* land redistributed to tenants would have to be taken from people who were themselves of the countryside. Conversely, if the rural *girasdars* and *barkhalidars* were confirmed in their holdings, the tenants would have to be evicted.

The government met the problem by fixing maximum limits on the *girasdars* in proportion to their previous holding. The Saurashtra Land Reforms Act of 1951 and the Saurashtra Barkhali Abolition Act of 1951 forced a substantial shift in the rural pattern of land control, tenure, and cultivation. The shift was most disruptive in the approximately one third of Saurashtra's land which had been under *girasdari* control. Here, about half of the *girasdars* and half of their tenants experienced a change in land occupancy. For the most part, *girasdars* actually expanded direct control, evicting tenants, or at least resuming part of the land which they had formerly leased out but which they had a right to recall under the provisions of the new laws. But the percentage of landlords in control of more than forty acres dropped from 26 percent of the total to 17 percent. Table 3, based on a sample of

Table 3 Changes in the Number of Holdings of All Categories of Cultivators between 1947–48 and 1954–55

SIZE OF HOLDING (ACRES)	PERIOD			
	1947–48		1954–55	
	NO.	%	NO.	%
Nil	129	2.6	98	2.0
0– 5	371	7.5	404	8.1
5– 15	994	20.0	1,250	25.2
15– 25	965	19.5	1,147	23.1
25– 40	1,207	24.4	1,215	24.5
40– 60	745	15.0	573	11.5
60– 80	291	5.9	175	3.5
80–100	123	2.5	51	1.0
100–150	112	2.2	33	0.7
150–200	8	0.2	6	0.2
200 or more	12	0.2	5	0.1

SOURCE: Mishra, *Effects of Land Reforms in Saurashtra*, 61. The data here reproduced from Mishra's table seem accurate, but in his original table, he has totalled the number of holdings for both 1947–48 and 1954–55, and both totals are grossly inaccurate. I have no idea how his errors resulted.

Graph 1 Distribution of Land Holdings, 1947–48 and 1954–55

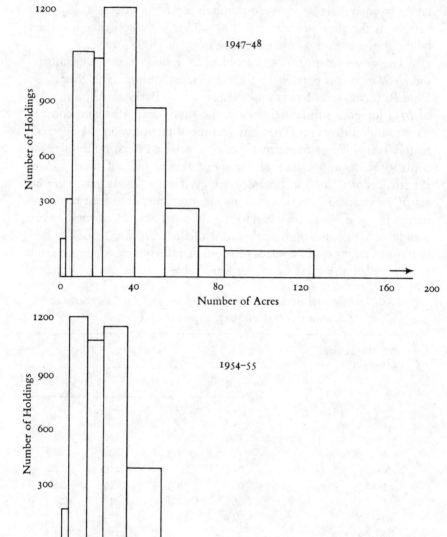

sixty-four villages, indicates the extent of change in the landholding pattern; Graph I reflects the land redistribution.

In cases where tenants gained control over previously *girasdari* land, they were required to pay compensation at the admittedly high rate of Rs. 85 per acre. The Saurashtra State Government organized the Land Mortgage Bank to arrange for the purchase money facilitating the transfers. Because *barkhalidari* rights ordinarily had been granted for only one generation and were not hereditary, *barkhali* tenants who now gained land were not required to pay.

Critics from the left found the state government's actions inadequate, for they treated the *girasdars* generously. But, as a whole the *girasdars* were not a remote *rentier* class; they lived and worked in the villages. Clearly the new government avoided root and branch reform. It wished to press forward economically, politically, and socially, but also recognized the conservatism of the region, and chose to move forward only so quickly as it could carry public opinion. The government urged "that while proceeding with the work of integration, we may not lose sight of the vital factors, viz., backwardness of the State and nervousness of the people at the loss of some rights that they feel are capable of earning a fortune for them."[36]

The Saurashtra government, however, did not fold under pressure. It achieved both land reform and increased productivity. It compromised with *girasdari* demands only from a position of great, proved strength, and it did so in order to achieve a combination of justice with social harmony. Many of the former rulers supported a movement of open opposition to the new government, backing outlaws who "caused a wide breakdown of law and order, committed many dacoities and murders, and intimidated the potential beneficiaries of the land reforms among the peasantry."[37] The Saurashtra government successfully apprehended the majority of these gang members. It implicated the brother of the last Maharaja of Bhavnagar State as an accomplice of the bandits, sentenced him to seven years' imprisonment, later reduced to five because he turned state's witness.[38] Resistance collapsed. Thereafter, the new government was willing to pay compensation at a generous level to the former princes, but would not allow them to obstruct land reform.

36 *Ibid.*, 13.   37 Daniel Thorner, *The Agrarian Prospect in India* (Delhi, 1956), 43.
38 Rasiklal Parikh, "Saurashtrani Raajakiya Tavaarikh: Maari Drushtie," a series of fifty-four articles appearing in the Bombay newspaper *Janmabhoomi*, 24 Dec. 1967–29 Dec. 1968.

By contrast, Rajasthan and Madhya Bharat, two other new states created from unions of former princely states, could not control land-lord violence and political pressures; they were unable to implement effective land reforms.[39] Uttar Pradesh was similarly crippled in land reform activities by the infiltration of landlords within the Congress party. The Saurashtra government vigorously enforced land reforms and, by 1953–54, had one of the most even distributions of land holdings of any region of India (see Graph 2).

Graph 2   Distribution of Land in Various States of India, 1953–54

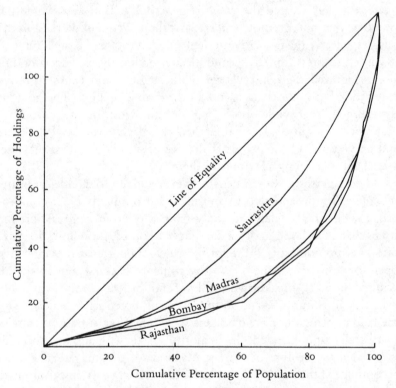

SOURCE: Government of India, Central Statistical Organization, *Statistical Abstract of India, 1956–57* (Delhi, 1958), 498–499.

Graph 2 clearly indicates the comparatively greater equality of land distribution in Saurashtra as compared with other states in India. Those states have been selected for graphing for which rather complete surveys had been done; these include some very large states and some

39   Thorner, *Agrarian Prospect*, 29–32.

composed primarily of former princely states. For greater precision, the Gini index of inequality was established for Saurashtra; for its large and progressive neighbor, Bombay; and for Rajasthan, a former princely region. The index was, respectively, 0.4041, 0.5880, and 0.5825.

Land-tenure reform presaged a diversified package of agricultural programs to increase productivity.[40] The package included: increased participation by villagers in the market economy by making all agricultural revenue to the state payable in cash rather than kind; establishment of a state-run land mortgage bank to assist farmers in buying land rights and financing improved farming operations; distribution of improved seeds and fertilizers; and a variety of major new irrigation plans.[41] The tax structure of the state was revamped to shift the burden from rural to urban areas (see Table 4).

Table 4 Incidence of Taxation per Capita

PERIOD	URBAN	RURAL
1944–47	Rs. 3.8	Rs. 18.7
1953–54	17.6	10.8

SOURCE: Government of Saurashtra, *Memorandum Presented*, 29.

Even the decreased level of rural taxation still left Saurashtra with substantial tax levels in the agricultural sector. Indeed, in terms of land revenue per acre, Saurashtra's rates were virtually the highest in India, exceeded only by tiny and remote Manipur and the Andaman and Nicobar Islands. In terms of agricultural revenue per capita, Saurashtra's was far and away the highest in India (it was, for example, three times that of Bombay). The harshness of the earlier rule left the new government in an enviable position: It could substantially reduce revenue

40 A recent comparative study of land reforms in various parts of the world at various times in history has found that "*the effects of agrarian reform, their extent and intensity, stem from the forces that create the reform in the first place more than from the reform itself.*" R. Laporte, Jr., J. F. Petras, and J. C. Rinehart, "Agrarian Reform and Its Role in Development," *Comparative Studies in Society and History*, XIII (1971), 485 (italics in original).

41 Mishra, *Effects of Land Reforms*, 51, reflects the following distribution of improved seeds and fertilizers, 1955–56:

>12,298 maunds of cotton seeds, enough for 80,000 acres
>4,113 maunds of wheat seeds
>18,215 maunds of ammonium sulphate
>1,956 maunds of super phosphates.

collection in the rural areas and still bring substantial sums to the state's coffers.

The introduction of *panchayati raj* turned over large portions of the taxes collected to newly created, elected bodies in the villages. Discretion over its expenditure passed from urban to rural hands. Table 5 indicates the growth in the number of *panchayats* and their disposable wealth in the decade 1950–51 to 1960–61.

Table 5 Panchayats, 1950–51 and 1960–61 : Number, Income, and Expenditure

YEAR	NUMBER OF PANCHAYATS	INCOME OF PANCHAYATS[a]	EXPENDITURE OF PANCHAYATS[a]
1950–51	593	Rs. 892,032	Rs. 375,699
1960–61	4,329	11,511,237	8,393,044

SOURCES: Gujarat State, *Census 1961. District Census Handbooks* (Ahmedabad, 1964), I–VI.

a   Income and expenditure of panchayats omit those of Junagadh District for both 1950–51 and 1960–61. These data were not available.

These innovations induced remarkable increases in productivity. Acreage utilized increased steadily throughout the years of the separate Saurashtra State from about 7.5 million acres to about 9.5 million acres, a gain of about 23 percent. (Cf. an all-India increase in cropped area of 15 percent between 1951 and 1961.) Production shifted sharply into commercial crops, a shift which began under the Saurashtra State Government and continued in full force after 1956. By 1961, almost two thirds of Saurashtra's cropped area was under commercial crops; 40 percent was under groundnut alone, which replaced cotton as the leading commercial crop of the region. Table 6 illustrates the transition.

The agricultural reforms were strongly oriented toward raising productivity. They attempted to tread lightly on vested interests except when the state's authority was attacked. This stress on economic expansion coupled with social conservatism ran throughout the programs of the Saurashtra government, which concentrated its efforts on traditional institutions, traditional units of production, and traditional forms of entrepreneurial organization. In the cities it supported small-scale rather than larger-scale industrialization and did little to foster urban population growth. In the villages, the socio-economic structure was largely preserved. As Schwartzberg found, "by and large the

Table 6 Area Under Various Crops (Acres)—Saurashtra

YEARS	TOTAL CROPPED AREA	AREA UNDER FOOD CROPS	% OF TOTAL CROPPED AREA UNDER FOOD CROPS	AREA UNDER COTTON	AREA UNDER OILSEEDS
1949–50	7,478,300	4,207,200	56.3	614,500	1,168,000
1950–51	7,507,200	4,102,300	54.6	1,093,400	1,693,200
1951–52	7,530,900	4,198,200	55.7	950,800	1,742,700
1952–53	7,910,100	4,933,200	62.4	961,200	1,592,900
1953–54	8,747,300	4,949,200	56.6	1,022,900	1,667,300
1954–55	8,851,500	4,538,700	51.3	1,199,900	2,562,700
1955–56	8,933,200	5,050,100	56.5	1,387,100	2,051,200
1956–57	9,225,700	4,535,700	49.2	1,455,900	2,757,300
1957–58	9,137,900	4,030,800	44.1	1,326,700	3,194,700
1958–59	9,147,800	4,155,200	45.4	1,318,600	3,246,900
1959–60	9,141,100	3,621,000	39.6	1,447,400	3,779,400
1960–61	9,182,900	3,429,600	37.3	1,310,100	3,888,600
1961–62	9,294,200	3,429,100	36.9	1,256,800	3,774,200
1962–63		3,101,400		1,107,700	4,041,700
1963–64		3,134,800		1,103,200	3,477,800

SOURCES: Gujarat State, Directorate of Agriculture, *Basic Agricultural Statistics of Gujarat State for the Period 1949–50 to 1961–62* (Ahmedabad, 1968); *idem, Statistics of Area, Production and Yield per Acre of Principal Crops in Gujarat State for the Period 1949–50 to 1963–64* Ahmedabad, 1965).

jajmani system of intra-village work allocation and reciprocal obligations appears to be more inact in Saurashtra than in any other study area." In light of village studies of other regions of India, this is not surprising. To the extent that villages grow wealthy by an increase in productivity per acre—rather than through the creation of wholly new sources of wealth such as industry might bring—the existing social structure is reinforced.[42]

42 Village studies carried out in Saurashtra in conjunction with the *Census of India, 1961*, affirm this view of the conservative social structure of the Saurashtrian village—even in the most economically progressive area, the Dhoraji–Upleta region of the former Gondal State. Joseph E. Schwartzberg, "Occupational Structure and Level of Economic Development in India: A Regional Analysis," unpub. Ph.D. diss. (University of Wisconsin, 1960), 169; T. Scarlett Epstein, *Economic Development and Cultural Change in South India* (Manchester, 1962). In Epstein's case study, new irrigation schemes provided the means of increase; in Saurashtra, it was a shift from less valuable to more valuable crops.

Increased commercial agriculture did, however, bring some structural change to the rural economy. Saurashtra began to depend on groundnut. The need to process groundnut into finished products provided new opportunities for small-scale industries, and even rural industries for preparing groundnut oil and groundnut-based fertilizers. The government responded by extending assistance to small-scale industries which were particularly suited to agro-industrial development, and these began to take root in the countryside. Indeed, small-scale factory employment increased more rapidly in the countryside than in the city (see Table 7).

Table 7 Factories

YEAR	NO. OF URBAN FAC- TORIES	% OF INCREASE	NO. OF WORK- ERS	% OF IN- CREASE	NO. OF RURAL FAC- TORIES	% OF INCREASE	NO. OF WORK- ERS	% OF IN- CREASE
1949	623 Total Factories, Not Divided by Location							
1956	702		42,723		133		6,602	
1960	962	+37	46,031	+8	229	+72	9,885	+50

SOURCES: For 1949, C. N. Vakil, D. T. Lakdawala, and M. B. Desai, *Economic Survey of Saurashtra* (Bombay, 1953), 243; for 1956 and 1960, *Census of India, 1961*, V, Pt. I–A (iii), 42–43.

URBAN DEVELOPMENT   The new leaders of Saurashtra, despite their Gandhian bias in favor of rural development, did not turn against the cities. They were themselves urbanites, businessmen and professionals in the most urban state in India. They wished to transform the cities from princely capitals to centers of industry and economic productivity, but at the same time to preserve the sense of identification which most urbanites felt with their cities.

To serve as Industries Minister they recruited Manubhai Shah, a native Saurashtrian who had long ago left Saurashtra first to study industrial management in England and then to return to Delhi as an official of the Delhi Cloth Mills. Shah, who was later elevated to Industries Minister in the central government in New Delhi, was credited with inspiring and guiding a variety of programs for industrial development, particularly for small-scale industries in rural as well as urban locations. The state invested large sums of its regular budget as well as monies of the first five-year plan on roads, electricity, and irrigation. It established a Small-Scale Industries Board and an Industrial Development Corporation—pioneering institutions later adopted throughout India—to provide credit and technical assistance to potential small-scale businesses.

Shah and the other leaders recognized the particular importance of Rajkot as a transportation and administration center and saw it as the likely hub for small-scale industrial development as well. They established there the central economic institutions for the peninsula. In particular, they sought to bolster Rajkot's economic importance before the anticipated merger of the Saurashtra State with the Government of Bombay in 1956 would terminate its political significance. In 1955, immediately after Shah moved to New Delhi to help guide industrial policy for the nation, Rajkot was chosen by the central government as the location for India's first industrial estate. The industrial estate—a government-built-and-financed center for providing worksheds and common minimum necessities such as power, water, repair shops, a bank, a canteen, etc., to a large number of private small-scale entrepreneurs—was expedited with remarkable speed.[43] The first shed of an eventual one hundred was completed and allotted to a small industrial unit in December 1955, within one year of the plan's adoption.[44]

The industrial estate confirmed the transformation of Rajkot from a central place for administration, communication, transportation, and marketing to a dynamic center of increasing productivity and the promotion of innovation. The capital was becoming an industrial growth pole.[45] The construction of a new dam over the Aji River emphasized development by securing for the city and its environs an adequate supply of water for growing population and industry.

The thrust of the new economic growth was toward agro-industries as a means of developing rural and urban areas in tandem. The need to process groundnut into finished products gave rise to new small industries. To supply the machinery needs of these new industries and to supply the irrigation requirements of the prospering farmers, a light engineering industry grew up specializing in the manufacture of

43 For an account of industrial estate development in India generally, see P. C. Alexander, *Industrial Estates in India* (Bombay, 1963).
44 *Ibid.*, 17–18.
45 For a useful, if facile, comparison of central places with growth poles, see Harry W. Richardson, *Elements of Regional Economics* (Baltimore, 1969), 106–107.

diesel engines. By 1969, Rajkot City was producing 50,000 diesel engines per year, one fifth of India's total. It supplied not only Saurashtra but other areas of India and an export market as well.[46] Table 8, concerning exports of groundnut by-products, indicates the extent to which the agro-industries centered on groundnut products.

Table 8 Exports from Saurashtra of Groundnut By-Products (in tons)

YEAR	GROUNDNUT SEEDS	GROUNDNUT CAKES	GROUNDNUT OIL
1938–39	162	54	2
1939–40	81	43	0.2
1940–41	3	12	0.1
1941–42	4	18	0.1
1942–43	5	12	0.1
1943–44	25	5	0.1
1944–45	46	2	0.05
1945–46	40	—	0.03
1946–47	8	—	negligible
1947–48	24	2	1
1949–50	Total groundnut product exports, 60,000 tons		
1954–55	34	59[a]	30
1960–61	140	196	22

SOURCES: For 1938–50, Government of Saurashtra, Department of Industries and Commerce, *Industries of Saurashtra* (Rajkot, 1950), Appendix IX; for 1954, Government of Saurashtra, *Annual Administrative Report for the Period April 1, 1954 to March 31, 1955* (Rajkot, 1955), xlvii; for 1960–61, Government of Gujarat, Public Works Department, *Gujarat State Ports Traffic Review 1960–61* (Ahmedabad, 1961).

a Includes all oil cakes, not only groundnut oil.

The production of food and food products employed more workers in more factories than any other branch of industry in Saurashtra (see Table 9). A modicum of small-scale industry was introduced to the countryside itself, as noted in Table 7, above.

The interaction between rural and urban areas also appeared in the increasing movement of farmers to the city. The new social as well as geographical mobility of the farming community was reflected in the enrollment of members of the dominant *kunbi* (*patel, patidar*) caste in urban high schools. Under most of the princes, the *kunbis* had been somewhat depressed in Saurashtra, particularly by comparison with

46 Interview with Jamubhai K. Modi, President, Rajkot Chamber of Commerce.

Table 9 Distribution of Factories by Major Industries, 1961

INDUSTRY	FACTORIES	EMPLOYEES
Food and kindred products	385	14,203
Textiles and their products	67	13,161
Metals and metal products	190	6,786
Chemicals and allied products	32	4,661
Mining	42	3,751

SOURCE: India, *Census of India, 1961*, V, Pt. I–A (iii), 42–43.

their thriving caste-fellows in mainland Gujarat;[47] new policies of the Saurashtra government aided the newly landed *kunbis* in particular (see Table 10).

Table 10 Members of *Kunbi* (*Patel, Patidar*) Caste Enrolled at Alfred High School, Rajkot[a]

YEAR	NUMBER OF *Kunbis* ENROLLED	TOTAL STUDENTS ENROLLED	PERCENTAGE OF *Kunbis*
1881	2	164	1
1932–33	4	485	1
1960[b]	69	801	8.5

SOURCE: Class lists of the Alfred High School, Rajkot.
a I chose Alfred High School for this study because it is the oldest in Saurashtra and because its records were made accessible. I had wished to extend my analysis to the composition of the Raj Kumar College which became open to the public after 1939, but has remained a very exclusive and expensive boarding school. Its enrollment would be a more accurate barometer of the rising and falling fortunes of various groups in Saurashtra, but I was not permitted access to its recent records.
b For 1960, examined about two thirds of the class records. The total student enrollment was about 1,200.

Within the urban area, the new light engineering industry was particularly profitable for the urban artisans, especially for the *suthars* or carpenter caste. The new state policies made it possible for them to find worksheds in the industrial estates and financing from newly created state institutions. They could thus overcome their shortage of capital for transforming their artisan skills into entrepreneurial productivity. Manubhai Shah, in particular, used the state financial institutions

47 Rajani Kothari and Rushikesh Maru, "Caste and Secularism in India," *Journal of Asian Studies*, XXV (1965), 35–50.

to facilitate business loans to new people. It was reported that more than 75 percent of the owners of the companies in the Rajkot Engineering Association by 1969 were of the artisan castes.[48]

The new government policies did not, however, promote rapid urban growth. They were policies for balanced urban–rural regional development. The overall percentage of urbanization in the peninsula did not rise, perhaps because the former princely capitals generally lost their historic political functions. The percentage of urbanization in Saurashtra has remained steady at 31 percent from 1951 through 1971, while the all-India percentage rose slightly from 17 to 20 percent.

Where urban growth did occur it was linked to industrialization, the increase of commercial activity, and the creation of productive job opportunities. This seems evident even from the marked shift in sex ratios of Saurashtra's cities. (Ideally, migration data should be used to illustrate the new attractions of the cities, but in 1961, with Saurashtra merged into Gujarat State, the census data on migration are not presented in a useful form.) Until 1951, the cities of Saurashtra had a higher ratio of females to males than did the rural areas. This pattern ran counter to the general pattern of Indian cities in which job opportunities induced men to come in search of work, leaving their families behind in the villages. In Saurashtra, men had evidently left their families in the city to seek jobs outside the peninsula. Saurashtra's cities had not generated adequate work to retain its own trading community much less to attract rural people.

Table 11   Sex Ratios

Females/1,000 Males—Rajkot Division (Saurashtra Peninsula + Kutch)

YEAR	ENTIRE DIVISION	URBAN AREAS ONLY
1901	965	985
1911	972	1,009
1921	977	1,008
1931	979	994
1941	979	984
1951	986	1,000
1961	961	945
1971	953	936

SOURCES: India, *Census of India, 1961*, V, Pt. II–A, 107; *Census of India, 1971. Paper I—Supplement. Provisional Population Totals*, 96.

48 Interview with Gatubhai Doshi, President, Rajkot Engineering Association.

Only after 1951 does the census report a shift in the sex ratios of urban as compared with rural areas. The percentage of males in the population becomes greater in the urban than in the rural areas (Table 11). The increase in urban job opportunities in small-scale industry and trade promoted by the new government attracted workers.

SUMMARY AND CONCLUSIONS   The urban system of Saurashtra, under the new political leadership was transformed to function in new ways to serve a new political philosophy which was economically progressive though socially cautious. The passing of political dominance from one urban group, the princes, to another, the Brahmin and Bania business and professional elite, engendered massive economic change in the whole regional balance of the peninsula. Saurashtra achieved an urban–rural complementary economic balance which other areas of India might envy.[49]

It achieved this balance because the new elite held values quite different from those which had dominated the area for 140 years. The new elite owed no political favors to the old, and committed itself to quite different political, economic, and social policies. Boldly and successfully it carried through the reforms to which it had pledged itself over long decades of opposition to the former princely policy: unification, reforms in land control and tenure, the provision of amenities to rural areas, government-sponsored rural finance, and tax redistribution. The shift in the urban–rural economic and political balance resulted from these massive, politically-fostered changes in the rural areas. The growth of cities was not encouraged generally, but where urban growth did occur, as in Rajkot and Jamnagar, it was largely aided by specific government policies, particularly for the creation of industrial estates. Small-scale industries were also favored through the creation of new institutions to provide both technical and financial assistance. Politics remained the key variable in the pattern of the growth of cities.[50]

The process of transforming the economic role of Saurashtra's cities from parasitic to generative differed from the strategy of China and from the patterns which marked many other regions of India. In

49   On the general desirability of balanced urban–rural development in India, cf. several of the articles in P. B. Dosai, I. M. Grossack, and R. N. Sharms (eds.), *Regional Perspective of Industrial and Urban Growth: The Case of Kanpur* (Bombay, 1969).

50   Because political decisions were so important in the development of cities, the cities competed aggressively for government favors. Cf. Howard Spodek, "'Injustice to Saurashtra': A Case Study of Regional Tensions and Harmonies in India," *Asian Survey*, XII (1972), 416–428.

China, after 1927, the organizational base of revolution was among the masses in the countryside. This inspired an anti-specialist, anti-elitist, anti-urban, and anti-gentry revolution. Many of the former economic elite were humbled; many were sent to the countryside for therapeutic work experience among the peasantry. Substantial economic progress as well as progress toward egalitarian distribution of wealth has been accomplished, but amidst great trauma. Private property has largely given way to collectivization. We know less fully what has taken place in the cities, but apparently the pre-revolutionary capitalist class, and the comprador class in particular, has been reduced in status if not totally stripped of wealth and power.[51]

If Saurashtra has not had so thorough a revolution as China, neither has it experienced the stagnation of many other regions of India. For instance, in the great north Indian state of Uttar Pradesh, holding one fifth of the nation's population, the landed aristocrats parried land reform. In the last years of British rule, they began to infiltrate the Congress to assure that land reform legislation after Independence would have loopholes and would not be rigorously enforced.[52] This pattern of evasion often coupled with violent resistance to peasant demands characterized most Indian states, at least in the first decade of Independence. The largest city in U.P., Kanpur, developed neither diversified industries nor the integration of rural and urban areas. Much of the responsibility for these failures has been attributed to the business community's willingness to invest their capital outside the region and to the lack of resolute direction within the faction-ridden, slow-moving bureaucracy of both local and state government agencies.[53]

By contrast with these examples from China and north India, Saurashtra's transformation has followed quite different paths. First,

51 John Wilson Lewis (ed.), *The City in Communist China* (Stanford, 1971), the most authoritative book on the subject in English, points out that no author represented in the collection had set foot in China since 1950. The opening of China may now give us a fuller view.

52 Richard Smith Newell, "Congress Agrarian Reform Policy: A Case Study of Land Redistribution in Northern India," unpub. Ph.D. diss. (University of Pennsylvania, 1966), esp., 325, 335–336, 343–344. Newell cites an unpublished manuscript of Peter Reeves stating that even in the wake of land reform legislation in the U.P., "'Those who traditionally held sway, the high caste tenant groups, continue to do so, while in the villages—where the zamindar has remained in residence, it has retained power or has conceded it only to the next highest land holding group'" (336).

53 Thorner, *Agrarian Prospect*; Desai, Grossack, and Sharma, *Regional Perspective*, esp. Ronald G. Ridker, "Prospects and Problems of Agriculture in the Kanpur Region," 55–72.

Independence transferred the mantle of authority to the well-established, but previously subordinated, urban commercial and adminstrative elites. Second, Saurashtra saw the integration of former city-states into a single, unified state. Moreover, this new state was now more closely linked with the political functions of New Delhi and the economic functions of Bombay.

In sum, during the first decade of Independence, Saurashtra's cities took on vastly more generative roles as a result of political changes analogous to the bourgeois revolution of Western Europe on the brink of modern times. An aggressive, rising bourgeoisie wrested dominant control from the hands of the landed, urban-resident, princely classes and joined with the power of the central government to consolidate their parochial city-states into a more comprehensive, more economically viable unit. More, they telescoped many processes of the economic revolution by immediately bringing the agrarian sector into fuller participation in a reciprocal urban–rural market economy.[54]

54 Cf. Karl Polanyi, *The Great Transformation* (Boston, 1957), esp. 62–67.

Paul Wheatley

The City Overseas

The City in Communist China. Edited by John Wilson Lewis (Stanford, Stanford University Press, 1971) 449 pp. $12.95

Urban India: Society, Space and Image. Edited by Richard G. Fox (Durham, Duke University Program in Comparative Studies on Southern Asia, 1970) 244 pp. n.p. (paper)

These volumes are sequelae to conferences arranged to investigate the phenomenon of contemporary urbanism in two of Asia's major cultural realms. Beyond that, they have little in common. *The City in Communist China* has a strong political science bias despite the contributions of scholars from other disciplines. It is also strongly institutionalist in orientation, generally inductive in approach, minimally functionalistic, and relies primarily upon empirically generated concepts. *Urban India* is more diversified in both authorship and methodology. It investigates a broader range of urban phenomena, includes a higher proportion of deductive studies, is more functionalistic in approach, and is more inclined to favor formalistic concepts. I suspect that the nature of the evidence upon which the authors were able to draw was partly responsible for these different emphases. Whereas those writing on China were forced to rely almost wholly upon secondary materials, the Indian specialists could utilize field studies as well as less rigorously regulated published records. Both works exhibit an unusually high level of scholarly competence and integrity.

The China volume is arranged in four sections that reflect the successive phases of the Communist Chinese government's policy toward the city since 1949. At that time, urban life in China was in a state of incipient dissolution, with the economy disrupted, and the old institutional framework inherited from the Republic near collapse. As early as 1945, at the Seventh Plenum of the Sixth Central Committee, the Party had announced its intention of replacing its primarily rural orien-

Paul Wheatley is Professor of Geography and of Social Thought at the University of Chicago and the author of *The Golden Khersonese: Studies in the Historical Geography of the Malay Peninsula Before A.D. 1500* (Kuala Lumpur, 1961) and *The Pivot of the Four Quarters: A Preliminary Inquiry Into the Origins and Character of the Ancient Chinese City* (Chicago, 1970).

tation with an urban-focused strategy. In March 1949, Chairman Mao
Tse-tung officially proclaimed the new policy and authorized a broad
coalition of urban classes to join the Communists in implementing this
program.

The highest priorities of the new urban policy were pacification
and reconstruction, the first of which implied, and the second of which
required, the maintenance of law and order. Part I focuses on this phase.
Jerome A. Cohen evaluates the extent to which the rules for the system
of mediation established by the Chinese Communist leadership reflected
the Party's urban experience rather than its previous preoccupation with
rural administration. Owing to a prevailing uncertainty as to the legal
institutions best adapted to the achievement of revolutionary goals, the
mediation committees were forced to compromise between competing
views of law as a coercive restraint and law as an instrument of social
change. In a case-study of law enforcement in Hui-yang county (*hsien*),
Victor H. Li investigates some aspects of law as a means of restraint. He
is particularly concerned with the types of persons employed by the
hsien-level public security bureau, their career patterns, and the channels
of vertical mobility within the organization. Ezra F. Vogel describes
how the security programs introduced an increasingly doctrinaire quality into the government's approach to social order, inhibiting innovation and encouraging collusion and concealment.

Part II investigates the nature of the leadership and bureaucracy
that attempted to bring about the economic and social modernization of
the Chinese city after law and order had been established. Ying-mao
Kau elucidates the manner in which the two antibureaucratic campaigns
of the 1950s paradoxically resulted in bureaucratic expansions, and
shows how cadre mobilization was subject to pendulum-like oscilla-
tions between recruitment and retrenchment campaigns. Paul F. Harper
discusses the efforts of Chinese labor unions to identify and prepare
workers for leadership positions, in response to Mao's injunction to
them in 1949 to rely upon the urban proletariat. He shows how the
urban bureaucrats recruited from the workers came into conflict with
entrenched technical elites. John Wilson Lewis explores the systematic
relationships at the local level within which political conflicts were resolved. In a case-study of Tangshan county, he demonstrates how new
alliances formed by cadres during the Great Leap Forward (1958–59)
induced a redistribution of power that went far toward bringing the
traditionally discrete marketing and administrative hierarchies of the
county into conformity.

Part III deals with the modernization of the Chinese city. John Philip Emerson turns his attention to the government's attempts to transform a substantial section of China's huge agricultural work force into an industrial proletariat. He expresses doubts as to the success of Peking's manpower planning in furthering the aims of industrialization, and demonstrates that the relocation, educational, and training regulations promulgated from time to time were often misconceived, owing largely to a failure to comprehend the essential functioning of the city. From a study of Shanghai, Christopher Howe illustrates how deceptive aggregate statistics can be even at the municipal level, and how the categories employed in Chinese national plans not only afforded an inadequate basis for measuring policy impact, but also obscured the workings of change. John Gardner analyzes the inequalities of opportunity existing between town and country, a dichotomy that was sharpened by the implementation of the commune policy. He discusses how the Maoist strategy was designed to eliminate not only these, but almost all other differences between the two modes of life in order to achieve sustained and, most desirably, rapid economic growth without relying upon a specialized, urban-based elite. In this context, Mao's significance lies in the fact that he "is one of the few leaders in the underdeveloped world attempting to deal seriously with problems that are largely ignored elsewhere" (286).

The final section of the book deals with the urban crisis that was induced when Mao, seeing the values of the revolutionary leadership threatened by the expansion and consolidation of an urban bureaucracy intent on according priority to industrial development, called for the adoption of more truly revolutionary forms of urban organization. Janet W. Salaff examines the impact of the Cultural Revolution (1966–69) on certain urban communities. She describes how the structural changes in neighborhood services, together with the vigorous politico-ideological educational programs that accompanied the Cultural Revolution, both intensified and broadened the scope of neighborhood community activities. "The combination of decentralization of urban administrative apparatus and intensification of local political controls," she writes, "was the solution of the Cultural Revolution to the problem of maintaining political commitment in the complex, differentiated urban setting of a developing society" (323). This conclusion is reinforced by the last chapter of the book, a study by Lynn T. White III of the conflicting interests of security-military, residential, educational, and labor institutions in Shanghai during the Cultural Revolution. In particular, he documents the way in which attempts to implement ideological prescriptions often forced the leadership to make decisions and formulate policies that were essentially unideological.

Not the least valuable part of this book is a perspicacious introduction in which the editor distills from the individual contributions a skeletal grammar of Chinese urban politics since 1949, and assesses the future prospects of the Chinese city. Fundamental to any such assessment, he writes, is the realization that what Mao anticipates is a wholly new model of urban society, the achievement "in hundreds of cities at different stages of industrialization [of] an ideal of local self-reliance and rural–urban cooperation that is only idly discussed in the West" (26). It is not without interest, as Lewis points out (380, n. 81), that Mao's regional ideal has much in common with the diffusion models proposed by geographers such as Hägerstrand and Gould.[1]

It is evident that in several chapters of the book there is no rigorous discrimination between specifically urban institutions and processes and those involving the society as a whole. In his preface, Lewis is inclined to attribute this to the fact that the evidence available for the study of contemporary Chinese urbanism often blurs the distinctions between urban and rural. But is this circumstance not a reflection of the fact that as a nation-state modernizes, its cities progressively cease to exhibit common and distinct patterns of behavior, with the result that the formulation of an independent nexus of concepts and generalizations applicable to the city as an analytically discrete entity becomes increasingly difficult, and perhaps unprofitable? As the late Oscar Lewis wrote on the study of social processes:

> The city is not the proper unit of comparison or discussion for the study of social life because the variables of number, density and heterogeneity . . . are not the crucial determinants of social life or of personality. There are many intervening variables. Social life is not a mass phenomenon. It occurs for the most part in small groups, within the family, within households, within neighborhoods, within the church, formal and informal groups, and so on. . . . Any generalizations about the nature of social life in the city must be based on careful studies of these smaller universes rather than on a priori statements about the city as a whole.[2]

[1] See Torsten Hägerstrand (trans. Allan Pred), *Innovation Diffusion as a Spatial Process* (Chicago, 1967); Peter R. Gould, *Spatial Diffusion* (Washington, D.C., 1969).

[2] Philip Morris Hauser and Leo F. Schnore (eds.), *The Study of Urbanization* (New York, 1965,) 497.

From the phenomenological point of view, the China volume mirrors a world of native experience. The Indian volume reflects the structuring activities of perceptual and conceptual assumptions and is thus organized on entirely different principles. Whereas the Chinese book is arranged to reflect a suite of categories perceived as inherent in the study materials themselves, the arrangement of essays in *Urban India* is "based on the three major visions or views of urban India which emerged in the course of the Symposium" (ix).

After a hortatory introduction by Ashish Bose urging the use of more refined tools of analysis devised specifically for probing the intricacies of the Indian cultural nexus, there follow three sections entitled "Urban Society," "Urban Space," and "Urban Images." The first investigates the structural modifications in Indian caste, family, and occupational categories brought about by the process of urbanization. Frank F. Conlon traces the preadaptations and subsequent accommodations of the Saraswat Brahmans to an urban environment characterized primarily by an impersonal organization of institutions, an English-style educational system, and British legal forms. In so doing, he reveals that an unexpected degree of adaptability to urban life styles is inherent in the traditional caste structure. Robert L. Hardgrave, Jr. evaluates the adaptive responses to urbanization of the Nadars of Tamilnad in terms of Mitchell's distinction between "processive" and "situational" change,[3] and proposes a suggestive analogy between the present-day organization of urban castes and the persistence of ethnicity in American cities. Harold Gould examines the changes induced in the occupational structures of four representative social groups: business and professional elites in Lucknow; menials in the same city; peasant farmers from the village of Sherupur, some eighty miles distant from the city; and students who had entered Lucknow University from villages or small towns. Generally speaking, he concludes that the modernization process acts selectively on the social forms of caste and kinship according to the status and wealth of the groups concerned. Although the urbanized peasant remains essentially a peasant, privileged business and professional elites within the city exhibit a nearly complete transition to modernity. In the last paper of this section, Joseph Di Bona discusses the socialization functions of the University of Allahabad, and elicits evidence of a grow-

---

3 J. Clyde Mitchell, "Social Change and the New Towns of Bantu Africa," in G. Balandier (ed.), *Social Implications of Technological Change* (Paris, 1962), 128; *idem.*, "Theoretical Orientations in African Urban Studies," in Michael Banton (ed.), *The Social Anthropology of Complex Societies* (London, 1966), 44.

ing parochialization of that institution as it absorbs an increasing proportion of students from rural backgrounds.

These four papers have all defined the city in terms of the behavior-
al realities of human social adaptation. The second section of the book
treats the city as but one aspect of a more inclusive system. John
Brush and Wallace Reed both examine the city as a generator of
"effective space," and the urban hierarchy as a spatial system differentiated by locational and morphological qualities. Brush recounts the
evolution of the Presidency towns from a common bureaucratic origin
and touches on some of their inherited demographic characteristics.
Reed investigates the hierarchical and regional patterns of direct management controls established by large-scale industrial and commercial
enterprises throughout India's urban system. Not altogether surprisingly, he concludes that regional and national decision-making is focused primarily in the largest cities. The remaining two papers of this
section define urban space through Indian ideological constructs and
social institutions. In what is one of the most insightful chapters of the
book, Fox seeks to isolate the specific urban organizational forms that
derive from the structural framework of Indian civilization at large. In
particular, he documents the formation, during the British administration of Uttar Pradesh, of incipient urban forms around the local centers
of Rajput stratified lineages. In so doing, he defines the urban hierarchy
in terms of "an attributional duplication of political style between national and rural society" (x). In a field of inquiry that is dominated
conceptually by attempts to explain the spatial organization of tertiary
economic activity, Fox's observation that the lineage leaders often
founded markets for reasons of status maintenance rather than commercial necessity is especially interesting (179). However, once established,
such lineage centers, by virtue of their political, economic, and ritual
functions, acted as local facsimiles of the state-level preindustrial cities.
In the final paper of this section, Leighton W. Hazlehurst delineates the
several types of urban space in a north Indian town that are defined by
internal equivalencies in status, the various members of such differentiated urban spaces being linked together by a mode of social interaction
based upon status inversion. He concludes that urban caste organization
can only be understood as a combination of space and activities, of
status equivalence and inversion, of caste and class.

The authors take a totally different approach in the third section,
abandoning objective investigation of the nature and structure of the
urban environment for what is thought and felt about it, the way in

which it is perceived. Mahadeo Apte describes how the optimism associated with urban images in Marathi literature prior to 1940 has yielded, during the past quarter of a century, to an alienation that allegedly reflects specifically the decline in living standards of the Bombay middle classes, and, perhaps more generally, the disenchantment with contemporary urban living that is common to many parts of the world. This alienation of the urban middle classes is also discerned by Eleanor Zelliott in an analysis of perceptions of the city as revealed in Indian fiction written in English. The urban personality, however, seems to be regarded as more malevolent by writers from Maharashtra and the north than by those from Bengal and the south. To certain minority groups, such as upper-class Muslims, Parsis, and Jews, for whom it has been their traditional locale, the city appears to be accepted as the natural and proper human environment. The section concludes with a fine paper by A. K. Ramanujan on the urban images of ancient India. After presenting what he aptly terms a "random reader" of city images, the author examines in detail ancient descriptions of the three cities of Ayodhyā, Pukār, and Maturai and finally speculates on the significance of the urban–rural dichotomy as it is manifested in classical Sanskrit literature (but not in Vedic or early Tamil writings). Methodologically, this essay is different from the two preceding in that Ramanujan takes account of the power of literature to refract, as well as to reflect, a life-style.

The Contributors

Reader on Industrialization and Urbanization

THOMAS W. AFRICA is Professor of History at the State University of New York at Binghamton and the author of five books and numerous articles on Greek and Roman history.

EDWARD ANTHONY WRIGLEY is Professor of Population Studies at the London School of Economics and co-director of the Cambridge Group for the History of Population and Social Structure. He is the author of *Population and History* (London, 1969) and *Industrial Growth and Population Change* (Cambridge, 1960).

FRANKLIN F. MENDELS is Associate Professor of History at the University of Maryland, Baltimore County, and the author of *Industrialization and Population Pressure in Eighteenth-Century Flanders* (New York, 1980).

WILLIAM H. SEWELL, JR., is Associate Professor of History at the University of Arizona and the author of *Work and Revolution in France: The Language of Labor from the Old Regime to 1848* (New York, 1980).

MICHAEL R. HAINES is Research Associate Professor, School of Public and Urban Policy, and Visiting Associate Professor, International Population Program, Cornell University. He is the author of *Fertility and Occupation: Population Patterns in Industrialization* (New York, 1979).

JON AMSDEN is an economic consultant at the United Nations and the author of *Class Conflict and Collective Bargaining in Spain* (London, 1972).

STEPHEN BRIER is President of Film for Thought, Inc., and the author of "Interracial Organizing in the West Virginia Coal Industry," in Gary Fink and Merl Reed (eds.), *Essays in Southern Labor History* (Westport, Conn., 1977).

STEPHAN THERNSTROM is Professor of History at Harvard University and the author of *The Other Bostonians: Poverty and Progress in the American Metropolis, 1880-1970* (Cambridge, Mass., 1973).

PETER R. KNIGHTS is Associate Professor of History at York University and the author of *The Plain People of Boston, 1830-1860: A Study in City Growth* (New York, 1971).

☐   ☐

VIRGINIA YANS-McLAUGHLIN is Associate Professor of History and Director of Women's Studies at Douglass College, Rutgers University, and author of *Family and Community: Italian Immigrants in Buffalo, N.Y., 1880-1930* (Ithaca, 1977).

DANIEL T. RODGERS is Associate Professor of History at Princeton University and the author of *The Work Ethic in Industrial America, 1850-1920* (Chicago, 1978).

STUART M. BLUMIN is Associate Professor of American History at Cornell University and the author of *The Urban Threshold: Growth and Change in a Nineteenth-Century American Community* (Chicago, 1976) and *The Short Season of Sharon Springs* (Ithaca, 1980).

CLYDE GRIFFEN is Lucy Maynard Salmon Professor of American History at Vassar College and the author of, with Sally Griffen, *Natives and Newcomers: The Ordering of Opportunity in Mid-Nineteenth-Century Poughkeepsie* (Cambridge, Mass., 1978).

GILBERT ROZMAN is Professor of Sociology at Princeton University and the author of *Urban Networks in Russia, 1750-1800, and Premodern Periodization* (Princeton, 1976) and *Urban Networks in Ch'ing China and Tokugawa Japan* (Princeton, 1974).

HOWARD SPODEK is Associate Professor of History and Urban Studies at Temple University and the author of *Urban-Rural Integration and Regional Development: A Case Study of Saurashtra, India, 1800-1960* (Chicago, 1976).

PAUL WHEATLEY is Irving B. Harris Professor of Comparative Urban Studies at The University of Chicago and co-author of *From Court to Capital: A Tentative Interpretation of the Origins of the Japanese Urban Tradition* (Chicago, 1978).